THE UNFAIR ADVANTAGE

THE UNFAIR

ADVANTAGE

Mark Donohue
with Paul Van Valkenburgh

Illustrated with photographs

BentleyPublishers®
.com

CONTENTS

Donohue sits in the cockpit of the McLaren M6B at the Road America 500 race in 1968.

Donohue in the cockpit of the Chevy Camaro in 1969 before the start of a Trans-Am race.

Donohue and Bill Blankenship scrutinize the famous #66 McLaren M16 Indy car.

Donohue and Penske confer over the Lola T192.

The AMC Matador at Daytona in 1971.

The Porsche 911 Carrera in the Penske shop just as it arrived from the Porsche factory in 1972.

Donohue's helmet during a rare moment of rest in 1973.

BENTLEY PUBLISHERS® | Automotive Reference™

Bentley Publishers, a division of Robert Bentley, Inc.
1734 Massachusetts Avenue
Cambridge, MA 02138 USA
800-423-4595 / 617-547-4170

Information that makes the difference®

BentleyPublishers®.com

This book is prepared, published and distributed by Bentley Publishers, 1734 Massachusetts Avenue, Cambridge, Massachusetts 02138 USA.

First edition published in the U.S.A. 1975

ISBN 978-0-8376-0069-7
Job code: GDDS-09

Library of Congress Cataloging-in-Publication Data

Donohue, Mark.
The unfair advantage / Mark Donohue, with Paul Van Valkenburgh.
p. cm.
Includes index.
ISBN 978-8376-0073-4 (alk. paper) -- ISBN 978-8376-0069-7 (pbk. : alk. paper)
1. Donohue, Mark. 2. Automobile racing drivers--United States--Biography. I. Van Valkenburgh, Paul. II. Title.
GV1032.D66 A38 2000
796.72'092--dc21
[B] 00-058655

Front cover painting and title-page drawing by Ellen Griesedieck

Chronology by Bill Cobb
Table of contents photo credits: (1) Cam Warren, (2,3) Pete Lyons, (4) Hal Crocker, (5) International Motor Speedway, (6) Donohue Collection, (7) Barry Tenin.

The paper used in this publication is acid free and meets the requirements of the National Standard for Information Sciences-Permanence of Paper for Printed Library Materials.(∞)

Manufactured in the United States of America.

202510R002

Donohue Collection

From left to right:
Bill Scott, Mark Donohue, Roger Penske

While many of our father's friends and colleagues have played important roles in our lives, there are two who deserve special mention. Bill Scott and Roger Penske, each in his own way, helped to guide us after our father's death.

Bill Scott was a fabricator at Sun Oil & Penske Racing for many years. Of the people who had been close to our father, Scotty was the only man who took an active role in our lives while we were growing up. He personifies the impression we have of our father and many of those who surrounded him during those early Penske days. Before passing away in 1998, Scotty helped teach us many of life's virtues. Scotty could always provide a solution to a problem, both professionally and personally. He was incredibly tenacious in a good and sincere way. At age 66 he beat paralysis from a broken back. Just a couple years later his wife suffered a stroke which the doctor's diagnosed as permanently crippling. Scotty put everything aside, took charge of his wife's rehabilitation, and proved the doctors wrong. He even managed to beat lung cancer after all this. He is often in our thoughts and prayers. We'll never forget him, or his influence on our lives.

Roger Penske met our Dad in the early '60's, so he was part of our lives from the very beginning. Throughout their collaboration, Roger and our father seemed to spur each other on to work hard and demand the best from themselves and those around them. Their partnership instilled in us the values of teamwork, professionalism, loyalty, and always striving for perfection. Roger has also played a major role in each of our professional lives and has been a true friend. His way of doing things has had a dramatic effect on who we are, and we appreciate that immensely.

While no one could take the place of our father, we are grateful to have had role models like Scotty and Roger. Because they each embodied some of our father's most distinguishing characteristics—such as integrity, sincerity, and determination—these two men were able to pass on to us the kinds of values our father would have taught us if he'd had the chance.

M.D., D.D.
September, 2000

PREFACE TO THE NEW EDITION

If history could be rewritten, and we were allowed to choose our father's career, we would both choose for him to have been a desk-bound mechanical engineer. This for the simple and rather selfish reason that he would likely still be with us today. Losing a parent early in life is never easy for anyone. But despite our loss, we are intensely proud that our father was Mark Donohue—a man whose many accomplishments in the field of motor sports continue to be both influential and widely respected to this day. And more significantly, a man who is remembered by his friends and colleagues in the racing world as extremely intelligent, always sincere, friendly and thoughtful almost to a fault, and as a man who approached all things with the highest integrity.

Since we have learned from experience that life on and around the race track continually tests all of these more lofty qualities, we have both developed a deep and lasting admiration for our father. We would like to thank all of the people that have approached us and recounted the endless stories, humorous events, and various ways in which our father played a role in their lives, however small it may have been. Although we were only eight and eleven when he died in a racecar accident, his fatherly guidance has always had an important influence on our lives as a result of the way he is remembered by so many. We are constantly learning more about him and about his significant impact on the world of racing through those who are willing to share their memories with us. Even though racing has taken him from us, it continually keeps giving him back to us. In a very real way, we know our father better now than we ever have, and that has helped to ease our sense of loss. We have come to understand his humor, his work ethic, his desire to do good things for others. These things have guided us in all the ways that a father hopes to guide his sons.

When we decided to re-publish *The Unfair Advantage* we knew we had the opportunity to share some of these memories. We also wanted to add more pictures to the book and give his story some historical context. We asked well-known motor sports historian and writer Pete Lyons to talk to some of the people who worked and raced alongside our father, making everything happen. We also asked many of the people who have photographs from our father's era of racing to dip into their archives and contribute new material to this project. These photos and personal recollections seemed like a wonderful way to let everyone know who Mark Donohue really was.

But very soon the proliferation of photos and the many funny, fascinating, and sometimes controversial stories threatened to eclipse the modesty and focused intensity of the original book. So we've decided to expand this 2nd edition of *The Unfair Advantage* by adding a detailed chronology of Mark Donohue's life and 32 pages of photos and anecdotes, while keeping the original text essentially intact. We hope to collect the remaining array of photos and stories in a separate volume that will be an answer to our father's wishes when he wrote as the last sentence of his book, "And hopefully, in a few years, I'll have another story to tell."

September, 2000

Michael W. Donohue David Donohue

FOREWORD

I now realize how much there is to say about so many people, cars, learning experiences, races, mistakes, technologies, and successes. I hope no one is disappointed that I've said almost nothing in this book about my private, personal life. Actually, I have had very little, because of the time and effort it took to do what I did. A race driver's life is never very private, and there was never enough time for strictly personal things.

In my first year of professional road racing—with Roger Penske in 1966—our mechanics said that someday I ought to write a book about our adventures. Now all of us are still together, and there seems to be a demand for such a book. Since we're still too busy, and too inexperienced in writing, I asked Paul Van Valkenburgh to do the job. He happened to be around some of the time while I was racing, and he saw me grow, and he even helped in technical areas before he became a writer. He's also been through some similar experiences as an engineer and race driver. So he has a feel for what it's like. He interpreted my words and feelings so well that I can't tell the difference between what I really told him and the extra material he supplied where I'd forgotten something.

Now that the book is finished, I'm satisfied that again I've done the best I could. You can criticize what I said or the way I said it, but that doesn't matter. It's me, take it or leave it. That's the way things were—the way I saw them.

MARK DONOHUE

INTRODUCTION

BY PAUL VAN VALKENBURGH

Mark Donohue wasn't born a great racing driver. Slowly and painstakingly he *made* himself a great racing driver—through sixteen years of incredibly intense hard work. It was the kind of effort that could have made him just as successful in any other career.

I've known and worked with Mark for a number of years, and I can safely say that he is as real a person as anyone who reads this book. He has many of the same faults, virtues, feelings, problems, illnesses, and worries as all of us "mere mortals" who have watched him rise to fame. Some less successful drivers have become racing legends through amazing traits or physical abilities, or a colorful off-track life, or a flashy driving style. But the quality that has made Mark a legend is his motivation.

From what I've learned about technology and psychology, and now about Mark Donohue, I'm sure that many drivers could be made into as good a race driver—given enough time and money and his intense motivation. That's not to say that Mark did it because he had wealth or a great deal of idle time. He started out like every other average, hopeful amateur racer. But he overcame his shortage of time and money through a natural friendliness, which caught the attention of people who could help him realize his potential. The question is not whether a person could become a Mark Donohue, but whether it is worth the personal sacrifice.

Over the past year, Mark and I managed to squeeze out 150,000 words on tape between races, engineering trips, and personal appearances. All I did was eliminate some words, add some, and rearrange some. He has an amazing memory for the details of all his cars, the names of all the people he has been exposed to, and all the times and places he has raced. And as anyone knows who has heard him give an extemporaneous talk, he is also an entertaining speaker. So the book is in *his* words, and its *his* story.

During our year of writing we often talked about his retirement, and he occasionally asked whether I thought he was doing the right thing. By then I knew a great deal about what he liked and disliked about racing and all the outside pressures. So it's possible that I could have influenced him one way or another. I'm not sure there is any conflict between his own personal comfort and security versus his value to the public as a great alter ego. However, I never did give my own opinion, because I would never want to feel responsible for encouraging him to be exposed to continual danger as a driver.

My last word on Mark Donohue is a point that he could never recognize, much less admit. But it is a flat statement that most other racers and automotive writers would agree with: Mark Donohue is his own greatest Unfair Advantage.

Chapter 1

1958–59

CORVETTE
Getting Started (with the Sporty Car Set)

In the spring of 1957, while I was a sophomore at Brown University, I started becoming aware of sports cars. One of my best friends from high school, Burge Hulett, owned an MG. Another friend, Dave Lawton, who had influenced me to go to Brown, had a Jaguar XK-120 roadster. My father was opposed to small, imported, two-seater automobiles, however. To him they were the peak of frivolous transportation. So we agreed that if I paid half, I could buy an ordinary, utilitarian, all-American Chevrolet Corvette. That seemed quite reasonable to us, since neither he nor I knew much about cars.

That wasn't my first car by any means. When I was fifteen Burge had a '34 Ford hot rod, and I wanted to have something like it. Eventually I found a cheap '37 Ford from which someone had cut off the top and the fenders. There was a big hole in the transmission and it had no exhaust manifold, but I drove it home and spent a lot of time getting it figured out and repaired. Since I didn't have a license, I drove it up and down the driveway, and broadslid it around in a field out back until it fell apart. That car was followed by a Willys Jeepster, then a '53 Ford convertible. Long before I was aware of racing, I was a fanatic about having a "properly prepared" car. I washed that car before school every day and waxed it weekly—until I wore off the paint.

With Dave's expert advice, and careful consideration of engines and gear ratios, I selected a brand-new, bright red '57 Corvette. It had a 283-cubic-inch, 245-horsepower engine, with two four-barrel carburetors and hydraulic lifters that limited it to 5500 rpm. Right after I bought it I left for a summer job with the Diamond Match Company in Cloquet, Minnesota. I was a little self-conscious about showing up there in such a spectacular new car, so I parked it some distance from the factory. When it came time to go to my hotel, however, I somehow got it jammed into reverse gear and had to back it all the way to a service station in town. From then on we became a bit of a sensation in Cloquet. I had problems with girls walking up and getting in whenever I stopped at a street light. It was a lot like an episode from "American Graffiti."

I had only seen one race in my entire life, when Dave and I had gone to Watkins Glen in upstate New York. It was interesting, but it hadn't made any great impression on me. But there wasn't much to do in Cloquet, so I drove down to Elkhart Lake to watch all the big-name stars at a Sports Car Club of America National Race. Paul O'Shea was there in his Mercedes-Benz 300SL roadster, and so was Walt Hansgen in Briggs Cunningham's D-Jaguar. Most interesting, though, were the Corvettes of Dick Thompson and Fred Windridge.

By the time the race was over I knew that if I ever considered racing myself, it was out of the question with my modest street Corvette. I had neither the money, the knowledge, nor the inclination to modify it into a race car.

In the spring of my junior year at Brown, Dave invited me to take my Corvette to a hill climb at Belknap, New Hampshire. I wasn't a member of the club that was putting it on, but I could run as Dave's guest. I immediately realized that I'd be handicapped by my street-stock sports car. For one thing, I had the three-speed transmission with a non-synchromesh first gear. At the top of the hill there was a tight traffic circle that required downshifting into first. The problem was having to make a double-clutch from second to first without tearing out my gearbox.

To make matters worse, a Providence real-estate man named Dick Jalbert appeared with a Corvette that made mine look sick. His was equipped with every piece of high-performance equipment that could be bought through a Chevrolet dealership: fuel injection, metallic brake linings, a four-speed transmission, heavy-duty suspension, quick steering, and so on. Somehow I managed to run the course slightly quicker than he did—in fact, I turned the quickest time of the day.

An even stronger competitor, Charlie Rainville, arrived with an aluminum-bodied XK-120 Jaguar equipped with Borrani wire wheels and a special C-type cylinder head. Charlie was a genuine big-time "real racer" to me. He was a top mechanic and driver who worked out of Jake Kaplan's Providence, Rhode Island, dealership for imported cars, and he had raced at places like Sebring, Marlboro, Cumberland, and Watkins Glen. Charlie made his run up the hill later than I did. Knowing he had to better my time,

Corvette *Donohue Collection*

he drove harder than he should have. He went straight on a tight left-hand turn near the top of the hill and bent one of those beautiful, hand-formed aluminum fenders, giving me the win.

I returned to school with no more reward than a mildly inflated ego. Because I had not been a member of the sponsoring club, I wasn't even given a trophy. It had been fun, but the hill climb added little incentive to my racing urges. I decided that my car had been better suited to the job than Jalbert's; his was a more satisfactory road racer than a hill climber. It seemed that I had won simply because I had the best car—the "Unfair Advantage," as any hard-earned advantage came to be called in later years.

I was majoring in mechanical engineering at Brown, which kept me quite busy. I didn't have a great deal of extra time to work on the Corvette. I did follow Dave's advice to purchase a four-speed transmission—a $300 expenditure that meant scraping the bottom of my bank account. I also added a set of the then-legendary Michelin X radial tires. They were known to break loose suddenly and without warning, but they wore like iron. On my budget the longevity was far more important than their handling quirks. I went back to Belknap twice and was beaten twice. As the months passed, that first moment of victory dimmed, and the entire adventure seemed nothing more than a good example of beginner's luck.

I kept the Corvette through my senior year, but I didn't race it again. Charlie Rainville and I were becoming better friends, and he suggested that I take my car to nearby Thompson, Connecticut, for some practice. The late George Weaver, a veteran driver who owned the track, opened the course on nonracing weekends, and anyone could run there for five dollars. Charlie was racing an Alfa Romeo Veloce, and we practiced at Thompson a number of times. Charlie and his Alfa were much quicker than me and my

Corvette, especially after three or four laps, when my brakes would fade away to nothing. As a remedy, Charlie suggested Ferodo brake linings, which were much better suited to competition conditions. He invited me down to Kaplan's shop one Saturday afternoon to make the switch. It was the first time I'd ever seen the inside of a brake drum. But with Charlie's help I removed the old Corvette linings and riveted the fresh Ferodo material in place. By that time it was late afternoon and Charlie had to leave.

There I was, alone in a strange shop, stuck with reinstalling my brakes. I struggled for what seemed like hours, trying to get the shoes, tensioner springs, and everything else into place. I did manage to get it all bolted back together, but I reversed the leading and trailing shoes on several wheels, which made the brakes grab uncontrollably on the street. It took some very careful driving to get the car back to Charlie the following Monday. My first exposure to "do-it-yourself" mechanics had been something less than a success.

The only other mechanical work I ever did to the Corvette was a valve job. After running the hill climbs and practicing at Thompson, the motor started feeling sluggish. I had been reading a lot about how to hop up the Chevrolet V-8, so over spring vacation I decided to grind the valves to racing specifications. I wasn't capable of doing all the work myself. I took the heads to a machine shop, along with a magazine article, and told them that was what I wanted done. I spent the week getting the heads off, getting them ground, putting them back on, and adjusting the valves—with the aid of a service manual. It was an interesting week, and the car seemed to run better.

On my way back to school I passed near Hartford, Connecticut. There were a number of traffic lights there, and I came up on a blue Corvette at one of them. Naturally, we did the normal thing for drivers of Corvettes in those days—we drag-raced between lights. After easily beating him again and again, he stopped and asked me to follow him to meet some of his friends. I didn't understand, but I followed him a ways, until I saw about fifteen or twenty Corvettes parked outside a drive-in. As it turned out, he had the second fastest car in their club, and he wanted me to race against the fastest one. I'd never gone anywhere with the express purpose of street racing before, but I was feeling reckless so I agreed.

It was just like the movies. Everybody got into his car, pulled out of the drive-in, and drove in a caravan to a deserted stretch of highway. I'd seen that the other car had a fuel-injection motor, drag tires, and a locked differential, and I figured I'd bitten off more than I could chew. He said that just for kicks he would give me a car-length head start, and he would start when I did. Everyone else drove a quarter-mile down the highway to see how we finished. I was really shaking by then. It was after dark, and I had to turn on my interior lights because there wasn't a light in the tachometer. Since it was a do-or-die deal, I was going to hold it at 2500 rpm, drop the clutch, and power-shift at 5500 rpm. When I left, he left, and I beat him by a little bit. They were all amazed! On our way back to town we had at it a few times from a rolling start, where his tires weren't such an advantage, and I pulled him every time.

I wasn't aware of the real significance of that exercise until many years later. After the 1968 Sebring race Chevrolet wanted to test the motor from my class-winning Camaro. They put new heads on it, ran it on the dynamometer, and it showed thirty horsepower more than when it was first built! The explanation was that as an engine gets older, friction is reduced in the cylinder walls and bearings—as they say, "the molecules get happy with each other"—and the valve seats deteriorate. The net effect is that horsepower remains about constant. But if fresh heads are bolted on, the power goes up. The ideal situation is to keep the block alive as long as possible, running it until it's "seasoned," or until the pistons are "friendly" with the cylinders, and then simply grind the valves. Everyone knows that now—Chevrolet, Porsche, or Offy—but I had seen that happen on my own Corvette in 1958, and I didn't recognize it for what it was.

I graduated from Brown in the spring of 1959 without having a real handle on what I was going to do. I had interviewed for several jobs before leaving school, but they all involved becoming an engineering trainee with large corporations. In fact, one of the companies I talked with was Goodyear, but when I mentioned racing, the representative looked blank. I didn't want to become a number, and because openings in smaller businesses didn't seem to exist, I decided to drift for a while.

I'd spent a few summers working in a gas station on Martha's Vineyard. My summer boss there for many years, Val Bergeron, ran the VW agency on the island, and he told me he'd bought a combination bus stop and delicatessen. He was planning to turn it into a lunch counter, and asked if I would like to run it. I accepted, and got Burge Hulett to join me in the enterprise, called "The Pit Stop." We didn't make any money, but we spent three months knocking around Martha's Vineyard, guaranteed of a place to sleep and all the food we could eat. What more could an engineering graduate from Brown University ask for?

The summer season on Martha's Vineyard closed down after Labor Day, and that meant getting serious again. I decided that a graduate degree in business administration, added to my qualifications as an engineer, would open the door to a really attractive job. I entered New York University and took business courses from accounting to marketing. It was fun, and by midwinter I'd also picked up a job with Raybestos-Manhattan in Passaic, New Jersey. The whole thing would have been better if my "junior engineer's" position with them had been more challenging. Their Passaic plant made conveyor belts and V-drives and apparently got along quite effectively without "junior engineers." I had nothing to do.

Bored with my job, I decided to try some ice racing. Weekend events were being run at Lake Naomi in the Poconos of eastern Pennsylvania, so I entered the Corvette. The first time out I spun and hit a dock, but managed to finish fourth in the race. The car was easily repaired, and I went again. That time I overtook a guy in a Porsche and gave him a hard clout in the rear end, which beat up both cars rather seriously. In fact, one of the Corvette's fenders was knocked off. I decided to make my own repairs. Working in my parents' cellar, I discovered—too late—that I had a bad allergy to fiberglass. I ended up in bed with my arms swollen and covered with open sores. It was a grim time, but the ice racing had increased my appetite for competition. When spring arrived, I'd had the Corvette repair job completed by a professional, and Burge and I were talking more seriously about getting into SCCA road racing. After all, I had some extra money now that I was working, and the whole thing seemed more feasible.

One evening an old high school friend of ours, Jim Haas, invited Burge and me to dinner at his home in nearby New Providence. He knew we were considering going racing and he wanted us to talk with his house guest, a former classmate of his from Lehigh. The guy had started out in Corvettes and was now racing Porsches with considerable success. Jim thought he might be able to give us some good advice. We had a good time sitting around talking, but I got only one tip of any great value. He stressed that if we were going to go racing, we should only go first class. Racing was very expensive, he said, and it was important to only compete with cars we could afford. I realized from what he said that there was no way I could do it with my Corvette, because I could barely afford the fuel for it, much less tires, spare parts, and repairs. The driver's name was Roger Penske. I didn't see him again for a number of years, but he did reinforce my enthusiasm for SCCA road racing.

Chapter 2

1960–61

ELVA COURIER
Immediate Success (with an Automatic Advantage)

Burge Hulett introduced me to the Elva Courier. Elva was a new British firm that built limited numbers of racing machines, plus a fiberglass-bodied Courier that could be raced or driven on the street. It ran with an MG engine, and competed against MG-A's in SCCA's F-Production class, although it was 600 pounds lighter. Burge located an Elva dealer in Hanover, New Jersey, named Lou Schulz, of S & R Motors, who specialized in off-brand imported cars—of which the Elva was a good example. But before I could buy the Courier I had to sell my Corvette. I accomplished that by giving demonstration rides on back streets in my home town—up to 60 mph in first, 80 in second, and 100 in third—which dazzled prospective buyers. The sale netted $2700, which was about what the Elva cost.

The Elva Courier was a better machine than we realized. Its high kick-up at the rear, clean sides, and sloping nose with a small radiator opening had most of the right principles of streamlining. Many chassis components came from the Triumph TR-10 sedan, including the entire front suspension. Its solid rear axle was suspended by coil springs and located by four trailing arms and a Panhard Rod. The engine was a stock 1500-cc MG with twin SU carburetors, driving through a four-speed MG transmission.

Dave Lawton gave the car his stamp of approval. After skidding it around on back streets, he said, "This car is perfectly balanced." I didn't understand what he meant by that remark—nor perhaps did he—and in fact I didn't realize its true importance for ten more years. But I was pleased that this authentic car expert thought the Elva was a good machine. It did handle beautifully. Through perhaps a coincidental combination of springs, shocks,

Donohue Collection

ELVA COURIER

chassis stiffness, and the rear axle location, I think the Elva was a neutral steerer—it had no severe understeer or oversteer characteristics. Four-wheel drifts could be set up and maintained with ease. One crank of the steering wheel as you entered the corner and the drift could be held with no additional steering movement. That was balance—a characteristic we worked weeks to develop in later years with race cars costing ten times as much. Thinking back, it's logical that the Elva's suspension, working through its small tires, would behave that way, but it was dumb luck for me to buy a car that handled so well. At that time I didn't know enough to understand or appreciate the Elva's excellence.

Before we could go racing, Burge and I faced the ordeal of joining the Sports Car Club of America, to get the proper competition license. Ed Brown, a well-known expert in British-built competition cars, sponsored our memberships in the Northern New Jersey Region of the SCCA. In those days the club was rather stuffy and exclusive (now they'll take about anyone they can lure through the door), and the NNJ people required candidates to appear at a dinner meeting and give a brief talk on why they wanted to become part of the SCCA. We wanted to join simply to go racing, but Ed warned us that we were supposed to have a broad interest in sports cars—rallies, classic cars, concours, and so on. Single-minded emphasis on racing was considered bad form. So off we went to one of their regular monthly meetings. With our knees shaking, Burge and I stood up and praised the virtues of the SCCA—its sportsmanship, comaraderie, our enthusiasm for all imported sports cars . . . I could see by Ed's satisfied nodding at the back of the room that we were telling them all the right things.

That was on a Thursday evening, three days prior to a driver's school at Marlboro, Maryland. We had to attend such a school before we could obtain a regional racing license, and we were anxious to get this part of our qualification over as soon as possible. So off we went, fat, dumb, and happy, as they say, heading for Marlboro. My mechanic, Lou Schulz, had installed a roll bar and the required seat belt, and the Elva had come fully equipped for the highway, so I drove the nearly 200 miles to the track. Burge had bought an H-modified Bandini, which he trailered behind an ancient Plymouth.

Pierre Mion, a driver of A.C. Bristols, was my instructor, and he appeared at the track with his race car. It was immaculate. I had never seen a first-class racer up close, and I was knocked out by the workmanship and attention to detail. The instructors were to drive each student a few laps around the track to give the novice an idea about line, braking points, and so on.

Pierre jumped into the Elva—with me as his passenger—and began to drive it as if he'd been at the wheel for his entire career. He was so smooth. It seemed effortless, as if he was driving in slow motion. He got out and commented on the fine balance of the Elva, warned that the brakes were fading, and let me drive. Trying to duplicate his rapid, unruffled style, I spun off the third turn. Realizing that Pierre Mion's driving skill was not something everyone is born with, I continued at a more modest pace. He was right about the brakes. They went away early in the going and never returned to full efficiency. We ran short races on the following day. Sam Perry, a guy who showed up with the only other Courier in the school, easily won my race. My general shakiness, coupled with the brake troubles, kept me out of contention, but I did return home with an official, certified SCCA Regional License.

Lou adjusted the brakes and I was ready for my first Regional race at Lime Rock in Connecticut—which, to me, was the epitome of the major leagues. Two changes had to be made to the Elva. Real racers didn't run with windshields and mufflers, so I set out to remove both. I finally decided I'd wait until I got to the track to take off the windshield, but figured it would be easier to leave the muffler home. I ripped it off, rigged up a straight pipe, and headed for Lime Rock, my MG engine rasping away in unmuffled splendor.

I drove six miles. A cop, his ears ringing, pulled me over, gave me a ticket for driving with a straight pipe, and escorted me home to be sure the car wouldn't appear on the streets until its muffler was back in place. I wired and patched the stock exhaust system back in place and got on the road for Lime Rock again. Dave Lawton met me there to assist in removing the windshield and muffler—and to give moral support. I needed it. I finished fourth in my race, and learned that it was going to take more than the Courier's inherent "balance" and my good track manners to turn me into a winner.

I was hooked. Remembering Roger Penske's remark, I decided to go first class, or at least as first class as $700 in scraped up pennies and nickels could provide. That was the sum Lou Schulz estimated would be required to turn the Elva into an effective racer. That would buy me the larger optional SU carburetors, a close-ratio transmission, a lower differential gear ratio for the short Eastern circuits of the day, and a few odds and ends. Those items would turn the Elva into a full race car and end its use on the street. That was just as well; the Courier is one of the noisiest, leakiest, coldest, most uncomfortable road cars I've ever driven.

With the Elva transformed into a full-time race car, I had to find a means of towing it to the races while lugging tools and spare parts. I found a 1954 Chevy station wagon and bought it for $175, although that was beyond my budget. We gave it some exotic flavor by dubbing it the "Scaglietti Chevrolet," and it dragged the Elva around for two seasons. The old crock probably produced as much fun as the race car, because it carried a secret weapon. Shortly after I got the Chevy, Burge and I rigged up a special "fogger" to signal people who ride my rear bumper with their high beams on. By mounting a reservoir of diesel fuel in the engine compartment, with a connection to the engine through the vacuum windshield wipers, we were able to produce clouds of black, oily smoke that would make a destroyer captain green with envy. The first time the thing was used on a busy highway, we produced such an impenetrable cloud of oily fog that traffic from both directions was halted for five minutes! We used our weapon with a certain amount of restraint, saving it primarily for surly gas station attendants. On the way out of the station, one shot of the "fogger" and his place looked like it was in a bag of cotton for twenty minutes afterward.

I went back to Marlboro with my full-race Elva and won easily over a strong field, including Sam Perry. That was my first SCCA trophy! After that, I made an arrangement with Lou Schulz to maintain my car between the races. I would drop the car off at his shop on Sunday evening and pick it up the following Friday. It was a good deal, simply because I didn't have any spare time to work on the car with my night school and all-day job at Raybestos.

The week after Marlboro I went to Vineland, a track in southern New Jersey that is now out of business. During practice a transmission seal failed and the clutch became covered with oil. Dave Lawton and another friend, Bob McCullough, yanked the gearbox out, right there in the sand dunes, and repaired it while I watched helplessly. Even though I won my race the following day, I was sore at Lou. I figured that race preparation meant you paid your money and the car was supposed to be foolproof. I complained to Lou, who in a patient, fatherly way explained that racing was an extremely unpredictable sport. He couldn't cover all the bases, not even with a complete teardown of the car between events—which I certainly couldn't afford. No one could guarantee against mechanical failure on a racetrack. I would have to accept that fact if I wanted him to continue to work on my car.

Lou was the key to my racing program, so I calmed down and carried on—to a string of convincing victories. There were only a few Elvas in Eastern racing circles at the time, and my car was as fast as any of them, and quicker than the MG's, Porsche Normals, Turners, and Fairthorpe Electrons that composed the rest of the class.

In the meantime I'd earned my SCCA National Competition License, which was equivalent to qualifying at Indianapolis to me. On the Fourth of July weekend I went to my first National at Lime Rock, and who should be there but Charlie Kolb! Charlie was the best Elva driver in the country. He had a Courier that was professionally prepared with every special piece the factory could create. When the green flag dropped, Charlie drove off into the sunset, building up a lead at an astounding rate. But then, about halfway through the race, his car broke—and I won. There I was, in my first National, and I was a winner. Instant fame and fortune! My friends said that I was on my way, that sponsors would be beating down my doors to get me to drive their Ferraris, Porsches, and Coopers. It didn't work out that way, but Lime Rock did teach me a lesson. It didn't matter how you won, only that you did win. When it was over, no one remembered that Charlie Kolb had been the fastest man on the track. They only remembered that I'd won.

Some of my friends continued to gripe that Lou Schulz was screwing me with his maintenance of the Elva, but he was in fact doing an excellent job. He seemed to have a sixth sense about when to grind the valves, replace the rod and main bearings, or check the brakes, to the point where we had an amazing record of finishes. I was sure I could win with the Elva—until a new driver appeared late in the season. His name was Jay Signore and he was to become one of my lifelong friends. Jay was a mechanic in Elizabeth, New Jersey, and had raced stock cars for a number of years before buying an Elva Courier. Jay quickly established himself as a strong rival, and in my opinion, one of the most naturally talented drivers I have ever competed against.

Finally Lou and I made our first chassis modification, and our only departure from the exact factory specifications. We put one degree of negative camber into the front wheels. We didn't even know why we'd done it, except that other guys were doing it, and it looked kind of racy having the front wheels splayed in at an angle. Suspension geometry was a total mystery. I remember seeing a new Courier with a front anti-roll bar, and I didn't have the vaguest idea what it was for.

The Elva, because of its speed, was moved up to E-Production for the 1961 season, where it would compete against MG twin-cams, Porsche Supers, and the fast but rare Siata V-8. Jay Signore and I decided we would try to win the E-Production National Championship, which meant racing every weekend throughout the summer. We began traveling together and encountering some of the more unpleasant aspects of racing. The Elvas were becoming less reliable under the heavy schedule of competition. The TR-10 chassis and brake components were never intended for that kind of flogging, and they began to break. Rear axle seals became a major problem. In 1960 I had done little more than take the car to the track and cruise around, but now I had to adjust the rear brakes after every practice session and be prepared to replace the seals if necessary.

Jay escalated our struggle when he obtained a set of optional 9:1 compression ratio pistons for his engine. I had the stock 8:1 pistons and tried to buy a set like his. But Hank Thorpe, an imported car parts supplier and friend of Jay's, had cornered the entire shipment of the new pistons from England and wasn't particularly interested in letting me have a set. In desperation, Lou Schulz and I tried unsuccessfully to raise the compression ratio in our engine by running without a head gasket. Milling the head was the easiest way to increase compression, but that was illegal, and in those days it simply never entered our minds that people would actually bend the rules to win.

The first time I was protested should have introduced me to the realities of racing. It happened at my first race in E-Production, which I won, with Jay taking second. Doug Diffenderfer, the driver of a very fast Siata V-8, was convinced that my motor was illegal, and he protested me. At the end of the day the officials hauled my car off and started disassembling the engine. Lou Schulz had built the motor, and since I never asked what went into it, I said, "Lou, we are legal, aren't we?" He told me not to worry. They took it apart to the last bolt and checked every component. It was legal in all respects. Then they loaded all the parts in a box and sent me on my way. I took them back to Lou, had him reassemble the motor, and sent that SCCA Region a $300 bill for his labor. In return, I got a check for $125. 1 wrote back that I'd like to get them to build my motors for that price, but my letters were ignored.

Before long I was protested by the mechanic of a Morgan driver who had been winning regularly. The motor was partially opened and again found to be within the rules. While that was happening, the Morgan driver came up and apologized for his mechanic's protest. He said that he had no personal suspicions, but that he had to support his own helper. The driver's name was Peter Revson.

Eventually I won so many races, and so many drivers were convinced that we were cheating, that Lou suggested we get some exposure out of the deal. Our Region was always looking for guest speakers, so Lou offered to assemble my motor right there at a regular meeting. Everything was prefitted, and he had two guys to help. There was a great turnout, including my father. They assembled the motor in two hours, sealed it, and announced that I would run it in the next race. I did, and I won again. That cut down on the protests.

Then I tried a protest myself. I was racing on Pirelli tires at the time, and I discovered that I could get recaps for ten dollars a tire, as opposed to twenty-five dollars for a new one. But the day before leaving for a race at Montgomery, New York, Ed Brown, my SCCA sponsor, called and told me that recaps were illegal in the SCCA. I went out and bought a new set of tires. Montgomery was an airport course, and because of the sharp corners and long straights, Doug Diffenderfer's Siata V-8 was outpowering me. If I could beat him I would win the E-Production Championship. But he had qualified ahead of me.

As we assembled for our race, Burge came up to me and said, "Diffenderfer is running recaps!" I jumped out of my car and told the officials, and they pulled him out of the field. I reckoned I had the race won. But moments before the flag dropped, Diffenderfer drove onto the track and took his place at the head of the pack. He had argued that it was too late to remove him from the race—that his recaps should have been spotted in technical inspection. He was allowed to run, and he beat me.

When it was all over we went back to the paddock, bitching about the outcome of the Diffenderfer affair and drinking beer. By the third or fourth can my team decided to protest Diffenderfer's victory on the basis of the recap rule. It took a $100 deposit to make a protest, but we anted up the money with revenge and alcohol in our hearts. The following day I received word that our protest would be allowed. I would be declared the winner.

Then I got a call from Ed Brown. "I suggest you drop the protest," he said.

"Why?" I asked. After all, Diffenderfer had broken the rule, and besides, it would give me the Championship.

"Look," Ed said. "You've proved your point, but he would have beaten you either way. You've got to win your victories on the racetrack or they won't mean much."

Ed was right. Once it was clear that my protest would be allowed and my point was proven, I notified the SCCA that I would allow Diffenderfer's victory to stand.

As the season progressed, Peter Revson became another serious competitor in the E-Production Championship. His Morgan was quick, and Peter had both the money to have it maintained properly and the skill to drive it quickly. Also, he had the time and money to race all over the East and

Midwest—and to pick up valuable points toward the title—while I was stuck by finances to the tracks along the Atlantic Coast. At one point Peter and I had just run a race at Bridgehampton, New York, when he asked me if I was planning to run the next National event at Meadowdale, a road course outside Chicago. I told him that my money was too tight and the Scaglietti Chevrolet would never make it. But during the week I managed to talk my parents into loaning me their new Olds wagon for the trip.

We took off for Meadowdale late Friday afternoon and drove all night. In the early morning we spotted Peter's rig parked outside a diner, so we stopped too. Peter was so shocked to see us that far away from home that he practically dropped his English muffin. It stunned him so badly that he ran a distant second in the race and never challenged me for the lead.

Throughout 1961 Lou Schulz put more and more into our effort to win the Championship. He was spending about $200 a week in parts and labor to keep me in the running. In exchange, I had "S & R Motors" painted on the fenders, and that seemed to attract business for him. It was working well for both of us, although it was a very expensive operation for me.

The year before I'd raced on the cheapest Pirelli tires available. They worked well on the track, and cost so little that frequent replacement didn't hurt my budget much. But in 1961 Goodyear made special, low-profile racing tires available for the Courier. They were more expensive than the Pirellis, but were about three seconds per lap faster. I was faced with keeping up with the latest technical developments such as pistons and tires, rising maintenance problems such as the rear axle seals and brakes, and the frustrations of rules disputes and protests. Each week it took more and more work to win. In the end I did win the Championship—which I had assumed would open the door to all sorts of driving offers from the big-time. Of course that never came.

I had no desire to turn professional, yet I wanted to somehow advance out of E-Production. Lou and I estimated that we had each spent about $6000 during the season, and we both agreed that spending an equivalent amount to pursue the same championship in the same car for 1962 made no sense. I had run the loyal old Courier for two seasons. It had been an excellent race car—better than I realized—but now it was time to move onward and upward. The Courier was easy to sell; cars that are proven winners usually are. A driver named Bob Gaunt bought it and ran it successfully for several more years. He paid me $3000, which I set aside for my next racing effort. I had no doubt whatsoever that it would be at least as successful as the past two years.

Chapter 3

1962

ELVA FORMULA JUNIOR
Facing the Professionals (and Getting Surprised)

After I won the 1961 E-Production Championship in the Courier, Lou Schulz and I felt rather impressed with ourselves. I had a desire to get into something with a little more power, but I didn't know exactly what it should be. I talked to Lou about it, and because he was close to the Elva factory, he knew about a new Formula Junior they were coming out with. He said it was so small and light that it was going to be a sure winner. They were building two of them for the upcoming Nassau races in the Bahamas. One was going to Jim Hall's brother Chuck, and we could get the other for only six thousand dollars. I didn't see any way I could raise that kind of money, though, so Lou finally said he would buy the car for us to take to Nassau, and we could work something out later. Lou was like a mother hen with *his* race car. He was obviously worried a lot more than he ever had been about my Courier.

That was the year that Roger Penske was driving for Team Rosebud, and he crashed his Lotus into the trees when the throttle stuck. But the really hot runners in Formula Junior were Pat Piggot and Pete Lovely.

It was my first race at Nassau, and the first time I'd even sat in an open-wheeled car. We assumed that the factory had already prepared it for racing, so we just fired it up and ran. I lost ground at the start of the race, when I had to get on the brakes just as the leaders were accelerating away. The course was so long that once they got a lead on me, I was all alone. It was a nothing race for me. I just motored around to a distant fourth. The only interesting thing about the race was getting used to the exposed wheels and the motor being behind me. Jay Signore was there too, and we managed to have a good time away from the track.

When we got back I decided that it was time to get serious about racing. Lou said that if I bought the car from him, he would do all the maintenance for free. It was the best deal being offered, so I took it. I had sold the Courier by then, so I had some cash. For the rest, I went to the bank and told them I wanted to borrow some money to buy a $6000 car. I didn't bother to tell them that it was an unregisterable race car. They kept calling me for a long time, wanting to know what the license plate and registration numbers were, but I kept putting them off. Somehow, I survived the year that way.

The next race was at Daytona. There were two qualifying races and one main event. Because of the way cars were split up in the qualifying races, I was able to win one of them. Two of the guys I ran against were Teddy Mayer's brother Tim (who was later killed) and Roger Penske, both in Mayer's Cooper-Austins. Walt Hansgen was there also, in a special Stanguellini, but he ran in the other race.

On our way into the pits after our race, good ol' Roger pulled up behind me and gave me a congratulatory tap on the gearbox. Because it was a Volkswagen gearbox with the external shift linkage, it knocked me back into gear and I went lurching into the paddock. I thought that was a little out of order. I didn't really know Roger that well yet.

In the main event I just made mistake after mistake. Every time I made a bad shift or took a poor line I'd slip farther and farther back. Eventually the motor backfired and caught the carbs on fire. I drove off the end of the

ELVA FORMULA JUNIOR

courtesy of Action Ltd.

straightaway, stopped, and put the fire out before it caused much damage.

We towed the car back to Lou's garage, and he rebuilt it as well as he could. It was a Ford motor, with racing modifications by Holbay, so we didn't know much more than to take it apart, clean it, and put it back together again.

We put out a banzai effort to get the car to Sebring for the next race. Since I had to work, I arranged for my friend Bob McCullough to tow the car down and back. Then I had to buy two new sets of tires. They were ungodly small—and ungodly expensive. Dunlops were the hot setup at the time, and you had to have a set of "drys" and a set of "wets." At about $60 each, that was a $500 investment right there. That took care of all the money I had in the whole world.

I put in no more than a few laps at Sebring when the frame broke and the right front wheel fell off. I was a real discouraged guy at that point. Peter Revson was there also, in a new Lotus 22. He "hit a bird," as we say when a driver makes a mistake, and broke the nose off his car. But he seemed to have the money to continue. I didn't.

We stored the car in my folks' garage while I tried to work my way out of debt a little. I was out of brakes, the gearbox wasn't shifting properly, the motor had less pressure, and finally, the frame was broken. Lou got the frame rewelded for me, but it was made of really thin-wall tubing and I didn't trust it. After looking at it sitting there for a long time, I decided that maybe I could be my own mechanic and pit crew, and go to some nearby races. I cleaned it up, started it in the garage, and drove it up and down the driveway a few times. I just couldn't leave it alone. I took it to a race at Lime Rock—and the frame broke again.

I was through at that point, for I just couldn't afford to do any more. I wrote a letter to the Elva factory: "I appreciate the fact that you built and sold us this special car, but I think I should tell you that I must stop racing it now. I don't have a lot of money, and I can't afford to replace the frame after every two races." I went on to describe where and how it broke. A while later I got a telegram back that said, "We read your very nice letter, and after talking it over, we have decided to send you a new chassis at no charge." They did, and it was beefed up in the same area where mine had broken.

The car still lay dormant for most of the year. It took forever for us to get the old chassis stripped and the new one assembled into a running race car—and for me to get out of debt. Finally I was able to take it to the annual Refrigerator Bowl at Marlboro, the weekend after New Year's, 1963. I won with it in the first heat on Saturday—and Charlie Hayes bought it from me that afternoon.

I was lucky to get out that easily, because I was really in over my head. I had spent so much money on the car that I couldn't afford to race it. A spare motor was out of the question, much less the repair of any broken pieces. The first two races broke me for the season. On top of that, I never spent enough time in the car to even learn how to drive it. I couldn't say whether it was oversteering or understeering, because I never drove it close enough to its limit. I was basically just tracking around the turns. I had to admit that I wasn't able to get the most out of it in such a short time. The car was faster than I was.

By running up front in a few races, however, I decided that if the Elva had a single Unfair Advantage, it was its lowness. They had sacrificed *everything* else a driver cares about to make it close to the ground. It was practically impossible to work on. It had inboard rear brakes—which was fine in itself—but they were drum brakes, and transmission oil leaked on them, and they were totally inaccessible. The engine and transmission had to be removed to adjust the rear brakes! It was a clever little car, but there were a few things like that which they forgot about when it was designed.

If that car taught me one thing, it was that I wasn't made out of money. I couldn't do any more than I had the cash in hand for. When I no longer could afford to buy new parts, it was time to get out. I didn't see the Formula Junior as any great steppingstone to a big professional racing career when I got into it, although it was obviously going to get me further than an Elva Courier. On the other hand, it was a big waste of money to just show up at Formula Junior races and not win. I had to get back into a class where I could win some races again.

Chapter 4

1963

DAIMLER

Advancing Backwards (Without Assistance)

I liked to race because it seemed to be the thing I did best. But I had to realize that I couldn't race in any class I wanted to, or the class that seemed to have the greatest future. If I was going to have a good time at it, I was going to have to have a potentially successful—and inexpensive—race car. Going back to the Courier didn't seem to be the answer. A guy named Duncan Black had been very successful in C-Production with a Daimler, so I thought maybe I should get one of those. They were big and heavy, they made a great noise, and Duncan's seemed fairly reliable. They had a 2.5-liter V-8 motor with hemispherical combustion chambers—just like a small Chrysler hemi—with two small SU carburetors stacked against each other on a very restrictive manifold.

Bob Grossman, an old friend who was a used-Ferrari dealer in New York, also handled Daimlers, so I set out to get one from him. I knew he had a lot of money, and perhaps he would give me one to race. But after talking in that direction for some time, I realized there was no hope. I had some money from the sale of the Elva, but there was no sense in buying a new car and stripping it, so I bought an old used one from Bob.

I wanted Lou Schulz to prepare the car for me as he had with the Courier. But he was disappointed that I sold the Formula Junior, and he wasn't very interested, even though I was paying him the regular rate. It seemed like he was taking forever. I was working as an engineer in the meantime, but when I saw he wasn't getting anywhere, I started doing a lot of the work myself in the evenings. It was a long time before it was ready to race. Finally

photo by Spanky Smith

DAIMLER

I took it to a Regional at Vineland—and won the first time out with it. I wasn't very happy with it, though. Oil was leaking everywhere, and it was junk compared to the Courier. I was so discouraged about it—and about all the money I had to pay Lou—that I decided to do it some other way.

A guy named Scotty, who had worked for Lou, was working at a truck garage at the time, and I asked him if he wanted to be a Daimler mechanic on the side. He agreed. The owner of his garage was interested also, so we worked on the car there. We took the motor out and disassembled it, and I took all the pieces around to various machine shops to have all the right things done. We had the cam ground, parts lightened, and the block line-bored. But eventually those guys lost interest also, and I ended up doing most of the work myself. I just wanted a nice car to take racing without too many hassles. But the Daimler turned out worst of all.

I finally got the car rebuilt and took it to another Regional at Lime Rock. Just getting it there was a lot of work on my part, since I was going to the races alone by then. Jay and Burge were usually around in the Courier days, but they'd had enough, and the Daimler wasn't particularly exciting. So I towed to Lime Rock, unloaded the car, and set out to practice.

In the confusion of doing everything myself, I forgot to secure the hood down properly. It opened at the front and hinged at the cowl, and when I drove up the back straight, it flew open. It bent back over the windscreen, hit me in the head, broke its hinges, and flew off into the woods. It didn't knock me out, but it was a big shock, and it hurt a lot. It was one of those days when a little thing like that can take all the enthusiasm out of a guy. I wasn't interested in driving any more. I talked to Ed Brown, who had helped me get my license and who was an important person in the SCCA. I said, "Is it so unusual for a guy to want to quit driving?" Ed said, "Listen, you've had a bad day. It happens to everybody. If you don't want to drive, just put it back on the trailer and go home." So I did. I went out and found my hood, loaded up, and went away. Since I was there by myself, it was my own decision.

I took the Daimler to a few more races, but there was a continual bad scene with the motor. It would inevitably overheat and wipe out the center main bearing. The temperature would go up and the oil pressure would drop. Then I'd have to pull the motor out again and go buy a new crankshaft. During those months I learned a lot about building motors from a good friend and machinist named Dickie DiBiasse. I learned how to do basic machine work, and how to balance and assemble motors. He taught me many things that were really valuable to me later on. Unfortunately, building motors was kind of a gamble, because no one had dynos in those days. So we just had to build them and hope for the best. I've always been interested in what goes into the motor, but that was the last time I ever built one myself.

After losing the crankshaft in three races, I finally decided to convert the Daimler back into a street machine. I put mufflers and the top and upholstery back on, drove it about a week—and lost the center main bearing again. When I took it apart and saw that, I didn't want to ever rebuild it. Hank Thorpe did me a great favor by selling the car through his imported car store to a friend of his in Florida. In the meantime, we opened up the main bearing clearance by one thousandth, and discovered that the old used radiator core was clogged. But the car left with the motor in a basket. The next guy reassembled it the way we said to and was much more successful. The motor cost me a lot of time and money, but in the end I was satisfied that I had solved its problem.

That car was simply an engine exercise to me. There was never any time to look into anything else. It had wire wheels and big tires, and I ran with the production brakes. It also had a Jaguar gearbox, which was a slow-shifting piece of junk, like a truck. Mechanically it was terrible. I don't think it even handled very well. It understeered a lot, which could be avoided by opening the throttle—but I couldn't do that for very long before the motor would fail. What little enthusiasm I had left from the glory of the Courier was practically gone. After the Daimler I never again owned my own race car. It wasn't by choice, but due to the fact that I was married, had kids, and just didn't have the money. I was on the verge of going through life as an ordinary career engineer.

Chapter 5

1963

COOPER-OFFY

The First Free Ride (Plus a Little on the Side)

The Elva Formula Junior and the Daimler had been so discouraging —after the successes I had with the Courier—that I sat around a lot in 1963. A friend of mine named Bill Claren told me he knew a guy who had a rear-engine USAC midget car he was going to enter in a road race at Lime Rock. The year before, Rodger Ward had beaten George Constantine's Aston-Martin with a front-engine Offy midget, which was a big deal to the sporty-car set. Now there was going to be another free-for-all, with USAC midgets against SCCA Formula cars.

Bill's friend, Kenny Brenn, had bought an old Formula Junior Cooper from Cunningham and rebuilt it into a midget. His mechanics installed a 110-cubic-inch Offy, shortened the wheelbase by eighteen inches, and mounted little twelve-inch tires on eight-inch-wide rims. So it became a mid-engine USAC midget—possibly the very first one. Bill kept bugging me to call Kenny, and finally I did it just to get him off my back. I never realized at the time how much Bill was doing to try and help me. Years later he came back and asked me for an interview, and because I was having a bad day, I was kind of rude. I felt terrible about it later. There have been so many people who helped me become successful over the years, and yet sometimes it's so hard to return their favors.

When I called Ken he asked me to come over and have a look at his car. He ran a construction business and had a lot of heavy equipment for building roads and highways. In their off hours he and his mechanics built and raced USAC dirt-track cars. He was a huge guy and I was kind of nervous. When I walked up he said, "Who are you?" I told him I was Mark Donohue, and he said, "Jesus Christ! You don't look much like a race driver." I was intimidated just by the way he looked at me.

We had a look at the car—they called it the "pusher" because the engine was behind and pushed the driver—while Ken told me all about it. He said one guy had hit a pole with it, another guy had gone over the wall in it, and another had backed it into a fence. Each time they had rebuilt it, until it was just one big scab on top of another. He wasn't sure he wanted to race it any more, because he was constantly picking it out of a fence and rebuilding it. Everyone knew that mid-engine cars were faster at Indy, but there were some doubts whether it would work in a midget. He was just a few years ahead of his time.

As it turned out, they knew how to build a car but not how to develop it—something that I was only learning had to be done. The Cooper had fully independent suspension, and the wheels looked all askew to me. When I suggested that we get everything all lined up, they didn't know what I was talking about. They were all solid-axle, left-turn-only racers. It was like a revelation to them that we should get all the wheels pointed in the same direction. I offered to take the car and get it aligned somewhere. I called Hank Thorpe, and he told me where to find a mirror-type alignment gauge.

I had no idea what the caster, camber, and toe-in should be, but I knew a guy named Tippy Lipe who had a Cooper Formula Junior. He had already made a million dollars designing helicopter blades, so I had a lot of respect for his engineering ability. Eventually he went off and started manufacturing the famous Lipe ski bindings. On the other hand, ten years ago he was convinced that someday someone with enough time and money was going to make turbochargers work on road racing cars and smoke everybody. Everyone laughed at him. Anyhow, he told me all about the proper alignment for a Cooper. The most important thing, he said, was to make sure the rear toe-in was one-fourth inch and equal from side to side.

The reason for that, as I learned later, was to help prevent the car from oversteering if the throttle was lifted while in a turn—which we now call "trailing-throttle oversteer." Most of the first rear-engined race cars had trailing-throttle oversteer. So everyone after that thought it was inherent in a rear-engine car, not realizing it was actually due to the suspension geometry. All the old hands said it was something the driver just had to get used to. There was a big difference in handling between front- and mid-engine cars, but it was due more to the suspension than the engine location. That was probably why the Cooper-Offy kept getting smashed up so frequently.

It looked like alignment was going to be the answer. Tippy said that the camber should be 2¼ degrees negative, so we spent hours making it exactly 2¼ degrees—without ever considering how the weight of fuel and driver would affect it. We cranked in the recommended toe-in at the rear, and figured that the chassis was developed. It was cured of trailing-throttle oversteer all right, but then it *understeered* badly—everywhere.

Ken wanted to take the car to an early practice session at Lime Rock, to see whether the car looked competitive. If it wasn't fast he wouldn't race it. It was a hot day, so I wore Bermuda shorts, which was the thing to do at sports car races in those days. When I walked into the construction company, everyone stopped what they were doing and stared at me like I was a freak. I might as well have been naked. One of the guys said, "Can I help you?" When I told him I was going to race their car, he laughed and yelled out to the other mechanics, "Hey! Look at the sporty car driver. What's that, a sporty car outfit you've got on?"

Looking around, I could see they were also taking a front-engine midget along for Len Duncan, who was the Eastern midget champion. They said he needed the practice, but it looked to me like a runoff between us.

None of those cars had clutches. They just used an in-out box for a transmission. But for starting there was a valve to cut out the front brakes. A truck would push the car up to some speed while the rear wheels were kept locked, and then the driver would let up on the brakes, watch the oil pressure gauge climb, and then switch on the magneto. I drove around one lap—and I was positive that something was seriously wrong. The whole car was vibrating like crazy. I pulled into the pits very carefully and told them that the motor must be falling out. They poked around for a while, and said, "Nope! That's just the way it is. It won't be so bad when you get going quicker."

Len Duncan and I both drove around, but I was quicker by quite a bit. In fact, I was turning better times than any of the Formula cars could. So we loaded up the cars and headed out. I suggested that we stop and have about twenty beers, but they said they had to get back to the shop. They had to pull the motor out and put a new one in for the race. I had never heard of such a thing before—to have separate motors for practice and racing. On the way back their kidding about my shorts changed somewhat. Ken told Len that maybe he would be quicker if he wore shorts also. But Len was a good sport about it. He gave me a lot of good advice about racing in midgets. When he showed up at the race with Bermuda shorts, I had to take my hat off to him.

In official race practice Ken told me not to go as fast as I could, so I wouldn't tip off everyone. First there was a sports car race, then a midget race. The top fifteen cars from each race would start the feature race. The hottest midget driver there was a guy named Mario Andretti, and when my gearbox broke, he went on to win the heat. I was devastated that we didn't finish, but Ken told me not to go away. They would try to fix the gearbox in time to make the "feach." We were late for the start, but another driver, Dutch Schaeffer, pulled his car up to the line—and left to go to the bathroom. Everybody was paging him, but he didn't appear and move until my car was ready.

I had to start way at the back, which was fortunate in a way. Len had warned me that there was going to be an accident at the start, because the track narrows from about five lanes to two going into the first turn. He told me to hold back and watch. Sure enough, two guys touched wheels. One car was fired up into the air like a rocket, landing upside down in the escape road and killing the driver. I just carefully passed everyone else, one by one, and won the race.

It was like the end of World War II to me—a history-making event. It wasn't such a big deal as the previous year, because I wasn't as big a name as Rodger Ward. But it was the first mid-engine midget, the car's first finish, and my first "professional" race. Ken was grandstanding in the winner's circle, saying, "The greatest thing about this win is that the kid's an amateur—he can't take any money." We won $1000, and Ken actually slipped me $600 under the table. The SCCA woulda' shit.

The next week about six midget car owners called me, wanting me to drive their cars. At the same time other midget drivers were challenging me to go to a "man's track"—an oval—and get smoked. So Ken and I went to an oval track race at Trenton.

It was like a nightmare. Everyone got only three laps of practice before the race. The car was understeering terribly, and I didn't know how to correct it or how to drive it with that setup. All I could do was turn the steering wheel more, which did absolutely nothing.

COOPER-OFFY

photo by Spanky Smith

The Cooper had two "saddle" fuel tanks, with a valve under the seat so that the outside tank could be emptied first. But the Hilborn fuel injection unit had a "controlled leak" with a high rate of return—which dumped into the inside tank. On the pace lap fuel was being pumped out of the outside tank and back into the inside tank. Pretty soon the tank got so full that it was pressurized, and the fuel started coming out the vent hole. It was a regular geyser, spraying up into the air, over the back—missing the tailpipe—and soaking the guy behind me. He was naturally upset about that, so he signaled me by coming up behind and crashing into me. I didn't know what was wrong, so I pretended nothing happened. He kept banging away, and when that didn't work he pulled up next to me and pointed to the geyser. I only had a few controls in the cockpit, and I knew it wouldn't help to turn the steering wheel or to use the brakes or ignition switch, so I reached down and turned the fuel valve—and the spray stopped. I struggled away with the understeer and finished the race in a poor eighth place.

Right after that we took the car to Flemington, a half-mile paved oval, and tried to improve the handling. Camber angles were the only thing I knew to play with, and that got me nowhere. Nothing had much effect on its "pushing." The car just wasn't fast enough. Another driver tried it, and he immediately spun by trying to get the tail hung out. Ken decided the car wasn't going to make it, and we ended our relationship with only two races.

My skill as a driver hadn't been the deciding factor in the Lime Rock race. The basic layout of the car was our Unfair Advantage. It would have won no matter who was driving. At least I learned something about chassis setup from that adventure. I always knew all those suspension adjustments were there, but I never before realized what could be gained by changing camber and toe-in. It was my first experience in suspension dynamics. It was also—unofficially—my first "professional ride."

Chapter 6

1963–64

COBRA
Awesome Power (for a Few Races)

By the end of 1963 I was a retired racing driver. But I was still interested enough to go and watch any race within driving distance. I went to one race at Lime Rock, although I couldn't even get a pit pass. I sat up on the hill and watched Bobby Brown's Cobra beat Dick Thompson's Stingray. It really turned me on to listen to the sound of those big booming V-8's. Brown would blow off Thompson so bad in the straights that I just couldn't believe it. Then Thompson would catch him back in the esses and somehow get ahead again. Then Brown would boot the Cobra past him again. After the race I went to the Lime Rock Lodge to have a couple of beers. I was just an ordinary spectator, sitting off in the corner. Brown came in with his wife—a stunning ex-stewardess—and he was really the hero. He was racing the Cobra for Jack Griffith, and he was generating quite a reputation as a colorful person. It wasn't uncommon to hear about him racing through cornfields in a Corvette or knocking down a motel wall with a hammer. There he was—all those fancy clothes on and his wife with almost no clothes on. He was really looking good. I looked over and said to myself, "It must be great to be famous like that—to have a beautiful gal, to win the big race, and to be king of the track." Actually, I was in love with his car.

Dick Monich, an old friend of mine, was trying to get Griffith involved in a deal to put Ford engines in TVR's. I thought the idea was insane, but they had the great Carroll Shelby Cobra dream. Dick's major interest was as a team manager-promoter-organizer, so Griffith decided to give him a project. The Cobra had already won the Championship, and it was just sitting around. So they decided it would be a good idea to take it to some local

Regionals, for the publicity. Dick, as manager of the "race team," asked me if I would like to drive it.

Strangely enough, I had just been called by Bernie Veal, the owner of all Bob Holbert's Porsches. He asked me if I would be interested in driving his RS-60 at that same race. That was the first time anyone ever called *me* to drive their sports car, and two called at once—and both had real super cars. But Bernie had been vague. He said he didn't know if I was good enough, but *maybe* I would get to drive. So I called him back and told him that I had to take the firmer offer. Bernie got pissed and told me he was going to smoke me and my Cobra.

That was the first time I ever went to a race not towing my own car. I drove up to the track and waited for the other guys. When people asked what I was doing there, I tried to very casually say, "I'm waiting for my Cobra to arrive." The mechanic was George Clark, a very competent but somewhat cocky guy. He and Bobby Brown had won the Championship, and it had gone to his head a little bit. He was complaining a lot, mostly about taking the car to a lowly Regional race for a nobody driver. Brown was the king and I was just another donkey.

I had never even sat in a Cobra before. They showed me how to start it and where all the controls were, then pushed me out onto the track. Fortunately my old friend Dave Lawton was there with me, to help me figure out how to drive it. He walked around the course while I was driving and watched my line through all the corners. He was a better watcher than I was a driver. He never said that I was doing anything wrong. He would just compare me to other drivers. My line might be higher or lower in some corner, or my braking point earlier or later. I could try his suggestions and evaluate them on my own. We could work together that way because we were such good friends, and we had done that a lot of times in the Elva Courier days.

There was no competition at Lime Rock that weekend. I just sat on the pole and won the race.

The Cobra didn't seem to corner as well as most of my previous cars, but it was much more powerful than anything I'd ever driven. It was tremendous on the straight. And what a great noise it made! Shelby was a pretty smart guy to recognize what a big motor, big wheels, and big tires would do to a mediocre car. No matter how bad the car was to start with, those things really brought it to life.

The last Regional race of the year was coming up at Vineland. None of the other guys wanted to go to a non-local race because there was less publicity value. But I was mesmerized. I called the track promoter and asked if he would be interested in having a Cobra show up at his race. He didn't know me from Joe Doaks, but he knew that a Shelby Cobra would bring in more paying customers. I told him that it would cost him some "tow money." When he asked how much, I said, "Well, how about $100?" He said, "Jesus Christ, kid, that's a lot of money—but I'll do it." So I called Dick, and he said that sounded like a great deal, especially for a mere Regional. It wouldn't cover the expenses, but it was a good excuse for Griffith and Clark. To me, it was sensational! Someone was *paying* me to race at his track.

At that point I became aware that racing could be more than an amateur thing with me. That's not to say I knew how to promote good deals. I still don't know how. But I knew that I didn't have to be a famous guy, as long as I had a famous car. I wasn't able to promote myself—but I found it very easy to promote the car.

We went to Vineland. That time I didn't want to arrive first and stand around waiting for the car. When I realized I was early, I parked outside the track and watched for the other guys. I was so nervous, wondering whether they would really make it, that I felt as if I was on my first date. I went to turn my car around for a better view, and smashed the rear bumper into a phone pole!

Eventually they did get there, we collected the money, and I led the

COBRA *Donohue Collection*

race—for a while. But a bolt broke in the front transverse leaf spring. Because the spring located both front wheels in camber, the wheels would flop over to the outside in a turn and stay that way until I got to the next turn. I didn't stop until the car became totally undriveable.

Then there was the annual "Refrigerator Bowl" weekend at Marlboro. Again I promoted $100 in tow money—under the table. That race was a little more exciting. I led a Corvette up to the last lap, when I spun and he caught up. I *might* have been able to get back on the track ahead of him, but I wasn't going to take the chance of getting hit in a car I didn't own. I managed to repass him coming out of the last turn, and I led at the finish line. It was a great thrill for the spectators.

Apparently the spin was caused by an oil leak in front of the left rear tire, and smoke was billowing off the tailpipe in right turns. George thought that was keen. He said it looked really hairy. But I was becoming worried about the car getting ratty. It was backfiring, and things were getting loose and rattling around. I was beginning to see the difference between a mechanic who really *cared* about his car and one who was living off his reputation.

After that race a reporter friend of mine named Ev Gardner sent me a copy of an article about my win, with a photograph of the car going around a corner. I looked at that photo for a long time, thinking, "Something looks wrong about the car. But what is it?" Finally I decided that the front tires were leaning too far out of the corner—as though the spring were still out of place. I'm not sure why I thought that was wrong, but I reckoned it was obvious that for better cornering the tires should be flat on the ground. I went to George and drew some lines on the photo, showing that the tires had about four degrees too much positive camber. I told him that we ought to do something to prevent that from happening. Apparently we would have had to roll new eyes in the leaf spring—which was the upper arm—or make longer lower control arms. As it was, the layout had a very bad camber change curve, although I didn't even know what that meant at the time.

George never gave me a good answer. He just said it was too much work to change it. Anyhow, the biggest problem was the front suspension bushings. They weren't designed for the weight of that big engine and the cornering power from those tires. Under braking, the front suspension would lock up solid and I'd have to get off the brakes to steer.

I got in one last race with the Cobra. The first National race of 1964 was at Virginia International Raceway, and I talked Griffith into letting us go. There were some famous guys there—like Howard Keck, in a similar Cobra. I wasn't as fast as Keck in practice. I had won there before, but never in such a high-powered car. So I spent Saturday night going over the course again and again in my mind, trying to analyze it the way Dave Lawton would have done for me. Since he wasn't there, I had to *think* the correct lines out.

The next day I was able to pass everyone. A large part of the credit, though, is due to George and his knowledge of Ford motors. He was especially good with Weber carburetors, and he jacked around with the jets and the timing until it was running perfectly for that course. In the race I pulled past Keck on the main straightaway. I guess it made him pissed to be shown up by a nobody. He tried to outbrake me, and ran into the back of my car. He went sailing off into the woods, while I went on to win—with a stove-in trunk.

I walked around the car when it was put on the trailer. I had just won my first National race in a high-powered car. It was really fantastic. And yet, there was a $ 10,000 car, with $400 worth of damage to the back end. That would have been a crisis if the car were mine. All I had to do was walk away from it.

After that, Griffith sold the car to raise capital for his TVR-Ford operation. I was really disappointed. I would have been happy with even a few more races in the Cobra—ratty as it was. But that ended our deal. They said that when they got into production with the TVR's, they would build a race version for me to drive at Sebring. I figured I'd believe that when I saw it.

If the Cobra deal didn't teach me a lot about cars, at least I learned something about racing mechanics. There are too many who think they know everything, not realizing how little the best men in the business really know. They don't give the driver an opportunity to think intelligently. For example, a good driver who is really wealthy, and yet doesn't know much about race cars, will go out and hire a guy who is known as a good mechanic. It's the reasonable thing to do. But then the mechanic says, "Okay, since you don't know anything, I'll prepare the car, and you pay all the bills." If the driver says something doesn't feel right, the mechanic says, "I know the car's right because I've done it before. Go back out and try harder." Or he says, "It's always been that way, and no one else complained." I reckon we've had a lot of potentially great drivers come and go for that reason.

George Clark and I eventually became good friends while working on another car—once we recognized each other's abilities. One of the most important things for a racing driver is to know what he wants, and to have the courage to try and get it—even if it means making some mistakes along the way. That's the only way to learn how to win. Ultimately, only the driver knows what is right or wrong about his car.

Chapter 7

1964–65

MGB AND FERRARI 275
Sharing Rides (with Walt Hansgen)

Walt Hansgen was the first good friend of mine who was a real professional road racer. He was a big-name driver for Cunningham until that team folded, and then he went with the John Mecom team. Mecom wanted him to move to Houston, where the race shops were, but Walt had so many interests in our area that he simply kept an apartment down there for short stays. I got to know Walt by driving to Road Racing Drivers Club meetings with him. We would talk a lot about our racing experiences and plans for the future. Walt had a service station, which included a Jaguar dealership, a BMC dealership, and a tractor dealership. He kept asking me to get into the business with him, but I didn't have enough capital and he didn't have enough volume to hire me. So I just hung around there a lot.

At some point Walt talked BMC into giving him an MGB to race. He was like Roger Penske in that respect—promoting rides and free cars. They sent him a new car and all the pieces he needed to make it into a race car, After he and his son Rusty got it all put together, Walt took it to a driver's school at Bridgehampton to try it out. When he saw that it was going to be uncompetitive in its class, he kind of lost interest. But that was a lean period for me. All my previous amateur cars—and my few attempts at getting a ride—had fizzled out. Walt offered the MGB to me, hoping I could make something out of it.

It was terrible. I took it to a Regional race at Lime Rock and finished way down. Winter was coming on, so I asked Walt to let me take it to my own place for some modifications. I took a good look at the other racing MGB's, most of which were lower and had a lot more negative camber. It wasn't obvious how they had done it, though. I cut the springs and bent the A-arms in a hydraulic press until the car was inches off the ground and looked like it had about the right camber. The car had lever-arm shock absorbers, which I had to find a way of making stiffer. First I took them apart to see how they worked. They had spring-loaded bleed valves, which I shimmed up, and I refilled them with a heavier weight oil.

When I thought the car was ready I took it to a 500-mile race at Bridgehampton. It cornered flat and fast but rode like a big rock. The suspension might as well have been welded up solid for all the work it did. The car was constantly hitting the bumpstops, because there was hardly any suspension travel at all. Whenever I hit a bump the car would leap to one side or the other, almost throwing me out of the seat. I'd just take another line, so that I didn't hit that bump again. For some odd reason—mostly a lack of competition—I won the race. I reckoned I was a hero. Walt was happy, and BMC was relatively satisfied with the deal. I drove it in one other race, without as much luck or success, before returning it to Walt. He gave it to his son, who converted it back to street use. But it rode too stiffly even for that, and he sold it.

When Walt wasn't off driving somewhere for Mecom, we'd sit around and drink his beloved martinis and swap stories. One time he told me that he'd get me a ride at Sebring in Mecom's Ferrari. I said, "Sure, Walter I'd be glad to." I grew to like martinis myself, but I'd get smashed on just a couple and have to struggle to keep a clear head. It seemed to me, once, that he said he had talked Mecom into letting me co-drive at Sebring. I didn't say anything about it because I didn't want to look foolish by taking him seriously.

One day he went off to Sebring on a tire test weekend. He also had a Firestone racing tire distributorship, and that was the period when their Indianapolis design was first being adapted for road racing. Firestone had already won a race with that tire at Elkhart Lake, and it was like a revelation. Walt came back from the tests with a lot of great stories about the car "I" was going to drive with him. I was getting frustrated. I didn't want to say, "C'mon Walter, be honest with me." He was such a dreamer. He loved things to be the way he imagined them, and if they didn't turn out right, he'd just go on to the next thing. I figured the co-driver deal was just another example of that.

Then he showed me a photograph of the car. It was a typical beautiful blue Mecom Ferrari, with a white stripe and the Mecom insignia. But on the side it had the drivers' names—Walt Hansgen and Mark Donohue. I was truly shocked! I decided that if they had gone to the trouble of putting my name on the car, maybe it was true.

Ludvigsen Library

MGB

When I finally realized that I was really going to get the ride, I mentioned the fact to another racing friend. He said, "If you go to Sebring and drive that Ferrari, and it turns out that you're doing too much too soon, you'll never get asked again by those guys"—meaning big-name teams like Mecom, Cunningham, or even Chaparral. "That'll be the end of you. You'll never get another ride." That was Bob Tullius, who probably could have done a better job at that point because he had more experience. But I had the Unfair Advantage—I was friends with Walt Hansgen.

I had driven at Sebring before, but never in anything like a 275 LM Ferrari. It was also the first car I'd ever driven with a genuine racing engine, instead of modified production engines. There was a world of difference between them and a 2750-cc V-12 Ferrari. Everything was so much more sensitive. Except for the noise, the most notable difference was that there was no "flywheel effect" to the motor, and it had a non-synchronized gearbox. I couldn't seem to adapt to shifting it, especially downshifting. I was used to giving the throttle a little blip, but with the Ferrari motor, wherever the throttle was, the engine rpms were also. On top of that, it was right-hand drive with a left-hand shift.

I had a really difficult time in practice. The pedals and steering were so responsive that I was "overcontrolling" it. I was about ten seconds slower than Walt, and just struggling along. It was making me sick that I wasn't getting the job done. But Walt was the eternal optimist. He just said, "Everything will be all right."

Walt drove the first two-hour stretch. When it was my turn, he came in and told me that the clutch linkage was out. It wasn't possible to disengage the clutch at any time. I thought, "Oh, shit! *Now* what?" He must have seen the panicked look on my face, because he got right to work explaining how to drive without a clutch. I could get going by using the starter with the car in gear. From then on I had to shift by matching engine rpms with the throttle. To upshift, I put pressure on the lever while still at full throttle, then let up on the throttle for just an instant, and it would slip into the next gear. The three-four shift was a little harder, because I had to move the lever laterally in the gate and match engine rpms better. Downshifting was somewhat like double-clutching without the clutch, with a little blip in neutral.

I did it exactly as Walt told me to, because I didn't know anything else—and it was easier than using the clutch! The shifting problem solved itself. I would have expected the gearbox to fail on the first lap, but I had absolute trust in Walt's advice. It was a valuable experience to learn that we could communicate that way.

Walt and I were turning about the same lap times, but he was just loafing and I was running flat out. For being such a sensitive and good-handling car, the Ferrari required tremendous physical effort to drive—at least the way I was driving it. It was a very hot afternoon; heat was pouring through the firewall, and I wasn't used to racing a coupe—in two-hour stretches. Toward the end of the first stretch I was on the verge of passing out. I began thinking that I'd never make it another lap—I'd just worry about getting

FERRARI 275

Donohue Collection

through the next turn. I was wondering if racing was all that much fun after all, and thinking, "Why am I doing this to myself?" When they finally called me in at two o'clock, I was at my maximum effort. I got out of the car and realized that if I tried to stand alone I would pass out. I couldn't collapse in front of all those people, so I quickly sat down against the pit wall, gasping as quietly as I could. As soon as I thought I could walk, I went to the Mecom trailer. John Cannon was driving another Mecom car, which had already broken, and he saw how destroyed I was. He told me he was going to take my place before I got hurt. I said, "No, John, I really feel perfect." I didn't think I could recover in time to go on, but I wasn't going to admit it. I had a sandwich and a lot of water, and when my time came again, it had cooled off a lot. Other drivers were getting out of their cars and passing out in the pits. I said to myself, "If I ever pass out while driving, that's when I'll stop racing."

That was the year it rained so hard during the race, and the Chaparral won—with Roger Penske as their crew chief. The water was so deep that tires were floating away in the pit lane. Walt told me to come in for rain tires as soon as it started, and he would drive while it was wet. But it kept on for so long that I had to drive in it anyhow. When it was my turn, Walt gave me some good advice. It wasn't exactly by the rules, but Walt sometimes bypassed rules if they weren't convenient to get the job done. He said that because of the great speed difference between cars at Sebring, it was foolish to drive into another car's spray on the straightaway. He told me that if I "accidentally" slid too wide on the right-hand turn leading into the straight, I might as well stay out there until the next right turn. That runway was wide enough, and the rain was heavy enough, that I could go way out, drive like a sonovabitch past all the slower cars, and cut back in ahead of them without anyone noticing. Then he said, "Whatever you do, no matter who passes you, slow down and go carefully past the scoring building on the track, so that everyone sees you there." It worked perfectly. I was going a helluva lot farther than anyone else, but I could pass a dozen cars at a time that way. I could see them all off in the distance to my right, jockeying for position, wondering where the next car was and how fast he was going, while I zapped past all of them.

Overall, we didn't do so well. The ignition got wet and the mechanics decided to change the plugs after dark. It was too hot, and too dark, and they had to give up on some of them. After they wasted a lot of time, they strapped it back together and sent me back out to do as well as I could. At the end I was having a hard time keeping up with an Austin-Healey. We finished twelfth. After that, Mecom was more involved with his Lolas, in shorter races where two drivers weren't needed, so that was the only time I ever drove for him in the Ferrari.

To get home, Walt and I had to take a plane from Tampa to Newark. We arrived at the airport and learned that every flight was booked and wait-listed until eight the next morning. On our way out of the airport we ran into Mecom's number-one racing manager, Bill Smythe, who became the top guy in USAC. Bill was on the early plane, and when we explained our situation he said, "Wait a minute. Let me see what I can do." He walked up to the ticket counter and said he wanted some more first-class seats on that plane. While the guy was explaining about waiting lists, Bill pulled out a wad of bills and started laying them out in front of him. The guy was talking away—and watching—and said, "What are you doing?" Bill said, "Tell me when to stop." The guy's eyes got big and he said, "Stop!" He covered all the money, scooped it into his pocket, and ran into the back room. We waited around a while, and when it came time to board the plane, the agent came out to announce the standby names. The first names on the list were Hansgen and Donohue! We knew that Bill was the kind of guy who went everywhere and knew everyone, but I still couldn't believe it. He really knew how to get things done. It was the first time I'd seen anything like that done in real life, and it was quite impressive. I was beginning to get educated in high-powered race cars and in high-powered financial operations.

Chapter 8

1965

LOTUS 20 (FORMULA C)
Getting It All Together (with the Right People)

Malcom Starr was the guy behind my Formula C and early Mustang racing programs. I met him through another good friend in racing, Jimmy Carter, who worked for Lou Schulz at S & R Motors. Jimmy was an enthusiastic racing mechanic who was getting frustrated working on production sports cars. Not only was he an enthusiastic race mechanic, but he figured he was a good judge of racing talent. Because he knew me, he was convinced I was destined for success. He came to me and said he knew this guy Starr, who had a lot of money and wanted to go racing. Jimmy figured that the three of us could work together, and I would get to drive some. Malcom could buy the car, Jimmy would maintain it, and I would provide the place to work and the tow vehicle. Malcom would take the car to drivers' schools and Regional races until he got his license, while I ran the car in National races. I wasn't too keen on the idea, because I'd just borrowed $8000 from my father and bought a $25,000 home, on an $8000 per year salary. The overhead was killing me.

Malcom came to talk to me about it, and I just couldn't say no. It seemed like a low-risk venture on my part. We made an informal agreement to share the driving and maintenance. Jimmy thought that the best car for us was Formula C. I wasn't very enthusiastic about it, from my experience with the Elva Formula Junior, but it wasn't my money. So Jimmy found a Lotus 20 with a 1100-cc Cosworth-Ford, which had won the National Championship the year before. It was a relatively conventional formula racer for its time, with A-arm front suspension and the rear axles acting as the upper control arms. I didn't know if that was good or bad, but the car appeared competitive.

My experience with the Cobra had shown that the first thing to do was to get bigger wheels and tires. The Lotus already had five-inch rims on the front and seven-inch rims on the rear, with the standard Dunlop tires that everyone said were perfectly adequate. They said it was foolish to get wider tires, because the little 110-horsepower motor wouldn't be able to push them down the straightaway. I didn't know whether that was true or not, but the car just *looked* wrong with those tiny tires. I'd heard an old saying that "What *looks* right is right." Going on that theory, the Lotus needed bigger rims and tires. I called American Racing Equipment and gave them the wheel dimensions I wanted. I'd decided to start with eight inches in the front and ten inches in the rear. I made a deal with Hansgen to get some Firestone road-racing tires, like the ones we had used at Sebring. When everyone saw the car with that setup, they said it looked impressive but that it wouldn't go worth a damn.

When we took the car to our first National race we just smoked everybody. I even beat most of the Formula B cars, which had 1500-cc motors. My main competition was from Gus Andre and Allen Gottleib, who had Lotus 22's, which were much nicer cars with upper control arms in the rear. Eventually they caught on to the big wheels, and we all ended up with the same capabilities. But it was a true revolution. There were no wheel regulations at the time, and we almost doubled tire width overnight.

The former owner of the car, Brooks Fryberger, who now works for Wester Porsche in Monterey, was at that race. When he saw what a great deal I had, he wanted to drive the car again. He tried to get Malcom to share the car with him instead of me. Malcom wasn't sure what to do, but he knew Jimmy and Jimmy knew me, so the deal stayed the same.

After a race or two I began to think the car was handling differently in left-and right-hand corners. We knew it had been in an accident before, and we thought that the chassis could have been twisted a little. Somewhere we got the idea that for a well-balanced car, both front wheels and both rear wheels ought to carry the same weight. So I went out and bought a pair of bathroom scales to put the car on. Two scales would support one wheel at a time, while the other three wheels were blocked up to the same height. It took a lot of spring shimming to get the weights anywhere near equal, but that turned out to have the greatest effect of any chassis improvements I'd ever made. That, and the big tires, were all we ever did to the Lotus chassis. In those days I tried to adapt to each car's particular handling characteristics, instead of trying to make the car handle correctly. All I knew to change were camber and toe angles and load distribution.

Donohue Collection

Lotus 20

With all the races that Malcom and I were putting on the car, we had to rebuild the motor quite often. We even had a regular schedule to follow. After a certain number of races we would grind the valves or replace the bearings or inspect the pistons and rod bolts. Someone at Cosworth told us not to hone the cylinder walls but just to replace the piston rings, if necessary. That was the "seasoned block" theory. We found that it was hard to get new rings to seat that way, and the motor would pump oil for a while. What we finally did with each rebuild was to let the motor run at a high idle for about three hours with a garden hose running water through it to keep it cool. Eventually all the molecules got very "friendly with each other." That motor ran the entire Regional and National race season with no failures—until it was time for the Championship runoffs in Daytona.

I won almost every Formula C National race I ran. In fact, there was so little real competition that I concentrated on trying to beat the Formula B cars. It was a remarkably fast car, even when the other guys caught up on tires. We considered going to even larger wheels and tires, except for the cost and durability problems. The wheels we had were starting to crack, and the next larger tires were so much bigger that it would have been a lot harder on the wheels. The problem was in the large amount of offset needed to clear the stock Lotus suspension, and the high cornering forces generated by the bigger tires. Besides that, the car looked ridiculous with bigger tires, and that couldn't be right.

We figured that our super maintenance would win the race at Daytona. We really went through the motor that time. In the process I discovered that the ring gap was too large in the cylinders. The cylinders seemed to be worn to their limit, and we couldn't legally bore them oversize. We could have bought a new block, but that would have required a lot of special machine work like line-boring and drilling and tapping for four-bolt main caps. So I made the executive decision to sleeve the block we had, and I took it to Dick DiBiasse, who was a good jack-of-all-trades machinist. In the long run that decision turned out to be a lot more complicated than a new block would have been. We took the car to Daytona, thinking I was gonna smoke everybody. In the race the sleeves shifted, breaking the seal and blowing the head gasket, and everything turned to junk. After that Malcom had his National license, so there wasn't an opportunity for me to drive the car again.

Malcom and I both learned a lot from that car. He learned a great deal about driving, and I learned that systematic race-by-race maintenance was the only way to succeed. We tried to concentrate on making the car reliable, so that it was capable of finishing races. We didn't take any chances with bearings or gears or valves or springs. That was the key to its success. Fortunately the car was fast and well-balanced to start with, because we still didn't know anything about chassis or engine development. Basically all we did was use bigger tires, change gear ratios for different tracks, and maintain the motor. Then we blew it all at the last race.

It seems like cars were much simpler then. There weren't that many components, and it didn't take a lot of check lists, schedules, and parts lists. Jimmy and I were both intimately familiar with the car, and it was just understood that we would replace certain things at certain times. As I became more and more professional over the years, everything got a lot more complicated. It's not just a matter of having the right check list or procedure for everything. You have to have mechanics who *know* those things—who have a feel for the right time to change something. If you have an unlimited budget you can replace everything in the suspension and motor before each race. But that's so expensive it doesn't make sense. The mechanic has to know the balance between what *has* to be done and what can be afforded—in time or money. It's very hard to find a guy like that, and it takes a long time before he really knows the car and recognizes the teamwork that's required.

Chapter 9

1965–66

MUSTANG
Forming a Racing Team (and Becoming Known)

The Mustang was a transition between amateur and professional for me. Not only that, but it really taught me a lot about chassis setup and team organization and sponsorship. It all started when Dave Lawton called me about halfway through 1965, and we started talking about the new SCCA sedan racing series. Dave was always watching me and analyzing my driving, and now he was about to influence my professional career. He told me that if I wanted to establish my name in racing I'd have to get in on the ground floor of this new series, and we both knew I was going to have to get a ride. He felt that the Mustang was going to become a very important car in racing. It was going to be a popular series and there would be lots of advertising connected with the factory.

In addition, a good friend of mine in Baltimore, Dr. Ben Poster, was also having a great deal of influence on me. He was a friend of Dr. Dick Thompson the famous dentist/driver, and a great supporter of the SCCA, although never an especially fast racer with his Elva Courier. He was also a Ford lover, and he had recently bought a street version of the Mustang race car, called the Shelby GT 350. I had already read about it in *Sports Car Graphic*, when Jerry Titus tested it at Willow Springs. But when I drove Ben's car, I fell in love with it. It was practically a "race car" as it was, and I thought it was the greatest thing to ever come down the pike. Everyone figured that this was the hot setup, that this was what I ought to do. And I wanted to, but I didn't know how. Shelby was selling fully prepared race cars at the time for $6000, with a good racing engine already installed, but I certainly didn't have that kind of money.

That was my first experience in assembling a race team. First I went to Malcom Starr, my Lotus sponsor, and said, "Listen, assuming I can find a way to get a mechanic and a tow car and a trailer and all the spare parts, and can get it to the track, will you buy the car if you can drive it in amateur races?" Starr said yes, he would buy it if I could get all these other things together.

Then I needed a mechanic. Because of his experience with Shelby and the Cobras, my first choice was George Clark, who was then a line mechanic at Hicksville Ford. I went to George and said, "If I can get the Mustang and a tow car and a trailer and all the spare parts, would you work on it?" He and Jack Griffith, from my Cobra adventure, were still talking about producing sports cars, but he was a real racer type so he went along. In fact, he even sweetened the deal more. He was about to buy a new car, and he decided to buy a station wagon that could be used as a tow car. When I asked where we might keep it, he said we could rent space from Griffith and work on it there at night.

Next I needed a trailer. I scouted around and found one that belonged to an old Corvette racer. If I came up with $1100 of my own, that part was taken care of, and all I had to do was find someone to supply the spare parts and tires. All that time I was working as a sales engineer, and four days a week I was calling on customers in Baltimore, where Dr. Poster was. We would sit around and have a few drinks and talk about racing. One night he said, "You know, you really ought to drive a Mustang. I'll call Lew Spencer, the manager at Shelby's shops, and tell him you ought to have the team car instead of Jerry Titus." Nothing ever came of that, of course, except that Lew probably heard my name for the first time. But Dr. Ben also knew Allen Abramson, who owned Archway Ford in Baltimore, and he knew they were involved with Howard Keck's Cobra team.

Ford had a parts assistance program through Shelby, and if you were one of a chosen few in the world, you could get free racing parts for your Mustang or Cobra. That adds up to quite a bit in a race program—extra engines, brakes, gearboxes, and all the other stuff that breaks. Not only had Abramson gotten the deal for Keck, but they were providing him with a tow truck and shop space as sponsorship. And Keck, the Cobra, and Archway Motors were getting a lot of promotion around Baltimore.

Naturally I started seeing Abramson every time I had a chance. I told him I had everything lined up, and all I needed were the parts. I just kept hanging on and hoping. Finally I walked in and Abramson said, "It's done." He had gotten me on the parts program with Shelby, and in addition, they thought I ought to be in on the Goodyear tire program also.

Suddenly it was all together. That was one of the most exciting times of my life. I had finally put together my first fully sponsored racing program. It had taken months, but now I had a car through Malcolm Starr, a mechanic and garage and tow car courtesy of George Clark and Hicksville Ford, and parts through Ford, Shelby, and Archway Ford, my official sponsors. By then it was late July, but there were still enough National races left to win the championship.

Because we were starting to look like professionals we began to operate like professionals. That was the first time we took a car to a track simply to test it *before* a race. We took the Mustang to Bridgehampton on a quiet weekend to find out what we had. The most notable discovery was that it must have had 600 pounds of aerodynamic lift on the front, because it went down the straight like a motorboat. Not only that, but the handling just didn't seem quite right. At the time, none of us knew much about vehicle dynamics, and I was merely able to recognize that it was very hard to control.

As we got it, the Mustang was too softly sprung for a race car. It understeered noticeably, but because of the soft springs the suspension deflected a great deal in cornering, and when I would apply the throttle, the rear end would break away violently. At the same time, we could see that the suspension was hitting the bump stops in front. It seemed like we should stiffen the front springs to fix the bottoming, the high amount of roll, and what I thought was oversteer. We dug through the Ford parts book, and from measuring spring coils, length, and wire diameter, we were able to identify stronger springs that would work. We went to the test track to find out that wasn't the correct solution. We immediately saw that we had to stiffen the back also, because it still had too much roll and the basic understeer was worse. The rear was easier, even though we didn't know the spring rates. We just added leaves until it looked right. Finally the car started becoming more balanced—more neutral all the way through a corner.

We were also trying to get on a shock absorber program with the Koni people. They were already supplying Shelby and other racers, but I thought that with a little experimentation we could work out better valving. I went to Kensington Products and worked with George Hayes and Mike Porter on their test machines, trying to produce what I thought I wanted. They have machines that stroke the shocks and tell you what they're doing at different speeds and deflections. That was 1965, and it wasn't until 1968 that we were able to learn how to improve them. Soon after we got the car we took it to our first race, at Lime Rock. Bob Johnson was there, and he had been running all season, so we didn't feel too bad about finishing second.

There was something else I started to learn around that time—about dealing with mechanics. I had known George Clark from my Cobra days, but I really had no control over what he did on the car. I would talk to him

Donohue Collection

MUSTANG

on the phone, but I wouldn't get a chance to see the car until we got to the track. He was very humble to start with. Then we started winning races and he became a very independent guy. George liked to leave things alone as long as he thought he could. I'd say that we ought to change the engine, or at least have a look, and George would say, "The engine is running good, let's leave it."

We went to an airport course in Pennsylvania and I ran in first place ahead of Don Yenko, until the motor broke. It was on the last lap, and I sat there and watched Yenko take the flag. A piston had broken, and it fairly well ruined the engine. George wasn't upset; he just said, "Well, call Shelby and get another motor." I did, but it still cost us a race, and I had an uncomfortable time explaining to his team manager, Lew Spencer, why it happened, when we could have replaced the pistons more easily. That should have been enough of a lesson in maintaining the car, but the situation eventually got worse.

My tire problems started with a 500-mile race at Watkins Glen, an important race I needed to win the Championship. Two drivers were necessary, and I thought, "Who could be a better co-driver than Walt Hansgen?" He'd been having bad luck all year in Mecom's Lola and was kind of down about it, so I said, "Come on, Walt, it ought to be a lot of fun." He looked at me like, "What the hell do I wanna do that for?" I didn't realize at the time that people should be getting *paid* for racing—it just never entered my mind that he considered himself a *professional.* Still, I was so excited that finally he agreed, if we would run on Firestone tires because of his deal with the Mecom team.

We looked around his garage until I found a tire that was bigger than my Goodyears, and I thought they might fit on the rear. When I got a pair and tried them out, though, they didn't quite make it—they rubbed on the fender a little. You weren't supposed to modify the fenders in those days, but it didn't take too much, so we just kinda did it. To make it a little less illegal, I made up a dimensioned sketch and sent it to Shelby's project engineer, Chuck Cantwell, who I didn't even know at that time. If the SCCA had any question, Chuck could produce some engineering drawings to explain it. In addition, my old friend Dave Lawton made up some quick-fill fuel cans, like they use in NASCAR, and we looked fairly professional. Everyone was all excited about the deal—a big name like Hansgen driving in my car—and it was promoted all over the area.

We smoked 'em. I could see that Walt was real happy about it, so I didn't even question the idea of him driving the victory lap. As it turned out, I think that was the only race he won that year. I thought to myself, "Gee, that's really great. After all these years I can finally do him a favor, in return for all he's done for me." I didn't realize that all the time he was doing me another favor. He didn't really want to drive that car, because he wasn't getting paid for it.

We got down to the end of the year, and because I had that one DNF—did not finish—I needed to win one more race to take the Championship. All that was left was one race in Gainesville, Georgia, and that was a long way from home in those days. But we had come down to the last nitty-gritty and we were simply going to have to win that Championship. That's what I said I'd do when I was getting the sponsorship, and that was it. We had a commitment to the sponsors and we were not going to give up, no matter how hard it was on me, no matter how hard it was to get the bucks up. Many people get to that point and say the hell with it, but when the going gets rough is when you usually have to spend the most money. Even now that's sometimes the way it is, even with Roger Penske. You do everything possible to accomplish your goals.

We went, and we won, but that's a minor part of the story. George and I had full-time jobs and couldn't spend days on the road, so I hired two of his unemployed friends to tow the car to the track, and we flew down with our wives. Don Yenko and Walt Hane were also there with their Mustangs, but they both had trouble and I picked up the Championship.

Then the trouble started. George and I flew back to our jobs and the two guys started back with the rig. But they lost control of the tow car crossing a bridge, and when they swerved off the end, the whole thing shot off an embankment and plunged into a swamp. Fortunately the trailer broke loose. The racer bounced up on the tongue and just plowed into the marsh. But the wagon rolled a couple of times and was a total loss. George's toolbox was loose and it sort of rounded out the insides. The guys were all right, but the wagon looked like there had been an explosion in it—the top and sides were bowed out, and the windshield was gone. When they got it all out of the swamp they had to put a new axle under the wagon, and then they started out again. Then the trailer lost a wheel near Baltimore and they had to borrow another trailer to get home. George's insurance covered the wagon, but by the time I paid them for the extra week, went after the trailer and repaired it, and patched up some creases on the race car, I was in bad shape. Still, we could at least go to the runoffs in Daytona.

We were going to come up with an Unfair Advantage over the West Coast Shelby team. We had Hansgen's big Firestones on the rear as a starter, and we figured the high banks were going to require some really stiff springs. And we couldn't simply use one of Shelby's engines as it was without some tricks the guys had come up with. George had a trick cam he had saved from somewhere and Dickie DiBiasse had some modified cylinder heads we could use in our home-built engine. We never dynoed it though—it just felt about right. On top of that, we were not only going to be faster, we were going to look better than Shelby's cars. We took the time to repaint our car just the opposite of the team cars. Instead of white with a blue stripe, we were blue with a white stripe.

Just as I predicted, we were faster than Jerry Titus' car almost immediately. Chuck Cantwell came over to our car and really looked that beauty over, while we sat back and smirked. But we had a serious problem with those big Firestones. We hadn't been on steep banks before, and the high "g" loadings were forcing the outside rear tire against the spring leaves. First we spaced the spring in, but that wasn't enough. We took a big grinder and cut away part of the spring; it was still rubbing just a little. Then we made a big mistake. I decided to let George take the day off and have a vacation with his wife. George had worked really hard to prepare for that race. It was the best effort I'd ever seen him put out, and it took so much time that he and his wife were having big problems. We were in pretty good shape anyhow, because class A and B cars were in the same race and we were second only to Howard Keck's "A" Cobra on the grid. The Shelby guys were crawling around under our car, and I was thinking, "We're really looking good." But every time I smiled, I would think, "That damn tire. I'm really worried about that tire rubbing." I was torn inside because I knew what we should have done—we should have ground the spring a little more—but I must have thought, "Maybe if I ignore the problem it will go away." I've had that idea many times since, and it has *always* been wrong.

The race started, and Keck and I charged off into the lead. I had a short battle with Titus, but near the end I was far ahead of him. However ... every time I got up on the banks I could hear a "sq-sq-sq-sq-sq," and I just kept thinking, "Christ, when is it going to go?" About that time there was a big smashup on the infield part of the track, and some cars spun just ahead of me. Just as I got to the accident the goddamn tire blew out, and I went sailing off the track.

Up to that point there had been some speculation that I might get the nod from Shelby if I won. Everyone was aware that I was faster, and they were wondering what was going to happen in the race. Titus and Shelby were very close, but there was a small possibility I could get a similar deal for the next year. So when the tire blew I didn't want to tell anybody. I didn't want Firestone to look bad, I didn't want George to look bad, I didn't want to look bad. So I said, "Well, I ran over some glass and the tire blew." I gave the tire to the Firestone guys and they went and hid it, but it was shredded on the inside.

That ended all my relations with Shelby. After that there was no more help, even though I went to him and sort of pleaded some. When I lost my deal with Shelby, I lost my deal with Starr as a result, and George was less interested. Really, I lost a lot more than that one simple race.

It wasn't the end, though, because a friend of Starr's named Yale Kneeland took over the car on the same kind of arrangement with me. And Bob Dockery, another Ford dealer, loaned us a truck for a while. But the problem was in getting enough spare parts. We had a bunch left over at the end of the year, and we ran some races in 1966, but when those parts ran out we just couldn't go anymore.

By going to a few races we did qualify for the runoffs again in 1966, when they were at Riverside. That year it wasn't quite so important to me anymore, because I was driving the Ford GT's in endurance races and the Lola for Roger Penske, but I went sort of as an obligation to George and Dickie DiBiasse. They wanted to go to California, and I wasn't opposed to the idea. We lost it again, though, because we were so low on parts. George put an old crankshaft damper on the engine, and it threw the fan belts off. There was a big crash into the pit wall that year and the race was stopped. We tried to fix the belts before the restart and were disqualified. Walt Hane won that one.

We learned some tremendous lessons from that Mustang program. I learned how to drive a different kind of "sports car"—with the different feel of a big sedan. I got a lot of experience in getting a team organized and dealing with sponsors. And I learned the grief and misery of putting your biggest bucks up, then not doing that last one percent and losing everything as a result. Losing that race at Daytona was really a tremendous blow to my racing hopes.

We also learned a lot about setting up a big production sedan for racing. About shocks and springs, and the kind of spring rates needed to keep a car off the ground on high-banked turns. Incidentally, what we had also done, although I'm not sure we realized it at the time, was find that by putting the big tires on the rear and raking the car forward, we had made some aerodynamic improvements. When we got through, it was a very well-balanced car. It was just on the verge of oversteer most of the time. We had made that Mustang into a really excellent race car for 1965. But by far the most significant lesson was that in racing, problems don't just go away when you ignore them.

Chapter 10

1966–67

FORD MARK II, MARK IV
Incredible Good Fortune (and Big Money)

One of the greatest lucky breaks that ever came to me in my racing career was getting to drive the factory Ford GT's, and I owe it all to one man—Walter Hansgen. We were already good friends from the Ferrari and MGB experiences, and another co-drive deal in a Mecom Lola at Elkhart Lake. At the end of 1965 Ford had their annual Motorsports Banquet to make awards to everyone who had won a race that year with a Ford product, whether it was in sports cars, stocks, drags, or boats. I got an invitation because of my National Championship in the Mustang, so Walter and I flew to Detroit together. All the way there he was telling me that we should make a deal to drive one of their Mk II's at Daytona. I thought that was a keen idea, but hopeless because they were hiring guys like Miles, Ginther, Gurney, McLaren, Amon, Bucknum, and Foyt. It was first-class effort, and they only wanted first-class drivers, not an amateur Mustang driver.

Walter introduced me to Jacques Passino, who was in charge of all the Ford racing activities at the time. They talked a lot about the GT program, with Walt trying to promote me into the deal. We even went to Passino's office the day after the banquet, but Foyt was already there, and he seemed to have cornered the market on negotiation time. I was amazed how friendly and personable he was, without a belligerent attitude as the press had pictured him. At the same time, he certainly was bold enough. I heard him tell Passino that if he couldn't make the right deal with Ford, he could always go to Chevrolet. I had to be envious, because Passino wasn't the least bit interested in me. In fact, he was downright negative. They had enough good drivers already, and Walter told me later that they wanted him to co-drive with Bucknum. That was perfectly valid and understandable to me, since I was inexperienced and they really didn't know anything about me. We left, thinking there wasn't any hope at all.

A few days later Walter called me and warned that I was going to get a call from Al Dowd, the team manager for Shelby. He wanted to know my uniform size because I was going to drive a Ford GT for Holman-Moody at Daytona! Then Dowd called—he didn't sound very enthusiastic—and told me that he'd send a contract, if $1000 plus expenses was adequate. One thousand dollars for *one* race? That was incredible! I would have done it for nothing, but that was the standard rate for all the drivers. What had happened was that Walter told them that if he couldn't co-drive with me he wasn't interested in going at all. And they ended up building another entire car for us, from parts in the Holman-Moody shops. I was so thrilled I just couldn't cope with it. I was afraid to even dream about it. I didn't even want to tell anyone because I was so afraid it wouldn't happen.

When we finally got to Daytona our car wasn't even finished yet. The two mechanics on it were Vern Houle, from Stroppe's shops, and John Sulley, who had been with Fred Lorenzen's stockers. Houle called himself a plumber, but he had been working on stock cars for years and could do anything—even though he was sort of set in his ways. I had met Sulley in Nassau when I had the Courier, and I knew he was very enthusiastic and versatile. At least *he* recognized me. He was the only one besides Walter that wasn't a little worried about me. But they were both happy and friendly and joked around a lot, even while working hard. The four of us got along well.

Walter showed me something about working with team members—especially with the mechanics. It's a good idea to be around the car a great deal, especially when they're building it, because you see all those things that go into it, and the mechanics know that you're interested in what they're doing. Walter surprised everyone else by picking up a broom and sweeping up around the shop, but it didn't seem unusual to me at all. I learned that when there's nothing else I can do with the car myself, sweeping and polishing is good relaxation.

I got to know John Holman pretty quickly. He was a good friend of Walter's and they were really very much alike. They looked, talked, and thought so much the same that I thought maybe Walter would go to work for Holman. At the time he seemed to be the best cross between Walter and Penske. When Holman came around the first time he quizzed me about my experience. "Have you ever driven 200 miles per hour?" No. "Have you ever driven on a high-banked track?" No. Actually, I had driven my Mustang on the banks, but I thought that was inconsequential under these circumstances. So Holman went to Walter and told him to get another guy, because I wasn't going to make it. Walter didn't argue or even make much of a comment. He just said, "He'll be all right." I think there was a lesson in that. People try to solve all their problems with words, when sometimes it's better to say nothing at all.

Our car looked beautiful to me, with its body neatly fitted and professionally painted. Although it had a monocoque chassis, it was still very heavy. It weighed around 3000 pounds, and we've since built a lot of production sedans that were a lot lighter than that. At least they said it was rigid. It had really small tires by today's standards, on eight- and ten-inch rims, which would fit neatly on a passenger car now. The engine was a factory built 427 Ford with stainless-steel 180-degree exhaust headers and a single four-barrel carb. It was good for about 450 horsepower, which seemed like a tremendous amount at the time. Now we can easily get that out of any 300-cubic-inch engine. The 427 was redlined at 6500, but we were supposed to keep it at about 6000 rpm to survive the twenty-four hours.

In the cockpit was everything a driver could possibly want. There were 50 million switches and guages that could tell you everything from exhaust temperature to the transmission oil pressure. The transaxle was built by Ford, and it used a Galaxy four-speed gearbox with synchronizers, so it was extremely easy to shift. It was also very huge, very heavy, and very expensive—I heard they were worth $15,000 to $20,000 each. Because of that they had a separate oil pump to insure a good supply of lubricant, and it was driven off the output shaft. In addition, there was a warning light to tell you when the transmission oil pressure was low, and the engineers indicated that if that happened the transmission would immediately turn to junk. Right away I noticed that the light was coming on in a certain slow corner, and that worried me and some of the others until we found out that every car was doing it.

The GT Mk II had been so well developed by Ken Miles and Richie Ginther that about all one had to do was bolt them together with the right springs, anti-roll bars, and geometry, and that was it. They were ready to race. Walter took our car first to check it out, and then turned it over to me.

I had never been so impressed with a car in my life, even though my appearance was a lot less than spectacular. My practice laps were around 2:10, and maybe eventually I got down to 2:06; the others were down around two minutes flat. I don't think I ever drove hard enough there to really know what the car would do. It was so heavy, and so fast, that I just couldn't tell what was happening. What was the most awesome, though, was to hold it flat out on the banking. It would easily do over 180 mph, and that was the fastest I'd ever been in anything on wheels.

I soon learned how to lose a lot of time on the banks. All I had to do was lift my foot slightly in one place—and the speed would drop so fast I couldn't believe it. At those speeds the air drag was so great that it acted like brakes. So I tried very hard to keep on it all the way through the banking, even though the high "g" loading and soft springs were forcing it down on the bumpstops. That made it very heavy. It made the steering stiff and unpredictable. The tires were even coming up and wearing through the fenders. Still, the car was very stable, and very, very impressive to me.

When I started going faster, though, I rapidly realized what the car's main weakness was. No one knew how to make brakes last on a 3000-pound race car. After the brakes warmed up—in two or three laps—I had to push so hard on the pedal that I couldn't concentrate on driving the car. I really began using the gearbox then, downshifting as early as I could without over-revving. Walter even showed me how to go around the banks low, then climb up them during braking to help cut the speed. Anything we could do to help the brakes. The engineers were trying everything: finned discs, cast-iron discs, copper-coated discs, meehanite discs. Nothing worked. No matter what, in a few laps they would all go to hell. Much later they found that part of the solution was to go to *bigger* discs. We were running 7/8-inch-wide discs at the time, and 1-1/8 inches turned out much better, even in good old cast-iron.

It was interesting to watch them tackle the problem. Those guys would take a problem and thrash it to death with exotic materials and processes—

FORD MARK II

courtesy of Penske Communications

and cost was no object. I have to admit, though, that at the time I didn't know any better way myself. The car was just too heavy for such a small "heat sink," and the rapid cool-off down the straight was too much of a thermal shock on the discs.

From the very beginning everyone knew that there was a bad brake problem. Holman fought the factory to get a quick-change disc setup because the original calipers and discs took so long to replace. Finally he came up with a way to get the caliper off in a hurry, and he just mounted the rotors loose on the drive pins so that they would slip off too. That came in very handy until we were able to make them survive longer.

The fastest qualifying time that year was 1:59.8—which can be done now with a Camaro, a Javelin, or a Porsche Carrera—and I can remember Miles and Hansgen fighting for the pole. I was amazed that the team managers allowed that, since we had to run practice *and* the twenty-four hours without an engine change. And Walter was surprising everyone by being as fast as Miles, considering that he didn't have as much development time in the car. When Walt came in, Vern and Sulley asked him if he thought he could go any faster. He said, "I'm sure—no matter what—that I couldn't go one bit faster." That really made an impression on me, because I'd never heard it before. I'd never heard anyone say they were driving at the limit of their—and the car's—capability. I don't really know if that was the ultimate limit at that time. Maybe it was, although it seems like you can always go a little bit faster. But the point is that he could admit to everyone that he was at his own personal limit.

Because it was all such an honor to me, and because it was my first big break, I was extremely nervous while getting ready for the race. I knew I couldn't drive fast enough for us to win, so I was mostly worried about finishing. That was all I had going for me if I was to get anywhere in professional racing. I told Walter how I felt, and he said, "The engineers have done the best they can; the mechanics have done the best they can. They've assembled the engines and gearboxes the best they can, and as long as we treat the car right, it's going to last the race." He was trying to tell me that once its done, it's done. No amount of worrying is going to make you or the car work any better. Walter really lived that, too, because even though he was a top mechanic himself, he would put all the technical details completely out of his mind before a race. Once the car was prepared, he wouldn't worry at all about mechanical problems. It almost appeared as if he didn't even care. But he was so concerned with driving he was putting full concentration into that, and you could always see he really enjoyed that part of racing.

Just before the race started we had a pre-race meeting in the Ford trailer with all the big shots: Gurney, McLaren, Amon, Shelby, Miles, Dowd, Passino, and the Ford executives—and even me. There were speeches about the importance of beating Ferrari and Chaparral, and last-minute instructions, and the assignment of laptimes to run. Our assigned laptime was what I was capable of running flat out—which is probably how it was selected—so I knew that I could keep up, but I was going to have to drive as hard as I could all the way to do it.

Walter started the race in our car, and a Chaparral surprised us all by pulling away in the lead. The Chaparral couldn't maintain the pace, though, and we generally ran in the first three positions throughout the race. It was such a thrill for me to see our names go up into first place on the boards that night. Even the next morning, when we were back in third place, I was still pretty happy about it.

When I was driving, though, my concentration was mostly directed to the brakes. Going down the straight I could hear clicks and dings that must have been the sound of the rotors breaking up, coming apart, and going through the fenders. Then the pedal would start to get rough and I'd know it was time to change the rotors again. Sometimes they would get really bad before we could make a stop. Over the long run it was kind of bad because of the long downtime, and if we had run a little slower and had taken it easier on the brakes we could have saved time. But none of the drivers was going to voluntarily take it easy. Each wanted to run as hard as he could. The crews were having a terrible time trying to get Walter to slow down, because he kept creeping his speed up. Not only was he always naturally trying to do better, but he may have also been trying to build an edge in case I had some trouble. We could have finished second but we were assigned third, and so that's how we finished—by a matter of seconds. Walter wasn't very happy about it, but I was elated! I had the last drive, and got the checkered flag, and it was such a great thrill to survive the physical effort required for twenty-four hours, much less finish third on the Ford factory team at Daytona.

I was still on the team for the Sebring race, and even though I was a lot more confident by then, it turned out to be far more traumatic for me. We never did do any testing or development work on our car because that was up to the full-time Ford employees. We still had the same car, but it was a little better prepared by then. And we had more time to practice—too much time, maybe. It gave me a chance to really screw the car up.

My big mistake was that I thought I was smart enough to understand more than I did. Walter had good self-control in that area. When he didn't understand something about a car, he didn't go around showing everyone that he didn't. He just didn't seem to do anything about it. He never even mentioned it. But he kept his eyes and ears open until he knew enough to at least ask reasonably intelligent questions. If we *all* did that, there would be a lot of silence around race cars. I'm sorry I didn't recognize that as a good quality earlier.

The problem we had was how to set the front/rear brake balance. Walter had no feel for that so he said nothing and did nothing, hoping the mechanics could get it right. "Let it fall where it will." I couldn't leave well enough alone, though. I had to do something, figuring that I knew enough about engineering to determine brake balance. That's a very important concept in race cars—and even in production cars today—but the way I tried to do it then was completely idiotic. Now, we usually adjust them to lock up the front wheels just barely earlier than the rears, on a high-traction surface. But a big problem on the Ford GT was that the brakes were so small that it was difficult to lock them up at all, much less know whether the fronts or rears were first. The standard procedure was to keep putting a greater proportion to the rear until the car felt unstable in braking, but there wasn't time enough for that at Sebring. We did have some night practice left, and I had noticed that you could see the brake disc glowing red through the ventilated wheels. So I had a friend go out and watch the car in the corner just after I braked the car down off the straightaway. He was to judge whether the front or rear disc was glowing more brightly, and we'd adjust the balance until they were equal. It was just totally insane. Anyone who knows anything about the dynamics of an automobile can see how dumb I was in 1965. But I figured that here was an area where I could make a contribution, and I reckoned it was going to be a good setup. On top of that, I made another mistake in asking for even more brake proportion on the front just before the race started—without any chance to test it.

Walter wasn't as fast as he had been at Daytona, and I was keeping up much better in qualifying. At the start of the race he was noticeably slower than Miles' Ford. Then he went off the track, hit some haybales, and knocked the door loose. He came in to get the door fixed and went out again, but came back into the pits right after that and got out of the car. The brakes were balanced so badly that he refused to run any more until they were readjusted. He was driving as hard as he could, but he claimed that the front brakes were far too strong because of my changes. I was heartbroken. Walter was so furious he wouldn't even talk to me. He had been tricked, and he was looking bad because of me.

We lost a lot of time because of that adjustment, and then when it was my turn to drive, I realized that we really had a problem. The pedal had to be pumped up for each corner, and in each straightaway it would sink down again. When we changed rotors the first time that problem went away, but the brakes were still underpowered and we were very lucky to finish a distant second. Gurney finished first but was disqualified for pushing his car across the finish line.

We couldn't figure out at the time how others could be driving so fast and not have more of a brake problem. Now I think that it was the mark of a really good driver in those days. Brakes aren't marginal on most racing cars any more, and no one develops those skills. Today we simply use the brakes as hard as we can. Other than brakes, the Mk II was a very well-balanced and well-set-up car. I was starting to understand what good handling was, and I could tell that the car was easy to control. It was one of the most enjoyable race cars I've ever driven, and I suspect that everyone else on the program would say the same things. Miles and Ginther really did a great job.

After the race Walter was still mad—and disappointed. Instead of having his usual martini, he just sat around in our room and read a book. There was nothing I could say. I figured that the only way I could apologize was to do the best I could in the future and never make the same kind of mistake again. He had a ride at Indianapolis that year so he was going there next, and then on to Le Mans for testing. When he left Sebring I never saw him again.

I was in Providence when I first heard about it on the radio, and they just reported it as a bad accident in testing at Le Mans. So I called John Cobb of the Mecom team and he told me how bad it really was. Walter died three days later in a French hospital.

As near as anyone knows what happened, he simply lost control on a wet track. Instead of spinning or trying to regain control, he drove down an "escape road," as he had done many times before. But what he didn't know—he never questioned it—was that they had installed a barrier that wasn't there the previous year, to protect spectators. By the time he could see it, it was too late to avoid. What made his death so awfully sad for me was not simply that we had been such good friends, but that we had parted on bad terms. It's such a terrible, terrible thing never to be able to correct bad feelings with someone. I couldn't even explain it to anyone at the time. He'd done so much for me, bringing me along and getting me my big break in racing, and now I was lost. I figured that was the end of it, and I didn't really care.

Strangely enough, it wasn't the end. Holman called me and said that he wanted me in on some brake tests at Riverside before we all went to Le Mans. Stock car drivers Dick Hutcherson and Marvin Panch were going to be there too, probably because we were the hardest on brakes, and possibly because we needed the most road course practice. The chief engineer was John Wanderer, a guy I'd met at Nassau when he was on the Scarab team. He was an undiplomatic hardnose and not too well liked, but he had a tremendous understanding of the car, and he was tough. He and I trusted each other, and I learned a lot from him.

The purpose was to evaluate different brakes until we found some that would last a trial twenty-four hours at Riverside. We ran the long straightaway with a slow-speed chicane at the end for a better simulation of Le Mans. I was unsure how to operate at first. They pasted thermocouples all over the brakes, and I went out and ran as hard as I could, because I thought that was the purpose—to fail 'em *now*. But they complained that the temperatures were too high. What they wanted was to know how hard we could run and still last twenty-four hours—not a solution to the ultimate problem, the braking capacity. I eased off, because I was getting a bad reputation for being hard on brakes anyhow, and that made everyone happy. It was a paradox to me. If we were testing, we shouldn't try to cover up or avoid failures. Of course, we had unofficial competition going on between us, with everyone trying harder and harder, and I was keeping up with them quite well. The other two didn't take it all quite as seriously as I did. Whenever we weren't driving, they'd be on the phone talking to some gal, or they'd simply disappear entirely. It was the first time I had ever seen this side of professional driving, but I learned about it right quick.

Finally we ran twenty-four hours off and on—actually putting in only about eight hours each day. That doesn't necessarily mean that we learned anything about brakes, but everyone was elated anyhow. We called Detroit and said, "The brakes are good. We're looking good for Le Mans." We couldn't have been more wrong. But that was how we had agreed to test.

When I got to Le Mans I discovered that I was going to be driving with a guy named Paul Hawkins, who I'd never heard of before. There were six cars between Holman-Moody and Shelby, and I guess the idea was to try to have an American and a European in each car. At least Paul had driven at Le Mans before—in an MG. The biggest problem for me was a scarcity of practice time, because the course isn't open that much and we didn't want to wear the cars out. So I rented a car and drove around the course a million times in the next few days while the roads were open to the public. It was very important to learn it well because there are extremely fast blind corners, and it was seldom obvious where one started or ended.

Just before the race I got a big disappointment when I learned that Paul was going to get to start. To me, that was a big honor, and I was kind of upset about not getting it. So I kind of let Holman know—in my dumb way—how I felt about it. He told me that it was simply because Paul had run here before. He said that if I started the car and made a mistake, it would be held against me. It would be bad for my career. I understood that all right, but it didn't make me feel any better.

It turned out to be a bad decision after all, because Paul clutched too fast on the start and broke an axle shaft. Our car was the first one into the pits. It took a long time to fix, but finally Paul went back out again and ran a few laps. Then he came in again and said it was pulling badly to one side. We checked everything out and it looked all right, so I got Holman to let me go out and try to diagnose the problem.

The first thing I discovered was that the engine was in bad shape. It wasn't hitting on all cylinders, and it felt like some valves or pushrods were bent. With the 180-degree exhaust system they had, though, it was hard to tell where the bad cylinders were by listening. I came into the pits, and when I gave my opinion they started looking for the engine guy. "Engine man! Hey, engine man!" All of a sudden, there's a scramble up in the stands, and he comes down struggling his way past the pit guards. It seems that with all the chiefs and backup personnel, there weren't enough pit passes for the engine man to get one. When he got the valve covers off we could see that the problem was bent pushrods, so he installed new ones, adjusted the valves, and we were off again. Apparently they got bent from over-revving when the axle broke.

So I'm in the car now, and we're a long way behind already. At the end of that ridiculously long straightaway, I back off on the throttle to apply the brakes—and the engine goes quiet. I look at the tach, and I can see that it's just idling. Then I think, "It's out of gear," and I try to shift it back in, but it's already in gear. When I rev it up to about 4000 rpm, it catches with a great jerk and becomes engaged again. I'm really mystified by then, so I take one more lap, to get a better idea of the problem. I get almost to the same point at the end of the straightaway, going about 210 mph, and there's this huge *snap*. It was kind of like before, but now the car is totally out of control! My first reaction is to look in the mirror to see what kind of traffic is coming up on me and to see if smoke and oil are pouring out the back.

I saw the *engine*—which is rather unusual in this case, because you can normally see the *track*! It didn't dawn on me at first, but then I did a double take and realized that the entire rear body section was off, and the upset aerodynamics had lifted the rear off the ground. I thought, "Hold the throttle and steering about where they are—don't move—and maybe you'll be in control when it settles down." It was like landing an airplane. Finally it straightened out and I continued slowly to the pits without rear bodywork.

The officials made a great effort to disqualify our car, and we started to pack up. But because it was a twenty-four-hour race, I wanted to try everything I could to keep it going. We hemmed and hawed a lot, and I explained to our interpreter that I knew exactly where the tail was, and that it was safe to drive around there to get it and bring it in. We could install it correctly in the pits. Of course they said no! But we kept at them, and the crowd started booing and throwing things, so finally they let me go.

I pulled carefully out of the pits with a cheer from the crowd. I didn't really know where it was, or what condition it was in, but I felt it was worth a try. Going slowly down the straight—I wasn't about to overlook the body or get up in the air again—I saw a bunch of people frantically waving at me. Sure enough, there was the tail section, blown way off into the woods. They all tried to help me, but I knew that would really get me disqualified. So I fought them off and single-handedly dragged it over the fence and back to the car. Surprisingly, it wasn't badly torn up. I had brought wire and pliers and "racer's tape," with which I was able to keep the tail on all the way back to the pits. The mechanics were ready, and they did a great job of installing a new window and latch brackets—and we were off again.

But the business of the engine disconnecting from the wheels during braking was still there! When I got back on the throttle it would reengage, but at 2000 to 4000 rpm. It was such a tremendous jolt that I felt it was going to break the whole car. I stopped and described the symptoms to our transmission man, and he finally recognized the problem. The transaxle had a Weismann locking differential, which uses rollers and ramps to wedge it tight, but when those parts get broken or deformed, it allows the driveline to freewheel. Our problem was created when the axle broke and put too much strain on the differential. We were so far behind at that point that we *finally* had to say the hell with it. That was the last I saw of the Ford people—until they came back and asked me to drive at Daytona again the next year.

I went to work full-time for Roger Penske at the start of 1967, but Ford still wanted me to do development and race driving on their GT program. Right away, they asked me to go to Daytona to test cars for the next endurance race. It was really pretty difficult, since Roger was so anxious for me to get his racing shop running well. But they were paying me $200 a day, and that was hard to refuse. That was my second big professional racing year, with the Ford GT's, the Lola Can-Am car, and the Camaro to run, and my income was fairly good. I did a lot of work with the factory Ford teams, which helped me a great deal in knowledge and experience ... and income.

Over the winter Ford had worked out most of the brake problems we had in 1966, so they weren't nearly as weak anymore. By going through materials like nodular iron, copper-coated faces, sintered this and kryptonite that, and by using wider rotors and extensive cooling ducts, they could keep them from coming apart and going through the fenders. We still had to be careful, but at least they were usable, and we could concentrate on other development areas.

The big things we had to work on at Daytona were spring rates for the banking and different induction systems. Carroll Smith was the chief engineer, with Ron Bucknum and me doing all the driving. We spent quite a bit of time going back and forth between various springs, anti-roll bars, ride heights, and camber angles to keep the car from bottoming on the banks and still have good handling on the infield. I wasn't kept too well informed, probably because my own knowledge was rather slim, and possibly also because I was working for Roger—even though he wasn't a direct competitor at the time. One curious thing we tried was an anti-roll bar that acted like a suspension spring sometimes. There was an arm in the middle of the bar, and when the car had gone down so far, the arm would hit a stop, making it effectively two simple torsion-bar springs. We couldn't really be sure what it was doing, but every time the arm hit there was a terrible "clank" and the handling would change, so we eventually dropped the idea. Looking back, it seems to have been a problem of spring rates changing too quickly, and a loss of roll rate as the spring rate suddenly went up. But the cars were still so soft and heavy that the tires were coming through the body, and we couldn't tell much of anything.

We also tried a lot of different carburetion setups—one carb, two carbs, open-chamber manifolds, and different tunnel manifolds. All of them had been run on a dynamometer at Ford, and they knew how much horsepower each would put out. But we had to learn how they responded in acceleration out of a corner. Two carbs on a huge open-chambered manifold obviously produced the most power, but it was no good because we couldn't get it off the turns fast enough. When we went to wide-open throttle the accelerator pumps simply couldn't squirt out enough fuel for all that air. The engine would take a great gulp of air, the mixture would go lean, and "poof"—it would just stop running. Sometimes it would backfire through the carb and start a big fire, which we referred to as a "flameout" or, more often, a "bangout." Finally we settled on two carbs on the familiar over-and-under runner-type manifold.

Some new safety gear had been added because of the crash experiences in 1966. There was now an automatic fire-extinguishing system that was triggered by photocell sensors and had nozzles in the cockpit and engine room. And there was also an extensive roll cage to prevent another disaster like Walt Hansgen's crash. I can't say that I was ever personally concerned about my own safety in the car, even after Walt's accident, perhaps because I'm something of a fatalist. I figure that no two accidents are ever quite the same, and even if you've prepared for *every* contingency—something else is going to get you someday. It's not that I'm *opposed* to safety gear, it's just that I don't *worry* about it.

That roll cage certainly meant a lot to Peter Revson, though. He and Skip Scott were testing later at Daytona, and he rolled one of the cars up into a ball. He flipped it in the fourth turn and it went end over end all the way down the straight to the start-finish line. Peter just stepped out and walked away. I saw the car later, and it was pretty seriously broken up ... except for the cockpit.

Peter was criticized a little for that, because he had said the car didn't feel quite right but he had gone on and run anyhow. Maybe he should have come in and had them go over it. Then—what really amazed me—after it was all over, Peter and Scott thought they needed a vacation, so they took a week off and went to the Bahamas. I was thinking, "Christ, I could never do that in a million years! When *I* have an accident like that, I work twice as hard to make up for it ... and they take off and go fishing."

We were also working on aerodynamics at Daytona. The engineers had a moveable lip on the tail, which we were moving up and down to change the car's aerodynamic balance. We were warned to expect a big difference in handling—although I had already experienced the absolute extreme when the tail came entirely off at Le Mans. At the time I couldn't understand why there would be any great effect, but looking back now, it all makes sense. That long, sloping rear deck couldn't have generated much aerodynamic downforce, which meant that the rear end would be teetering lightly at high speeds. Anything like a little lip would have to help quite a bit. Because of wind tunnel tests of air drag, though, the engineers were concerned that we shouldn't move the lip up more than one or two inches. But all the drivers liked it up as high as possible because it made the car feel so stable, and we couldn't believe it had that much negative effect on speed. Personally, I couldn't tell any difference in handling between lowspeed corners and high-speed corners, so the car must have been balanced very well . . . or I just wasn't experienced enough yet to be a good judge.

A couple of weeks before the Daytona race, Homer Perry, my team manager, got the word that I was also going to be driving another car that same weekend. Up in Roger's shops we had put together a Camaro to run in the Daytona Trans-Am sedan race that preceded the twenty-four-hour "Ford GT race." Homer was rightly upset about me doubling up, especially since it was in "Brand X" instead of a Mustang or a Cougar. I got the message, and I went to Roger to tell him I couldn't throw away their deal of $3000 a race simply to compete for a share of the purse in the Trans-Am. Roger got kind of excited at first, but then he thought about it for a while and told me that he would pay me $3000 to drive the Camaro in *both* the twenty-four-hour and the Trans-Am races, and the hell with the GT's. He guessed their position fairly well. Ford was short on road-racing drivers with experience in their cars, so they relented and let me run in the Camaro also.

All that dealing didn't matter, as it turned out, because neither of my cars finished its race. That was the time when all the Ford GT's broke an identical shaft in their transmissions. After all the testing we had done, it was hard to take . . . and hard to believe. We had always tested more for durability than for maximum performance anyhow. I was able to keep up better all the time, with some of the fastest practice times, but the big thing was durability. Speed wasn't supposed to matter all that much, as long as we could keep the engine, gearbox, and brakes together. We assumed that everything had been tested and proven by race day, and that the car was foolproof. Someone, however, was really worried about the possibility of Ferrari beating us, and made the last-minute decision to switch from aluminum to cast-iron cylinder heads. The reason was that iron heads always produced more power and were more durable. But they also weighed more, so the explanation of the moment for all the transmission failures was the increased power and weight. It was decided later, and more rationally, that it was due to a poor heat treat in the shafts. It just goes to show that no matter how much time and care you put into a race car, you can always be beat by something beyond your control. There are so many people, and processes, and pieces that there will always be random failures.

I didn't get to break the transmission on my car, though. The first problem to crop up was a shock absorber mount that tore loose from the chassis while I was up on the banking. With those loads and speeds, anything that goes wrong can be critical, and it was a fairly bad experience, trying to get down in a straight line. While they were patching up the mount, I learned that some of the shafts were breaking, and that it was probably just a matter of time before ours went. My co-driver, Peter Revson, got the honor while I was asleep. Someone woke me up to tell me the car had failed, and when I went around to the garage, there it was, parked and forgotten. It was a black day for Ford.

FORD MARK IV

For Sebring, Ford decided to run only two cars, and I got left out. I was paid to be there as a standby driver for Ford, but the only racing I did was in the Penske Camaro we brought for the Trans-Am that same weekend. I didn't even do any testing between Daytona and Sebring. McLaren and Andretti were there in the first Mk IV, which had longer, swoopy fender lines and a long, low tail. They won the race—easily.

I have to admit that I was jealous of Andretti at the time. He was good, all right, but he wasn't as experienced as I was on road courses. To me, he was really an unusual person in many respects. He was one of the hottest drivers in USAC—young, upcoming, a frequent winner—and he was having exciting wheel-to-wheel battles with Foyt in the Indy cars. But he still seemed like a very young guy most of the time. At drivers' meetings, for example, he would start talking about anything that entered his head, without any concern as to whether it was relevant or not. I thought he was making an ass of himself with his ridiculous comments. He was usually pretty funny, but that wasn't appropriate to the time and place. My reaction was, "We're getting paid all these dollars to race, and I'm not going to insult anybody or offend anybody. I'm going to pay attention and do a good job." He couldn't care less as long as he could get a few laughs. That was just his off-track behavior, though. On a racetrack I thought he was spectacularly reckless—the way he seemed to drive with absolute total abandon.

Actually, it was more like tremendous skill . . . *and* reckless abandon. He seemed to mature a great deal over the years, but then he isn't winning so

Donohue Collection

Ford Mark IV

many races now either. You never know. . . .

Then there was Dan Gurney, another driver in those cars. He never used up as many break pads or rotors as anyone else, and nobody could understand how he did it, unless he was stopping the car out on the track and replacing the parts himself. He was really spectacular from an engineering standpoint. He never complained—he just got in the car and drove it. Apparently Dan was never too concerned with balancing the car to the *nth* degree in a long-distance race. The idea was simply to be comfortable, and he could be because nothing was ever particularly wrong with the setup. Due to Miles' chassis development, the cars were always well balanced. But Dan was always clearly superior—and there were a lot of good drivers to compare him to. Trouble was, a lot of the other guys were from USAC or NASCAR oval tracks, like Andretti, Foyt, McClusky, and Ruby, and they weren't familiar enough with road courses. Homer Perry, the team manager, was selecting the drivers, and I guess he didn't think there were enough good professional drivers in American road racing. He didn't realize how hard it is for most drivers to adapt from oval tracks. Perry made that decision and it turned out to be rather unwise, but it's hard now to second-guess just who else should have been chosen.

We did have to do some testing for Le Mans that year. We had learned that there was absolutely no time to do any fixing at Le Mans if the cars weren't perfect when they arrived. There's a deserted Army airfield not far from Holman's shops, where I had tested the Mk II before, and we were going to use it to check out the cars before they were shipped to Europe. We were just to run up and down the runways to make sure everything worked right—the brakes, oiling, lights, and other stuff. The cars were loaded for the trip from Sebring to the airfield late in the afternoon of the day we were to test, as usual, but we needed some night driving anyhow, so they started out. Since one of Homer Perry's men had a twin-engine Queen Air, the rest of us decided to have dinner and then fly over. The airfield was unlit, naturally, but the truckers were going to have their headlights on, marking the ends of the one good runway—the only one that wasn't broken up and overgrown with weeds. So a bunch of us flew over there.

Somehow, I ended up sitting next to the pilot, and when we came in for the landing I could see that he was lined up with the wrong runway. I'd been there before and I knew it had three feet of weeds on it, but the pilot was convinced the truckers were marking the wrong one—or he just decided to show us that he could do it by himself. I tried to yell at him, but you can't tell a pilot anything. It's strange how they can understand all that squawking on the radio and can't hear the guy in the next seat. So he comes down ... down ... down ... and then his lights get buried in the weeds and he loses the runway. He can't see it when he gets too close. I can see the drivers blinking their lights at him So he starts to pull up a little for another try, but he's looking back to see where the runway was, and the plane is wobbling along close to stalling. Then I look out over the nose, and I'm looking into a dining-room window at a family eating dinner. The pilot was slowly flying right into a house on the side of a hill. I wasn't going to bother him again—I know my business and pilots know their business—but the situation started looking pretty grim. So I tapped him on the shoulder and pointed, and his eyes got as big as the landing lights. He nosed over to build up a little speed, and just barely hopped over the house. I can tell you for certain that they didn't have a television antenna. Finally, he figured out where the right runway was, and we landed easily. When the plane stopped, one of the Ford guys was so shook that he jumped out and kissed the ground—literally! I've never seen that before or since. He rode back to the shops in one of the trucks.

That kind of flying seems to be all too common among racing people. When we tested at Virginia International Raceway after Le Mans in 1966, Ralph Moody flew us up in his Beechcraft Bonanza and used the straightaway for a landing strip. It was so short, however, that he had to take off under some telephone wires. It's like Curtis Turner's flying escapades—some of those guys think that crashing an airplane is no more serious than crashing a race car. So many racing people have been in airplane accidents that it seems if you fly to tracks a lot you're as likely to get it in a plane as in a race car.

For the early Le Mans practice weekend, there were only two Ford team drivers present, Bruce McLaren and I. He was there for Shelby's cars and I was there for Holman-Moody. I considered it quite an honor to get sent to France for a weekend of testing. John Wanderer was the team manager, and we communicated very well. He had enough experience with race cars so he understood when I tried to tell him something. About the only thing we had time to try was some new anti-roll bars with serrated ends, which made it easier to change them in a hurry. The problem was that the links were so short that the ball joints bound up, and we cured it by simply raising the bar. Really, we only worried about that and the brakes. It rained most of the time and we didn't get much practice on a dry track. Based on previous experience, we knew that the suspension was already proper for the track, and the aerodynamics on the Mk IV had been worked out at Ford's proving grounds in Kingman, Arizona. The cars had been around.

When we all went back to Le Mans for the race, I somehow ended up not driving the Holman-Moody cars I had worked so hard on. Instead of driving with Revson in a Mk II again, I was teamed up with McLaren in one of Shelby's Mk IV's. There were three updated Mk II's and three new Mk IV's between the two teams, and somehow in the melee of executives, managers, drivers, trucks, trailers, caterers, and maids, I was shuffled to Shelby's team. It didn't matter as far as Ford was concerned, because the paycheck always came from the same place, but there was a lot of subsurface rivalry between the two teams.

I didn't know Bruce at all then, and it was the first time I met his team of Teddy Mayer and Tyler Alexander. Bruce obviously didn't know anything about me either, because he didn't seem to be very happy about being teamed with me. I felt Bruce was so much better at driving and engineering that I was really over my head. Neither one of us set up that particular car. There isn't any time for that. At Le Mans you run one or two laps and then you race. Bruce knew what he wanted, although he didn't want to let me know what he wanted, so he just told the mechanics to jack this or that around, and all I was supposed to do was drive it. I listened a lot, but all I learned was that he really knew what he was doing. Obviously it was important to know what you wanted, instead of saying, "It's doing something wrong." You've got to know what it ought to feel like. That comes mostly from experience. Now I know what *I* want . . . most of the time.

Bruce had a surprise for us that weekend: a bunch of new tires from Goodyear. It was a wider design, which he was going to use on his new cars in the Can-Am that summer. They were much wider than our Firestones, even though they'd really be skinny by today's standards. He had warned the Ford engineers to get wider rims, which was no trouble since Halibrand was doing all their wheel casting. We just barely got everything under the fenders. If I had talked to Bruce—if I had any idea of the car he was designing around those tires—I wouldn't have been looking forward to the Can-Am in my old Lola.

Bruce easily qualified on the pole—for whatever that's worth at Le Mans—and when it was my turn to drive, I just got in and drove. We hardly said a word to each other for the entire twenty-four hours. Still, we kept falling further and further behind because of failures, and it seemed as if everything was happening to Bruce. He had the rear body section fly off on him as it had on me the year before, only this time it got smashed up a lot worse, and by the end of the race it was half tape. Losing tails really plagued our lives. That's the way he got killed in testing a new Can-Am car in 1970, and I survived a similar accident in the 917 Porsche in 1972. In spite of the failures, Bruce and I finished fourth, behind Dan Gurney and A. J. Foyt in another Shelby Mk IV, and two Ferraris. Andretti had an accident that took out three Fords, and none of Holman-Moody's cars finished.

As it turned out, I guess it was good fortune that I was transferred to one of Shelby's cars at the last minute. Not only did it appear to improve my finishing position, but it gave me a chance to get to know some other valuable team members. The three key guys on Shelby's team were Al Dowd, Phil Remington, and Carroll Smith, and they were all a lot more organized than anyone with Holman-Moody and John Wanderer. Dowd was mainly concerned with arranging the people, passes, transportation, reservations, rental cars, and that sort of thing. Remington's area was pieces—engines, gearboxes, wheels, tires, bodies, fabricated parts—whatever it took to keep the cars going. And Smith was the so-called "chassis expert," who had to make sure that the cars went fast and felt right to the drivers.

What really made Shelby successful was that those three guys worked so well as a team—and it didn't matter whether they liked each other or not. I remember marveling . . . Dowd didn't like Carroll, Carroll seemed to resent Remington's fabrication skills, and so on, but during a race each had his own jobs and did them well. Shelby never even had to come around at all. He just looked around and said, "Fine . . . that's good . . . keep it up." When the race started, each one had his blackboard, notebooks, stopwatches, or whatever, and when the time came for a pitstop, each one did his own thing in an organized manner. None of them were together by choice, but they worked well as a team for a long time.

I think Remington knew more about more different things than the other guys. He could weld, shape metal, build engines or transmissions, sort a chassis . . . he was like the universal person. He works for Dan Gurney now, and he's probably the most valuable man on the team because in addition to all his technical skills, he has the ability to get along with people. He is so sincere, and so capable himself, that everyone else just naturally goes along. I would guess that Remington is one of the boulders at Gurney's shop, one of the guys who holds the roof up. I have a great deal of respect for him. In fact, maybe I'm a little jealous. I wish I could do so many things with so little apparent effort.

Carroll Smith knew more about chassis setup, though, so he and I spent a lot of time talking about calculating spring rates, anti-roll bars, roll couple, how drivers could tell what was right or wrong, and that sort of thing. He thought I knew more than I did because of my old role of keeping my mouth shut and trying to listen intelligently. Carroll had a lot of ideas, though, and I didn't know enough to judge whether they were right or wrong. At least they all sounded right—to start with. Later I learned that there are very few hard-and-set rules. But I was most impressed by his orderly system of doing things—keeping records, making check lists, solving problems—as opposed to the average chief mechanic who says, "Because we're under this shade tree now, we've gotta put in six beer cans and four rubber grommets." Carroll always tried to work from *some* prior knowledge. He tried to keep *some* degree of sanity in the operation. We had long, interesting technical discussions about what went into those cars, and I learned a lot by listening to Carroll. He was always quite straightforward with me, and I liked him for it. Trouble was, it was his job to deal with all the drivers—to try and keep them all happy with the cars some way or another. Maybe he would have gone a lot farther if he could have been more diplomatic with some of them. Sometimes that's more important than your technical ability. It's damned hard to find someone who's outstanding at both.

One of the things we talked about was bump steer, or roll steer, which is the way the wheels steer due to their particular suspension geometry whenever they travel up and down over bumps. That was a new term at the time, and if you said "bump steer" it automatically raised your status because it implied that you knew what it meant. It was a very important term just from the standpoint of impressing everybody. Holman's guys obviously didn't know anything about it. Anyone who is familiar with NASCAR could tell they would have no idea what it was. Those guys didn't *need* to. But Carroll had been to Ford's KarKraft shops in Detroit, where he learned how to measure bump steer with plates and dial indicators. They spent days getting it to within twenty thousandths of where they wanted it by moving the steering rack around and bending the steering arms. Even though I never actually did it myself, at least I was aware of what was going on, and I learned how it could affect stability in bumps or turns. Carroll later wrote an excellent article on it for *Sports Car Graphic*.

After the race at Le Mans the Ford executives held a big party in their hospitality center at the track. Everybody was pretty happy about Ford's big finish—especially Shelby's guys, because they had beat the Holman-Moody cars again. Almost everyone was getting really drunked up, and Remington and Smith came up to me all full of nostalgia, and they told me what a good job I'd done. They said that this would probably be the last time we would be racing together with the Ford team, but if the program did continue, they really wanted me to drive for them. They didn't need to say that, so it was a vote of confidence that I really appreciated. In the end, what they were saying was true—about the program not continuing.

At the same time John Holman was telling me to leave Penske and go to work for him. He said he was going to land a seven-year contract for a racing business with Ford, and we'd be lookin' good. I have to admit I was tempted because it sounded really interesting. But Ford finally got out of all racing—even the NASCAR stuff—and Holman was up a creek without any contracts. He had a lot of parts, and he survived, but he had to do things a lot differently. You never can predict the right people to be hooked up with from one year to the next.

The Ford program did a great deal for my professional racing career. If it weren't for Walter Hansgen and the GT Fords, I might just be an ordinary mechanical engineer for some company today. And I guess I was also lucky not to sink with the program when Ford got out.

It's hard to imagine an ordinary amateur guy like me, with very little experience, getting to drive for a major professional team with all those engines, and parts, and engineers, and managers, and caterers, and maids, and butlers. Try to imagine that! It's indescribable how prestigious it was! I was so honored that I didn't even want to talk too loud. And then to get *paid* for it . . . I would have paid *them* to let me drive! That's exactly how I felt. If they had said, "Look, we can't pay you next time, but will you come and drive anyhow?" I would have said, "Gladly!"

I have nothing but good feelings about the cars, too. I saw where some guy had a Mk IV for sale a while back, and I suppose that if I had a million dollars I might have bought it. They were very well built, considering all the production pieces that went into them. They seemed so strong, so safe, so thoroughly tested, that nothing would break or fall off, no matter who put it together. At the time they were by far the highest performance cars I'd ever driven. They were the fastest cars on the track—except for the Chaparral, maybe—and yet they'd still last twenty-four hours. They were very durable, very powerful, very fast, and about as easy to drive as a big Cadillac. The easiest part, though, was that they were backed by such a big team that I wasn't required to do much of the work. I just went to the track and drove. Those were the last race cars I drove that I didn't have to feel personally responsible for. That could have a lot to do with my comfortable feelings toward them.

There were probably many amateur drivers around at that time with a lot more talent and potential than I had, but I got the breaks. Once in a lifetime an opportunity like that falls in your lap, and I have only Walter Hansgen to thank for getting me started.

Chapter 11

1966–67

LOLA T70
Going Professional (with Roger Penske)

Roger Penske and I were just barely acquainted when I saw him, looking very upset, at Walt Hansgen's funeral in 1966. I had met him in 1959 when I had the Corvette, and whenever we were racing at the same track he would always say hello. But I didn't think he had ever paid much attention to my driving. I remember an incident one year at Vineland, New Jersey, where he was driving a Birdcage Maserati. He was just bubbling with enthusiasm for the car, and when I walked up he said, "This car is so fantastic. You really ought to drive it." So I said, "Okay, I will." He was a little shocked at that, because he obviously didn't mean it—it was just an expression he used. That was his way of getting so much cooperation in all of his deals—by being so enthusiastic. It's very seldom that you can put Roger back very much, but he didn't quite know how to respond that time.

Aside from that, most of what I knew about him was what I read in the papers: about his racing retirement and his dealership. But when he saw me at the funeral, he came over and said, "Hello, Mark. How are you?" That kind of surprised me at the time, but I've since learned that he prides himself on never forgetting anyone. He told me he was feeling around for a driver for his new Lola, and had tentatively considered Dick Thompson. Then he asked me if I would be interested in trying it out on a race-to-race basis, for fifty dollars a day. It wasn't much compared to the Ford GT arrangement, but I figured that program had just about gone down the drain at that point. Later I found out that the guys at Traco who were building all of

Roger's engines were pretty disappointed about me. They wanted Roger to get Parnelli Jones to drive.

When I first saw the new Lola in Roger's shop I was really impressed. It just looked like a real race car ought to look. In fact, I still think it was one of the most beautiful race car shapes I've ever seen. But it seemed like we all just sat and stared at it a lot. I was worried about that being indicative of the season—that there would be too much thinking and not enough action—but Roger kept pulling everything together. From his experience with the Grand Sport Corvette at Sebring that year, he already had an Unfair Advantage in mind. Instead of the cast-iron smallblock Chevrolet engines that everyone else was using, or the aluminum smallblock engines that the Chaparral racing team had, Roger was going to shoehorn the new bigblock 427 into the Lola. He was in close with all the right people who could get him the right stuff from Chevrolet, and he had a good relationship with one of their racing engineers, Gib Hufstader, who knew a lot about the new engine.

When the chassis and the engine were delivered in Philadelphia, however, there wasn't anyone there to put the two together. The motor mounts and transmission were the same for both engines, but it needed all new water lines, exhaust headers, and more clearance everywhere. So Roger got his good friend Bill Scott, a machinist from Sunoco, to make the installation.

There were a lot of other race car details that Roger insisted on, like all Aeroquip fittings and super-immaculate appearance, so he also hired Karl Kainhofer. I remember being there when Karl came in for the first time. He carried all his tools in two little plumber's toolboxes, and I thought, "Gee whiz, what kinda guy is this?" I had gotten used to all the professional mechanics with the Ford racing team, and their huge chests of tools, and I was sort of judging his ability by the number of tools he carried. I was pretty busy with my regular job plus the GT Ford testing and Le Mans race plus the Mustang I was still trying to win a Championship in, so I more or less just left it up to those guys and kept an eye on what they were doing with the Lola.

In those days we still didn't appreciate the value of thorough track testing before going to a race. I had learned a little about chassis setup from my previous cars, and I simply tried to adjust the suspension to Broadley's factory specifications right there in our shop. I didn't quite know what caster and camber and toe-in did, but I figured that they were pretty important and ought to be exactly right. We spent hours trying to get each wheel adjusted to within one fourth of a degree in every direction. We even adjusted rear caster, although we didn't know why. We didn't know that it was a way of changing roll steer, because we'd never *heard* of roll steer.

The first problem we ran into was that all the adjustments interacted with

courtesy of Penske Communications (photo by Peter C. Borsari)

Lola T70

each other, and we were continually going back and forth. Then everything would be just perfect. We'd move the car and something would be off again. It turned out that we weren't allowing for fuel and driver weights, and for suspension friction changing the ride heights, and for the fact that even the floor—our reference surface—was crooked.

I figured later that Karl knew about that stuff all the time, and went along just to make me feel good. He's very patient, he seldom complains, and he probably thought that as long as it was all right in my mind, that's all that was necessary. That's the way it's worked, anyhow, as I have absolute confidence in a car prepared by Karl.

We finally got the car built. With a couple of your ordinary "all-nighters" we got it fairly well set up and took it to St. Jovite in Quebec, Canada. The United States Road Racing Championship was already four races old, but there were two international FIA races in Canada that we could use for development-and possibly even win some money. That was pure insanity . . . we never should have bothered. There were so many things wrong with that car that it was all I could do to just hang on.

Right away we discovered that the big engine wouldn't maintain oil pressure in the corners. Within half a lap the oil pressure would go to zero and smoke would roll out the exhausts. Hufstader was there from Chevrolet, and he dropped the oil pan a million times, welding in baffles, and trays, and extended pickups, and *still* it was the same—smoke and no oil pressure. It was a long time before Chevrolet discovered the real problem: The oil wasn't even *getting* to the pan. The greater lateral acceleration in sportsracing cars was causing all the oil to be trapped up in the rocker covers, and it would smoke out past the valve guides. But that engine would last longer without oil pressure than any other engine I've ever seen. Pressure would only come up on the straightaways. I had to keep running it just to qualify for the race.

On top of that, I had no tachometer because we couldn't wire it into the transistor ignition, and the chassis was a mess. The biggest problem was the clutch, a triple-plate affair that I broke the linkage on almost immediately. I was trying so hard—driving without oil pressure, without a clutch, without a tach (and I'm sure I was over-revving about 1000 rpm sometimes)—that I couldn't have said whether it was oversteering or understeering. Still, I knew something was wrong with the handling, too, so we tried to fix it up a little. Now I can probably guess that it was understeering badly, with that heavy engine back there on those soft stock springs. I had just enough engineering to know about spring rates and how to calculate them, but I certainly had no idea what was needed. So we did all we knew how to do—we adjusted the camber. But since the front was so hard to work on, especially without a nice neat alignment setup, all we changed was the rear camber.

Roger was there, of course, and so were all the big international stars like McLaren, Amon, and Surtees. They would drop by and stare at that great big motor while Roger told them how we were really gonna smoke 'em off. Then they would sort of smirk and walk away. So we sat there and worked on our unfair *dis*advantage, while trying to think of ways to catch up. For one thing, it was raining off and on, but it was drying up, and Roger decided to have one of the few cars to start on dry tires. In addition, Roger always wants new parts on the car, so Karl was told to install new, unburnished brake pads, without me realizing their tendency to "green-fade." Ever since then I've hated to break in new pads. If I could find someone else to do it for me, I would.

So I start the race on a damp track, with dry tires and a bigger engine and new brakes. On the first lap I come down the straight right behind John Cannon. He brakes—I hit my brakes—and naturally the car won't stop. Instead of running up his tail pipes, I pull out to miss him—and I get out of the dry groove and into the water. Then things really get serious. I spin and run up an embankment and a rock punches a hole in the radiator.

I got back on the track and ran a few more laps because everything seemed to be all right. I could see water pouring out of the nose, but I thought it was just accumulated rainwater. Finally it turned to steam, the temperature gauge shot up, and I pulled into the pits with the engine banging away. By that time it was junk. Roger looked a little disappointed about the whole weekend, and I figured I was going to have to write the whole project off to bad experience. "It was nice while it lasted, Mark, but I'm sorry . . . ." Instead, he actually told me to stick around. We would get everything fixed, and we would win the next one at Mosport, near Toronto. That was a very valuable vote of confidence for me at that point.

We took the car back to Philadelphia, while Hufstader did more work on the oiling system in Detroit. Again we had all-night sessions. Karl and I left midnight Friday and drove the truck nonstop to the track, just as everyone else does when they first start out in racing. Naturally I can't remember much of the weekend, except that none of the previous problems improved a great deal. But one incident in that race made a serious impression on me. I was behind Jerry Grant in another Lola with the new lightweight Weslake Ford engine. There was a lot of oil on the track, and Jerry spun off and hit a flagman. The guy went twenty feet in the air—all arms and legs—a really horrible sight. While driving under the caution flag I looked around me and the passenger seat had an inch of oil in it. I didn't think I was spilling any, or I would have spun in it myself. But still, I thought, "Grant has just killed some guy, and here I am carrying around a gallon of loose oil. Maybe I contributed to the accident." The engine started smoking about then anyhow, so I pulled into the pits. I just said we ought to stop . . . and no one argued about it. Before we left the track, I told Roger that maybe we ought to go back to a smallblock engine like everyone else. And so we did.

The week after that I went to Le Mans with the Ford GT's. By the time I got back to Philadelphia, Roger's men had the little motor in and were all ready for Watkins Glen. This was a USRRC race without all the international FIA drivers, and the competition wasn't quite so rough. I qualified third, and actually led the race for about twenty laps. Wow! Finally everything was going together! Just before total disaster.

We were already having trouble keeping the fuel filler cap closed, and it came open again when I bumped a car I was lapping. Fuel ran out the open cap, got on the rear tires, and caused me to spin through a flag station. I got out and closed the cap. Even though I lost quite a few places with that, there was still a chance to catch up again. But there's a high-speed blind section of track where a right-hander goes over a crest and down into a left-hander, and a couple of cars got mixed up there just before I arrived. I stormed over the crest really making up time, and there they were—a Porsche off on the right, and another Lola sitting crosswise right in the middle of my path at the apex of the turn.

Those things usually happen so fast and so violently that you have a hard time sorting out the details later, but some WFIL television guys caught it on movie film, so I have a vivid image of what happened from two vantage points. I was aware that there was a spectator tunnel under the track at about that location, which was new and not very well protected with guardrails yet. Normally the smart thing would have been to go outside of him, except for that tunnel and a gulley where I would have ended up. Instead, I tried to go inside. But I was already at the limit of adhesion, and there just wasn't any extra cornering power to get me inside the line—plus the fact that I was braking, which made the car oversteer badly. It was quickly obvious that I wasn't going to make it.

There's an old theory in racing that when you know you're going to hit another car, and there's *nothing* you can do to avoid it—hit square, head-on. Instead of being all crossed up and out of shape from evasive actions, just line up and plow right into it, and you'll come out better off. So at the last instant, when there was *no* hope, I straightened out and drove right through the other car. All I can remember is everything breaking up ahead of me. The fenders came up and I couldn't see a thing. My car was badly broken at that point.

There's another old theory that is more often proven: When you lock the brakes up solid, the car will keep sliding in about the same direction it was going. So, not being able to see where I was going, and knowing that going off the road on either side wasn't such a hot idea—and I probably couldn't have steered what was left of the car anyhow—I just locked it up and skidded down the track. But a fire broke out immediately because of all the fuel that spilled from the loose gas cap, and flames started spreading back over my body. At first it wasn't so bad, but by the time the car stopped, flames were all around me—and I couldn't get out! Finally I remembered the *seat belt*! I had to put my hands back down in the flames to unlatch it, and that was really pretty excruciating because I had no gloves in those days. But I was finally able to scramble out, and I started rolling in the grass to put out the fire on my legs, where my old fireproofed cotton uniform was burning. The gas cap must have popped open in the collision again, because the car began burning like a paper balloon, even though the fire trucks arrived almost immediately.

Believe me, I got a couple of real good lessons out of that. In the first place, *every* time I get in a car of any sort any more, I fasten the seat belt, just so it will always be a reflex action to unlatch it *every* time I have to get out in a hurry. Secondly, the very best fireproof racing uniform is pretty cheap insurance. That's why I always wear—and market, incidentally—the best all-around suit I can find. If that sounds like a plug, I'm sorry, but I really believe it.

I was really lucky not to have any broken bones, but I was in the hospital with painful burns for a while, and I had a lot of things to think about. Roger surprised me by asking if I wanted to continue racing, and I said, "Yes!" So he said, "Okay, we'll have to get another car." And Elmer Bradley from Sun Oil Company came in and boosted my hopes with a lot of moral support—and, later, the finances to back it all up. But we still hadn't even finished a race with the Lola, much less won one, and we still hadn't really developed it or even learned much about it.

Five weeks after the accident we had a totally new car put together, hauled it out to the next USRRC race at Kent, Washington, and *won*! It was kind of a hollow victory, though, because everyone else just fell down around us—Grant, Motschenbacher, Parsons, Cannon—and we moved up by attrition. Maybe it was because most of the other cars had run the whole season, and there we were with an all-new car, our second T70 of four we were to run through eventually. Charlie Parsons won the USRRC Championship that year, but at least we had one win to our credit.

That was the first year of the Can-Am series, the real prize that Roger was aiming for. After the Kent race we had five weeks to get the Lola in shape for it. But we *still* didn't know what we had. Since we were out West, Roger had arranged through Chevrolet for Karl, Al Holbert, and me to take our Lola to Jim Hall's Chaparral test track for development work. I had never met Hall before, and he had probably never heard of me, but I was supposed to learn everything I could in a few days. I really had no idea what to look for.

Hall's people were already busy getting their sensational new winged cars ready for the Can-Am, but they appreciated having my car around because they wanted to have a good idea just how strong the other Lolas were going to be in competition, and we were sort of on the same team through our Chevrolet connections. Jim took the time and interest to show me around his shops himself—although I never got a hint at that time of the wings they were about to use. That was the first time I had ever seen a monocoque chassis being assembled, and it was obvious that a great deal of design work was involved. It was remarkable what tremendous facilities they had—so many mechanics, a machine shop, an assembly building, and all that understanding. Yet as I looked around, I couldn't see how it could all happen right there. It never dawned on me that Chevrolet Research and Development was so much more strongly behind the scenes there.

All the time we were talking—or *he* was talking, anyhow, while I asked questions—I picked up things about bump steer, rear caster, ride heights, spring rates, and torsional rigidity, which were all news to me. But to Jim, it came out just like lighting a cigarette. I really admired him at the time. There he was, a successful driver and a brilliant designer, taking the time to explain all those things to me. Our relationship changed very quickly after that, when I became a strong competitor, and we were a lot less friendly for many years. When I saw him strictly as a car designer in the 1973 L&M Series, I got to know him again. I can see now that he's always been the same kind of guy—nice, easy-going, sincere, smart—while *I'm* the one who has changed so much. I was so ignorant about cars then that I had no idea how stupid I was.

My attitude was that I wasn't going to act surprised—that I was going to listen and learn. When we went there, we had no idea what other racing teams knew about building and setting up cars, but it rapidly became obvious. We were exposed to so *many* things. Because I loved racing, and because I wanted to become a success at it, I wasn't about to go around telling everyone that I didn't know anything by asking a lot of stupid questions. Just listen and learn. I kept that philosophy throughout my relationship with General Motors, and it really paid off. Even today there are so many people who know so many valuable things about racing, like spring and suspension frequencies, and wings and aerodynamics, it's very hard to keep up.

While *I* was learning, the Chaparral engineers were learning. They really 'scoped our car over. They measured it, looked at it, and oohed and aahed over things like the aluminum hubs. Then we took it out to their track to run it around the skidpad, a big, unobstructed slab of asphalt with a 200-foot-diameter circle painted on it. Skidpads were commonplace to GM and Chaparral at the time, but this was the first time I had ever seen one. To determine just how the Lola handled, Jim drove it around and around, right on that 200-foot circle, right up to the limit of adhesion. Just by watching, it was obvious to me that it didn't have enough front traction, that it understeered badly. Jim didn't seem to be very impressed either. Then they put a speed recorder on the car, and both Jim and I drove the Lola around his private two-mile racetrack.

After a little practice I was turning reasonable laptimes, but it could be seen from the speed recordings that Jim was really taking it easy. I assumed he was just being careful with my car. Later I learned that he simply wasn't interested in "racing" against me during a test session, especially with the car set up so poorly by his standards. After our short personal visit, we left the Lola there for a week so they could optimize it for a more accurate comparison with their own car. I've heard that Jim eventually demolished my laptime with the Lola, but I still don't know how it compared with the Chaparral at that time. I'm sure that Chevrolet figured we would finish one-two in the Can-Am that year.

Altogether, we learned that the Lola was actually a good car when it was set up right. It had been unbalanced in handling—that is, it was faster in one direction around the skidpad—so they balanced that out while installing a larger rear anti-roll bar to reduce the understeer. The Lola was also about 400 pounds heavier than their car, with its aluminum engine and all, but it was still out-accelerating the Chaparral in certain speed ranges. To find out why, they took our engine out and shipped it to Chevrolet for a dynamometer test. According to Bill Howell, one of their liaison engineers, Chevrolet was really shocked at the horsepower our simple 333 Traco-Chevrolet put out. Since then, I guess we've all sort of taken Traco for granted. They're just a bunch of honest blokes trying to do a good job. They've stumbled and thrashed with those engines for years, and they still build the best racing engines you can buy.

The most obvious changes on the Lola, when we got it back from Chaparral, were the spoiler on the tail and the dam under the nose. Those guys were mostly interested in aerodynamics at that time, and they wanted to see how good other cars could be made without using the wing like they had. Paul Lamar, their chief engineer, had tacked on simple aluminum spoilers that did fairly well on both their downforce instrumentation and in laptimes. They were rather rudimentary, so Chaparral was generous enough to leave them on when they returned the car. Hall may have regretted that later, when we were racing against each other. But they must have learned quite a bit themselves, because they didn't show up at the first race. The whole thing was quite an experience for me.

One other important thing we did with that car was to go tire testing. Roger promoted that deal with Firestone—he was tied in with them until he got his Goodyear distributorship—because he wanted me to get more time in the car on different tracks. I reckoned that it was another vote of confidence in my driving and engineering ability. Most of it was done at Riverside, though, because the weather was more dependable there. It was a lot of work, too, with Karl Kainhofer and I doing all the changing. I would be running for gasoline while Karl changed the tires each time—which took quite a bit of time because we had bolt-on wheels and we kept stripping lugs. George Follmer was there with his car too, and Bruce Burness was helping him. It turned out to be sort of a contest, with both of us trying to get more laps and faster laps than the other. Firestone was getting a lot out of us.

Something else that turned out to be wasted effort was changing *all* the tires at once. Years later we discovered in testing on the skidpad that, with our understeering cars, you should deal with the fronts first, then work on the rears separately. Changing more than two things at the same time is insane—you almost never learn anything that way. It was a long time before I convinced the tire engineers of that. In the early days I just let them tell me how to do everything. We would put on a full set of tires with a different compound of rubber and I'd go out and run laps as hard as I could. I'd come in and say, "This feels such-and-such," or "That felt so-and-so," when in fact I was working so hard that I couldn't feel anything at all. Since then we've all decided that the ultimate feel is in the laptime. If the time doesn't drop, the tire is no good for those conditions. We tried lots of tires and ran lots of laps, but we didn't really learn very much. That happens most of the time. Tire engineers will be the first to admit that they don't really know a great deal about racing tires.

But it was an interesting experience. I got quite a bit of practice in, and we got a chance to try out some different things on the car. I was putting a lot into it because it was such an honor to me. And I was getting my strength built up to resist the "g" forces and heat of racing, even though the cars were only cornering at about 1.1 "g's."

I remember working on the brakes at Riverside, due to a little trouble we had. We didn't understand much about the brakes then, but Airheart had a lighter caliper than the Girlings, and Roger wanted the best of everything. The Airhearts hadn't worked too well for us before, because the pads would retract too much. So we took the car to Airheart's shops to fit a new system. During the installation one brake line was placed too close to the disc.

There are a couple of places at Riverside where a sudden loss of brakes can be instant disaster. Fortunately, turn seven wasn't one of the places back in 1966. Instead of a bluff on the outside of the turn as they have now, there was just a bunch of haybales and a chain-link fence. Coming into turn seven at well over 100 mph, the brake line melted through where it had been rubbing against the disc, and the brake pedal went to the floor. Naturally I drove right off the turn, through the haybales, and through the chain-link fence.

Karl arrived before I could get out of the car—he was that quick—and after he made sure I was all right he took a look at the car. The first thing he said was, "I'm glad *you* didn't make a mistake." I didn't know what he meant at the time, but I've learned since then just what a perfectionist Karl is. I think the most important thing in his life is not making a mistake, and I think he blamed himself a little bit in that case. But he and I were already good friends, and he didn't want the car ruined because I made a mistake. I trust Karl, and even if maybe that *was* his fault, in all the years I've known him, the only other mistake was not getting a wheel on right in a pitstop at Phoenix. But the rest of the time he's been perfect, and that's *truly* incredible for anyone who's been racing that long. And the guy is so terrific, and so conscious of that sort of thing happening, that he can drive you nuts sometimes because he's so slow and careful.

That was the end of Lola T70 number two. The tub was too badly bent to race anymore. I think that eventually we repaired it and sold it as a coffee table or a show car, but most of the other stuff off of it was used in Lola number three. I'm not sure anyone else ever knew about that accident.

We tried a lot of other things besides brakes that first year, few of which made much difference in the car. We even experimented with engines, in trying to find the Unfair Advantage. Some of them were aluminum small-block Chevrolets that Roger either had left over from an earlier program or got from someone close to GM or Chaparral. We also tried a long-stroke 377-inch version of the cast-iron engine without much success. That one was so touchy that if you over-revved to sixty-six hundred and *one* rpm, it would *destroy* itself. In the end we always came back to the old reliable, bulletproof 333 engine. An example of its durability: One time a screw came out of the headlight covers, flew into the Webers, was swallowed by the engine, and imbedded itself in a piston. We pulled the head, removed the screw, and were able to put the engine back together and race with it. We put the screw back in the headlight cover too—with a little more care.

Other things we played with were gear ratios, camber, ride height, shocks, and headers—mostly just because we were *able* to change those things, That was the first time I'd been able to experiment with different gear ratios in the transmission, and we finally concluded that they don't effect the ultimate speed very much. But they *can* make it a lot easier to drive, when you select ratios for individual short straightaways. The same was true for shock absorbers. They don't mean a whole lot in terms of improving a car's ultimate capability, but they can make a driver feel better. Since then, we've verified these things many times over on many different cars.

My first year in the Can-Am series was less than spectacular. I remember watching those guys get away from me at every race. We would all start together, but they would just pull away and pull away. It was pretty tough on me, because I was driving as hard as I knew how. I didn't know how to make the car go any faster. I felt I wasn't really in complete control, and I was out of shape physically and not as capable as those other guys. I was driving at my maximum, not the car's maximum, so I wasn't really getting the most out of the car. Roger was always giving me the "go faster" sign, but I absolutely *couldn't*. It almost killed me, even though I knew he had a lot of pressure on him for not getting a more experienced driver. He never gave me the "faster" signal much after that, mostly because he knew I'd probably go berserk and crash.

One race in the 1966 Can-Am stands out in my mind. The last race of the series was at Las Vegas, and the attrition rate was high because of the stress that all the cars had been under. I had been racing with Surtees all the way up to the end, when he began to fall back. I was in the lead! I was beating him! Then, on the last half of the last lap, I ran out of gas. I coasted across the finish line—but Surtees beat me there by seconds. Still, it gave me a lot of confidence, because Surtees was the Superman then—he was the one who won the Can-Am that year.

I was in pretty good spirits going into the last race of 1966, down in Nassau. That was the last big race they had there, and the year the wing flipped up on Hap Sharp's Chaparral and he crashed into a tree. In the feature race for all the big cars, a pitstop was required, whether your car could go the distance nonstop or not. We had good mileage calculations on the Lola, so Roger figured that if we added eight or nine gallons of fuel capacity, we wouldn't require a pitstop. According to the rules, it was mandatory for the driver to get out of the car. So all I had to do was stop, get out, get back in again, and go. That was going to be our Unfair Advantage for that one race. My strongest competitors were Peter Revson and Skip Scott in Holman-Moody Ford McLarens, and they practiced fueling stops all week, while we sat back and quietly laughed. All that time we hadn't shown anyone our auxiliary tank—until the morning of the race. When they saw that tank, they knew they'd been had.

When the race started, though, I had some doubts about just who had been had. The extra tank was installed in the passenger side of the cockpit, and I immediately discovered that gasoline was sloshing out the filler cap. I don't know why we hadn't tried it out somewhere before. Peter and Skip were pulling away from me, while I was being fumigated. It was hard to concentrate properly, too, from thinking about the Watkins Glen crash and burn. But I kept holding on because I knew that the extra tank was designed to empty first. In the meantime, those guys were getting farther ahead.

Then, to make matters worse, I made a mistake. I lost control and spun. I hit a tree and knocked off half the nose. I got back on course all right, but I thought, "We're history. From here on I'll just drive to finish." But soon Peter lost his brakes while leading the race, and I started gaining on Skip. Finally he had to pit for fuel, and I was in the lead! Roger was bringing everyone up to a fever pitch by waiting until almost the end of the race—the next-to-last lap—before calling me in. So I came screaming in, jumped out, jumped in, they pushed me off like crazy . . . and Skip went by me as I pulled out of the pits. But on the *last* lap, Skip spun behind a back-marker—and I won!

At that point I decided I should stop racing. I decided to retire. I remember thinking about it on the cool-off lap. Scott and Revson were much faster—much more capable drivers—and the only reason we won was because Roger had psyched everyone out. In all the effort I had put into racing that year, in the Lola, in the GT Fords, in my Mustang, I had only won two major races, at Kent and Nassau. I went through all the post-race interviews and signed autographs, and when I was ready to leave, everyone else had gone. There was no way to get to the hotel. I ended up hitchhiking in the back of a garbage truck. By then I was really feeling sorry for myself.

Over the winter holidays I did a lot of thinking. As hard as it was to quit, I just decided that I had to get out. Roger was paying me fifty dollars a day for racing or testing on the weekends, but that didn't cover all the weekday preparations that were necessary. It simply wasn't worth it for the amount of work that was involved, considering my other full-time job. I had been to Ford's KarKraft racing shops in Detroit, and they offered me a job as a quality control engineer, with "some driving work." So I drove down to Roger's dealership in Philadelphia to give him the news. After all he had done for me, I thought it would be kind of rude to call up and say "I quit" over the telephone.

Roger was surprised to see me. I didn't normally drive to Philadelphia just to have coffee with him. He listened, then said, "So you're going to drive for Ford, are you? The first thing you've gotta remember is that you're going to have to race against us, and you'll be running behind us. And in the second place, you'll probably end up just testing cars for Foyt and Andretti. On the other hand . . . if you want to race with me, I'll pay you $13,000 a year and 25 percent of what you win. If you like it at the end of the year, stay on—or go try something else."

That weekend I talked it over with my wife and my folks. I had decided not to do it because of them—because of what I thought their feelings and my obligations were—but they all said it was *my* decision. I didn't think it was fair to my wife and kids to become a professional racing driver, because I felt I was throwing away all responsibility. But Roger had guaranteed me an income, so there was no financial mystery involved—I wasn't dependent on winning prize money. At the time, there weren't many people getting paid to race full-time. And I don't even think I had demonstrated any particularly great driving talents for Roger to recognize. It's just that we worked well together. We agreed in the necessary areas, and otherwise we went our own way. I didn't get involved in his areas, and he didn't get involved in *my* things. That sort of relationship has remained the same all the years since.

Another thing that had a sudden influence on my decision was a little legal matter at work. At that time I was working with my old Cobra partner, Jack Griffith, on the Ford-engined sports car that was later the Omega, and then the Italia, and so on. Griffith and a guy named Petri had signed me up—unknown to me—as a third member of their corporation, for check-writing purposes or something. But when the going got rough they disappeared to South America or somewhere, and left me watching the shop. Some guys who had done a lot of work for Griffith and not gotten paid went to the government. The bureaucrats saw my name and came after me for back payment of wages. Those guys were friends of mine, but even if I had the money, I didn't think I should have to pay, so I went to a lawyer. I wasn't perfectly clean myself, because I had gotten a tip that the sheriff was coming to padlock the shops, so I loaded up my Mustang and all my own personal stuff as though the place were on fire, and pulled out the back door while the sheriff was coming in the front. My lawyer suggested that the most efficient solution was to get out of the state.

I moved fast. We had just bought a beautiful new house in Stoneybrook, Long Island, and that had to go. After a few days we found a schoolteacher, Barry Hildas, to take it off our hands for a $4000 loss. But he didn't have any money, so I took a second mortgage and walked away. He still sends me a check every month.

So, at the first of the year in 1967, 1 decided to go pro. We moved to Philadelphia and I made the decision to build and race cars full-time.

About all we did to start the 1967 series was update the old car to the latest Lola specifications in chassis and geometry. We did experiment with aerodynamics a little, because Hall's wing seemed to work fairly well and because we heard that McLaren was trying one also. We didn't know what it was all about, but Roger said that we needed one too. We had Troutman and Barnes make us up a small airfoil, with supports to mount it out behind the tail section. At least we had heard from our spy system at GM that it wouldn't work if it was mounted close to the body.

The car was *very* good that way, and we didn't really know why. We had the airfoil hanging out the rear, like no one else has done until recently. On the other hand, we could have used a much larger airfoil, and the one we had was tipped way up so that it was probably stalling. But there was no reason we couldn't have had the same aerodynamic shape then that works so well on the Porsche Can-Am car now. We just didn't realize what was happening.

We were on the verge of achieving a major breakthrough—we could have revolutionized aerodynamics back in 1967—if *only* we had worked on it, if *only* we had recognized what was going on. When I think about what we could have done back then it drives me crazy, because I wonder, "How many times are we missing something just as obvious, *right now*?" You just never know. Now, every time we test, whenever something happens that we can't explain, I ask myself, "Just *what* is happening? Maybe we're looking at something that we don't see." And I feel that every team can gain a lot from that kind of thinking.

The same thing can be said about anti-roll bars. We were getting the word from West Coast racers that all you had to do to the Lola was stiffen the bars. Follmer and Burness were "big bar" nuts, and they were going faster, so again we gave it a try without really knowing why. We knew that the '66 Lola was understeering badly when we tested in Midland. George Follmer was putting great big anti-roll bars on the rear of his Lola, so we copied it, and we went faster too. None of us really knew much about oversteer/understeer yet; we just knew that the car felt better that way. Many other teams had very strong understeer, and they though it was oversteer. What was happening was that the front end wouldn't bite, so they woul apply more and more power until the rear end would break away and they would "dirt-track" out of the corner. They called that oversteer, but it wasn't. With all the power we had on those small tires, it was very easy to power-slide, but it wasn't any way to win races. Until you know what you want, and until you can try it out on the skidpad, it's pretty hard to arrive at good handling just by accident.

Then there was a wheel battle that year, too. The factory Lola came on eight- and ten-inch-wide wheels, so somebody—I think Parnelli Jones was first—decided to solve their "oversteer problem" with wider wheels. He had Halibrand cast up some ten- and twelve-inch wheels, and he smoked everybody. Then we all had to have the bigger wheels to keep even. And when twelve wasn't enough we went to fourteen. Along with that we always needed heavier suspension components, and that meant more weight. It's an old story—one I should have remembered from my experience with the Lotus Formula C car—but ten-inch rims sure seemed wide enough on the Lola back then. We still don't know what the limit is today, and we're at nineteen inches. The only reason we don't go wider now is that it's too *expensive*. Hmm. It wasn't too expensive then. But that was the era of watching the other guy—whenever he went faster, we followed.

The 1967 USRRC series was quite a bit better for me, with six wins out of seven races. The only problem was at Laguna Seca, where I came in third because of some fuel pick-up problems. The car was a lot better due to our Can-Am experience, and there wasn't so much competition. There was Follmer and Revson and Posey and Skip Scott, who were all better drivers than I, but they had terrible cars that weren't set up well. We won a lot of races on consistency and reliability. And I myself had improved. I was running all the time and was more familiar with the car, the tracks, and Karl. The all-important combination.

For the 1967 Can-Am, Roger decided to run two Lolas. He had made a deal for Chris Amon to drive one—which I didn't like at *all*! It made it look as if I wasn't capable of doing the job against the European drivers, and Roger was getting someone who was. But at the last minute Amon backed out, and Roger brought in George Follmer. I was a little bit happier with Follmer, but I didn't like the idea of running on a two-car team then, and I don't to this day. It's a matter of spreading your resources too thin. Still, he was a very good driver for us, and in fact he was usually faster than I was in practice. He made me work really hard to outlap him in the races. He didn't know much about engineering and development of race cars, but he's always been capable of getting the most out of a given car. I feel he's hard on cars, but he's a good compensator—he makes up for what a car lacks in handling. On the other hand, he finished more Can-Am races that year than I did, because I was trying out a lot of new things that broke, and he ran a more standard machine. That was our fourth Lola T70.

Dan Gurney was one of the first to modify the basic Lola chassis, in addition to using a Ford engine, which was rare in the Can-Am even then. By watching the car and talking with him I learned a lot—about public relations, not about cars. The first race was at Elkhart Lake, and his car was all screwed up. He just couldn't seem to do anything with it no matter how hard he struggled along. I was going faster than he was, so I walked over and said, "Dan, if I were you [which of course I wasn't] I'd cut some of the bumpstops out, because when I did, my car felt a lot better." I don't remember his exact words, but he gave me some kind of remark like, "Christ, kid, I think I know what I'm doing, and I'll eventually get it squared away." I don't blame him for that, because I was just a new, snot-nosed kid. I think that if some amateur driver came up to me now and told me how to fix my problems, I'd hit him over the head with a hammer.

When Dan showed up at the next race he had a different rear suspension and the car was lots faster. He had moved the control arm brackets around and fabricated new wishbones, probably based on his experiences with the Ford factory team efforts. I didn't understand why, and I was really curious about it. Even though I still didn't know him, he seemed like such a likeable guy that I asked him. "Please, would you mind telling me what you've done here?" Dan sat down and said, "Look, we all work really hard in racing to be a little bit better than the next guy. Roger has a lot of ins that I don't have, like getting pieces from Chevrolet and cars from Lola. Now maybe I understand suspensions a little bit better than other people, and that may give *me* some small advantage. I would be stupid to tell that to anyone." I thought that was a really good answer. He could have said, "Go shove it!" but instead he calmly and sensibly said what I always say now when asked a similar question. After that I never asked a competitor a question, and I seldom offered any solutions. Whenever I did, I'm sorry to say, I usually lost somehow because of it.

One of the things we tried on my car was a cold ram-air system. That's another thing that has been making a comeback recently, on Formula cars. We had gone to bigger fifty-eight-millimeter Weber carburetors for more power, but they were only available as sidedrafts and they starved out in the turns until we learned how to use pressure regulators. Anyhow, for those carbs we mounted huge pontoon-shaped cold-air boxes off to both sides of the roll bar. They were the greatest things! They made the car look like a spaceship. We didn't realize that they were interfering with airflow to the rear spoiler, which probably offset any gains in horsepower. And they would crack, and they would fall apart, and we even sucked their screens into the carburetors. Still, it was beautiful. It was a very impressive car.

The experiences with those Lolas did a lot for my career. For one thing, I was making more money than I'd ever seen in my life at that point. I still wasn't a "star," though. I didn't have any great spectator following like Foyt, Andretti, Hall, Gurney, Parnelli Jones, and of course, all the European drivers. I had run with them before, in the Ford GT program, but I was sort of lost in the immensity of that thing. Even with the Penske team, I was still kind of an outsider. Roger was noticeably in charge—getting all the outside work done, arranging, phoning—and I didn't have much authority. I was still just coming and going. I was "one of the guys who came along and did the driving."

But to me, that was *my* first total effort against the best American and European cars and drivers. And we did tie John Surtees for third in the final standings, which was fairly good, although maybe it was by default. We usually ran relatively standard and proven equipment, while everyone else tried to trick up their cars with new gimmicks, then dropped out. We certainly had that happen often enough ourselves. That was a very, very good lesson, and it's still true.

Chapter 12

1967–69

CAMARO

Learning the Engineering (Electronics and Dynamics)

I had only been working full-time in Roger Penske's shops for a short while when he asked if I'd be interested in putting together a TransAm Camaro. Our original program was to run the Lola in the USRRC and Can-Am, but since those races didn't start for months, we didn't have a lot to do. Roger has always liked to go to the endurance races at Daytona and Sebring. Now, here it was January and he didn't have a car to enter. He could get George Wintersteen to buy the Camaro some way or other, and his mechanic, "Murph" Mayberry, and I could put it together. Roger said that with my experience in the Mustang at Daytona, I should to be able to quickly set up the Camaro the same way. I said, "Sure," knowing in the back of my mind that the Mustang was successful not because I was so smart but because I had been lucky. I had done the right things mostly by seat-of-the-pants decisions, as opposed to intelligent thinking.

We figured that we had to start with Chevrolet's five-liter Z/28 Camaro package, so George went somewhere in the Midwest and picked up a new street-stock production Camaro and drove it to our shop. I had a rough idea what to do with the car to prepare it for racing. In those days there were certain simple basics: install a roll bar, strip the upholstery, fit big tires, and so on. In the meantime, Traco was putting together a 302-inch version of the 333 smallblock we had been running in the Lola.

Roger was in touch with the engineers at Chevrolet, and they kept asking him what spring rates we were going to use. Then Roger would ask me. But I didn't want to answer . . . because I really had no idea. When he saw that I was unsure, he became unsure that I knew what I was doing. All I knew was that the springs had to be pretty stiff for the banks at Daytona. So when it finally came time to make the decision, I pulled the rear leaves out and took them to a spring shop in Philadelphia. I just asked them to make me up some bigger ones to fit, with "say . . . four leaves," and about "oh . . . yea thick." When I got the springs back I measured the rate by loading weights on them, and they were about 400 or so pounds per inch.

For the front coils I got a Triangle Spring catalog and went down the lists of production springs, checking free length, wire diameter, and number of coils, and I bought three or four different sizes. All were intentionally long, so that I could cut coils out until the ride height was about right. I wanted something really stiff, and that turned out to be about a 1200-pounds-per-inch spring rate.

Those were actually fairly good guesses for Daytona. There was just one thing I forgot. When you lower a car, you have to check for bump travel in the suspension components. There wasn't much to start with, and now there was almost none. But that car was low . . . and it was *stiff.* It even had an "anti-windup bar" mounted to the rear axle that would wind up and hit a rubber stop, which was supposed to be the answer to all our axle-hop problems.

We got the car put together as good as we figured it needed to be, then went to test. Roger knew that Jim Hall did a lot of testing at his Chaparral test track—so we should test. I had no idea what to test for, but Roger insisted, so we just took the car out to drive it around and see if anything was wrong. (It's funny, but now the situation is just the opposite. Roger doesn't think we need to test so much and the rest of us insist on it.) We went to Bridgehampton, and as usual we were late, arriving at about sundown. It was midwinter and there was ice on the track, but we put the lights on, and George and I drove around the course. Under those conditions it was hard to tell if it was right or not—but to me it felt terrible. I didn't want to say anything because I had built it. But I was saying to myself, "Something is really wrong with this car and I don't know what it is."

Our development time was gone, though, so we packed up and went to Daytona anyhow—and doggone, if the car wasn't fast! I didn't know if the car was oversteering or understeering, but at Daytona—who cares. There are few turns, and if the car is sprung stiffly for the banks and fast on the straight, you can just drive it around with no problems. We were clearly faster than the Mustangs. I qualified fourth, but I zapped them on the start. I just pulled out and passed them going into the first turn. The car really wasn't handling right, and it wouldn't stop because the brakes were terrible, but we couldn't tell because it didn't run long enough. The engine started cutting out and I had to stop. I kept telling the crew there was something wrong with the carb, but they went all through the electrics before they found out that the sintered iron filters in the fuel line were clogged. We had made a thirty-seven-gallon fuel tank by cutting and welding two stock tanks on top of each other, and apparently we didn't get them cleaned out well enough. That was it for the first Trans-Am race. George Follmer drove the Camaro in the twenty-four-hour race while I was driving the Ford GT with Revson.

We went back to the shops and reprepared the car for Sebring, and at Sebring we just couldn't do anything! It was the *worst* handling thing I had ever driven. It was so bad it was beyond belief. It had the same springs we used at Daytona, because we didn't know any better—and it was just awful. Then the brake problems started to show up, and I crashed it and tore the nose off. I qualified way down, and got in the race, but the Fords all ran away from us. The brakes went and we struggled along to finish second after Jerry Titus. At least we survived.

Surprisingly, after two unsuccessful races the Chevrolet people were interested in seeing us continue. They had been sending us special rear ends and transmissions, but everything else at that point was our show. We used an optional production anti-roll bar up front and none at the rear, just hoping that it would somehow turn out to be right. We used our own Traco-prepared engines with the optional factory tube headers. And we had production front disc brakes with drums in the rear. So it was obvious we had no brakes at all. Still, it was a lot of work for Murph Mayberry and me to prepare for those races.

An interesting thing happened about then. Because of the surprising showing we made the first time out at Daytona, *Car & Driver* magazine wanted to do an article on the Camaro. So when Murph and I took it back to Bridgehampton to test again, we invited them up to look at it and ride in it and see what it was all about. Pete Hutchinson was their technical editor at the time, and he had quite a bit of engineering experience from working at Chrysler. They came and saw the car, and listened, and watched what we were doing—and then they went away quietly and didn't write an article about it. No article ever came out. I'm sure they recognized all my mistakes. The car had lots of punch but it was too stiff, it was on the bumpstops, and it had terrible handling. When they ignored us like that, I got the impression I was in the woods somehow. I was in trouble.

The third Trans-Am race was at a converted dragstrip in Green Valley, Texas, and if we were going to run the series for the honor and glory of Chevrolet, we had to be there, problems or not. We had slightly softer springs by then, since I had taken a leaf out of the rear, but we still didn't have any brakes. They would last for about ten laps—but this was going to be a four-hour race. If I took it easy the brakes would usually recover somewhat, so that I had some reserve in case I really needed it. This situation also caused a great deal of trouble for one particular competitor of mine. A guy in a Mustang was dicing with me at one point, trying to pass me at the end of that long dragstrip straightaway. He could tell I was having brake problems because I was braking very early every lap. At the same time, I could tell he was setting me up for the pass. So I saved my brakes until I knew he was going to try it, then I drove about fifty feet past my normal braking point . . . and threw out the anchor! I think I had both feet on the brake pedal.

The poor guy had decided he was going to brake after I did, and *that* time it was entirely too late. I glanced over to see where he was, and I caught the most shocked look on his face as he went sailing past me with all four wheels locked up. He just kept right on sliding. Pretty quick there was a bang! ... then another bang! . . . and then a bang-bang! . . . as he flat-spotted and blew out all four tires. But he kept on sliding—and he even flat-spotted his *wheels* before he ran off the end. I guess you would say that's the breaks of racing. He's still racing today, and if he reads this, he'll thank me for not using his name.

Dan Gurney won that race in a Cougar and I was fourth, but what I remember most is getting so exhausted that I didn't think I could last four hours. It wasn't like driving a race car at all. The car was so hard to drive I just had to fight it all the way. The worst thing was that I didn't know what was wrong. I was very unhappy about the whole project.

After that experience I decided that no matter how bad it handled, if it wouldn't stop, I was in the worst trouble. Gib Hufstader had been using his experience on the competition Corvettes at Chevrolet Engineering to help us a little. We tried automatic adjusters on the rear drums, we cut out the backing plates, we tried bigger air ducts, and we used sintered metallic linings. Still the brakes wouldn't last. Murph and I went back to Bridgehampton and spent a week there, trying to get the brakes to work. Vince Piggins and Dick Rider came out from Chevrolet with all kinds of parts and instrumentation, and they put pressure and temperature gauges everywhere. They came to the conclusion that the temperatures weren't too high but hydraulic pressures were. And taper wear on the brake pads was also bothering us. What we failed to see—what all those instruments couldn't tell us—was that we were exceeding the hydraulic capacity of the master cylinder. After all the pieces in the brake system warmed up and expanded, the pedal would go full travel and bottom in the master cylinder. The pedal was rock hard and yet the car wouldn't stop. It fooled us, because that was a sure indication of fade. All we concluded was that if I didn't use the brakes "too hard" they would last a "reasonably" long time.

The situation didn't get much better after all that. I came in second to Revson at Lime Rock, and Roger hired Follmer to drive the car to a third at Mid-Ohio while I was at Le Mans with the Ford GT's. Finally someone in a high place decided that it wasn't such a good idea to let Chevrolet look bad in the series, and we got an invitation to take our car to General Motors' Proving Grounds at Milford, Michigan. I never dealt personally with whoever makes such decisions, but I got the impression that they were doing it as much as a favor to Roger as they were for their own reputation. I knew it was quite an honor.

The Camaro was delivered to GM's Proving Grounds after Mid-Ohio, and I showed up a day later. I had been exposed to a skidpad before at Jim Hall's test track and I knew that it was useful for determing stability, but I wasn't prepared for General Motors' version. They had an unobstructed sea of asphalt over a quarter of a mile square to run large-radius circles on; a two-lane, pool-table-flat straightaway two miles long; and all kinds of electronic instrumentation to measure aerodynamic forces. Dick Rider was working with me again, and this time there were also engineers from Chevrolet's Research and Development Department, including Al Rasegan, Don Gates, and Paul Van Valkenburgh.

Rider's test driver had already been running our Camaro when I arrived, and he showed me the way to take it around the skidpad—very smoothly and steadily. I thought, "Christ, I can certainly get it around better than that!" So I got in and jumped on the throttle and tried to hang the tail out all the way around the circle. Naturally, there's no way you can get around fast in a broadslide, especially in such a poor handling car. They must not have been too impressed. On the other hand, our positions were clear. I was the guy who had to race the car, who had to live with the problem, and it was their job to help me make it work. Actually, they were all very nice about it—if possibly too noncommittal. They thought that maybe it was sprung too stiffly, and perhaps it understeered too much, and just possibly it would be faster if it had softer springs in front. I agreed completely, but when I asked for suggestions, they didn't exactly know what would be better.

Then we went to the straightaway and instrumented the car for aerodynamic lift and drag, and we spent a lot of time getting a little bit of data. We learned that at 100 miles per hour, the body with spoilers gave us about 300 pounds of drag, 50 pounds of lift at the front and 100 pounds down at the rear. I thought that maybe such information would mean something to us in the future, but at the moment we had much more serious problems. The car was "bucking" so badly on the slightest roughness that it would almost throw me out. I could hardly keep my feet on the pedals. I complained about that a lot, but I never got much response. I'm not sure there was even any indication that they understood what I was talking about, because there wasn't enough roughness on their tracks to create the problem.

At the end of the session I said to myself, "Skidpad and aerodynamic work may be keen, but they don't apply to a 3000-pound production car that is leaping and bounding around on a racetrack." All I got from that first session was a little awareness of their capabilities. I had expected a lot of practical advice, but no one would commit himself to any actual numbers. They wouldn't tell me whether to put in 600-pound springs or 100-pound springs. I didn't realize that they had no experience in this area either, that they were going to have to work on the problem and couldn't give me any immediate answers. So I said, "All right, now I have to decide for myself what to do."

In the meantime someone had gone to Fisher Body and arranged to have some lighter body panels made up. They weren't acid-dipped, as we learned to do later. They were simply stamped out of lighter gauge sheet metal on the production line. There were fenders, doors, a hood, and all the inner panels, and they were really light. They were really expensive, too. I heard they cost someone over $15,000. We immediately mounted them on our Camaro, painted them very carefully, and took the car to Bryar in Loudon, New Hampshire—where I promptly crumpled the entire front end into junk. A rear axle broke, throwing the car into a wall, and we lost *all* of our lightweight sheet metal at once. I was heartbroken, because the panels were too thin to repair, and we had put *so* much work into them already.

We also found out that it wasn't a good idea to foam the gas tank in. We had originally cut out the trunk floor and strapped in the larger tank. Then there was a bad case of gaposis to fill, so we made cardboard walls, poured in some foam-in-place polyurethane, and "baked" it up solid. But when the wheel and tire came off, the tank was torn up so badly we had to replace it. We had to hack that stuff out with an axe. It was such a mess that ultimately we welded a floor in the trunk and set the fuel tank on top of that.

We shouldn't have been too surprised about the broken axle, because Vince Piggins and Paul Pryor at Chevrolet had predicted that racing stresses were too great for stock Camaro axles. They already had drawings made up for larger axles with greater radii in the critical areas, so we had them in before the next race. They were just one race too late.

The next Trans-Am race was at Marlboro, in Maryland, and the time had come for me to make a decision on spring rates. The Chevrolet engineers couldn't produce an analytical solution fast enough for our needs, so they had made up a series of front and rear springs with various rates between 250 and 900 pounds front, and 100 to 400 pounds rear. I had to find the right combination for a Camaro race car. I made a quick guess of about 750 pounds front and 350 pounds rear. They sent those springs to us, we installed them in the car, and we went to test at Marlboro. Jim Musser, an engineer who was to become head of Chevrolet R&D, drove down to meet us with a technician and all the rest of the springs. Secrecy was still important, so I borrowed Pennsylvania license plates to get their Chevrolet tool truck into the pits. I had given up on skidpad development for the moment, because it didn't matter so much whether the car oversteered or understeered until I could get it to ride properly on the track. We started jacking around with all those different springs—and the *minute* I drove it with soft springs, I knew everything was going to be all right. We found the right rate by trial and error. The final answer turned out to be 550 pounds front and 180 pounds rear, less than half the spring rate we had started with at Daytona.

Then we started playing with the front camber angles to get the outside front wheel to corner right. We hadn't learned to replace the standard rubber front suspension bushings with a harder material, and the wheels were practically laying down from cornering loads. It took four degrees of static negative camber to get what we wanted—and it looked horrible, with the wheels all splayed in. It was fairly well balanced that way, though. Musser drove the car, and he came to the conclusion that the addition of a rear anti-roll bar would finally get the excessive understeer down to where we wanted it.

Part of our solution was to also remove the anti-windup bar, or traction bar, on the rear axle housing. The geometry was all wrong, and it caused the springs to bind up as though they had an even higher rate. We still had the classic condition of strong understeer, which had to be overcome in a turn by the driver inducing throttle oversteer. But now we were down to a more acceptably soft transition between the two.

While I was at Le Mans with the Ford team, I came to the conclusion that the Camaro ought to have a stiffer chassis also. I had been reading the rule book very carefully, and I noticed that the SCCA allowed roll cages like they use in NASCAR. I had never seen one before, but I thought this was a perfect opportunity to tie everything together into one welded unit. While the car was apart after the Bryar crash, I got a welder in, and in one day he and I cut and installed the basic, waist-high ladder structure. We picked up the front spring towers, the rear of the subframe, the roll bar, and all four rear spring perches. Then, to make it look like a legitimate safety roll cage, we installed tubes up around the windshield and tied them into the roll bar in the roof. All the tubes were 1 1/2 inches in diameter, with .060-inch wall thickness. But when the car was later rolled off a fifty-foot cliff in a towing accident and nothing in the cage was bent, we decided to go to .040-inch thickness on the next car. I guess you would call that a very realistic—but expensive—strength analysis.

We really got our act together between the Bryar crash and the Marlboro race. In that short period we not only solved all the leaping and bounding problems with better spring rates, but we came up with our two Unfair Advantages for the season—the structural roll cage and the understeer-reducing rear anti-roll bar. Finally, I knew that we were on equal terms with all the other Trans-Am cars, and better than most.

Roy Gane, a new mechanic who had replaced Mayberry, and I went back to Philadelphia after the Marlboro tests and *totally* rebuilt the car for the race—engine, transmission, brakes, plumbing, and paint. We went without sleep for days. We sent out for sandwiches and showered under a hose in the driveway. We loaded the car up and drove all night to get back to Marlboro the day of the race. I qualified on the pole—and won my first Trans-Am.

We had a very strong, fairly well-developed car at that point, and we won a few more races that year. But it wasn't without a lot of trouble and strain from other complications—mainly in logistics, or getting the right people and the right things in the right place at the right time.

After we lost all our expensive lightweight body panels at Bryar, Roger got his spy system working and found out that the other team cars were much lighter because they were acid-dipping entire bodies through an aerospace company in Los Angeles. If we were going to uphold the honor of Chevrolet, we had to put together something more special than our converted street sedan. We got started building a second, superlight Camaro. We figured that if we were going to acid-dip, we might as well dip like crazy. I think we finally got that car down to about 2550 pounds. But it was taking forever to get it built, and we had given our original Camaro to Craig Fisher and Bob Johnson to run as sort of a backup in the West Coast races. On the way to California, however, their tow rig went off a cliff and destroyed everything—truck, trailer, and our Camaro. We had just days to finish the new car. We finally air-freighted the unfinished car out to Modesto, and we painted and wired it the night before qualifying. Then we discovered we had the wrong gear ratio for that track, and I spent Saturday night driving 200 miles to find another differential—which wasn't much better. In spite of the reduced weight of our new car, the wrong gearing held us down to third place.

The old car was so badly smashed that no one wanted to have anything to do with it. But the chassis was still straight, so I practically forced the guys to rebuild it, by searching junk yards for Camaros and sending them a new body, piece by piece. That period was really quite a strain on me. Our "team" had doubled in size, but I had no real authority over the new people. We were very loosely associated, and Roy Gane was the only one who' actually worked for me. I couldn't get the other guys going very well, I didn't know how much time and money to spend on their car, and I wasn't sure how to keep everything all together. Also, we were way out on the West Coast where I was unfamiliar with the people and available facilities.

We spent a lot of time rebuilding the wrecked car in a Chevrolet dealership in Oakland. The owner was a member of Roger's "Chevrolet Twenty Group," an association of non-competing dealers around the country who meet quarterly to compare notes on how to improve business. Then we worked in Alan Green's dealership in Seattle for a while, surrounded by his own bunch of local racers. Those dealers were all friendly enough, but I had no idea how far I could push people who were helping us. In the meantime the Can-Am had started, and I was having to fly back and forth between races. At least Karl Kainhofer was taking good care of the Lola, which left me more time for the Camaro headaches.

We got both Camaros to the Las Vegas race only because we all worked night and day. A win there reinforced our hopes somewhat—but then everything went to hell again. After the race we discovered that all four of our engines had a chronic valve train problem and would have to be rebuilt before the Kent race a week away. At the same time, a tow truck we had borrowed from George Follmer was on its last run and would barely pull itself, much less a race car on a trailer. So I rented another truck for Gane to tow our car to Seattle, while I limped into Traco's shops in Los Angeles with the four engines in George's truck. We had two days to rebuild and dyno four engines, and we weren't even sure how to solve our problems.

The symptoms were high wear in the rocker-arm pivot balls and pushrod sockets, which showed up only at the high rpms we had to run to be competitive. We had seen this coming early in the season, because we had to give up our roller cam and rockers for the Trans-Am rules. By now, we heard, Chevrolet engineers had a solution. Bill Howell had developed some new pivot balls with lubrication grooves and special coatings, which seemed to be our only answer for survival. I called Vince Piggins, and he told me that for some reason Howell had all the parts we needed at his house, and there was no way we could get them by the next day. I explained very carefully that we couldn't be competitive without them, that one engine had burned its rockers in warm-up at Las Vegas and that we had to rebuild and dyno the engines the very next day. He could send a guy to Howell's house, get some of "Bill's balls" to the airport, and ship them to us air freight—that *night*. Piggins said, "We can't do that." I said, "Why not?" He said, "We aren't involved in racing. We don't have spare people to go running around town picking up parts for you. It takes the proper paperwork, and it would be three or four days before we could ship them." I was really getting mad, but I just said, "Okay, Vince, I'm glad you told me that, because it saves us a trip to Seattle. We aren't going to run there with engines that I know aren't going to last the race. I don't know what arrangements you have with Roger for getting us special pieces, but I'm going to call him now and tell him that there's no damn reason to run at Kent. It would look bad for us, and it would look bad for Chevrolet. It's that simple." And I hung up.

In a couple of minutes he called back and said the balls would be on the midnight plane. I didn't say a word. I had to hang up quickly, or I might have said something like, "I told you so," and ruined the whole deal. What made me so mad was that I felt we were busting our asses to win those races for Chevrolet, and the least he could do was go a little bit beyond his job to help out. I don't know whether he thought twice and decided that my request wasn't unreasonable, or whether he didn't want to incur Roger's wrath. But apparently he reckoned that I meant business—and he was right! I wasn't going to put that much work into racing with engines that I knew were going to fail. I became a little wary of Vince after that. I had called his bluff, and I didn't figure it would be long before he tried to return the pressure. So I stayed away as best I could. I had worked with Piggins and his engineers before, but this was the first time I had come right out and asked them directly for parts that I knew existed.

We got the parts and we got the engines rebuilt and dynoed. I drove them up to Seattle, where Gane installed them in the two Camaros. Then we had another unhappy surprise. We had been running on Firestones all season, and suddenly Parnelli Jones showed up with some special new Firestone Indy-type tires on his Cougar—and the tires weren't available to our team. But Dan Gurney was the fastest, and he was on Goodyears. So we put on a set of their tires, and our car was about one second faster. As a matter of fact, that put me on the pole. Roger Penske showed up just before the start of the race, and he said, "Okay, let's get those Goodyears off and put our Firestones back on." I jumped up and said, "Wait a minute! *Why*? Roger, we don't have any deal with *either* tire company. Are we going to win this race for Chevrolet, or are we going to play favorites with Firestone?" He knew how hard we had worked to get to this point, and he could see how serious we were about that one-second difference. We ran on those Goodyears and won the race. Shortly after that, while we were racing at Laguna Seca, Roger and I met with Larry Truesdale of Goodyear, and we made a profitable deal for all concerned. That began a long and very good relationship with Goodyear. Before long, Roger also picked up a Goodyear tire distributorship in Philadelphia.

Between the two Camaros and the two Lola T70's, 1967 was an extremely busy and hectic year for Penske Racing. It was our first year together as a professional team, and it was a mess of typically amateur problems that caused all the trouble. There was ignorance on my part; we were trying to hold costs down; we started the season unprepared; we had engine-development problems; we had wrecks and failures in both the race cars and tow vehicles; and we were outnumbered by Ford's factory effort. Still, we managed to win three races, and by the end of the season we were really looking good—on the track anyhow. There is a kind of perverse pleasure in loading the winning car on a trailer behind a beat-up rental truck, while the factory team is winching their "also-rans" into their exotic tractor-trailer rig.

By the end of the season we knew we had a number of Unfair Advantages.

Our engine was more powerful and more durable for one thing, and our handling was probably better also. We still had rubber bushings in the suspension, so the car was soft and floppy, but at least it had smooth traction and not too much oversteer or understeer. We couldn't change anti-roll bars to adjust the handling anyhow, because all we had were the factory bars on the front and rear. What we had been trying to do was change the front-to-rear roll rate distribution by changing the compression on the bar-mounting grommets. We had extra-long bolts holding them in, and if we wanted to reduce the front roll resistance, we would simply loosen up the bracket bolts. With that, of course, there was no roll resistance at all until the rubber compressed again, but we didn't know any better at the time.

CAMARO 1968

In the winter of 1967 we spent most of our time building an all-new '68 Camaro and updating the lightweight '67 to keep as a spare. We had a good idea what we wanted in the way of spring rates, anti-roll bars, geometry, and shock absorbers, so we didn't do any chassis development. The new car was built primarily for the long-distance races at Daytona and Sebring, so it wasn't nearly as light, but there were quite a few acid-dipped pieces in it anyhow. We got an all-new body shell and built the car around it. We had all the time we needed, and by golly we were going to do the best job we knew how, everywhere we could possibly make it better.

The new car would incorporate everything we had learned in 1967, plus it would have a neater roll cage, would be easier to maintain, and would be virtually bulletproof. The body was built with sensible fender flares for the widest tires we could imagine, and the entire front end could be easily removed and replaced with just a few bolts. In the suspension, we finally went to spherical rod ends, and began using delrin bushings in the control arms. We acid-dipped the subframe, built stronger motor mounts, and used higher-grade nuts and bolts everywhere. I spent weeks developing better headers on Traco's dyno, and we recessed the pipes into the body where they wouldn't get squashed. When we got through, that was a beautiful race car.

That time we were ready early enough to do some serious testing before the race. Jim Travers and Frank Coon of Traco, Roy Gane and Peter Reinhart of our shop and Craig Fisher and I all went to Daytona to try and run a complete twenty-four hours just to make sure we hadn't overlooked anything in durability. I knew that Smokey Yunick was working closely with Chevrolet, including a Chevelle he had run in NASCAR and a Camaro he was now building, so I thought that would be a good place to work on our car. I gave him a call. He said he wasn't sure if he had room, but maybe he could squeeze us in.

We ended up in this little shed between two of their buildings. On one side was their machine shop, and on the other side they were building the Camaro—I guess. I don't know for sure because they didn't want us to look around very much. And that was the noisiest place I've ever worked. They had a jukebox that constantly played their particular brand of country and western music, and I think they hired a professional door-slammer just for our benefit. Somebody would open one door—slam it—walk through our area—open the other door—and slam it. Back and forth, all day long, slamming the hell out of those doors. In spite of the fact that Smokey let us use their space, I felt they didn't really want us there. Maybe they just wanted a good look at our car. Later I discovered that there was some sort of rivalry among Smokey, Roger, and Piggins, but I didn't know—I didn't even care. All I wanted was space to work on our car, and Smokey seemed to be a straight shooter, in spite of what anyone said.

We got everything ready, towed the Camaro to the track, and set up to run a full twenty-four-hour test. Craig and I were trading off on every pitstop, and we ran, and ran, and ran. Pretty soon little odds and ends started to happen. The brakes got weak, some seals started to leak, something in the valve train broke and fell down into the pan, and oil pressure was down to about ten psi. A cylinder head broke, "Crabby" Travers changed it, and we kept on running the hell out of the motor—even with ten psi oil pressure.

About halfway through the test, when we were starting to get worn down, Smokey pulled in with his beautiful new car all clean and polished. Coincidentally, I guess, that was when the Chevrolet engineers decided to show up also. I suppose Smokey had waited a while to make sure he would look good by comparison. But he hadn't brought a driver, so Craig and I were talked into trying out his car. Even as tired as our car was, they were both still about equal overall. It's an old line—what we were lacking in the straightaway was made up by our better handling in the corners. Before long the tail pipes fell off his car, and we got back to our own business. We actually only ran about twenty hours. The car was still running, but by that time we were all so tired we just couldn't move any more. One of us would bring the car in, and no one would even have the energy to get up and put fuel in it. We were even driving much slower by then, so we figured twenty hours was close enough. Everything we were worried about—the brakes, transmission, front wheel bearings, and such—had held up.

We had even taken time to test a dual four-barrel carburetor setup that Bill Howell brought from Chevrolet. It looked good on the dyno, but we had to find out how it would respond on the track. Howell had it all tricked up right because he knew what we needed, and it was *really* good, right out of the box. It was so much faster than the single four that we reckoned it was another Unfair Advantage. We went back to the shops in Philadelphia and rebuilt the car again for the race.

As it turned out, we couldn't keep up with the Mustangs. If they weren't faster on the track, at least they spent less time in the pits. For one thing, they could make brake pad changes much faster than we could. Not only did they have a better design to work with, but their crew was more practiced at changing them. Then, at about the halfway point, we cracked another cylinder head. Chevrolet would never admit it, but I'd hate to guess how many hundreds of cracked cylinder heads I've seen on racing engines. I don't know whether it's due to porting or poor coolant flow, but they inevitably crack across the intake valve seat. That's been a problem for as long as I can remember, and it's still a problem today. We changed the head again. That dropped us so far down that we were hard-pressed to finish second in class.

Because we looked so bad at Daytona, Roger said that we'd better have two cars at Sebring. So we started preparing the old acid-dipped car from the year before. Meanwhile, Bill Howell from Chevy had seen the problems we had changing brake pads at Daytona, and he went to Moraine with an idea to make us faster. The problem was that when we slipped the old pads out, the pistons slid out, preventing the new pads from going in easily. The Ford guys had developed some special tools that pushed the pistons back into the caliper, but that took some time also. Bill's idea was to put a vacuum on the master cylinder to *pull* the pistons back in. We already had a source, in the brake booster vacuum, so all we needed was a pressure regulator to prevent sucking air in past the pistons, and a valve so that the driver could actuate the system. Bill put it together on a production sedan and drove it around in Detroit to make sure everything worked right. When

CAMARO, 1968

courtesy of Petersen Publishing Company

Roger heard about it he said, "Forget it. Those guys don't know anything about racing." But I was intrigued with the idea, so I went ahead and plumbed it up on our cars anyhow. When we got to Sebring and Roger saw the system, we had to show him that it worked. We jacked the car up in the garage with the engine running to create a vacuum. By the time the wheels were off the pistons had retracted, and the mechanics whipped the old pads out and the new ones in—just like popping bread into a toaster. When Roger saw that he changed his mind. He told us not to let anyone know, so that this might be another Unfair Advantage.

We were still kind of nervous about going through tech inspection with the old acid-dipped car. After we first ran it at Modesto the year before, the SCCA had called Roger and told him that it was illegal and that we couldn't race it anymore. Roger really laid it into them about that—and rightfully so. He said that Ford had been using that against us for a long time, and now that we had gone to the expense also, we were going to run it. Now there it was again, looking like a new car, and we didn't want anyone to notice it for a while. So we pulled a tricky stunt. I carefully shaped the number circles so they could be easily interchanged between the number 6 for one car and number 15 for the other, First we went through inspection with the heavy number 15 car, then we went back to our garage on the far side of the track, put the number 6 on it, and went back through inspection again. Nobody said anything. In fact, the two cars were very similar except for the dipped body. Actually, there wasn't all that much advantage in acid-dipping because there were minimum weight requirements we had to meet. Dipping merely allowed us to redistribute weight around to where we would rather have it. But it was funny to think we could put one over on them like that. By changing the numbers around again, and entering the track where our garage was instead of through the pits, we even used the dipped car to qualify for both cars. That one car got quite a workout.

For the race, Craig Fisher and I drove the new number 15, and Joe Welch and Bob Johnson drove the old lightweight number 6. Or maybe number 15 was the lightweight car for the race. It was even confusing for us to keep track by then. Smokey brought his Camaro back to race also, with Al Unser and Lloyd Ruby driving. They weren't too familiar with this type of racing, but they caught on quick. We just barely squeaked ahead of them in qualifying. A couple of hours or so into the race, those guys blew Smokey's engine sky-high in the pit straight, which left Jerry Titus and Dick Thompson in a Mustang as our only real competition. But we figured that we had the advantage in pitstops this time. All of us came in for new brakes at about the same time, because the pads would only last about three hours, or through every other fuel stop. Our cars came screaming in, were jacked up—wheels off—throw the old pads out—throw new pads in—wheels on—car down—and out again. I think we could fuel, change all tires, and change front brake pads in about one minute forty seconds, while it took the Ford guys about four minutes. We could gain a lap on them at every brake change. The second time that happened, they were watching a little more closely. Our mechanics looked as if they were just throwing parts everywhere, but we gained another two minutes on them. The next time, Ford's team manager, Fran Hernandez, came over and stood right behind a mechanic and watched everything he did, and still Hernandez walked away scratching his head. He was a good sport about it though. He later admitted that he'd really been screwed—and he didn't know how.

By the end of the race we were about four laps ahead of the Mustang. Even our second car, with Welch and Johnson driving, finished ahead of them, and that car had gotten air sucked into the brake system—the pressure regulator was set too high or something. I don't know how they drove it, either, because I could hardly get it to the garage area after the race.

We were first and second in the GT class, and third and fourth overall, behind a couple of Porsche's. In terms of crowd enthusiasm, though, it was as if we had won the race. We were in the victory circle and everyone was screaming and yelling—it was really a thrilling thing. It took Hernandez about six months to figure out what we had done, but there were no more long-distance sedan races, so it was academic by then.

At that point we were even-up with Ford, with one long-distance race each, and we knew our cars were good for the season. Chevrolet was really interested in what we had, so they invited us to bring our Traco engines in to run on their dynos. Traco was getting 410 to 420 horsepower, while Chevrolet engineers figured we ought to be getting at least 450 horsepower. So we hauled our engines to Detroit, set them up on their dyno, and watched them blow the first one apart in warm-up. It's no wonder, either. They fired it up and ran it wide-open throttle without even waiting for the oil temperature to come up. On top of that, both of those engines already had twelve hard hours of racing. The second one survived that ordeal somehow, and sure enough, it showed about 420 horsepower.

Then they gave us a slide job about what *they* could do. They pulled our cylinder heads off and snapped on some high-compression heads of their own. They hooked up their doodads that maximize everything like spark advance, and fuel mixture, and so on—and they showed us 460 horsepower. That was when we began to understand the principle of "seasoning" a short block assembly. You run a newly-built engine carefully for as long as possible, so that all the parts get "friendly" with each other, then you pop on a fresh set of heads and it will give you another twenty horsepower. Anyhow, they demonstrated that they could get more power with some of their parts, on their dyno, with a prime setup including cold carb air, open headers, and careful monitoring. But we still had to build all our own engines regardless of what they did. We considered that exercise to be kind of a dig at Traco.

We knew that there *were* things to be learned from Chevrolet, because they had made hundreds of hours of durability runs on that engine. They regularly ran hard upshifts at 8000 rpm, and blew engines left and right until they had considerably improved the connecting rods and valve gear. When they suggested trick parts and other odds and ends to improve both durability and power, we were anxious to try them out. We eventually spent four months putting together one super motor out of all the best parts. They didn't want us to test it, though. We were to ship it to them, and they would run it in and make the power checks. So they bolted it up to their dyno and blew it to smithereens. The previous engine they had on that dyno had blown, and no one cleaned the junk out of the lines to the oil cooler before they hooked up our engine. Four months and one engine wasted because of their carelessness. I guess they had the attitude that engines were pretty cheap and easily replaced somehow.

We went to Tulsa, Oklahoma, next—it was really mud city—and won again over Parnelli Jones' Mustang. He was really coming on very strong, but he took himself out because of his recklessness. We had some trouble there too, for the tech inspectors were starting to crack down. We had welded the subframe to the body for rigidity, and they made us cut them apart. Also, to get a lower nose, we had sectioned the radiator cowling and nose the way Bud Moore had done to the Mustangs. That was a trick they brought from NASCAR. We were also gradually putting acid-dipped parts back on the new car without being too obvious. Our job was to win the Trans-Am, and if we had to bend rules as everyone else to be competitive, then we would just bend rules *better* than anyone else. We had a pretty good idea what to do. We had our cars well sorted, and we had good guys working on them. We could simply concentrate on maintaining them properly to finish races. Sometimes it seems as if we spend entire seasons just putting bandages on bleeding sores, but that year we were really looking good.

With everything we did, the cars always got faster or better somehow. We won all but two other races that season, and I had an amazing string of eight in a row. We also had Sam Posey driving our backup car, and he regularly picked up thirds and fourths. He was a good person to have around because he was an up-and-coming guy at the time, he wanted very much to drive for Roger, and we didn't have to pay him very much.

After the Meadowdale race we got another "invitation" to go to Detroit—this time with the whole car. We thought it was because they wanted to help us, but as it turned out, Piggins' group was writing a manual for the independents to use in setting up their own Trans-Am cars, and they wanted to measure our car as a reference. If we had known that at the time we might not have gone. However, we did learn a great deal from R&D Chaparral people like Musser, Gates, Rasegan, and Van Valkenburgh. I hadn't been too impressed with what I'd gotten from all their instrumentation before, like the brake temperature test at Bridgehampton and all the aerodynamic data. I didn't see the potential in it, and I just hadn't paid attention. This time I really had my eyes open, and my mouth closed.

By the summer of 1968 Chevrolet R&D had changed their emphasis from instrumenting in narrow areas like brakes or aerodynamics to measuring and analyzing *total* vehicle dynamics. Gates had put together a rig that could measure all kinds of information on a running race car and record it in a special van parked miles away. They had set it up on their quartermile-square sea of asphalt they called "Black Lake," and were using it to demonstrate their new high-performance 1969 models to the press. There was also a nine-turn, eight-tenths-of-a-mile road course laid out on the asphalt, plus two square courses with corner radii of 100 and 400 feet. All of them were computer-designed to reduce or eliminate shifting, to avoid driver variables. When I arrived and saw my Camaro wired up to record speed, cornering power, acceleration, braking, accelerator position, rpms, steering-wheel angle, laptime, and brake points—I began to suspect that this time I was going to learn something.

I thought I was pretty hot stuff, from winning all those Trans-Am races, but I was humbled right away when the top R&D engineer, Jim Musser, went out on the circular skidpad and turned slightly faster laptimes than I did. Of course, I was quicker on the square corners and the road course where transient responses were required, but he showed me that I could make some improvements in smoothness. A lot of information was generated that was of no value to me, like what the throttle position was and how hard the car was accelerating. Still, the 10 percent or so I did use was invaluable. Roy Gane, my mechanic, was perplexed. He couldn't see how all that was related to racing. But I was beginning to find out just how much there was to learn about the vehicle dynamics of race cars.

Possibly the most important concept was the "friction circle" technique of driving. Basically, that is the knowledge that the car—or its tires—has relatively equal traction capabilities in any direction, whether accelerating, braking, or cornering. The theory is that you get maximum performance when you pass from one condition to the other without going through the center of the circle. In other words, the fastest way into a corner is to gradually trade off braking traction versus cornering traction, until all traction is being used in cornering. I began calling that the "American technique," as opposed to the traditional "European technique" of braking, cornering, and accelerating totally independently. I still think that "filling the circle" is one of the hardest things a racing driver has to do. Few drivers are aware of the theory, but most have a natural tendency to do it anyhow.

The value of having Black Lake to drive on at that point in my education was that it made my mistakes harmless. I can't take risks like that on a racetrack, where it's critical. That's just not my style. But there was nothing to run into on Black Lake. I could skid off the course and just slide forever. I knew that was a tremendous opportunity to learn the upper limits of both me and the car, and I was really being selfish at that point. I was going to run there until they kicked us out—and I don't think we left until we eventually wore out the motor.

The data that they were recording in the instrumentation van helped a great deal also. For one thing, whenever I slid off the track I could drive over to the van, and by the time I got there they could tell me exactly what happened, why it happened, and how it happened. They knew as much about the mistake as I did! "You locked up the left front wheel, didn't you?" Or "You went to wide-open throttle about fifty feet sooner," or "The car rotated 340 degrees and slid for twelve seconds." But what really interested me about the instrumentation was that it could be used to record suspension movements. It wasn't precise enough to tell us exactly what was happening, but we were able to get a better idea how the springs, shocks, and suspension geometry worked—such as the way high roll centers caused jacking in corners, and what anti-dive was doing in braking. I knew some of the theories, and this equipment demonstrated how it was working on my car.

We experimented with camber and caster and anti-roll bars, and we studied the effect of different types of differentials. When we first built the '67 Camaro with stiff springs, we were burning up the limited-slip clutches in the differential. The problem went away when the car was made softer, because it had better traction and didn't spin the inside rear wheel so easily. Now we were learning that uneven action in various types of locking differentials was causing an instability in cornering, and we adopted the fully-locked rear axle. It didn't seem to have any effect on the circular skidpad, but it avoided the slipping and jerking as the clutches grabbed when I came out of a corner, as on the square course. It made the car a lot more stable and easier to drive. For some reason locked differentials weren't approved by the SCCA, though, so we left the positraction in and merely stacked up the clutch springs so that there was about a million pounds of pressure on the clutch packs. We figured this knowledge was another Unfair Advantage, and we went to a lot of effort not to let anyone see how the tires chirped and skidded when we moved the car around in the pits. The next season we lobbied to make locked differentials legal, but it was a long time before anyone else realized they were an advantage in some respects.

There was a similar situation in our brake system. All our fade problems were being overlooked since the rear axle began hopping all around in braking. That was limiting the amount that the brakes could be used, leading us to believe that we had a reasonably good system. We didn't even know what good brakes were then. So we used the test gear to find out why the axle was hopping. We didn't have time to solve the problem right there, but at least we discovered what the precise problem was.

I also learned to appreciate the effects of aerodynamic forces on the car at high speed. As it was, the Camaro had a little bit of oversteer on the low-speed skidpad, and yet it understeered a lot on the high-speed skidpad. This knowledge, combined with the measurement of front and rear aerodynamic downforces, told us how to make it more constant in handling characteristics. All this exposure to suspension movements and aerodynamic forces and driving technique made me so familiar with the car that whenever a problem came up after that, it was much easier for me to pinpoint exactly what the cause was. I learned how to establish a baseline, make simple step changes in the car, and always go back to the baseline to make sure any changes we saw—whether good or bad—were really there.

When we stopped working with Chevrolet and went with the American Motors Javelins, we put together much simpler and more inexpensive instrumentation, so that we could keep on learning on our own. Eventually we used the recording gear on practically every car we developed in TransAm, Can-Am, Formula A, and USAC. We still have the equipment, although we don't rely on it as much any more. Part of the reason is that we can seldom afford the time to set it up regularly, partly because we have learned to trust the skidpad, and partly because we know so much more about geometry in general. That kind of information is so valuable that more racers ought to be exposed to it. But the problem is that you have to know how to use the data. The information just gives you the big clues. On the other hand, a million monkeys, working on a race car for a million years, will eventually put together a car that can beat anyone. There are a lot of guys who build cars with no idea of what instrumentation is, and they still go out and smoke everybody.

After I found out how valuable a skidpad could be, I told Roger that we really ought to have one of our own. It had to have an inner diameter of 200 feet and a 20-foot-wide path. The price I was quoted was $14,000! That's more expensive than your average driveway, but our big sedans would be generating a lot of cornering power, and we wanted something that would stay awhile. I went to Roger and told him how much it would cost. He coughed a bit, but he told me to go ahead with it, and I got exactly what I wanted.

From then on we almost always took every car we had to that skidpad before every race. Sometimes it seemed like we didn't gain very much, but at least we made damn sure that we hadn't *lost* anything. It was always dirty and either too hot or too cold, but we worked for at least a day each time, and when we finished we were prepared to race. That is one good reason why our cars always seemed to run properly, right off the trailer. We've run a lot of cars at our skidpad, from the 917 Porsche to production sedans, and we've made a lot of strong conclusions. Some cars just haven't responded correctly there—and they've gone on to perform poorly on the track also. I've discovered, almost without exception, that if a car looks good on the skidpad, and if I can qualify it without having to make changes at the track, I can put it on the pole. That is a rule that's applied to every kind of race car.

We used that pad for five years, and I figure we got every bit of our money's worth out of it. By 1972, however, we moved our shops further away to Reading, Pennsylvania, and we incorporated a new skidpad right next to the shops. It's identical in size and surface, although it probably cost twice as much the second time. But we couldn't get by without it. It's one of the best tools we have.

We were doing real well at the time I went to Detroit and learned all about instrumentation and skidpads and vehicle dynamics and driving techniques. After that we were much quicker. We really had some great advantages with the Camaros in 1968. The only races that stick in my mind are the ones I lost. At Watkins Glen I used up my brakes trying to keep up with Jerry Titus. That was a longer race than usual, and we were just barely able to make brakes last the shorter races. Sam Posey had the lead in our backup car for a while, but he let Titus get past somehow and we finished two-three. I don't think Roger ever forgave Sam for that. We had won the Championship by Riverside, so I ran alone there, and lost the motor for some reason.

I usually drove the new car that year, and by the end of the season it was fairly well worn out. I was very close to the car, you might say, and I usually knew just how far I could push it and still survive a race. All the other racers accused me of sandbagging, or holding back. They said I wouldn't race, but just hung around until the hot dogs broke. I guess I did keep more or less to myself, but by the end of the race I was usually ahead somehow.

After the last race, at Kent, Washington, we had to decide who our second driver was going to be for the two new Camaros we were going to run in 1969. So we invited five or six very good racers to drive my Camaro the day after the race. There were a couple of experienced sedan drivers, and a B-Sports Racing Champion from Washington, D.C. Roger drove too, although I suppose more for his own entertainment than anything else. I was presiding at the test, and I kept careful records on each driver—laptimes, maximum rpm on the tach, and consistency from lap to lap. Roger was a little slow, at least compared to my expectations, probably because he hadn't raced for a number of years. For some reason, the B-SR driver couldn't get close either. I suspect it was because a sedan has to be driven so hard. That doesn't mean you have to abuse them mechanically, but you really have to manhandle a 3000-pound car on a road course. You have to force it into a drift. Braking and turning together is the key, and that's hard to do, both mentally and physically.

The car was pretty well beat up by then. The front ball joints were worn, the rear brakes were about gone, and the engine was tired. All the drivers were complaining that I had ruined it, that they weren't as fast because the front suspension and brakes were chattering badly. I wasn't sure but what they were right, so I hopped in the car, went out on the track—and turned laps two seconds faster than their best. None of them said anything more about the car after that. The two fastest drivers were Skip Scott and Ron Bucknum, but because Ron was more consistent, we chose him to drive the backup car in 1969.

CAMARO 1969

Over the winter we built two all-new cars for the 1969 season. We hadn't learned a lesson, though, in simply making small detail improvements in what we had. Instead, we tried to come up with too many radical Unfair Advantages, and they cost us so much wasted development time that we almost never caught up again.

All during 1967 and 1968 we had to run with a billion degrees of negative camber up front to make the car handle right, and I just didn't figure that was the best way to set it up. That was what the skidpad told us to do, but it didn't look right at all. So I kept going back to Chevrolet and telling Al Rasegan to design an optional geometry that would give us a better camber change curve. He worked all winter to come up with one that could be adapted to production and yet still satisfy the racing rules. Then we tried it on the car, and it was terrible! He had increased the camber change in a turn all right, but to do that he had to raise the front roll center, which caused "jacking" of the front suspension in a turn. The outside front suspension was made so stiff under lateral weight transfer that it didn't deflect at all. So we never did have a really good geometry for the Camaros. The use of solid bushings allowed us to reduce deflection camber, but other than that, it was pure stock.

As soon as we got the first '69 car running, we took it to Detroit to show Chevrolet what we had. Roger had arranged another test trip, and we were going to impress them with our best and greatest efforts, based on what we had learned in 1968. It was our big presentation, and the car really looked wild. It had a low drooped nose and special front fender flares. We took it to the Research and Development shops in Warren to baseline it against our '68 car.

Our beautiful new car was awful. We worked on their skidpad for a solid

courtesy of Petersen Publishing Company **CAMARO, 1969**

week trying to figure out what was wrong with it. It started out slower than the '68 car, which was slightly discouraging. But what really hurt was that no matter what we did, we couldn't make it consistently faster. We jacked that car up and down and changed anti-roll bars for a week, trying to find a workable combination. It would run right for a few laps and then would get worse again. We would stop and rebalance wheel loads on the scales, take it back out and it would be okay for a few more laps. It would start out understeering, then slowly begin to oversteer. I would turn around and run the opposite direction around the circle. It would understeer badly and then begin to oversteer. Since we were confused, we randomly tried a bigger anti-roll bar up front—and the same thing happened. Then the bar preload would be way off, and when it was readjusted we got more of the same.

We were tearing our hair out. We guessed that maybe the tires were slowly heating up and changing the front-to-rear traction capabilities. It was so cold at the track, though, that our minds weren't even working right. We struggled along for a week before realizing that the anti-roll bars were yielding. They were heat-treated enough to hold up when they were mounted in rubber bushings, but when we mounted them solid, they would bend under large deflections. The front suspension preload changed by the minute. We spent another day getting the bars heat-treated properly and balancing the car correctly, and then it was at least as fast as the other car had been.

Then we wasted another three days trying to get bigger tires on the front. We figured that since there was so much weight on the front, it ought to have bigger tires than the rear, or at least as big. We were so convinced of it that we already had the front end all clearanced for big tires. So we mounted up rear tires for the front—and spent three frustrating days trying to get the car balanced again. When we finally got rid of the understeer on the skidpad, I took it out on the track, and it was undriveable. It didn't even feel good on the track or the skidpad. But I had it in my mind that it was going to be the Unfair Advantage, and I wasn't going to quit until I found out why it didn't work. Cornering power was about equal on the skidpad, but it was unbalanced and unpredictable—virtually uncontrollable. We put the small tires back on the front, and it was normal again. Jerry Titus ran with big tires up front all year, and it never seemed to work for him either. All NASCAR sedans are required to run equal front and rear tires, though, which may account for their poor handling on road courses. To this day, I still don't know why it didn't work.

Altogether, we wasted a couple of weeks of development time getting nowhere. We ended up with a car that was barely as fast as the old one. At least it was better to do it there than at the racetrack.

The Detroit trip wasn't a total zero, though. That was the point at which we finally solved our braking problems again. We had tried to cure the rear axle brake hop at the previous summer's test by installing various tricky linkages. First we mounted horizontal shock absorbers on the axle housing, and that didn't do anything. Then we did a long study to determine where the exact center of rotation of the rear suspension was, so that we could use a solid traction bar that wouldn't bind up. The pivot point turned out to be way inside the car. We cut a hole in the floor, built a pivot bracket on the roll cage, ran a rigid link from the axle to the pivot, and fitted a rubber boot in the hole. When we got all that stuff built, and tried it at Black Lake, the thing hopped just as bad as ever. Maybe it was a little better, but it worked best in acceleration instead of braking. Then we discovered that the SCCA wouldn't let us use it anyhow.

That was when the instrumentation came to our rescue. By mounting displacement transducers on the axle, and making high-speed recordings of its movement in braking, we discovered that it was hopping due to a *vertical* axle movement, not a rotational movement as we suspected. Between test trips we got together with Koni engineers and came up with a different concept in shock absorbers. What we did was to increase the low-speed leak in the shock valve, so that there was less damping of the smaller movements. The idea was to let the axle have more freedom to do its hopping on minor bumps, and just try to control the major bounces. Before, we had gone stiffer and stiffer and it just got worse. So we made the shocks softer in one mode, and that cured the problem. The ride got a little worse, but it was already so bad with those Konis that it couldn't have hurt much.

We had to start out the 1969 Trans-Am season knowing that our new cars were only just as good as the '68 cars. We did have an interesting pit gimmick, however, which we hoped would be an Unfair Advantage. Over the winter I had looked at our fueling rig and poured through the rule book, and I was sure we could come up with something better. There didn't seem to be any maximum height rule in the book, so I suggested that we build the tallest tank that was practical, to give us the maximum fuel flow pressure. A Chevrolet engineer named Don Cox had started working with us by then, and he made the point that we didn't need such a huge tank. All we had to do was mount our ordinary twenty-two-gallon supply tank as high as possible, and run a four-inch hose down to the nozzle. The Sun engineers designed a tripod that put the head tank up about twenty feet, and they calculated that it would take a seventy-three-mph wind to knock it over. The tripod was built out of aluminum tubing with slip-fit joints so that it could be easily assembled in a hurry.

When we were finished we erected that beauty at our shops and ran a test—which turned out to be a little scary. The fuel came out of that nozzle so damn fast that it sprayed all over *everywhere*! And the pressure head was so high that shutting the nozzle off created a kickback that could knock a man down. We were filling a fuel cell that was lying there on the ground, and I thought we were going to blow it up like a cheap balloon. It was a fantastic setup. Warren Agor was our fueler at the time, and he was a little afraid—no, he was very *much* afraid—of what could happen. But it didn't violate the rules, and it seemed to be as safe as anything else we had used, which isn't saying much.

The first race of the season was at Michigan International Speedway. Our plan was to wait until Sunday morning to erect our secret fueling rig, so that no one could see how hard it was to put up—and so that it would be too late for anyone to complain about it. We got to the pits at about 6 A.M. and had it up before anyone arrived. The first guy to see it was Homer Perry, who was the head liaison man between Ford and Bud Moore and Shelby. He took one look and walked away. Pretty soon he was back with the head SCCA official. He stood there and looked at our rig, the rule book in one hand and scratching his head with the other. Then the American Motors team came over and stared at it. By that time a crowd had gathered, and everyone debated it for hours while we sat back and waited. No one could find anything wrong. No doubt it was the Cadillac of fuel rigs—a true example of the Unfair Advantage.

Actually, however, it didn't save us any time in that race. That was the year it rained so bad, and we went back and forth between rain tires and dry tires on each pitstop. Besides, Agor was so afraid of it that he wasn't really fueling much quicker. Interestingly, a very quiet team, Titus and Godsall, had come with a rig that was better than ours in one way. They had a slide-valve nozzle that was safer and had less restriction than our butterfly valve. Also, Rusty Jowett's mechanic had invented a much faster hinged quick-fill cap. I looked both of them over very carefully and realized that those teams had done their homework. We eventually copied their nozzle and filler cap, as everyone else did, but *we* were the ones who got all the publicity for it.

That was the race where we also tried—and gave up on—power steering. In anticipation of the large tires on the front, we had developed a power-steering system made up of a Bendix gearbox and a Saginaw pump. The gears were one of the first variable-ratio setups, and the pump was driven by a Gilmer belt. We ran it for two weeks at the GM tests without any problem. Roger didn't want to take a chance running it on both cars in the race, so we only used it on Bucknum's car. Sure enough, the drive belt broke during the race, putting Bucknum out of the running. Ron didn't like it very much anyhow, and we were under the gun at that point so we never ran it again. The mechanics should have changed the belt after that much use, but they were unfamiliar with the system.

The mechanic on Ron's car was John Woodard, and that was his first race with us. Woody had walked into our shops that winter looking for a job, and since the Datsun dealer he had worked for was a friend of mine, I tried him out. We had the shell built on the number two car, but the mechanic on it wanted out of racing. Woody seemed to be a kid who didn't know much, so I showed him where all the parts were and told him to put the gas tank in and plumb it. Then the rest of us went to the Detroit tests with the other car for a few weeks. When I got back that car was all put together—and it was gorgeous! It was as if he had been building race cars all his life. That was outstanding enough, but I soon learned that he could catch on equally fast with any kind of project. The Michigan race was difficult for Woody, because he was in charge of a new car and had a new driver. But what was amazing about him was that no matter how miserable the conditions, he always dug in and got his job done ... and without complaining.

The Michigan race was a disaster for me. Firestone's rain tires seemed to be much better than ours, and we lost a lot of time in the pits. Everything got very confusing, and the officials said I was the winner even though our timer, Judy Stropus, showed Parnelli Jones to be the winner. We figured the SCCA could find any mistakes on their own, so we didn't make any noise. Judy and I left as soon as possible, taking our own lap charts with us. Who knows—we could have been wrong. Roger was the only one who stayed. Since he was sure Parnelli had won, he waited around to see what was going to happen.

The Ford guys did something at that point which probably changed the outcome of the whole season. That was our third season in the Trans-Am, and it had lost its novelty and challenge to Roger. We did have a deal with Chevrolet to run the series, but we were already well developed, we had all the equipment we needed, and we had convincingly won the Championship the previous year. The program was more or less running itself and Roger didn't have to be too involved. His big interest at the moment was Indianapolis.

After the race there was a meeting because Bud Moore, Homer Perry, and Parnelli Jones were violently protesting Roger and the SCCA's results. Roger just sat there listening, but pretty soon some of those guys went over and started insulting him. Apparently they had been drinking, and they became more vocal than usual. First they told Roger that their cars had outrun him on the track and in the pits—and in fact, they had actually blown us off. But then Perry made the mistake of getting personal. I don't know his exact words, but it was something to the effect that Roger was a spoiled rich kid who didn't have the honor to stand up and admit that he was really being supported by GM. They said that he was doing things in a backhanded, sneaky way. Of course, they were finally declared the winners, and that didn't help Roger either.

When Roger came back to the motel he was furious. He couldn't say much at the meeting, but I've seldom seen him so mad. Roger told me at that point, "I don't care what else we do this year. It is my firm intention to beat those guys, no matter what it takes." In fact, they had beat us fairly at the first race, but then they started insulting Roger, and they just went too far. As a result, Roger was very upset. What started out as a relatively conventional "let's see what happens" year became a personal vendetta. He was going to make sure we won the Championship, all right, even though we had gotten off to a poor start.

Right after that we ran into a confrontation with Chevrolet. The next Trans-Am race was at Lime Rock, and it conflicted with Indianapolis. Roger was sure we could win the Championship anyhow, so he entered me at Indy and hired Bob Johnson to drive the Camaro in that one race. A rift was growing between Roger and Vince Piggins, and Lime Rock seemed like an opportunity for Vince to make Roger look bad. So he called Roger and told him they had made arrangements for him to run the Trans-Am, and they figured that part of the deal was for me to drive the car. Roger suggested that they come to Indy to discuss the situation. When Roger, Piggins, and Jim Musser got together, he showed them what we had invested in the USAC car and spares, and told them flat out that he was going to race at Indy. If they wanted to come up with a great deal of money, then he could afford to get another driver and crew. The way he explained it sounded quite reasonable, but of course there was no way Chevrolet could do anything like that, and they had to back down. I picked up quite a few dollars by finishing seventh at Indy, and Bob Johnson took a third at Lime Rock.

For the next race at Mid-Ohio, we started getting things back together again. Since the track is so close to Detroit, we were able to persuade Chevrolet to send their fabulous instrumentation van down, and Don Gates came along to wire up the cars. We recorded things such as speed, lateral acceleration, throttle application, and brake points, with Bucknum and me doing all the driving. I was generally faster than he was, and by comparing the recordings we were able to see exactly what and where the differences were. "Keep your foot down longer here. Make a longer radius turn there. Do this, that, and the other thing."

At first Bucknum was reluctant to trust the machine, but by carefully following our suggestions he picked up a tremendous amount. His laptimes were what convinced him. He never was quite as fast as me in the same car, but he was damn close by the time we were through. His biggest problem was that he was anticipating brake trouble, and he would back off early and apply the brakes too conservatively. We could see on the recorder charts that he was using the European technique of braking and turning separately. It took a lot of practice for him to convert to the brake-and-turn combination, which I now believe to be the secret of going quickly in road racing. I led the race most of the way, but when I lost a wheel bearing Ron was able to pick up the lead and win—thanks to our electronic driver-training, I like to believe.

An important thing happened between Lime Rock and Mid-Ohio. The SCCA sent a little bulletin to all competitors: "As of right now, no fueling rigs will be over twelve feet high." They didn't consult with us or warn us—they were just saying, "All right, we're gonna change the rules now." We were a little upset, because we had put over $7000 into that rig, and one day we get an arbitrary change in the mail making it illegal. What next? If they could do that, the next day they could say blue paint was illegal and make us repaint the car.

We rebuilt the rig for Mid-Ohio anyhow. But then the SCCA guys came up to me at the track and started laughing about it a lot. They said, "That really was a funny joke you pulled on us. But we did a job on you. We legislated fueling rigs so quick, you never knew what was happening." Then I really got mad. I said, "If you think it's so goddam funny when you legislate thousands of dollars out the window, then you've got a mixed-up sense of values. You're going to put us all out of business. When we make a mistake we have to live with it. When you make a mistake you ought to at least be fair about it." In the end I guess it really hurt me to say that, because they later got me on another deal. They weren't about to let me have the last word.

In preparing the new '69 Camaros we had come up with some ideas that weren't covered one way or another in the rules. For one thing, we opened up the front fender wells, cut holes in the door pillar and door panels, and ducted air through them all the way back to the rear wheel wells. It wasn't of critical importance, but it let a little more air out of the engine room and cooled the rear tires and brakes a little better. Everyone could see the holes when the doors were opened, and you could see signs of engine oil in the rear wheel wells, but no one bothered us for a long time.

Another thing was the vinyl top. We were constantly repainting our cars, and it cost about $400 just to paint the top alone. So we figured that a $50 vinyl roof ought to last the entire season. Well . . . actually it wasn't just a cost consideration, because we *had* acid-dipped the top a little too heavily, and it was wrinkled enough so that it looked bad in paint. But it wasn't aluminum or chopped full of holes as some competitors claimed.

After our little disagreement at Mid-Ohio, the SCCA guys started complaining about our cars. They said they didn't like the holes in the doors, and the vinyl top wasn't homologated in the manufacturers recognition papers. They also said the nose was too low. Bud Moore had started that, but he hadn't chopped his as much as we did. I told them that when Moore brought his Mustang noses up, we would too. The way I read the rule book, everything else was legal. I was running the whole team by then—sorting out the cars and parts and trucks and mechanics, and that was a major effort for me. I didn't need a lot of other trouble.

At Bridgehampton I guess they decided to crack down. Dave Tallaksen was the Chief Steward there, and he happened to be around when we took our cars through tech inspection. He and I had known each other for years, and Dave took his job as seriously as I took mine. When he saw those holes in the door, and the vinyl roof, he said, "I don't know exactly what's wrong about your car, but when I see something like that, a little red light goes on in my head." I thought, "Christ! First I have to put up with guys making instant legislation on our fuel rig, and now I have to deal with a guy who doesn't like our car because there's a red light in his head. We're dealing with insane people in this Neanderthal SCCA system." So I said, "Fine, Dave, but here we are, and unless you can show me any rules against vinyl tops and holes in the doors, we're going to race it like it is." He said he didn't care *what* the book said, he wasn't going to let us run.

According to the system, my next move was to appeal to the Stewards of the Meeting, and they would rule whether the car was legal or not. So Dave explained to them about the red light in his head, and I explained how I was trying to rationally follow their rules. I won because the board was made up of some really straight shooters like Tom McNeil, Henry Zamota, and Ed Brown. Those were guys who had built and raced their own cars, who could read the rule book, and who knew that it pays to be reasonable in this business. They let me run as it was—and that *really* pissed the "Red Light Kid."

That wasn't the end of it. I qualified on the pole, then broke my motor in warm-up just before the race. Bucknum had qualified his car in fourth, and according to our arrangement, I was going to take it over for the race. Well,

"Red Light" told me that I had to start at the back of the pack because I hadn't qualified that car on the pole. He was right of course, according to the book, but I was still mad about it anyhow. When we came around for the start of the race, I got back about 500 yards behind everyone else, just to make sure there was no confusion. I drove the hell out of that car. I got up to second place before I broke a pushrod and had to finish on seven cylinders.

We seemed to have done everything wrong so far, so we decided to go test at Donnybrooke in Brainerd, Minnesota, before the next race there. That's an expensive proposition, mind you, to keep two cars out there for a week and a half. Then Ron Bucknum had a highway accident on the way to the track and broke his wrist, and we had to get Ed Leslie to come and drive for us. Ron was out a long time because of that, and I really think it hurt his career. As for the vinyl top controversy, Homer Perry had gotten it in his mind that there was something wrong there, and he just wouldn't shut up about it. After Bridgehampton, the SCCA called us and said that it wasn't unreasonable for us to take them off with enough warning. Roger finally agreed, but by that time the cars were at Donnybrooke, and it would have to be after that race when we could get the cars back in the shops.

When we unloaded to test at Donnybrooke, one of the first persons I saw was Dave Tallaksen, who was going to be Chief Steward again. We said "hello" and had a lot of friendly small talk, and he didn't say a word about the tops. So we ran our tests, and I went away on some other business. When I got back on the Friday before the race, I heard that Dave had told the tech inspectors not to pass our cars until the vinyl tops were off and the doors were patched up. At that point Roger came in and said we were leaving. Really, we had no other choice. He told us to go back to the motel and wait while he tried to negotiate. Our agreement with the SCCA was to have the tops changed by the next race at Bryar, and that was it. We probably could have done some kind of quick and dirty job, but now it was the principle of the thing—we had to force some kind of consistency in our dealing with them. Dave stood his ground too, saying that he knew Chevrolet wouldn't let us withdraw. So Roger called Piggins and Musser and told them he was taking a stand. He said he was prepared to end our arrangements and stop right there. We weren't afraid to let the press know what was going on either. Everyone thought it was just a bluff, but when we sat there in our motel all day Friday, people started getting the idea that we were serious. The SCCA was being unreasonable again, and we figured that our other racing interests could take the place of the Trans-Am, if necessary. Don Cox was there from Chevrolet, and he was just blithering. Not even he could imagine us staying out of a race. Finally, at the last minute, both Roger and the SCCA gave a little, and they allowed us to run if we blocked the door vents and had the vinyl top off by Bryar.

That was an interesting race. There were four factory Mustangs, with Parnelli Jones, Follmer, Revson, and Horst Kwech driving—versus me and Ed Leslie, who wasn't quite as quick as the rest of us because he was new to the series. The five of us ran together in a tight group for a long time, before they all eliminated themselves and dropped back. Follmer made a mistake and hit someone head-on; Revson overused his brakes and fell back; Kwech hit me and got a flat tire for it. The race ended up between Parnelli and me. We were fighting it out tooth and nail. We were about equal everywhere—in the pits, in power, and in handling. Finally he made a mistake, and I got ahead by about twenty seconds with five laps to go. And then I broke a connecting rod, and the car just stopped. Parnelli went on to win, and Leslie, who had been holding back, came in second. We were all a little mad about that connecting rod, because Chevrolet engineers had told us it was all right not to polish their stock parts. The production rod was supposed to be perfect as we got it. At that point we told them that no matter what they said about engines, we were ultimately responsible, and we were going to build them our own way. After that, we won every one of the remaining Trans-Am races, and the second car finished all but two.

At Bryar we had the cars all fixed up the way the SCCA wanted. We had the doors patched, and the vinyl tops were off. Actually, it turned out to be cleaner to cut the entire top off and weld a new one on, since the old one was wrinkled and covered with glue. Maybe we should have done that earlier in the season, because we finished one-two at Bryar. That course is fairly hard on cars, and every one of the Mustangs broke there. I had set such a fast pace that even I was about to break by the end, and I had to slow down drastically. The differential was cooking and smoking, and I was thinking about Donnybrooke, where my engine broke in the lead. Then Ed Leslie caught up to me in our other Camaro, and I began having mixed emotions. Roger gave Ed the signal not to pass me, though, and we both circulated at a reduced rate to the end.

Ed was a little upset about that, but he didn't say anything. Everyone else was down on Roger, though, because Ed could have won easily. Horst Kwech went up to Roger and said, "Roger, Ed deserved to win and you should have let him do it. If I was driving for you, I would have gone by Donohue no matter *what* you said." Roger just very calmly said, "Well, Horst, that's why you aren't driving for me. And in fact, you never will." I was confused about it all. Naturally I wanted to win fair and square, but it really didn't matter which one of us was first since it was a team effort. But I appreciated what Roger and Ed did for me. I guess it was Roger's way of repaying me for all the extra effort I was putting into the team.

The next race, at St. Jovite, was where we introduced our new fast fueling rig. Don Cox had gone through some calculations, and he reckoned that if we used slide valves both at the nozzle and in place of the ball valve at the supply tank, we could fill in three or four seconds. So we made up the pieces, which involved a lot of gears to slide the valves open, and specially shaped flow cones in the tank. It took two guys to operate the rig—one to stick the nozzle in the spring-loaded filler cap door and the other to open the valve—and it took a lot of practice. But it was truly incredible! Putting twenty-two gallons of gas in a fuel tank in 3-1/2 seconds is unreal. I could actually feel the back of the car sink as a couple hundred pounds of fuel went crashing into the tank. Of course, we also spilled gasoline everywhere. It was all over the trunk and the ground, and we had to dig holes to wash it into. We had made hints to the press that our pitstops were going to be a little quicker at St. Jovite, so for our first stop of the race everyone was crowded around with their cameras ready. I screamed into the pits and stopped, there was a splash of gasoline, and I screamed right back out again. We left everyone standing there with their cameras in hand, saying, "Hey, wait a minute! Let's see that again!" We were so fast that no one even got a picture of it. That little exercise really shook everybody up. The few seconds we saved didn't mean all that much over a two-hour race, but it demoralized everyone else and provided us with a lot of publicity.

It did save the day for us at one race, though. At Sears Point, in California, Parnelli was catching me at the end of the race, and we figured that I only needed five gallons to finish. It actually took less than a one-second stop—zip in, zip out—and I was only *two* seconds ahead of Parnelli at the finish. Crowds would gather to watch, and Ford was going berserk. The more they practiced, the slower they got. We were finally on top of the game, both on the track and in the pits.

Ford was in the game fairly deeply and they had arranged to rent each track just before every race. I was still rather naive, so before we went out to Laguna Seca, I called Homer Perry and asked if we could run there a little bit on one of their days. He said, "Oh, yeah, come on out." We went to California a few days early and wasted a lot of time standing around waiting. They never did find time to let us in. Maybe Perry should have just told us no. But then again, their secrecy could have had something to do with a new Firestone tire they came up with. When we finally saw it at the race we were quite impressed. It was a beautiful tire. It was lower and wider than anything we had ever seen before, and it just flat smoked us. Those tires must have been at least a second a lap faster than anything we had in Goodyears. I think the only reason we won there was that they broke some wheels, and one of their cars caught on fire.

I hadn't been faced with such a tremendous disadvantage in a long time, and the only difference I could see was in those tires. I knew we had to get some to try on our car, so I either borrowed or stole a set, depending on who you talk to. Actually, I made a deal with another car owner to share test time at Sears Point with us, if he would let me try out the new Firestone tires he had on his car. So while everyone else was drinking it up in the bar on Sunday night, I made arrangements for the tires and the track, and we hauled the cars up to Sears Point. The next morning we were testing tires. I ran for a long time on the best Goodyears we had, to get familiar with the track and to establish a baseline. When I figured I was at my limit—which included going off the track and scraping up my tires—we switched to the Firestones. They clearly had an advantage of 1.5 to 2.0 seconds over us.

I made one big mistake, though. It's hard to know how careful to be in this kind of a deal, because there's no way of knowing how serious the reaction will be. I had let too many people in on our quiet little test session, and Firestone got the word almost immediately. I don't know who told them, but it might have been another Firestone driver who lived close to the track. Right away, everybody was mad at everyone else; Firestone, Ford, and Parnelli Jones were furious with me, Roger, Goodyear, and especially the guy who loaned me the tires. It became quite a problem. On top of that, when the Goodyear engineers saw how fast the tires were, they flew them back to Akron for more tests. There were a lot of rumors and threats about that—Goodyear was going to cut them open, Parnelli was going to lean on me, we were going to fight back, and so on. I was in the middle, and it didn't take me long to grasp the seriousness of the situation. I wanted to return the tires and get it forgotten, because I figured Goodyear was smart enough to produce a better tire on their own. I couldn't blame Firestone for their reaction, but at the same time, if they were that concerned they should have kept closer control over the tires.

Another crisis created when we started to look bad at Laguna was the need for another car. Jim Musser at Chevrolet told Roger we ought to have a third car to back up the program just in case the Ford team "accidentally" sacrificed some of their five cars to eliminate ours. A third car? Damn! It was hard enough to keep two together. But we got the word that cost was no object and not to spare any extra effort. We had sold our best '68 car to Sam Posey, and he had just stored it. So we bought it back, and the guys in Philadelphia updated it to 1969, painted it, installed a new engine, and we ran it on the skidpad—all in two weeks. For some reason, that was the fastest sedan we had ever run on the skidpad, so we figured it was going to be a real ace in the hole. We could air-freight it to the West Coast and press it into service on a day's notice. But we never had to use it. It was sitting there ready to go, and no one ever even saw it.

By the race at Kent, two weeks later, Goodyear had come through. They produced a better tire. At the same time, the Firestones started blistering and coming apart under severe use. At Kent I blew my engine and Ron Bucknum won in our other car, with Parnelli coming in behind him on a flat tire.

Parnelli was so furious at Kent that he couldn't even talk to me. We had been friends—at least professionally—up to that point, so I went up to him to apologize for the way things turned out with the tires. That was really the end of our friendship, though. He reckoned that I had knifed him in the back when it came down to the point where our success, and our jobs, were on the line. I can't say for sure, but that could have had something to do with a bash Parnelli and I got into at Riverside.

Follmer was leading the race there, and when I came out of the pits after a fuel stop, I was right ahead of Parnelli. Going down through the esses I was a lot heavier, and since I still had fuel running off the rear of the car, I was relatively slow. Going into turn six, which is the slowest turn on the track, I put my brakes on normally—and Parnelli came up and rammed me in the back. I thought, "Christ! Now what did he do *that* for? Did he skid on my spilled fuel, or is this the big showdown?" I knew it couldn't have hurt me very much, and I figured it didn't hurt his car either. So I continued on. But I looked back and I couldn't see him any more. A few laps later I went into the esses—and there was Parnelli again, going real slow. I thought he must have gotten a flat tire or something, so I started around on the outside—and he turned into my path. I pulled up behind him, and *then* he put on his brakes! I ran right into him. I spun off the track and stalled my engine, while Parnelli drove around to the pits.

However, we had built those cars from the very beginning to take that kind of punishment and keep running. Naturally we wanted most of the weight to the rear for better handling, but we also made sure there was nothing vulnerable in the crush space in the nose. The oil coolers were back in the fenders behind the front tires, all electrics were isolated, and there were no sharp objects ahead of the radiator that could puncture it in a collision. I took a tremendous hit, but everything flexed around and there was no serious damage.

Follmer was still in the lead, but I was running quicker by then. Finally I unlapped myself from him, and as I passed I gave him a sign to indicate that I had one lap to make up yet. I guess he got incensed at that somehow. He started trying harder, and he took himself out of the race. He broke a front wheel in a turn and limped all the way around to the pits on the brake disc—where he ran into the pit wall and destroyed his car. I came in first, with Bucknum second, and we won the Trans-Am Championship again.

In the meantime, Parnelli had gone to the press and complained that I put my brakes on and busted his radiator intentionally. He told everyone that I was really a dirty guy, when in fact *he* had obviously waited around to finish me off. I hadn't meant to cause trouble, but what he had done was totally unnecessary. I was kind of pissed when I heard that, but racing is racing, and we had won after all, and Homer Perry was looking bad. So I went down to their pits to apologize. I guess that was the wrong thing to do at that point, but I figured that if Parnelli was so mad he was going to punch me in the nose, it was better now than waiting for it. Everyone had been drinking it up, though, and they became very, very nasty. What stands out in my mind is that they said I had a halo reputation with the press and the public, but really I was a rotten SOB underneath. All I could do was just stand there and take it like a man. Parnelli had already left by then. The next day I tried to call him at his Firestone tire dealership to apologize, but he wasn't in. I really made an effort to reach him, but he was not here . . . and not there . . . so I finally gave up, Much later I heard a rumor from one of his guys that there was nothing really wrong with Parnelli's car he was just so mad that he drove it in and parked it. He and I raced against each other some in the next year's Trans-Am. We would say hello occasionally, but we never really had any conversation after that.

That was also the end of our relationship with Chevrolet. We were doing very well for them and we didn't feel we were getting enough in return. Actually, we had a lot of reasons for leaving. From a technical and rules standpoint, all Trans-Am sedans were about the same. There were no great advantages for us from one make to another. Financially, we just couldn't afford to race Camaros if another company offered us a great deal of money, because Chevrolet was extremely limited in that respect. Professionally, we had to show all our business associates that it was the Penske Team that was winning races, and not GM with us as a front. And finally, we were getting personally annoyed at comments such as Homer Perry had made, to the effect that we were being sneaky and dishonest. Chevrolet wasn't happy to see us go—well, maybe Piggins was—but their hands were tied by corporate policy.

We sold all three of our Camaros, and all the spare parts that went with them. One went to Jim Hall, and Craig Murray of Sears Point bought one. But no one ever really did much with the cars after that. I occasionally still hear about them being raced by people who don't really realize what they have. It's the same old story. Successful racing is not in the basic materials you have to work with—it's all in the team and the preparation.

Chapter 13

1968

EAGLE-CHEVROLET
Trying USAC (and Getting Humbled)

In 1967 George Bignotti asked me if I'd like to drive his second USAC car in the Rex Mays race at Riverside. I didn't see why not, because the Penske team wasn't too busy at that time of year. So, thinking we might be able to learn something from the experience, I asked Roger. He said, "No! What if a wheel breaks or something falls off, and you get hurt? Then where am I?" That's always been his standard policy—he doesn't want me driving for anyone else because he has so much invested in me. It makes a lot of sense to me now. I'm around my cars constantly. I know the mechanics who do the work, and I know what is being done. It can be very risky to get in a car you know absolutely nothing about. Roger said, "If you want to run USAC road races, I'll buy a car and *we* will run it." I didn't think I was that interested.

But the idea drifted around in our heads for a year, and in 1968 Roger bought a new USAC Eagle from Gurney. We figured that we might not be too competitive on the oval tracks right away, so the first plan was to go to the Mosport USAC road race in Ontario. Everybody else was running their 305 stock blocks, 255 OHC Fords, and Offys on alcohol, but since we had no experience with it, we decided to run our 305 Chevy on gasoline. We reckoned that what we would be giving up in power could be regained by carrying a lighter fuel load. We also figured that Gurney ought to know what kind of chassis setup was right for these cars, so we ran with the chassis as it was delivered.

It was a typical last-minute operation. We got the engine at the last minute, we put the car together at the last minute, and we arrived at the track

courtesy of Penske Communications (photo by Richard George)

EAGLE-CHEVROLET

a little *after* the last minute. I was only able to get a few laps of practice on Saturday. There was no time for development at all. We just unloaded the car, tried it out to see if it was running, qualified, and raced.

Anyone else who had a decently set-up car was easily faster. There were some junkboxes with two-speed gearboxes, asymmetrical suspensions, and turbo-Offys, but there were also some very good cars. It was kind of a "run what you brung" type of race. That was my first experience with those cars, and I didn't know what was right or wrong about our Eagle. It seemed to be stiff and not responding too well, On the other hand, I had never been in a powerful open-wheeled car before, so I had no idea what to expect. I did feel they weren't cornering as hard as our Can-Am cars, which used all sorts of wings and spoilers for aerodynamic downforce.

What was surprising was that I didn't see anything different about anyone's driving. I had heard some pretty horrible stuff about USAC drivers on road courses, but they seemed quite normal to me. They were very hard on their cars, however, since most of them weren't used to shifting and braking. We had hoped that my experience at road racing would be our Unfair Advantage, but as it turned out, the best I could get was a fifth place, behind Gurney, Andretti, Bucknum, and Al Unser. But even after the race we had no idea whether that was due to chassis setup, my driving ability, or the engine. Because of our inexperience with alcohol motors, we didn't want to push ours any—and those guys were really good at pumping up an engine, especially for short qualifying runs.

We went back to the shops and began preparing for the Rex Mays race at Riverside. We had Traco build us a couple of 320-inch Chevys to run on alcohol. They weren't inclined to raise the compression ratio very much on those engines, however. We had already seen too many problems with leaking head gaskets, and there was the eternal problem of cracking cylinder heads, which we never did zero in on. We were afraid that more compression would accentuate the problem. We got a Hilborn injection setup, and Jim Kinsler put it all together on a manifold and flowed it for us. Then we got the Champion Spark Plug dynamometer engineer to show us how to set the jets and mixtures, and so on. Later on we did try a little nitro, and we broke the motor immediately. Other racers got away with it sometimes—and sometimes they didn't. It was like Russian roulette.

We went to Riverside a week early, assuming that it would be possible to somehow improve the Eagle's handling. Over a period of a few days we learned that it really would respond to changes in spring rates and anti-roll bars. I hadn't learned what I could do with a skidpad at that point, but I did know that we could change the degree of oversteer or understeer. The hard part was in trying to sense, or even define, how much understeer was best, for I was able to induce oversteer at any time with the throttle. This was—and is—complicated by the changing aerodynamics between lowspeed and high-speed corners. It's very difficult for a neophyte to distinguish the difference between aerodynamic and mechanical effects.

Eventually I began to realize that if it was understeering a little too much, we wanted softer springs and bars in front, and reasonably stiff ones in the rear. But then I discovered that the front springs had such an extreme inclination that the suspension would stiffen up just due to binding in the ball joints. This could be why there was such a strong tendency to understeer. When we got through, I had selected what seemed to be a very low spring rate, about 175 pounds per inch. But the chassis didn't bottom anywhere on the course, and I thought it handled very well.

For both qualifying and the race we ran on straight alcohol. Those who wanted to take a chance used unknown amounts of nitro and improved their grid positions over me correspondingly. But in the race I soon found myself running in second place behind Dan Gurney! I think it was as much a surprise to me as it was to Dan. He almost *owned* that track, and yet he couldn't pull away from me. It must have been a shock to everyone, especially all those big-name USAC drivers that I was ahead of. It was such a big deal for me to be keeping up with Dan, in fact, that I was driving a little over my head. I remember thinking, "I can't get by him, and I can't stay so tense. I've got to cool it—and wait." So I relaxed. I relaxed about one tenth of a degree. But that was too much. I lost my concentration, cut an apex too close, and grazed some marker tires. Nothing happened right away, but within a few laps my outside front upright broke and sent me flying off the road at turn six. I had gotten so caught up with the fact that I was staying with mighty Dan that I didn't do a good job of driving my own car. I didn't even make it to the first pitstop.

Our Eagle was supposed to be identical to Dan's, except for the engine. When our cast-magnesium upright broke, however, we noticed that it was different from Dan's. We were a little disturbed about that, at first. But when we researched the problem in more depth we concluded that the responsibility wasn't solely with my driving or the Eagle's design. The hub would have broken eventually regardless.

As is customary, we had torn the car down after our test session and had the suspension inspected. Then Karl Kainhofer, who was chief mechanic on that car, had to be somewhere else, so Peter Reinhart and Peter Law put the car back together. There were three front uprights, one of which had shown cracks in inspection, and somehow or other they put the cracked one on the car. Karl disassembled the car after my accident, and he could see the marks where the crack had been. I was really upset with those guys for making such a mistake, when we were looking so good in the race. I told Karl not to mention it to them—that I would handle it. I put the broken upright in my drawer, thinking it might be useful information someday. But I never said anything about it. I don't know why, but I just didn't want to bring it up after the race. I guess that I didn't want the guys to feel like I had "caught" them at something. Roger never did that with me, or anybody else, and they certainly hadn't done it on purpose. That broken upright sat in my drawer for four years as a reminder, and those guys never knew about it. But occasionally I thought, "Well, so much for Roger's faith in the absolute security of only driving our *own* cars with our *own* mechanics."

After those two races we reckoned that we ought to be competitive with

RIVERSIDE 1968, KARL KAINHOFFER LOOKS OVER WRECKED EAGLE-CHEVROLET

courtesy of Petersen Publishing Company

the USAC guys at Indianapolis. Roger wanted me to get some practice there before the '69 season started, so he arranged for us to go to a Goodyear tire test. Because of all the work we had done with Chevrolet's instrumentation on our Camaro, we were also interested in what we could learn with it on a USAC car. At the same time, Chevrolet engineers wanted a chart of speed and accelerations on the Indianapolis track, to run through their computers so they could figure out just exactly what was needed to make the Chevy engine competitive. They sent us a data tape recorder, and instructions on how to wire it up to the Eagle. We took out the right-hand fuel cell to make room for the recorder, and we installed a speed transducer on the right front wheel.

Gurney sent us a crate of miscellaneous springs with all different rates so I could try and get the car rebalanced for constant left turns. The trouble was—none of them came in pairs, because nobody worried about chassis symmetry at Indianapolis. Not knowing anything about their trick of diagonal weight—jacking with different rate springs, I managed to get them all mixed up and on the wrong corners of the car. I just assumed that because the car always turned left, the heavier springs should always be on the right-side suspension.

At the speeds I was running, however, it really didn't make any difference. At the time the record was about 170 mph, and rookies who hadn't taken their driver's test were only allowed to run 150. So I never got the car up to a point where I could tell if it was understeering or oversteering, and consequently we never changed very much. Even at 150 mph, though, I felt like I was barely hanging on. I didn't know what to expect, because I had heard that once a car got away from you there it was too late—you could never catch it. I was really trying to avoid that, and I didn't feel comfortable at all.

Then I got called into the pits. One of the very alert driver-observers on the back straight had radioed in that he thought he saw sparks coming from the right front wheel. We looked the car over really carefully but couldn't see anything wrong. I went back out and ran a few more laps—and the nut came off the right front spindle! Going into turn one the wheel started wobbling, and I started getting very nervous. I knew I was going to crash. Somehow I slowed down, though, and went grinding and scraping my way through the turn. The wheel never came completely off because the brake disc was trapped in the caliper—which is probably where the sparks had been coming from in the first place. Our last hub and upright were ruined, so we called it a day. As it turned out, that was the last time I ever drove the Eagle.

There were a number of reasons why we abandoned the Eagle-Chevy for USAC racing. In the first place, we didn't get much encouragement from

Chevrolet. We gave them the speed and acceleration recordings of me going around at 150 mph, but nothing much came of it. I wasn't too sure what good the data was, and I never got much feedback from the Chevrolet engineers. There were few people who could analyze that stuff anyhow. The next step would have been to use the instrumentation van for more channels of information, as we had done with the Camaro, but no one was interested enough for that. They could have simply decided that the engine wasn't competitive at that point. At the same time Roger was under some pressure from GM and the press, because it was apparent we were getting some back-door help with the Camaro and with the instrumentation at Indianapolis. Using the traditional Offy engine would solve a lot of those problems for us.

That was the start of 1969, when we tried to form an all-inclusive deal with Eric Broadley, to race nothing but Lolas. But the Eagle was a great car, even though we never spent much time developing it. The only other areas we experimented with were some little aerodynamic spoilers on the rear bodywork and side-scoops for the side-draft injectors. I only raced it twice, and then we sold it to Ron Bucknum. We learned one thing from it, though. Roger came to the conclusion that if he gave me enough time to research the problem, we would be as competitive as anyone else. Ultimately we did become successful in USAC, although it took a little longer than we expected.

Chapter 14

1968

MCLAREN M6-B

Keeping Up with the Factory Team (—and No More)

Toward the end of the Can-Am season in 1967 we could see that our old Lola T70 just wasn't going to do the job against McLaren's new cars. We did well against the amateurs that year, but nobody's car—not even the Chaparral could keep up with McLaren's M6-B's in the professional series. When the races got out to the West Coast, Roger started dealing to buy the car that Bruce himself was driving. I remember keeping a close eye on that car at Riverside and Las Vegas. I was convinced that we were getting some pretty good machinery from the way Jim Hall was having to work to keep up with McLaren. Even with his radical wing as an advantage, I've never seen Jim drive so hard and so well as he did trying to outqualify the McLarens. The car was to become ours after the Las Vegas race, so I had more than one reason to be happy about it dropping out early with engine problems.

McLaren's chief engineer, Tyler Alexander, came to Philadelphia to show us how to keep our new car running—adjustments, maintenance, repairs, replacements—all those things you don't usually get in an instruction book. All the time he was there I kept asking, "You're selling us such a great car. . . . what do you have in mind for next year?" And Tyler—he's so casual—just said, "I don't really know yet. We'll just get together and build a better car."

To me, the car we were buying was so much better than what we had that it was beyond me how he could say something like that so casually. It was kind of depressing, actually, to know that we had a hard time just maintaining our cars, and they were so far above us that they were going to build two or three *better* cars. Now I understand how all that works. They had spent a season with that design, and they knew all its weaknesses—or at least what they didn't like about it. They would simply go back and change the drawings a little bit and update what they had. We've even done that ourselves quite a bit since then. The later McLaren's, which we beat with the first Can-Am Porsche, were basically six years old in design.

We had our own scheme in mind for an Unfair Advantage in 1968, though. We were going to take out the cast-iron Chevrolet smallblock that had served us all so well and go back to the 427 engine. Hall had run an aluminum version all season, and it had stayed together most of the time, so we figured it was fairly well debugged. But all we could get from Chevrolet was a cast-iron block with aluminum heads. I felt that was unreasonable, considering that we were also doing such a good job with the Camaros.

Part of the solution to our previous problems with that engine was the new dry-sump system. Hall's engines were rigged up with dual gear pumps in the ordinary distributor-driven location, plus a scavenge pump driven off the nose of the crankshaft. However, the rest of us had been successful with the multiple stacked-rotor Weaver pumps on our smallblock engines, and it turned out to be the best system on all counts. GM tried it out too, and it obsoleted their self-contained system. The first engine that Traco built for us was just under 600 horsepower at 6500 rpm. We can get that at 5500 rpm now, but it was a lot more than the smallblocks were good for.

Right away—before the year was out—Roger wanted us to run a simulated race to see whether it looked as if the combination was going to work. So we went to Riverside in November with the idea of running a 200-mile test with the 427 engine. All we did to prepare the car was to stick the new engine in and haul it to the track—no suspension changes at all. Looking back, I don't suppose it entered my mind to increase the spring rate at the rear, even considering the experience we had with the same kind of engine swap in the Lola T70.

My laptimes at Riverside were two seconds slower than McLaren's had been in the same car with the smaller engine—and I had no idea why. The car was so unfamiliar to me that I didn't know whether it was the engine, the suspension, driver ability, or simply a slower track. I can imagine now that the increased rear weight on those soft springs gave it a lot more understeer, making it feel more stable but limiting its speed through the corners. And the engine didn't feel much more powerful, but it survived and that was what we went to learn. Still, I wondered where I was going to get those two seconds. I was going to have to keep my eyes open.

The first amateur race of the 1968 season was in Mexico City. Everybody else in that series still had smallblock engines, although Lothar Motschenbacher had bought Hulme's McLaren and was running a Gurney-Weslake Ford engine. The first problem we had was in getting into Mexico at all, because we didn't know the border guards wanted to be "tipped" for their services. But we finally got that straightened out and got the truck to the track.

When practice opened, the blasted motor wouldn't start. Both Jim Travers and Frank Coon of Traco were there with Roger, and the three of them were climbing all over that engine. They tinkered with the fuel injection and the ignition—which was still a point-type at the time, because we used such low revs—and they replaced the tiny Varley battery that everybody was using. Finally they got it started, somehow, and I went out and ran half a lap—and the engine locked up. Actually, I could feel it start to freeze, and I shut it off before anything was damaged. So we towed it back to the pits. After cooling down it loosened up a bit, and I took it out again. And it locked up again.

That time we decided we would have to take it out of the car and look into it. We didn't have a spare motor, but Jim and Frank had engineered that one so we reckoned they should be able to fix it. When we turned it upside down and opened the pan, we discovered that all the bearings were shot. Jim and Frank could replace them easily enough—if they *had* some—so they called George Bolthoff, who worked for them at the time and who had actually assembled the engine. They told him to grab some new bearings and take the next plane to Mexico City. When he finally arrived he still had to smuggle or bribe the parts past the customs blokes, so Roger got some guy with influence to pay off everybody in sight and we got the bearings. Meanwhile, I was carrying the bare block around in the bilges of the pits, while everyone else was practicing and qualifying. Finally I went to bed, while they got it back together and back in the car.

I had an opportunity to qualify again in the morning before the race. I carefully warmed up the rebuilt engine and took it out on the track. It went two

McLaren M6-B

photo by F. David Stone

or three laps and seized again. By that time we'd had enough, and we loaded it on the truck. Ultimately we found out that the cause of our problems was simply the wrong size bearings. Somehow George had used undersize bearings—they were mismarked or were on the wrong shelf—in both the original build and in our pit rebuild. Because they were only two thousandths off, the crankshaft would rotate, but there wasn't room for oil flow. I don't know why they weren't checking that, but I'll bet it's never happened since. I'll bet that also had something to do with the engine being so hard to start. Anyhow, the week was a total disaster. Roger had arranged everything in his own fantastic way, spending all those dollars to get the equipment there, and flying all those people in, and getting the engine rebuilt, and because of one tiny mistake we never even started the race.

There was a lot of time before the next USRRC race. I went back to Philadelphia to finish up the new Camaros, and the Traco guys settled down to making the engine right. I was still upset because we couldn't get an aluminum block, but I decided that maybe we could reduce weight by acid-dipping the iron blocks. I thought that ultimately it might be cheaper and more reliable. The owner of Automation Industries—the place where all the Trans-Am competitors were getting their sedan bodies acid-dipped—was enthusiastic about the idea, except for the problem of masking off all the critical machined surfaces. We masked one ourselves and built one engine that way, which ran fine, although we didn't get a lot of weight off. I told our problem to our Chevrolet liaison engineer, Bill Howell, because he was sympathetic with our difficulties in getting the aluminum engines. With a little urging on my part he was able to get us some raw block castings, and he said he could arrange to have them worked back into the production machining line at the factory after we had dipped them. We had ten blocks shipped to Automation Industries. Since it was a totally unfamiliar operation, I told the dippers to vary the time each one was in the acid, so that we could learn how much we could take off and still survive the machining operations. All we had to mask off were the alignment ears that locate the blocks on the machining line. Eventually we got back ten raw blocks in varying degrees of lightness, and we shipped them to the Chevrolet engine plant at Tonawanda, New York.

Then there was the problem of how to identify our blocks in the machining line, so that we could get the right ones back. The whole procedure is automated, with remote-control operation, and there are a lot of people involved. I heard that finally they decided to paint our blocks a different color. Well, our engines got lost in the system. I called all around, and the most reasonable story I got was that there was a shutdown somewhere in the line, and during that time there was a shift change. The new guys didn't know there was anything different about pink blocks, or purple, or whatever they were, and so they were assembled and installed in production sedans. We had never even weighed them to see how much lighter they were, because it was purely academic in the unmachined form. But somewhere there are a bunch of very high-nosed 427 Chevrolets running around with funny-colored blocks.

The weight problem resolved itself after that, however, because Chevrolet decided to go into limited production with the all-aluminum 427, and they were made available to everyone. What had happened was that Roger heard that the McLaren team was going to get aluminum blocks, and then he wouldn't take no for an answer. They were very, very expensive though, at about $3000 right out of the crate. That's before Traco would do their own expensive magic. The new engines were somewhat unreliable to start with, because of leaking castings, pulled studs, shifting cylinder liners, and a myriad of other things. But Roger kept calling Jim Hall, and fortunately Jim was willing to help us out from his experience. I don't know if our engines were the most powerful that season, but Traco was able to keep them together better than most of the other builders.

By the third race of the season, at Laguna Seca, we had the aluminum engine in, and it was worth an easy win. But at the next race, Bridgehampton, all that extra torque caused a little difficulty. We were using a Wisemann differential for the first time, which is essentially locked up under acceleration—and one of the stub axles broke! I was running about ninety miles per hour over the crest of a hill at wide-open throttle, and when I came down it was in one-wheel drive. There was no warning, no time to react in any way—suddenly the car was just totally out of control! It had immediately gone into critical violent oversteer and was spinning down the track. Like the Lola wreck at Watkins Glen, all I could do was lock up the brakes and at least skid in a straight line in the same direction—rotating all the way. Finally it slid off the road and into an embankment, bending up the tub a little bit.

That was a valuable lesson to me, since that sort of thing has happened many times since. It's good to know what the car is going to do when an axle snaps—which is really quite a bad experience. Still, there is just no possible way a driver can react in time to keep the car from spinning. When the axle breaks under power the car is going to spin immediately, and all you can do is try to minimize the damage. The whole violent maneuver really gave me an understanding of oversteer. It makes me wonder how race cars with a locked differential will go around corners at all.

In repairing the chassis after the accident, I began to understand that the fastest race cars aren't built to run forever. I could see where rivets were popping out and pieces were bending, and I remembered how easily the front suspension broke when I had hit a tire marker in practice at Riverside. It became obvious that this chassis was only good for so many races. I had never seen that before. I had always assumed that you might have to replace the running gear, but the chassis ought to be indestructible. Now this one was in its second season and already was getting old.

By that time we began to realize that the aluminum 427 engine was causing too much understeer because it was heavier than the cast-iron 327, and we began to work on the problem. We never did think to experiment with anti-roll bars, but I had experience with coil springs, so I got my spring formula out and tried to design some stiffer ones for the rear. I guess I could have called McLaren and asked for help, but I was too proud to let them find out that I really didn't know what I wanted. I talked with West Coast racers Phil Remington and Charlie Hayes about it though, because springs were a big thing then—the answer to all your problems—and those guys were experts to me. And of course, the Indy and NASCAR guys had been juggling springs for years. I knew that the engine was about 100 pounds heavier, but not what was needed in terms of spring rate. I finally drew some up and had them made by a local spring company in Philadelphia. But they were cold wound and overstressed, and they would sag before we could finish a race. I suspect that cost us a lot of finishing positions over the season. Eventually I got Dick Rider from Chevrolet to help me out as he had with the Camaro and Lola T70, and by the end of the year we were in pretty good shape. We worked out of the problem slowly—we struggled along on our own—and ultimately we learned something, which is probably better than buying a canned solution, if you don't go crazy in the meantime.

The way we decided on spring rates was whether or not the car would bottom anywhere on the course. We just kept stiffening the rear springs until nothing hit, and then stiffened the front springs until the oversteer was balanced. By the time we got through, I thought it was a very good-handling car, especially considering that huge—at the time—engine in the back. I could apply lots of throttle coming out of the corners and it would gradually approach oversteer, which I now know to be typical of high-camber-change suspensions. I was very comfortable in the car.

The only other USRRC race of any great consequence that year was in the rain at St. Jovite. John Cannon and the English drivers were known to be much better rain drivers for some reason, and I really expected them to show me around. But I had gotten some practice on a wet track, and after I sat down and analyzed it for a while, I came to an odd conclusion. It seemed that performance was not diminished equally in all stages of driving. Acceleration and braking were reduced, naturally, but not nearly as much as cornering power was. So I tried to avoid my ordinary style of braking deep into the corners, and adapted to the "European style" of braking and accelerating only in a straight line, and cornering at a constant "steady state."

I was on the front row for the start of the race, and I remember sitting there under an umbrella in a rain that was so bad you just couldn't believe it. It was torrential. Finally they started the race anyhow, and I picked up my new style immediately. I *charged* into the first corner—*jammed* on the brakes—and creeped around on tiptoe. Then I *rushed* into the next corner—*jammed* on the brakes—and creeped around. I didn't know what the others were doing, but that seemed to be working for me. When I got to the back straight, however, I looked in my mirrors and there wasn't anyone behind me! I thought, "Christ, either they didn't start the race and here I am running like a fool, or there was a big accident and everyone is wrecked." They were way back there all right, and I went on to win by a large margin over Cannon.

Up to that point I don't think either Roger or our guys had a great deal of confidence in me. But everyone knew that if you could win in the rain in those big cars, then you were some kind of Superman. That was a big ego thing to me, even though I knew it wasn't because of any great driving ability. It was because of my engineering knowledge and careful reasoning that I was able to analyze the situation and come up with a solution. And you've got to be able to control yourself a lot in the rain. You have to have different moods. You drive *violently* down the straight as if you want to break the car in half, then you stomp on the brakes like there's no tomorrow. Then you calm . . . down . . . and . . . tiptoe serenely around the turn. Some drivers can't make the adaptation, I guess. I've seen a lot of drivers who either creep around everywhere or who give it everything in the straight and go flying off the turn. I certainly haven't dominated every rain race since—like later coming in eighth at Laguna in the Can-Am—but St. Jovite was the first race where I saw it work.

The rest of the USRRC races that season were relatively uneventful, except that an engine failed while I was in the lead at Kent, and the gearbox broke while Jerry Hansen was co-driving at Elkhart Lake. During the season we were again preparing for the fall Can-Am races, and that included coming up with another Unfair Advantage.

We had been having little problems with our body panels that year. They were always breaking up, and every time we patched and repainted them they got heavier. Roger thought we ought to have our own bodies made, so he got Berry Plasti-Glass in Long Beach to make a mold and incorporate a few improvements. This was about the time of all the high wings and moveable spoilers, and we decided that we had to have one also—only better. Our rear spoiler was going to fold down into a trough in the rear deck so that it would be perfectly flush for low air drag. A hydraulic lever in the cockpit allowed me to trim it out on the straights. We really didn't understand what we were doing, but it was based on the success that Chaparral was having with their wings. So Bill Scott came over from Sun Oil again and made the spoiler and lever, and Berry Plasti-glass produced a rear deck to fit it into. By the time we got through, those expensive new bodies were only about ten pounds lighter. That was hardly enough to justify the time and expense of making our own mold, so it turned out to be an exercise in futility. But we had our own body, and it was a real beauty. It had that fantastic spoiler and a beautiful paint job with 20 million pinstripes. We were really proud.

Before the first Can-Am race we went to Bridgehampton to have a little test . . . but mostly to show off to the press. We got all set up and I went out to try our new moveable spoiler. I was going to trim it out on the straightaway, and that car would take off like a rocket. So, about halfway down the pit straight, going well over 170 mph, I released that beauty—and I damn near lost it! On the *straightaway*! It happened so suddenly that it was like being hit with a brick. Naturally I backed off immediately and kept it in a straight line, but that scared me *so* bad that I could never bring myself to use it again. The problem was that we had a lot of downforce ahead of the front wheels, and when the rear spoiler dropped, we actually had a little lift in the rear. The combination may have been lower in drag, but it was just flat undriveable from a stability standpoint. Our one Unfair Advantage for the Can-Am was history, seconds after we tried it the first time. We had made a giant step backward. I don't think we let on to the press at the time—I mean, I hope they didn't know how scared I was—and finally we even took all the operating mechanism off.

We started into the 1968 Can-Am with a note of mediocrity. The first race was at Elkhart Lake, and the McLaren team showed up with spectacular new cars as we had expected. They were truly gorgeous and much faster than anything we had. All we could hope for was that they weren't as well developed and as finely tuned as we were. That almost happened, too, except for a little slippage of the tongue on my part. We all had the same aluminum 427 Chevrolet engines in our cars, but the McLarens immediately broke some of theirs for unexplainable reasons.

But to go back a little bit. Roger had been trying to help Sun Oil get their transmission fluid approved through GM's standards tests. Along with that we were also evaluating Sunoco racing oil in our Camaro program. It was becoming known, or we were learning on the dynamometer, that mineral-base additives in the oil would cause combustion chamber deposits, the deposits would cause detonation, and the detonation would rapidly destroy a high-compression racing engine. Sun Oil gradually switched away from those additives, and we finally worked out the problem. Then we learned on Traco's dyno that the aluminum engines had an even more critical problem. They had a dip in the torque curve at about 5500 rpm, where they would go lean, detonate, and blow black smoke out the exhaust. This was later avoided by using the staggered inlet stacks, but we minimized it then by using Sun's "ashless" oil.

When McLaren suddenly started losing engines that were otherwise running great, I thought, "What could be more obvious? I'll bet they're failing from detonation." I started feeling cocky, thinking that I knew something about engineering that the great McLaren team didn't. After a while Bruce came walking up and started joking around, and he very casually said, "Why do you suppose we're breaking these motors?" And dammit, I stood there and listened to myself tell him exactly what I thought the problem was! I guess it was because they always seemed to be one up on us. As one engineer to another, I just couldn't resist giving an engineering answer to show that we had some smarts too.

I don't know if that really was the problem, but I heard they were looking for some Sun Oil oil at the track, and there was a bit of a scene about that, of course, because their sponsor was Gulf Oil. Sure enough, they had no problems, and they came in one-two ahead of me. They never mentioned it again, so I don't know for sure, but that looked like the tipoff. Even at that, I don't think I ever learned to keep my mouth shut. Fate evened us up at the next race, though, when both of them broke, and *I* won—my only win of the series.

There was one other thing I discovered at Elkhart. I was very close behind McLaren and Denny Hulme at the start of the race, while they were throwing a lot of trash up off the wet track. My car had a scoop, or ram air box, on the injector stacks, and it collected a rock or something. Going into a turn, I backed off and the throttle butterflies were held open a little bit. I had to apply the brakes harder—and I spun off the track. That must have gotten more trash in the stacks because it happened again. Finally I discovered that all I had to do was give the throttle a hard blip to let the rock fall into the engine and get digested, and there was no more problem. That happens all the time nowadays, but I didn't recognize it early enough, so I had to drive like hell just to catch up to them again in that race.

Our McLaren was the first car I had driven that had truly indestructible brakes. I could push them as hard as I needed to and not have to worry about fade or failure. Simultaneously, the engines were so unreliable, and the gearboxes were so hard to downshift, that it was about the time I started learning not to downshift for braking. We were also learning that early downshifting was upsetting the very carefully set up front-to-rear brake balance, and it would tend to lock up the rears early. I still see some Europeans and drivers with weak brakes do it the old way—they rush into a corner and downshift about twenty times. But it's really only necessary to downshift once, to the next gear you'll need.

Although I won at Bridgehampton, and we all thought it was a big hope for us, I realized down deep that it was just a fluke. They had still outrun us easily until their engines broke again. Apparently they hadn't gotten them totally debugged, and that particular course was very hard on engines. We simply won by default.

I can remember realizing after that race that I wasn't even in as good shape *physically* as those guys were. By the end of a Can-Am race I was absolutely, totally physically exhausted. I finally realized that working full-time in the shop and eating poorly wasn't going to keep me in shape. So I started getting up early and taking long runs around the neighborhood. It was killing me in more ways than one. I remember people making jokes about it—my wife, and the neighbors—and I don't like to be laughed at. It hurt quite a bit. The only thing that kept me going, when I wanted to stop so badly, was that I'd paint a mental image of those orange McLaren's in front of me. Just that one thought kept me running for a long time. I was hoping that I could develop my stamina into a personal Unfair Advantage. I finally stopped doing it because of all the ridicule, but I kept in fairly good shape with regular indoor exercises like pushups and situps. Apparently it didn't help much that season, because we didn't win any more races in the Can-Am.

At Edmonton I had more of the trash problem, only that time it was leaves in the radiator duct causing overheating, and I had to stop to get them all cleaned out. Revson finished second ahead of me with his Ford-powered M6-B, which showed me that he was becoming more competitive in our own quiet rivalry than I cared to admit.

That all led up to my poor showing at Laguna Seca in the rain. Before the race Karl was talking with me about pitstops, and he said, "You know, there's something about you that's really good. You never come in unless the car just won't run at all. If the engine loses a cylinder, or the gearbox loses a tooth, or the clutch isn't working—you just keep driving as hard as you can. A lot of those Formula One guys will come in and complain about the gearshift sticking or not enough free play in the clutch—and take themselves out of the hunt." Karl was telling me he hoped I never did that.

I was wearing an open-face helmet and goggles in those days, and for some reason they started fogging up in that rain race. It must have been the heat or poor circulation or something. The crew was holding up dry spares in the pits, but I had it in my mind that I wasn't going to pit for something as inconsequential as that. There were two extra pairs taped to the door, so when it got to the point where I just flat couldn't see anymore, I stopped out at one of the slowest turns and changed goggles. They were all soggy and foggy too, by then, and I had to stop again. The crew had some properly prepared goggles for me, but because of what Karl had said, and because I was too proud, I wasn't going to come in. I drove as hard as I could in the rain and still finished eighth. I eventually learned that you simply have to make your own decisions.

Between Laguna and Riverside I got a lesson as to why some of our competitors don't do so well sometimes, even though they have the same equipment. A lot of people run with Traco engines, but they complain that we get better service and more reliable stuff. That's not true. Traco has a policy that engines are rebuilt on the basis of when they come in—"first in, first out." It's always been that way. One time it happened that Sam Posey got in first, and since we were both rebuilding our cars in the same garage at Reath Automotive in Long Beach, I was there when they got their car back together. We were still putting our engine in when they fired theirs up — and ruined it right there in the garage. They didn't prime it or warm it up or wait for oil pressure, and they raced it while it was cold. When we went out to practice, Posey was way off the pace—and he blamed it on Traco. But in fact, that time I knew his engine had produced more power on the dyno than mine did, before they left the shop. It's what happened later that made the difference. And it wasn't Sam's fault either. He had some mechanics at the time who couldn't handle a sensitive motor. A Traco-Chevy is a pretty reliable lump as long as you give it a reasonable amount of care, but they're sensitive to certain kinds of abuse.

I've seen that happen a lot. It's caused Traco to lose their enthusiasm for building engines for amateurs, no matter what the price is. They do the best they can, and then some guys will ruin the engine before even getting it on the track. Then they go back and complain, or spread the word that they got a bad job. And you can't tell a racing mechanic how to treat an engine. They're all experts already. If you took a poll, probably 70 percent would rather be engine builders, since it looks like such an easy job. It's exciting to run engines on the dyno because they make a lot of noise. But what Traco does is really very, very difficult, and it takes a lot of skill and hard work—and pride.

The Riverside race was typical of the season. I ran behind the McLaren team until one of them broke, giving me a second place. But there was one interesting engineering—or political—point that's worth mentioning. That was the first race where we really ran into high operating temperatures. We had always raced in cool weather or rain, and I'd never seen the oil temperature up to 270 degrees. I told myself that we had to step up to the problem, no matter what it took, because I knew the engine wouldn't live under those conditions. So I went looking for a larger oil cooler, which we mounted sticking up out of the body like a big mistake, and we tacked some quick bodywork around it. Karl almost refused to do it because it ruined the looks of the car. Roger didn't want it done because it was different from what everyone else was doing. I had to take a stand at that point. We were going to do it and that's all there was to it.

It was ugly, all right, but we ran hard in the race while everyone else overheated, and we finished the race. I had decided that there were going to be times when I—as the driver and engineer—knew what I *had* to have, and I wasn't going to take no for an answer.

The last race of the Can-Am that year was at Las Vegas. Because McLaren and Hulme had been splitting their wins, we still had a good chance to win the Championship. Hulme was three points up on me, and McLaren and I were tied, and in Sunday practice I had been turning some faster times. Roger had a bunch of his friends at that race—ball club owners, restaurant owners, and so on—even though probably 80 percent of them didn't know what a race car looked like. But by the start of the race there they were, all standing at attention on the back of the truck because that was Roger Penske's big show.

We pushed the car up to the line and sat there waiting for the one-minute signal to start our engines. Because of the desert heat we were going to wait for the thirty-seconds signal, even though there had been some doubt about the engine starting ever since the Mexico incident at the first of the year. We still had the same point ignition and the same tiny Varley battery, which is marginal at best. It's like a Polish hand grenade; you can never be sure whether it's going to go off or not. Then you've got to follow the proper sequence in starting, with fuel pumps, ignition, starter, and so on. So they gave us the signal . . . and it wouldn't fire! It just wouldn't *start*!

We didn't use booster batteries in those days, so they held the race up long enough for us to change the battery—and it still wouldn't start! The plugs must have been wet by then. We pushed the car off to one side and kept at it while the rest of the grid started up and moved out. It's a terrible, terrible feeling to see *your* race start without you. It's the kind of thing you can have nightmares about. Here we had worked all year with that car. We had run in fourteen races, and now by some chance of fate we had a mathematical opportunity to win the series . . . and the car wouldn't start. It was more than I could take. I was about to cry from the frustration. No one could tell but Karl, and he said, "It'll be all right. Don't take it so hard." But I think that's a problem I've always had in racing—taking it too seriously. As they say, "Show me a good loser, and I'll show you a loser." Maybe winning was too important to me.

After about fifteen minutes we finally got it started. We got ready to go out, but someone decided there wasn't any money in it by then. Sometimes we made the mistake of running—using up the car and taking chances—when there was no possibility of breaking even. Roger had a hard time explaining it to his friends, I suppose, but we went to the victory banquet and I made a funny little speech that got a few laughs. Roger never said a word about it to anyone on the team. Not that we had any idea of who to blame, anyhow. Roger had come around before the race and told us all, "Now this is the *big* race. It's important that you look everything over very carefully and not screw anything up." Someone said later there was white smoke coming out the exhaust pipes and blue smoke coming out Roger's ears. But he's really not that way. He reckoned everybody did his best, and in this case it wasn't good enough. By the end of the race he was already off on his next project, as usual.

Our next racing project was a trip to Japan. There was an invitational race over there that was after the last Can-Am and therefore didn't count toward any championship. It was simply for money. The McLaren team, the big stars, didn't go, but Carroll Shelby took his car for Peter Revson, and that looked like the only competition. I was sick most of the time with the flu or the twenty-four-hour grip, or maybe even from the Las Vegas fiasco, and I spent most of the time in my room while everyone else ran around town to the geisha baths and whatever.

Roger and Shelby spent a lot of time huddled together over their high-minded financial dealings. Shelby may have been a strong competitor of ours, especially in the Trans-Am that year, but he and Roger have always been friends in a professional sense. It was interesting to watch them work. Eventually they got to talking about the race we were going to run, and how they could make it more interesting for the spectators and maybe even make a more assured profit for themselves. They figured there was no reason for Peter and me to beat both our brains out competing and maybe not finish, maybe not get any dollars, when we could play it smart and save the racing until the end. Their idea was for us to run just ahead of the pack for the first two-thirds of the race, then sprint to the finish. I didn't know whether that was quite legal or not, but I soon decided in my own mind that I couldn't do it. I didn't know if I could convert from running slow to running fast without making a disastrous mistake on the track.

I was on the pole and Peter was right next to me, and from the start I pulled into the lead and ran as hard as I could go. Peter stayed right with me. Not only was he even with me in the corners, but he seemed to have more power and could pass me on the straightaway. There we were, fighting it out, dicing around, changing the lead, and the guys in the pits thought we were just fooling around. I started getting worn out, and I was wondering, "Is Peter running hard too, or is he just barely keeping up?" Then, at about the two thirds mark, we started lapping in heavy traffic, and Peter used his straightaway advantage to pull away.

That's the part of racing many drivers fear the most—where you start looking bad as a driver. I started thinking, "That guy has been stroking it all along while I've been running flat out, and now he's putting the pressure on." I had a lot of respect for him at that point. He was looking stronger and I'd had it. I don't know to this day whether he started running harder or whether I got off my pace, because I never could bring myself to ask him and he never mentioned it either. It was very, very embarrassing to me at the time.

Then a fortunate thing happened—to me, anyhow. I started running out of fuel. It was a disaster for the team, but it saved my pride. Apparently we hadn't maintained the fuel system properly and a one-way valve wasn't working, which kept it from picking up the last few gallons. I had to pit for more fuel. They weren't prepared for that, of course, so Bud Poorman of Goodyear picked up a rubber marker cone to use as a funnel and Karl started pouring gas in. Sometimes it seems to take forever for fuel to gluggle into the tank. Roger was estimating how much was needed, and he started yelling, "That's enough! Pull it out!" There must have been a couple of gallons in the funnel, and of course it was poured all over me. I roared out onto the track anyhow, thinking, "I can do anything for five laps." Then it's four laps to go . . . then three laps . . . and I was just flat burning up from all that raw gas in my open pores. Finally I couldn't take it anymore. I couldn't even get around to the pits. I pulled to a stop on the edge of the straightaway, jumped out of the car, and started pulling my clothes off in front of thirty thousand Japanese. There I was, crouched down in the bushes, naked, while Peter went on to win. Finally somebody came around with some woolen towels and rescued me, but it was a very embarrassing end to my year with the M6-B.

We could see that wasn't the way to go racing—to run against the factory team with their year-old car. Not only was the car obsolete, but we had trouble getting pieces for it since it wasn't anywhere near production. Once we even had to weld up a crack in a magnesium hub carrier, which isn't the smartest thing to do but we had no choice. We weren't getting any great help from Chevrolet either, because they were still working closely with Chaparral and they didn't really consider us a serious competitor. We certainly weren't the leading team to beat. There was that one win, when everyone else fell out, and we came very close in the final points standings, but that's not much of a claim to fame.

I really liked the car a lot. It was light, it had a short wheelbase, and it was easy to drive even though I didn't really know why. But it was frustrating to run behind the McLaren team. I could be close in practice, but they would build up while I stayed the same. Our team was actually at its peak most of the time.

We never had a very close relationship with McLaren. They were way above us all the time. Roger approached McLaren's manager, Teddy Mayer, at Edmonton with a deal to buy one of their "next year's" cars instead of a new "old design." Bruce said no, which you can't blame him for. So Roger let them think it over, and when they still said no at Las Vegas, he made a deal with Eric Broadley. We sold our M6-B to a friend of Roger's in Minneapolis, and we began our "all-encompassing" program to run only Lolas in 1969.

Chapter 15

1969–70

FOUR LOLAS—T70, T152, T163, T150

The Exclusive Lola Deal (Four Cars, Few Wins)

LOLA T70

In 1969 Roger Penske decided that we were no longer going to race someone else's used or year-old design car as we had with the McLaren M6-B. He was trying to tie up Eric Broadley's Lola factory as McLaren had done with his own race car operation. The trouble was that Roger didn't have a very strong position to deal from and Broadley wasn't that tieable. We did get a few privileges, though, such as the use of a four-wheel-drive Indy Lola that never did very well, and a special lightweight Can-Am Lola that was unsuccessful. And we got one of two new Lola T70-Mk III coupes for the World Manufacturers Championship.

Daytona and Sebring didn't include Trans-Am races in 1969, so along about December we went through the same story we did in 1967 with the Camaro—Roger started wondering what we ought to run at Daytona. We were sitting around the shop and Roger said, "Say, I hear Lola has a coupe." Actually they had been around for some time, but they were relatively unsuccessful and unreliable. James Garner, the movie star, was involved in a team that was running a couple of them that year. But in our dealings with Broadley we heard he had a new version, which was supposed to be basically the T162 Can-Am car with the old coupe body on it. So Roger called England and said, "Can you make me one in blue . . . and send it right away." Then we called Traco and asked them to build us a couple of 305-inch Chevrolet engines like we used in the Camaro, but with Lucas fuel injection.

On January 1, New Year's Day, the car was flown in, and Roy Gane and I picked it up at the airport. Roy and I had about three weeks to get an engine

courtesy of Petersen Publishing Company

LOLA T70

in it and get it put together right. It was one of those "We're gonna drag it outta the woods" type of things. We had to make an exhaust system, plumb it up, make a lot of odds and ends, and just generally try to make it look nice. It was a monumental job.

In going to Daytona we had our annual problem of choosing the right spring rates for the banking. I had at least learned by then that the first consideration was to be sprung just hard enough to keep the chassis from bottoming on the suspension or the ground. Without giving it a lot of thought, I guessed at initially setting the car up with about 400-pounds-per-inch springs in the front and 600-pound springs in the rear. This was very stiff for such a light car in those days, but we had a test session in which to experiment with spring rates, shock absorbers, and ride height.

When we went to the Daytona test we took a lot of different springs left over from the McLaren 427 experience. At first the car seemed to have a lot of clearance everywhere on the track. But then, with no other changes, it started rubbing the ground. We measured the ride height, and sure enough it was falling down. We put a stiffer set of springs in, and they did the same thing. We would jack the car up on its springs—it would sink. We jacked it up again—it sank again. Right away it was obvious that the stresses in compression on the banking were so great that all our springs were yielding. When I saw that, I made some simple calculations that showed our basic spring design wasn't strong enough for those loads. I called my engineering pals at Chevrolet and asked if they could design something better. I gave them weights, deflections, space requirements, and approximate rates, and they produced a spring design and selection chart for our new Lola. I had some springs built in Philadelphia, and after our test we installed what I thought was right.

We eventually ended up with some very good springs, which we kept for years and used on many different cars. They were extremely stiff, to keep the bellhousing from bottoming, and purely by accident they were also the right selection to balance the car on our new skidpad. We weren't able to run the Lola on the skidpad before we went to test the first time, since it was January and everything was covered with a foot of ice and snow. But we did run it before the race, and it turned out to be a very good-handling car.

Another thing that made it feel good was our experience with aerodynamic downforce and spoilers on the Camaro and the McLaren M6-B. We had learned the value of balancing downforce between the front and rear axle to prevent a change in oversteer/understeer as the car went faster. However, because Daytona is a relatively straightforward problem of mostly left turns, we decided to try and change the downforce balance from side to side. We had seen the new long-tailed Porsche 908's, with their separate left and right suspension-actuated flipper spoilers. We knew we couldn't come up with something that complex in a hurry, but we did use a fixed, split, asymmetrical spoiler on the rear.

The most remarkable thing about that car was that we were able to develop it so well in such a short time. When we started it was so unstable that it was almost undriveable, but by fooling around with springs and spoilers we finally did a very good job of sorting it out. Roger was there at our test session, and he kept saying, "Why aren't you faster? Why aren't you faster?" I told him to let me get it handling right first, then we could worry about laptimes. Once we made it stable I started going fast—and the car was about *twenty* seconds a lap quicker. It was quite a remarkable performance, and Roger seemed truly amazed.

Ron Bucknum was going to co-drive the long-distance races with me. At the last minute, however, he broke his thumb on a motorcycle, and we got Charlie Parsons to take his place. I didn't know Charlie very well, but he had been driving Lola Can-Am cars for the distributor, Carl Haas, so it was a good tie-in. In a long-distance race, ultimate driver ability doesn't make that much difference anyhow. A Porsche 908 got the pole, with Vic Elford driving, because they were smart enough to qualify early in the morning when it was cool and there was less traffic. Because my mechanic, Roy Gane, was so meticulous—and so slow—I was lucky even to get out in the afternoon qualifying session, where I picked up the second fastest time. Jo Bonnier was a ways back in the other new Lola T70-Mk III.

At the start I was thinking, "Boy, I'm gonna do a job on those Porsche guys," and I jumped them about four car lengths before we crossed the start line. I didn't figure anyone was going to "yellow-flag" a twenty-four-hour race. But the Porsche blokes went crazy. Three of them drafted past me like a big train on the next straightaway. We all had quite a big dice going on for a while. They had the aerodynamic shape to give them the edge on the straightaway, but I had a bigger motor and better brakes. Bonnier even got his Lola into the lead for a while by banging his way through. But he broke the car up doing it, and went out with shredded fenders and flat tires.

After about twenty-five laps my car started starving for fuel. We should have gotten the fuel system down perfect by then, after our experience with the McLaren in the last race in Japan. But we kept struggling along. Then the exhaust manifolds started to break up. One of the biggest problems we had in building the car was fabricating our own headers, and now they were coming apart. It took almost an hour and a half in the pits to get them cooled, off, welded, and back on again. We lost a lot of laps from that, but what kept us going was the knowledge that the Porsches were having a similar problem. What's more, their cars were so identical, we knew that if *one* car had a problem eventually *all* their cars would have the same trouble. Then our headers broke again, but we were more experienced by then and it only cost us about fifteen minutes to fix. After the race we learned from Chevrolet that our basic construction was all wrong. We learned to make headers from stainless steel and weld them with a heli-arc, and we never had that particular problem again. As it turned out, all the Porsches were held up with the same trouble, followed by a string of failures in all their jackshafts—and we finally outlasted them for first. Leslie and Motschenbacher finished a distant second in their older James Garner Lola.

We were looking good in the Manufacturers Championship at that point, so we rushed the car back to Philadelphia to get ready for Sebring. We had to make new headers, of course, which we opened up from 1 3/4 to 1 7/8 inches for a little more power. And by then we had finally learned how to select some reasonably proper spring rates between Daytona and Sebring. We also replaced the fuel injection with carburetors, over Traco's objections that it would cost about thirty horsepower. We were using Lucas fuel injection, and it just didn't have the throttle response I knew I was going to need at Sebring. We know better now. There is a cam in the fuel metering device that can be reground and tailored to fit almost any conditions. But it takes a lot of time and experimentation, and we didn't have enough experience with it then.

We spent a lot of time at the pre-race tests developing an unconventional set of transmission gear ratios. We tried to choose our ratios so that we could use all five of the Hewland's ratios in the race, instead of reserving the lowest one for starting only. By knowing the power curve on our engine, we were able to graph rear-axle torque in each of all the available gear ratios, and cleverly select the ones that gave us the greatest net acceleration. As it turned out—and as everyone knows by now—we learned to step ratios so that the faster we went, the less the ratio drop should be between gears. By the time you get to fourth and fifth gear, the ratios are very close. Previously we had selected gears primarily to give good acceleration out of particular corners. This was the first time we used a mathematical approach, and it seemed to give us the Unfair Advantage we needed over the Porsches. To combat the strain from all that extra shifting, we went to a bigger Borg and Beck clutch from the seven-liter engine, and we adapted the softer Salisbury clutch-pack locking differential. The most important development work in a long-distance race is to make sure everything is going to last. We put a lot of thought into that.

But you can't beef up everything that looks weak or you'll have a car that's about 1000 pounds fat. In going over the car before Daytona, one of the things we had doubts about was the point where the upper rear control arm mounted to the chassis. Because the tub was so low, there was a little tower there, and we thought it looked weak. The guys welded a cap over it, but there wasn't much else we could do in a hurry.

In the race at Sebring we were a lot faster than the Porsches. A new Ferrari 312P was there for Andretti and Amon, and they outqualified us, but we were leading the race. Then we got the word that Bonnier's Lola was out because that rear control arm tower had broken off. We thought we might avoid a similar failure because of our "Band-Aid patch," so we just hoped a lot and kept up the pace. We were way ahead at the time—on fuel stops, brake changes, and even speed. When Bucknum took over the car—his thumb was better by then—I went off and slept.

Hours later, Roger came and woke me up. Bucknum was complaining that there was something wrong, and he was falling back. Roger reckoned I should go try to figure it out. I got in the car, and Christ! . . . before I'd gone half a lap I could tell that the rear suspension was broken. One of our mounting towers had broken off just like Bonnier's. We somehow thought that because they had taken the stiff springing and the banks at Daytona, they ought to be heavy enough, but apparently the pounding had taken its toll. The brackets were buried so deep in components that we could hardly see them, much less get a welder in there, so we had to quit.

We had won one and failed one at that point, but we were looking so strong that we had bigger plans in mind. Because our car seemed so much quicker than anything else, Chevrolet had started to get interested in us going to Le Mans. They weren't going to fund us, but they could supply lots of parts and people and development time, and Sunoco was interested also. We had gone so far as to make an entry for our car along with Broadley, who had one for Paul Hawkins. The commitment from Chevrolet was to let us use Black Lake and the instrumentation again on this car as we had with the Camaro. We could probably reduce drag a great deal, and we could use their computer-controlled dynamometers to test our entire driveline for durability.

The timing was critical if we were to make it to France for the April tests. It was very important that we get the Lola patched up right after Sebring, and to Detroit a week later. Peter Reinhart and Murph Mayberry were driving the tow truck, however, and they wanted to stop off at the Paleface Bar in Daytona on the way back. Murph had always been sort of a party guy, and he had made some good friends there. I was so disappointed about not finishing the race that I decided one day probably wouldn't hurt. So they started out, and the rest of us flew back to Philadelphia.

The next morning Peter called me from Daytona and said the truck had been stolen. Everything was gone—the truck, the Lola, the spare engine, parts, tools—everything. Murph had parked it in front of a motel near the Paleface, and by morning it had disappeared. I really panicked. I figured we had to find that stuff in a hurry or we were out of business. I called everyone I knew in Daytona. I even arranged for a plane to go up and start making circles around the area, because the rig was too big to hide very easily.

About that time—less than twenty-four hours after it was stolen—the police found the truck in a marsh with what was left of the car tossed on the back of it. Anything that was of any possible value had been torched out of the Lola, and the truck had been stripped of anything not needed to drive it into the marsh. They had even taken the wheels, gearbox, headers, and other stuff that could only be used on a Lola race car, and what was left was all torn up. It was a mess. It took three days just to get the truck fixed up enough to drive it to Philadelphia. That was the end of our effort in the Manufacturers Championship. I had to call Chevrolet and tell them there was no possible way we could continue at that point, considering the upcoming Trans-Am, Indianapolis, and Can-Am series.

I was really furious. I spent a lot of time and money after that trying to track down the missing stuff. Then, about a month later, I got a call from a guy in Maryland who said he had some information if I was willing to pay for it. So I scrounged up the bucks and bought his tip. It seems that this guy had met some girl in Florida, and she got drunk and bragged that her boyfriend or husband had done this unbelievable thing. He had stolen a race car from the great invincible Penske team. My tipster hadn't believed her, so she showed him this huge barn full of stolen stuff. As it turned out, a group of guys had a nice little car-stealing ring. They would steal a car up north, drive it to Florida, wreck it, and sell it to a junkyard. Then they would turn around and steal one to go north again. In their spare time they stole boats, trailers, race cars, trucks, and anything else you could imagine.

Donohue's 1957 Corvette (left) and Dave Lawton's XK-120 Jaguar. This was taken at Donohue's first competitive driving event, the Belknap Hillclimb. Lawton, Donohue's life-long friend, dared him to compete as his guest. In return, Donohue achieved the fastest time of the day. *Photo by Dave Lawton*

> "We arrived in Daytona in early afternoon after driving all night. Mark wanted to see the track right away. There were hardly any cars around and it was the oval which was open. We hurriedly unloaded and Mark went out for a few laps. After a while, he pulled in and with a big grin on his face said, 'You've got to try it. It's fantastic.'"
>
> ***-Dave Lawton***

Donohue in his first race car—a 1960 Elva Courier—at the 1961 SCCA National Championship run-offs in Daytona. Donohue would race this car for two SCCA seasons, entering between 25 and 30 races and winning the SCCA E-Production Championship in 1961. *Photo by Dave Lawton*

Donohue removing the windshield of his Elva Courier at Lime Rock, CT, in 1960 with the help of Dave Lawton in the background. This was Mark's first SCCA race after getting his competition license. He would finish fourth (see page 9). *Donohue Collection*

Mark would become good friends with fellow competitor Jay Signore, seen here in a matching Elva. Little did anyone know they would work closely together in Penske Racing for many years. *Donohue Collection*

Donohue's 1960 Elva Courier in the garage area at Daytona before the 1961 SCCA National Championship run-offs. In right foreground is the infamous "Scaglietti" tow vehicle, complete with "fogger" as described on page 10. *Photo by Dave Lawton*

"The 'Scaglietti' had a wooden platform permanently attached to the roof used for race watching. Access was over the front fenders and hood. Little effort was made to preserve the bodywork from the effects of the scrambling race watchers. Thus, the comparison to the beautiful Scaglietti-bodied Ferrari of the time. This vehicle was also fitted with the infamous 'smoker.' A device which produced a smoke screen any World War II Navy destroyer would have been proud of." ***-Dave Lawton***

Donohue in the Elva Formula Junior in 1962. He had one of his earliest "run-ins" with Roger Penske in this car when "...good ol' Roger pulled up behind me and gave me a congratulatory tap on the gearbox. Because it was a Volkswagen gearbox with external shift linkage, it knocked me back into gear and I went lurching into the paddock." (see page 16). *Donohue Collection*

Donohue approaching the start/finish line at Thompson driving his own Daimler SP 250 in 1963. This was the last car he owned and raced as an unsponsored amateur driver. *Photo by Ed Picard*

Donohue looking over the mid-engined midget (Cooper-Offy). Although Bermuda shorts were the thing to wear at sports car races in 1963, Mark took a ribbing for this outfit when he stopped by the constructor's shop to check the car out before a practice session at Lime Rock (see page 24). *Donohue Collection*

Walt Hansgen (left) converses with a young Mark Donohue. An inscription written by Donohue on the back of a similar photo of Hansgen reads: "Walt Hansgen, who did more to get me started than anyone before." *Ludvigsen Library*

Donohue in the Shelby GT 350 Mustang in 1966. Note it was painted blue after a transporter accident before the run-offs in 1965. The team wanted to differentiate themselves from the factory team at the run-offs, so they painted the car blue with white stripes instead of the traditional white with blue stripes. *Photo by Ed Picard*

The Ferrari 275 that Donohue would co-drive with Walt Hansgen at Sebring in 1964. This is the photo Walt gave to Donohue to show he was serious about wanting him to co-drive the race (see page 33). *Donohue Collection*

Donohue drives the Ford Mark II for the Ford factory team at his first 24 Hours of Daytona in 1966. He co-drove the race with Walt Hansgen and placed third over-all. *Donohue Collection*

Donohue (driving the Lola T70,) leads Phil Hill (driving the Chaparral 2E) in the "chute" just before Moss corner at Mosport in 1966. Donohue would finish first and Phil Hill second. This was the first year of the Can-Am series. *Photo by Don Markle*

"I have always felt that his achievements were somewhat understated in the book. He was modest by nature. He always recognized that luck and being in the right place at the right time helped him in his career. It is also difficult to write about your own successes without sounding like a braggart. Somehow, it would be great to see him get all the recognition he deserves without the understatement. Some of his achievements and records are just amazing." ***-Dave Lawton***

This sequence shows the Lola T70 accident in 1966 at Watkins Glen as described on page 74. Donohue wrote, "At first it wasn't so bad, but by the time the car had stopped, flames were all around me—and I couldn't get out! Finally I remembered the seat belt! I had to put my hands back down in the flames to unlatch it, and that was really pretty excruciating because I had no gloves in those days." *Donohue Collection*

At Riverside in 1967: Donohue in the #6 Lola T70 rounds turn 8 with his Penske teammate George Follmer following close behind in the #16 Lola T70. The rear spoiler that was used in 1966 has been replaced with a wing, and the fenders are wider to accommodate larger tires. *Photo by Bob Tronolone*

The '67 Camaro at Lime Rock. This is the first year of the Penske Team's incredible performance in the Trans-Am series from 1967 through 1971. In those five years that Donohue and the Penske team competed in Trans-Am, they won three championships ('68, '69, & '71), won 29 races out of 57 starts, and finished outside the top five twice (not including the 11 DNFs). *Photo by Ray Jeanotte*

Donohue in the McLaren M6-B at Riverside in 1968. *Photo by Barry Tenin*

Roger Penske and Mark Donohue talk before the 1968 24 Hours of Daytona, which was the start of the Trans-Am Series that year. Donohue started racing full-time for Penske in 1967, and by 1968 the teamwork between the two was really coming together. *Photo by Barry Tenin*

> "That was probably one of his biggest hang-ups, that he would be too hard on himself. And I guess that was one of my jobs, to try to kick him in the pants and say, 'Hey, let's go racin' here. There's a lot more to this than a bad day or a good day.'"
>
> ***-Roger Penske***

The McLaren M6-B with its elaborate pin stripping at Riverside in 1968. Note the oversized radiator extending from the bodywork on Donohue's left as described on page 137. *Photo by Barry Tenin*

Data acquisition was truly in its infancy in 1968. Here is Mark with the instrumentation roped into the passenger seat of the Camaro at the General Motors proving grounds (see page 103).
Donohue Collection

A victory lap for anyone who can cram into the '68 Camaro at Lime Rock. *Photo by Barry Tenin*

Donohue on the way to victory with Charlie Parsons in the Lola T70 coupe at the 24 Hours of Daytona in 1969. This pit stop is well into the race, as evidenced by all the tape holding the front fender together.

Photo by Pete Biro

> "But Mark was a complete race driver, and he would race. That's what people forget about Mark — there was a lot of tiger in Mark. He wanted to win a race, and if he had to he'd abuse the car to do it. You know the old story about engineers don't make good race drivers, 'cause they don't want to hurt the machinery? Bullshit!"
>
> ***-Carroll Smith***

Donohue and the Lola T152 receive lots of attention in the pits of the 1969 Indy 500. Donohue would place 7th in his first Indy start to become USAC Indianapolis 500 Rookie of the Year. In left foreground is mechanic Bill "Scotty" Scott; Penske in pink shirt; Penske chief mechanic Karl Kainhofer, second from right; and mechanic Jim Schofield in the right foreground. *Photo by Barry Tenin*

The now comically controversial vinyl topped '69 Camaro testing in the rain at Michigan. Note the sensor on the front wheel (see page 114). *Photo by Harry Kinnison*

> "I think of when we were dipping the bodies and putting vinyl roofs on. The big fuel tanks. We had a slider valve for fueling in the Trans-Am. We worked on getting the right wheels on the Trans-Am cars, and being able to execute faster pit-stops. All those were Mark's ideas. He really was an innovator in all those things that could save two seconds." ***-Roger Penske***

The infamous 20+ foot tall fueling tower that would cause the SCCA to legislate that fueling rigs could not exceed 12 feet in height (see page 110). *Photo by Pete Luongo*

Once the 20+ foot fuel tower was illegal, Donohue and Don Cox came up with new ways to fuel quickly. By changing the valves and other pieces, they could put in twenty-two gallons of fuel in 3 1/2 seconds. "Of course we also spilled gasoline everywhere. It was all over the trunk and the ground...." (page 117). *Photo by Pete Luongo*

> "But he also was an experimenter. Constantly. Usually there was something new on board or something that he was thinking about. I think he was among the first to use the lockers, and he was certainly among the first to use a lot of caster. He understood the friction circle and all of that before anybody else was putting it into play."
>
> ***-Sam Posey***

Putting dry ice around the fueling tank. This was yet another pit-stop strategy to try and fit more fuel into the tank. It became quite an issue once when the pace car came out right after the car was refueled. The team began to panic when they thought the fuel might expand faster than it was being burned off. The result would have been a disastrous blown fuel cell.

Photo by Barry Tenin

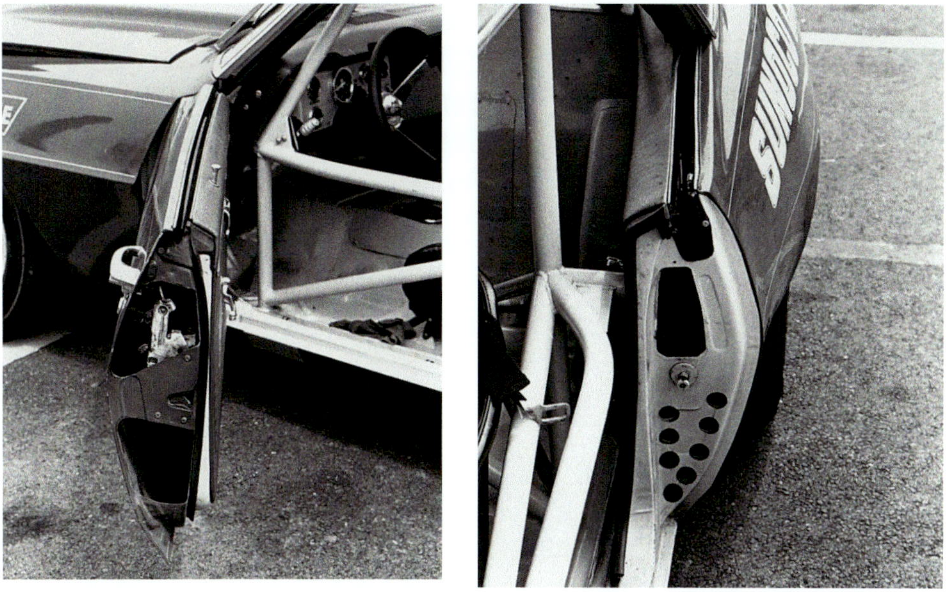

These photos clearly show the holes in the door pillar and door panels of the '69 Camaro which were another example of Donohue and the Penske team pushing the SCCA's rules to the limit in an effort to make the car a few seconds faster. *Photo by Pete Luongo*

Donohue races past the grandstand in the Lola-Ford at the 1970 Indy 500. He placed 2nd after Al Unser in this race, after qualifying a disappointing fifth on the grid. *Photo by Barry Tenin*

The 1970 Javelin at speed at Laguna Seca. Donohue came in second behind Parnelli Jones in this Trans-Am series race. *Photo by Cam Warren*

"He did have a lot of mechanical sympathy, that's why he was so good at setting cars up. But I remember one instance, a Trans-Am race when he was driving the Javelin, God help him. We were at St. Jovite, and nobody to my knowledge had ever gone down the hill past the pits there flat in a Trans-Am car. Mark was doing it, and the rest of us were sitting there with our mouths open, when Roger arrived. And the first thing he saw was Mark going down the hill flat, the car bounding from pillar to post but totally under control. His jaw dropped as far as ours."

-Carroll Smith

Donohue's AMC Javelin being prepped for a Trans-Am series race in 1971. Donohue (on left) is observing from the truck in the background. *Photo by Pete Biro*

Donohue, driving a Lola T190, close on the tail of Graham Hill at the 1971 Questor Grand Prix, Ontario Motor Speedway. This was a one-off race that had Formula One cars racing against Formula 5000 cars, thus pitting the Europeans against the Americans. The Europeans would rule the day, with Mark dropping out of both heats due to a clogged fuel-tank vent (see page 219). *Photo by Barry Tenin*

Donohue, driving the AMC Javelin, leads the 1971 Trans-Am series race at Lime Rock, CT, in the rain. Following him in second place is George Follmer in a Ford Mustang. Donohue was the 1971 Trans-Am Champion. *Photo by Barry Tenin*

Donohue driving the McLaren M19 before his first Formula One race, the 1971 Canadian Grand Prix at Mosport. Despite—or perhaps because of— heavy rain throughout the race, he would place third behind Jackie Stewart and Ronnie Petersen. *Photo by Barry Tenin*

Donohue at the wheel of the Ferrari 512M in the first few hours of the 24 Hours of Daytona in 1971. He co-drove the race with David Hobbs.
Photo by Pete Lyons

"When I signed on to drive the Ferrari 512M, we did a test at Sebring and I remember driving this car which Mark had set up, and it was damned near impossible to drive. He'd become enamored of this locked differential, ie. no differential. [The Ferrari] understeered like a pig, of course, because when you have no differential the back wheels are just pushing you forward all the time, like on a go-kart. On real power you can throw it sideways, break it loose and then even with it going slightly sideways you still have good traction because both wheels are driving. It made it a bit difficult to drive, but it's a technique which he was pretty good at." ***-David Hobbs***

A very tattered Ferrari 512M in the final laps of the 1971 24 Hours of Daytona. After Donohue got tangled up in a nasty multi-car crash during the night, the Penske team borrowed some suspension parts from a Ferrari that had already dropped out of the race and finished third overall (see page 226).
Photo by Barry Tenin

Donohue leads two Porsche 917s into the esses at Watkins Glen in 1971. Notice that the rear wing of his Ferrari 512M is much larger than the one damaged at Daytona earlier in the year.
Photo by Barry Tenin

Penske mechanics Karl Kainhofer and Bill Scott confer in pit lane before Donohue's 1971 Pocono 500 win in the McLaren M16. Donohue worked closely with both of these mechanics during his tenure with Penske, in his tireless quest to perfect the engineering of every car he raced. *Photo by Barry Tenin*

Donohue's Lola T192 (far right) sliding off turn one at Mosport just ahead of David Hobbs's Surtees. Donohue actually slid into the guardrail at this turn, slipping into second behind Hobbs (see page 214). He was able to regain control of the car, passed Hobbs at the hairpin, and remained in first place to the finish. *Photo by Dale Von Trebra*

The AMC Matador at speed. Donohue would only compete in six NASCAR events between 1972 and 1973. While they struggled on the ovals, winning the 500 mile, 5+ hour Riverside road race by more than one lap proved not only Donohue's endurance, but that the team was one to watch. *Photo by Pete Luongo*

Donohue in the McLaren M16B on his way to victory in the 1972 Indianapolis 500. In this race he set records for the fastest average speed of 162.2 mph—a record that stood for more than a decade—and the fastest race lap of 187.539 mph. *Photo by Barry Tenin*

Donohue leads teammate George Follmer in their matching Porsche 917-10s at the Donnybrook Can-Am race in 1972. This was Donohue's first race following three months in a cast after breaking his leg during a practice session in the Porsche 917-10. He spun the car in this race after his left rear tire blew out, narrowly missing Follmer's car, but walked away unhurt (see page 301). *Photo by Pete Lyons*

Donohue, still recovering from his devastating crash at Atlanta, bends down to give some tips to George Follmer, who drove the Porsche 917-10 to an easy victory at Elkart Lake in 1972. Donohue describes the experience of watching Follmer drive his beloved Porsche 917-10: "But what made me even sicker was seeing George drive that beautiful car, which I had spent so many months building exactly the way I wanted. It must be like seeing another man in bed with your wife." (see page 297). *Photo by Barry Tenin*

"I spent quite a lot of time with Mark and his family and hanging around the shop with him. He used to call me 'Mate,' or 'Matey.' I suppose the first thing that hit me was that, for a guy that was a multiple Trans-Am champion by that time, he was, I suppose humble would be the word. Apart from his astonishing thought that he would be superior to an Englishman behind the wheel. But apart from that, very humble. He would do everything in the shop. He'd spend all his time working on the car and then at the end of the day sweeping up the trash and taking it out to the dumpster."

-David Hobbs

The team of Mark Donohue/George Follmer in the #6 Porsche 911 Carrera going head-to-head with Peter Gregg/Hurley Haywood in the #59 Porsche at a six-hour manufacturers race in 1973. Both cars were Porsche prototypes, and the #6 car was sold right after the race for $20,000 in cash (see page 319). *Photo by by Bob Brandle, courtesy of Mezzacca Motorsports Photography*

The first Porsche 917-10 during its development. From left to right: Donohue, Roger Penske, Helmut Flegl (Porsche factory engineer), Don Cox, and Peter Falk (also of Porsche). *Donohue Collection*

> "In my opinion, Mark gave too much credit for his successes to his engineering ability, and not enough to his driving ability. I don't think he ever realized just how good a driver he was."
>
> ***-Carroll Smith***

Donohue doing some aerodymanic testing in the quest for front down-force in the Porsche 917-10 during its development. *Donohue Collection*

Donohue in the dominant Porsche 917-30 talking with mechanic John "Woody" Woodard. Donohue would be the Can-Am Champion in 1973 with six series wins. The Porsche 917-30 represented one of his proudest engineering accomplishments. *Photo by Bill Oursler*

Donohue returns to the Indy 500 in 1973 driving an Eagle with an Offenhauser engine. After qualifying on the front row, he dropped out of the race with a blown engine. Penske teammate Gary Bettenhausen finished fifth in a Penske McLaren. *Photo By Dale Von Trebra*

The Porsche 911 Carrera at the 24 Hours of Daytona in 1973. *Photo by Barry Tenin*

> "Mark was a thinking driver. He knew when to go and when not to go. He wasn't going to win it on guts, he was going to win it on using his head." ***-Roger Penske***

Donohue drives a Lola T330 in a Formula 5000 race at Road America, Elkart Lake, WI in 1973. *Photo by Barry Tenin*

The 1200+ horsepower 917-30 Porsche at Mosport in 1973. This was its first race and Donohue would not win due to an accident. Aside from Mosport, whenever the 917-30 finished, it won. *Photo by Don Markle*

Donohue checks the wing angle on Hurley Haywood's 917-10 while Eckart Schneider, one of Haywood's mechanics (on left) Haywood (second from left), and John "Woody" Woodard (behind Donohue) look on. *Photo by Hal Crocker*

Donohue and the Porsche 917-30 leading the field at Laguna Seca in October 1973. A hopeful George Follmer in the 917-10 tucks in close behind, but Donohue would go on to win this race as he did most of the others with the 917-30. *Photo by Cam Warren*

The skid pad at Sun Oil's Marcus Hook facility. Donohue works on both the 917-30 (left) and the Lola T330 (right) at the same time. Both cars are not even fully painted yet and the aerodynamic louver modification to the front fenders of the 917-30 is clearly visible in primer. This is where the suspension of many cars was sorted out. *Photos by Tom McKeon*

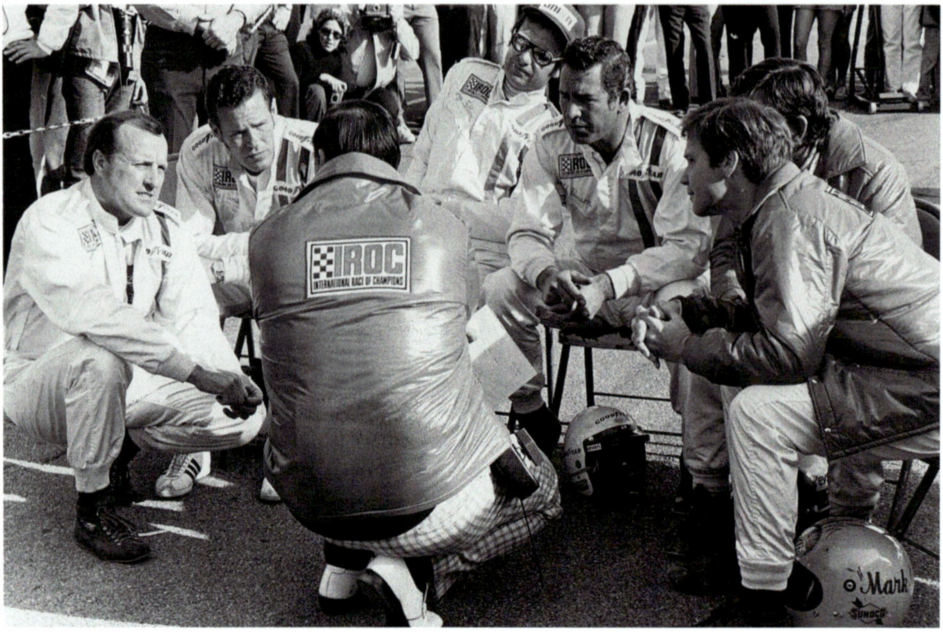

Les Richter addresses the drivers on behalf of the Daytona Motor Speedway prior to the final IROC race in February, 1974. Donohue would become the first ever IROC Champion at this race. From left to right: A.J. Foyt, Bobby Unser, Les Richter (back to camera), George Follmer, David Pearson, Peter Revson (hidden), Mark Donohue. *Photo courtesy International Speedway Corporation*

> "I think he contributed an incredible amount [to racing]. In a strange way he not only defined road racing in America during its period of growth, its most significant period. But he added to it immensely by focusing that world of road racing on one person as an exemplar. He was the best. And I think that meant an awful lot. It raised the bar for the rest of us. It defined the sport in excellent terms, and made everyone else take a second look."
>
> ***-Sam Posey***

The IROC Porsches at Riverside. Never knowing if he was successful due to his mechanical "unfair advantages" or his driving ability, Donohue saw the International Race of Champions as a true contest among his most formidable competitors. He was more than simply successful, winning three out of the four rounds, having dropped out of one race due to a stuck throttle (see page 321). *Photo by Hal Crocker*

Donohue and Penske, with Donohue in the unfamiliar role of team manager after having retired from driving in 1974. He eventually came out of retirement to take on the new Penske team project of Formula One, an opportunity he saw as the ultimate engineering challenge. *Photo by Hal Crocker*

"The humidity was right off the peg. And by the time he actually got on the track it was raining. And the idea of going around Talladega at 235 or whatever it was in the rain while he stuck to the upper lane, of course, which was the sensible thing, I mean he just managed to eke out the record. And it was something that gave no one any pleasure at all. I mean there was no sense of celebration. They just loaded up and left. It was just like, 'Thank God that's over.' And all it came down to was, did Mark sort of have the nerve to hold this thing on the mat. It had to be one hellish ride."

-Sam Posey

In 1975 Donohue sets the world closed course speed record of 221.12 mph in the Porsche 917-30 at Talladega Speedway. *Bob Tronolone Archive*

Heinz Hofer, team manager of the Penske Formula One team, talks to Donohue at the 1974 Canadian Grand Prix at Mosport. *Penske Archives*

Donohue in the first Penske chassis, PC1, at Watkins Glen in 1974. Donohue was entered into two F1 races in 1974, the Canadian Grand Prix and the US Grand Prix, in preparation for a full assault in 1975. *Photo by Bob Brandle, courtesy of Mezzacca Motorsports Photography*

Everything was stored in a huge barn, where people came around and bought from them. It was a regular stolen-car market.

I described all this to the police, and they located the place and staked it out. Finally they gave me a call and said they thought they had the guys, if I would come down and identify my things. That was at 5 P.M., so I got a plane, flew down that night, and went to the place and looked around for anything that was left. I was raging around there, still furious about what they had done to our racing program. I tore the place apart looking for our engines and tools. The manifold and carburetors were hidden in the rafters over the porch. One Traco-Chevrolet had been painted red and was being installed in a stolen Cobra. Ordinarily we might have had trouble identifying some of the more common stuff, but the proof was that they had forgotten to throw one of our loading ramps on the truck, and there it was.

Those guys went to jail, and we finally got a lot of our equipment back. Most of the tools had been sold, and the engines were junk by then, but we recovered some things. We got someone to rebuild the Lola with mufflers and air conditioning, and we installed a stock 350 Chevy. We sold it to a guy in California who drove it around as a street machine for a while. It turned out to be a bit of a problem, though, because he kept wanting our mechanics to go to California to tune it up for him. The last I heard, the car thieves were still in jail. They had to be pretty dumb, anyhow, to steal such a well-known car as the Roger Penske-owned Daytona twenty-four hour winner.

LOLA T152

There wasn't much time left to get ready for Indianapolis. Part of our attempted exclusive deal with Lola was to get one of two T152 four-wheel-drive USAC cars built to take a turbo-Offy. At the same time Roger was dealing with Larry Truesdale over expanding our Goodyear tire sponsorship, and Truesdale brought in Bobby Unser. Bobby had won the last Indy 500, and he was convinced that four-wheel-drive was the right thing to have for 1969. Truesdale decided it would help the Goodyear cause if Bobby got the other Lola T152. Bobby's chief mechanic was Jud Phillips, a typically good USAC-type mechanic, although maybe not as neat as we tended to be. So the five of us went to England to get set up with our new cars. I soon became aware that a large share of those trips was just a big party. Roger rented a limousine and had us all driven around—which I thought was a little out of order, but they all accepted it rather easily. I was kind of out of place in that society, so while they fooled around here and there, I kept a low profile.

Ever since I can remember, delivery dates have been a problem with Broadley, and this car was no exception, I was to get the first car, but I sat around and waited a long time for it, while Bobby told me how important it was to be ready early. He said that to be competitive you have to be running well the first day the track opens, and he was never more right.

As soon as I got my car and we put the engine in it, we rented the Hanford oval track for a few days. Rumor had it that if your car was good there, it would be good anywhere. But I didn't run half a lap before the front driveshaft slipped apart and I lost front-wheel drive. Because there was an open front/rear differential, I lost *all* drive, and the car had to be towed in. The problem was that the shaft was too short, and when everything shifted a little bit here and there, the splined end pulled out. We spent the first day building new pieces to hold it all together.

When we got back to the test, Bobby Unser was there. Roger was in communication with him, and had invited him over to watch me—and possibly even drive the car a little. I felt somewhat strange, with this Indy winner standing around watching me experiment with a totally unfamiliar car on a new track. I didn't know Bobby very well yet. But he kept an eye on me in the corners, and he could tell I had something to learn about USAC racing. Slowly but surely, in a very diplomatic and polite way, he showed me a lot of the tricks of the trade. Woody Woodard and Karl Kainhofer were there to help me change the car around, and Bobby told us a lot about camber angles, cross-jacking, toe-in, springs, and so on. We had a lot of variables to work with in the area of handling. Over a period of two days we tried just about every combination of springs in existence to fit that car. We could also vary the torque split between the front and rear wheels by changing gears in the front/rear planetary differential. But no matter what we tried, the car seemed to have a chronic case of oversteer going into a turn and understeer coming out. None of us understood four-wheel drive enough at that time to have the slightest idea what changes should cause what reactions. It was like starting over from scratch in the field of race car development.

My laptimes at Hanford were not at all competitive, so I finally let Bobby drive the car. When he turned almost the same laptimes, I had mixed feelings. It was heartening for Roger to learn that I could do about as good a job at driving as Bobby. But at the same time it was disheartening for me to learn that Bobby couldn't make the car go any faster. When last year's winner couldn't make it go, I began to reckon something was basically wrong with the Lola, and I had absolutely no solutions in mind.

At least Hanford proved that the car would run. One thing Broadley wanted to do was mount the turbocharger low on the left side of the chassis, for a lower center of gravity and a lower polar moment of inertia. This required long exhaust and pressure pipes, and screens to avoid sucking in track dirt. As soon as the Indy establishment saw that, they assured us it wouldn't work. As far as those guys are concerned, nothing will ever work if it hasn't been done before. There was a little problem of too much engine

photo by Tom Patterson

Lola T152

oil siphoning down to the blower, but Karl put a shutoff valve in the line, and that was our only trouble with the layout. There was nothing obviously, basically wrong with the car—it was just slow.

Bobby figured it was time to take the car to Indy for tire tests, but I was tied up somewhere else with the Trans-Am or something, so he took the car. He didn't get very far with it at Indy either. I showed up for a few days and drove a couple of times, and then we watched it rain a lot. We didn't learn much about which way to go from the tire tests. Obviously the car wasn't going to be a winner "right outta the box." George Bignotti, one of the best mechanics at Indianapolis, had a four-wheel-drive car going good, but we didn't know why, and since he was on Firestones there was no way we could share the information. Bobby's car was to arrive by the time official practice opened, so we thought the only thing to do was to have Broadley come to Indy with the second car.

Bobby was getting an identical car, which is why he was helping me set up mine—so that he'd be ready when his came. Still, he got rather anxious to be developing his own car. When Broadley arrived Bobby went his own way, and there was no information exchanged between us after that. He gave me a great start, though, and I've always been grateful for that. Roger and I couldn't have asked him for more. Broadley brought two mechanics who had previous experience at Indy, and they all worked mostly with me. Still, that was my first year there, and I didn't really know what I wanted in the car, whether it was four-wheel-drive or two-wheel drive. I went through my rookie test, and that was no big deal. The maximum they would let me go was 160 mph. Everybody knew I was having a hard time holding it down. But then they took all the restrictions off—and the fastest I could go was 161.

I brought the car into the pits, and Roger asked what was wrong. I just said, "Roger, I don't really *know* what's wrong." And that's where we started.

Broadley has always been a guy who believed that correct suspension geometry is the answer to what ails you, that the last final tweak in geometry will bring any car to life. Maybe that time he was right. We worked night and day, changing more springs and anti-roll bars and suspension mounting points. I stood around and watched everything they were doing without understanding much of it. Whenever I asked what was going on, Broadley would say, "Don't worry about what I'm doing. You just drive the car and tell me how it feels." That seems to be the British approach to developing race cars—separation of power, I guess. I hadn't experienced that since Bruce McLaren set up our Ford GT at Le Mans in 1967. It was very much unlike what I had done with Chevrolet. But since *I* had no idea what to do, I had to go along. Pretty soon I stopped going to the garage area at all. I would drive the car, tell Broadley how I thought it felt, he would go back to work on it, and we would go on from there.

I didn't learn much about Indy cars for the entire month I was there. I'd just wander around for a while, then go out and run whenever they wanted me to. Eventually, somehow, I qualified the car fourth—0.3 mph behind Bobby in the other four-wheel-drive Lola. But as qualifying drew to an end and we began to prepare for the race, a sudden realization hit me. There I was on the second row, and the whole time I was practicing and qualifying I had never gotten close to another car on the track. If there were too many cars out, Roger would have me pull in and wait for the track to clear. I had raced with those guys on two road courses before, but I had no idea what they did on an oval at over 160 mph.

I suppose that the start of a race means different things to every driver, especially the "Gentlemen . . . start your engines!" at Indianapolis. When I look at films of drivers getting into their cars, with faraway looks in their eyes, or obvious nervousness or apprehension, I sometimes wonder myself what is really going on in their minds. But I have almost always looked forward to that final moment, when I could get into the car and get on with the job. I felt that once I was in the car and on the grid, finally all the hassles of preparation were over. I could be left alone to the simple problem of me, the car, and the race. And Karl and Woody were always good about that. They never bothered me with a lot of distractions, and they kept the spectators from bugging me then. It was almost a relief to be on my way. As the saying goes, "When the flag drops, the bullshit stops."

Unfortunately, that particular time at Indianapolis I was a little worried about what was going to happen when the flag dropped. When we went around on the pace lap it was the first time I had been near any other car, much less thirty-three in one pack. I was really wondering, "What am I *doing* here?" It was extremely important that I not make a mistake—not only for my own safety but because of all those people, and because of all the time and money we had put into that one race.

When the race finally started, I almost pulled off onto the grass going into the first turn. I wasn't in control of the situation, and I just didn't know what was going to happen. I got passed by almost everybody. Guys who were much slower in qualifying just drove right on by. I must have dropped to about fifteenth in the first few laps. If Roger was disappointed, he never let me know it. Obviously, it was going to take me a little time to figure out how to get close to other cars and repass them.

About halfway through the race I began to figure out how to do it, and I worked my way up to second place. There I was, far behind Andretti and just ahead of Gurney, who stayed on my tail for a while but then he dropped back with a bad wheel or shock absorber. At that point, after all my carefulness and learning, the engine started to pop and bang. The magneto had failed. Davy Crockett, who was our engine man at the time, put a new one in, and I went back out about eight laps down. I just cruised around as well as I could from then on, and finished seventh. After the race everybody looked the magneto over very carefully, and it looked perfect. My only guess is that it was misfiring due to extreme heat in the car.

Someone was making a film about the race, and they got Gurney and me to talk about it—the veteran and the rookie. Dan surprised me by mentioning retiring. He was saying that he'd gotten a lot out of racing but he didn't know how much longer he could keep it up. He sounded really tired and worn down. I couldn't understand what he was talking about at the time. But later, when I was in the same boat, I could relate to his feelings. There he was—a somebody—and a nobody like me comes up who he can't get away from. We were running about the same speed. A lot goes through your mind when that starts to happen. He finally did retire at the end of the next season.

That was my first attempt at Indianapolis, and I ended up getting the "Rookie of the Year" award for it. It's given by Stark-Wetzel, a local food producer, and the decision is made by a vote of the press. They had a big banquet—a great occasion—which was quite an honor for me. As Karl pointed out, you can come back and win the race anytime, but there is only one opportunity to be Rookie of the Year. Later on, I heard that Peter Revson was a little upset about it. He was a rookie that year also, and he worked his way from last up to a fifth-place finish, two up on me. He figured that it was only Penske's public relations that got me the honor instead of him. I just accepted it without a thought, because I had been lapping Peter until my magneto went out. I wondered later who he was upset with. It certainly wasn't me, because the press makes the decision. At the time I guess Peter wasn't very good with the press.

LOLA T163

We were tied in closely enough with Lola that it was a natural for them to build us a Can-Am car also. While we were in England setting up the Indy car deal, we told Broadley to build us a car that would beat the McLarens. We didn't have any trick Unfair Advantages in mind, so we just told him to make it lighter than anything else. He could use titanium, or whatever was more expensive, for just this one car. Broadley didn't like the idea, but he went ahead and gave us what we wanted.

When we got the car we were right in the middle of our USAC program and our '69 Camaro crisis, and we just didn't have the time or the crew to get into the Can-Am. I told Karl Kainhofer to put a new 430 Traco-Chevy in it in his spare time—that was a joke—and we would just go to whatever race came up. Karl prepared the car as best he knew how, while I devoted all my attention to the Camaros.

At some point we did take the car to our skidpad, but I could only afford a few days with it, and it really needed some major development. Something was seriously wrong on the skidpad. The car was definitely not right. We gave up on it and decided to take it to Mid-Ohio, the fifth race in the Can-Am. After Indianapolis we had six very important Trans-Am races in a string, so that really was our first opportunity to try the new Lola.

The car was really bad at Mid-Ohio. It oversteered and understeered, naturally, but worst of all it was breaking rear axle half-shafts for some reason. With a lot of time for hindsight, I can probably explain it. To try and cure the oversteer, I pulled out the rubber bumpstops Broadley had built in the rear suspension. With that, we had a lot of travel in the rear because of the soft springs, and Mid-Ohio is hilly enough to accentuate the problem. There probably wasn't enough travel in the axle shaft, or the universal joints were binding. At any rate, I broke one in practice and another during qualifying. Somehow I managed to qualify third, for what that was worth, considering both McLarens were over three seconds faster.

Nine laps into the race, while I was running fourth, the axle broke again. Mid-Ohio is no place to go off-course, so I considered myself lucky that the car was only bent up when I hit an embankment. The broken axle got loose and flailed around in the rear, tearing up the chassis quite a bit. We could have repaired it, but Roger made a momentous decision on the spot. We abandoned the Can-Am right there. The series was five races old, the McLaren team had it fairly well wrapped up, and we had an unsorted car to compete with. We patched the car up and sold it to someone as a show car.

Fortunately, in those days it was easier to get out of a series commitment. The most valuable lesson we should have learned that year is that we couldn't go off like we wanted and pick up a new chassis that could beat a

LOLA T163 *photo by Cam Warren*

well-developed team. It takes time and effort to make a successful race car. That's all there is to it. There's no easy way out.

LOLA T150, FROM 4WD TO 2WD

There was one other Lola chassis we ran in our big 1969 "exclusive" year with Eric Broadley. After the Indianapolis 500, Eric sent us a shorter version of the T152, which was designed to take a Chevy motor instead of the Offy. We were figuring that four-wheel-drive was still the answer, but for shorter tracks, and especially the Riverside road race, a Chevy would provide more flexibility. Actually, this car was converted to four-wheel drive from a two wheel-drive car that had been wrecked. In the conversion to four-wheel drive, the wheelbase was shortened from 104 inches to 98 inches, but otherwise the two chassis were identical.

We got that car about the middle of the year, so there was time to take it to our new skidpad and set it up right. At the time USAC was limiting four-wheel-drive cars to ten-inch-wide rims at front and rear, which still left us a lot of things to adjust. We played around with the torque bias front to rear—which didn't seem to make much difference at those low torque requirements—and we adjusted the spring and anti-roll bar rates. With the given rim size, we still had a lot of choices in tires, and after trying just about everything that existed, I decided on Indy tires front, with a Trans-Am design on the rear. We got that chassis so well set up on the pad—at 1.45 "g's"—that we couldn't wait to get to a USAC oval. We selected Indianapolis Raceway Park for our first big appearance.

Our ideal skidpad combination was so bad on the track that I could hardly drive it. It oversteered terribly going into the turns and understeered terribly coming out. But with all the complications and interrelated factors, we didn't know where to begin to start fixing it. Considering the fact that it had taken Eric a month to get the other four-wheel-drive chassis sorted at the Indianapolis 500, I reckoned we were lost. I called Roger and said I simply couldn't drive the car the way it was. He understood, so we withdrew from the IRP race and went home.

courtesy of Petersen Publishing Company

LOLA T150

We finally converted the chassis back to two-wheel drive. The Riverside Rex Mays race was coming up, and from my experience there with Gurney in 1969, I knew that a well-set-up conventional chassis could win. That was also our first experience with nitro. We decided that if everyone else was using it, we were going to have to learn how to make it work in our Chevy motor. So we broke one cylinder head in practice, and one cylinder head in the race. While it ran, it was strong enough to qualify second and lead the race for a short time, but it looked as if we needed another expensive development program. And at that point we had just severed any racing association we had with Chevrolet.

Since we had the car, and since it was competitive on road courses, we ran it some in 1970 also. There was a USAC road race at Sears Point, California, which we didn't finish. I was sitting on the pole, with an engine that was already sick from warm-up, and my chassis tore apart on the first lap. Then, in mid-year we went back to another short-track race at Indianapolis Raceway Park. I qualified third behind Andretti and Al Unser, and finished second behind Al on a terribly rain-slick track. It was a poor second as far as I was concerned, but that was the only race that car ever finished. We took the car back to the shops and prepared it for the next Rex Mays race in the fall—which was never held. It looked like there was no future for a road-racing car in USAC, so we got rid of that combination. It was no great loss to me, for the Chevy-Lola-USAC car was never one of my favorites.

Chapter 16

1970–71

JAVELIN
Making a Nash into a Race Car (in Two Years)

The first time I ever talked to any American Motors people was in a motel room in Century City, California. We had just won the Riverside race and the Trans Am Championship with our Camaros, and we were having serious problems with Chevrolet. But we had heard that American Motors was going to drop Ron Kaplan and Jim Jeffords for another team, so Roger had set up a meeting for us with Bill McNealy, their Vice President of Marketing. Since we hadn't broken off with Chevrolet yet, I felt a little out of place—as if we were cheating on our wives or something—although it was really a legitimate business meeting. Roger was being almost too honest with them about our position. He came right out and said we needed exactly "so many" dollars to run the Javelins for a season. McNealy said it was about the range they had expected, and we got into negotiations over terms and bonuses. Roger was so mad at Chevrolet at that point that he said he wasn't interested in any bonus dollars in the contract for second in the Championship—it was going to be first or nothing.

We all had separation anxieties over the deal. Roger didn't know if he could break away from racing Chevrolets or not, as long as he had his Chevrolet dealerships, so we asked for a few weeks to think about it. Finally, Roger went to John DeLorean, the General Manager of Chevrolet and later to become a close friend, and explained the opportunity we had. DeLorean said, "You're a good Chevrolet dealer, and as long as you are, we don't care what you do about racing." After that there never was any difficulty with Chevrolet—as a company—although some individuals in the racing programs weren't very happy with us.

So Roger signed up with American Motors and we were in business. They announced the program at a big press conference in Los Angeles, because that's home base for so many motorsports writers. Roger and I both got up and said a few words about how happy we were with the deal. That's when I first heard Roger announce that we were going to win at least seven races in our first season with the Javelins. I was as surprised as the press was—perhaps scared is a better word—because I still hadn't even taken a good look at the cars we had to race. All we knew was that in addition to Ron Kaplan's work, Traco had done some development on the engines, which were quite similar to the Chevrolet engine. We reckoned that as long as all cars had to weigh the same, and have the same size engine, we could do the job. Within those parameters we could make a Javelin just as fast as a Camaro. Unfortunately we didn't anticipate the detail problems.

The first step—of about 10 million—was to find out what Kaplan had done. We inherited his entire team operation right after Riverside, including cars, trucks, trailers, and parts. Compared to what we were used to, it was the sorriest mess I've ever seen. The most valuable asset they had was an International tow truck, which we used for many years after that.

We sold most of the stuff, but kept one car to use as a reference for a while. I had our best sedan builder, John Woodard, fly out to California and get it running as best he could so that we could test it at Riverside. He spent a solid week getting it in good enough shape so nothing would fall off. The biggest problem was that it had been lowered and lowered and lowered in the front, without decreasing the length of the shock absorbers or bumpstops, and it was sitting on hardware instead of springs. There was practically no suspension travel at all. How Jerry Grant and Ron Grable were able to run them as fast as they did is absolutely beyond me. We couldn't take time to find shorter shocks or different springs, so I had Woody cut a hole in the hood and make a higher bracket with more clearance. Then something else was bottoming. We cut that away and there was something else, then something else. Finally we just raised the front up until we had three inches of travel, and ran it. Obviously, it was going to require some serious development work.

When we recognized that we were going to have to engineer and build an entire car, we went looking for more help. Our last liaison engineer at Chevrolet had been Don Cox, who was reluctantly loaned to us from the Chaparral project. Neither one of us was too happy about it, because he preferred the more abstract and advanced racing technologies and I felt that he was a hard person to communicate with. But even if we did have difficulty understanding each other at first, I figured that anyone was better than no one. As we worked on the Camaros through 1969, though, it became obvious that Don was no bullshitter—he was a doer. Whenever we had a problem in brakes or axle hop or whatever, he could solve it with his technology. He didn't tell me to drive differently, or change tires, or change ride height, or any of those things we could handle ourselves. He did what only he could do, and usually in completely unbiased ways—something that always impressed me about a lot of the people in Chevrolet's racing program. I started to realize that those capabilities were something we were going to need.

Roger and I invited him down to our shops to look around. When we left Chevrolet, Don came with us, primarily to handle the engineering on the Javelin. He probably wouldn't make that same decision again. Roger also went to Traco and made a deal with them to develop the engines. He promised whatever they needed to make us competitive.

JAVELIN *courtesy of Penske Communications (photo by Floyd D. Harvey)*

We found the engineer who had designed the American Motors V-8 engine, Dave Potter, who had retired, and we put him on retainer. He was to design any special engine pieces we needed, such as connecting rods, pistons, rocker arms, or crankshafts.

Whatever we had to have, though, we produced ourselves. About the only nonstock components American Motors provided was billets to make connecting rods from. We saw the Javelin project as the ultimate challenge. We were young and enthusiastic, and we were going to make it or break it. There weren't going to be any more automotive writers spreading rumors that Chevrolet was actually building our race cars for us.

We started our first Javelin as a stripped chassis from the factory. We needed hundreds of other stock parts, though, such as hinges and brackets and linkages and things, which are really quite a problem to order individually. For some reason American Motors didn't want us to strip them off another complete car as they were needed. After we had installed the roll cage and widened the fenders we had to have some parts to continue with, and none were coming. I was getting desperate, so I called the factory and said, "Look, you've got to give us a car to take odds and ends out of. We have to have parts *now*!" So they agreed to loan us a car, on the condition that we would rebuild it as the parts we ordered arrived. I was promising anything at that point. We picked up a running Javelin at a dealership and it got stripped . . . and stripped . . . and stripped . . . until it was virtually useless.

By the time we had the racer running the stripper was a pile of junk sitting in the corner. In the meantime, American Motors had supplied us with six loaner cars for the team to drive. But somehow, everyone else seemed to need them worse than I did. Don Kean and I were the only ones without cars, and he felt slighted since he was our chief fabricator. He came to me and asked if he could have the stripper if he put it back together in his spare time. I waited until the right moment—when the American Motors blokes saw their racer running, and when their smiles seemed widest—and I said, "Oh, incidentally, we have this other car . . . etc." They okayed it, and I called Kean before they could change their minds.

We had seen earlier that the suspension was going to be a major problem, so Cox spent the majority of his time from November to February designing and producing an entire new layout. He drew up new A-arms, uprights, spindles, hubs, wheels, brakes, and steering linkage. There were hundreds of parts farmed out to small machine shops all over Philadelphia. The biggest problem was not geometry but stiffness. Because of deflections in the Camaro, we'd had to run a lot of negative camber, and we planned to eliminate that by strengthening everything. Also, it was easier to lower the front of the car by raising the spindle on the upright, which also used up less suspension travel. To keep costs down a little, we had the factory provide us with the stock upright, specially forged out of better 4130 steel. Then we made up our own heavy-duty spindles, and plates to bolt them on the upright.

Cox designed the entire rear end also—housing, axles, full-floating hubs, differential spool, locating linkage, brackets, and brakes. We could have gotten away with a simpler setup, but that was where we were going to have a secret Unfair Advantage. We knew we were going to be down on power, and we couldn't make the chassis much better than we had on the Camaro, so we had to come up with a trick. From our experience with the camber effect up front, we decided to put some camber into the rear wheels by bending, or "gronking," the axle housing. We had seen housings come out of production with as much as one degree of accidental misalignment, so we designed-in one degree of negative camber. Because of the full-floating axles, the wheel-bearing surfaces could be pressed into the housing crooked. There was no provision for the drive axles to align themselves, but they were splined at both ends so we figured they could just grind themselves into position.

We took the "gronked" axle to our first test at Daytona, and it made such tremendous grinding noises just pushing the car around in the pits that we were more than a little worried. After a short test something else broke, and we took the car back to Philadelphia to have a look at it. The splines were torn up so badly that we had to make a choice between dropping that trick or going on to a more sophisticated design. So Cox sat down and spent days adding universal joints to the outer ends of the axle shafts. He used modified Toronado front-wheel-drive joints, and even at that the torque strength was marginal. The whole thing was very expensive and very complicated to jig up, but I figured it was the answer, so I said we ought to make five or six axles at once. Roger came around, though, and he said, "Hold on a minute. Let's make *one* and try it first."

We went back to Sebring to try it again. After setting the car up and running baseline tests with a normal rear axle, we brought it in and changed to the new, improved gronked axle. I took it back out on the course to see how much faster the car was—and it *wasn't*! The laptimes weren't one bit better. Cox and I were completely mystified. We went back to the straight axle and saved a great deal of money on any more development. It wasn't until the next winter's development tests that we came up with the explanation. It appears that very heavy cars running on relatively small tires just don't respond to camber the way a small race car does. The tires have a great tendency to conform to the road regardless of the camber angle.

Then we got into the brake system, which was no small job either. We had an option between four designs, none of which were really what we wanted. We could use the Kelsey-Hayes brakes as Ford and American Motors had. Or we could go back to the Camaro's Moraines, which we knew were weak. Airheart's brakes weren't big enough, and it would take them months to build what we needed. Finally there were Girlings, which had been very successful on small sports cars but might require too much line pressure to stop a sedan. About that time Kelsey-Hayes came to us and said, "We have the new hot setup—the latest and greatest." But Bud Moore and Parnelli Jones were testing the prototypes, and we had to wait until they were finished. They tested for two months while we sat around and waited. Finally I got so angry that we made the decision to go with Girling.

Cox calculated that we would need a two-to-one force ratio between the front and rear brakes, but we wanted to use Girling's largest caliper, and we wanted them to be the same front and rear, for parts standardization. Girling had an inline booster, though, which I'd had good experience with before. It adds a vacuum boost anywhere in the line between the master cylinder and the caliper, and since we had independent front-to-rear systems, we could boost the front brakes separately. We worked with Girling's representative, Tony Cross, who juggled parts until he got the right ratio by combining a seven-inch diaphragm and the piston from a five-inch unit. That was the primary balance ratio, but of course we also had a balance bar for fine adjustment between the two master cylinders. When other Girling engineers realized what we were doing, they panicked. They said it just wouldn't work. We said, "Doesn't that give us a two-to-one ratio?" They said, "Yes, but . . ." So I asked, "Then why won't it work?" Apparently their only logic was that it had never been done before. We even checked the booster characteristics for vacuum supply, because if that ran low the brake ratio would change. When we discovered that a lot of pedal pumping caused a critical shortage, we added an extra vacuum tank—a Corvette headlight-opening tank that cost about twenty cents.

In the first brake tests we found that the rear brakes would come on slightly early and lock up because of a delay in the vacuum booster to the front. To compensate, we tried installing restrictor orifices in the rear brake line. Finally we got down to about a .030—inch hole, which gave us a very good brake system—strong, well balanced, and durable. The durability was not only from Girling's thick and even-wearing pads but from the brake rotors Cox had come up with. We had suspected that our rotor—cracking problem on the Camaro was due to the tremendous offset in their centers. Chevrolet said there was no way that could be true. But on the Javelin, Cox eliminated the offset by using Lincoln-Mercury rotors on a separate hub flange, and we tripled rotor life even though they were the same diameter and thickness. Not only that, but Cox arranged the mounting flanges so that the rotors could be changed almost as quickly as pads. The final system looked complicated, with lines and cylinders and hoses and bleed screws everywhere, but in fact it was really quite simple in operation and almost foolproof.

Aerodynamic development of the Javelin was more of a political than a technical problem. We knew at the outset that we had a big battle on our hands between all the factory teams—Bud Moore and Shelby Mustangs, Gurney's Plymouths, Hall's Camaros, and so on. It was a matter of life or death for us to get everything we needed, especially the homologation of optional equipment.

For rear aerodynamic downforce, Ron Kaplan had used a small wing on the trunk. Maybe that would have worked, but we had no experience with wings on sedans, and we did know a lot about spoilers. So immediately after our Riverside test I went to Detroit and began pleading for a run of production spoilers for the car. We had made up an aluminum version that was about the right shape, even though it wasn't the best-looking sales model I'd ever seen. Everybody said, "No! It would take too long and cost too much!" But it was so important to me that I quietly stood there and said I wasn't going to take no for an answer. I went away and let them think about it for a few days, and ultimately they decided they could do it after all. If they hadn't, I think we would have been in serious trouble aerodynamically. As part of the deal, though, I had to agree to put my name on the back of it. I sent them a legible copy of my signature, and they made a "Mark Donohue" decal that went on the spoiler. Unfortunately, that was about the end of the era when people's names were supposed to be an important sales gimmick on cars.

Eventually American Motors built 2500 "Mark Donohue Javelins," which had the spoilers we needed, plus slightly different engines with four-bolt main bearings and open-port heads. To help promote them, Roger purchased the first eighteen off the line for Sun Oil Company. Sunoco had hired eighteen young girls to drive around the country checking service stations on a "beautification campaign." They would drive into a Sunoco station and go through a check list to see if the johns were out of order, or if the windows were dirty, or whatever, and the owners could win prizes. All the girls came to the shop to pick up their cars—and our guys just about went crazy. I think some of them started dating, because I saw the girls around sometime later. In the end there was one left over—a Javelin, that is—so I bought it myself and gave it to my mother. She had no idea I was going to do it, and when I delivered it to her house she went berserk. She's a very enthusiastic racing person—my greatest fan, I'm sure—who has been to at least fifty of my races. Sometimes I never even know she's there. Dad takes everything very calmly, though. He's pleased that I'm successful at something, but he's stoical about automobile racing. Anyhow, they had a Mark Donohue Javelin to drive, and it caused a lot of confusion among their friends. They didn't understand that it was a production car. The most common reaction was, "Say, Mrs. Donohue, I saw someone else driving your car the other day," or "Are there two of them?"

After we got the spoiler we needed we took the car to Sebring for comprehensive aerodynamic tests. We developed a system of pressure taps to measure air pressures all over the car, which was hard to do and very time-consuming, but it gave us a good idea as to what things we needed and where they should go. That was how we decided that we had to have the reverse-opening hood scoop, the flush grille, and the special front valence panel that came out on the 1971 Javelin. There were a lot of other changes we would have made to reduce air drag, but we couldn't expect American Motors to make special body dies for just 2500 cars.

I went to Detroit a couple of times to convince them that there were certain things we *must* do for the car to be functional and look right, and eventually they all became reality. I felt that was a great accomplishment for me—for an average guy who wasn't a qualified automotive engineer to influence their designs. I may have been slightly prejudiced, but I thought the 1971 Javelins were about the most attractive Trans-Am sedans on the street. The front spoilers may not have been too practical, since they were frequently broken off in parking, but the styling was great. In the end the SCCA liberalized their rules to the point where we could use almost any kind of spoiler on the front, so we made it larger, to better balance rear downforce, and we made it out of unbreakable Lexan.

When we took our Javelin to its first race at Daytona we knew we were low on power. The first motor we built was only good for about 375 horsepower on Traco's dyno, which was about 100 horsepower shy of the equivalent Chevrolet motor. But I figured that everything else was about as strong as it needed to be. Peter Revson was co-driving, and we only ran a few hours before the motor broke. We thought we had lost a rod bearing, but in fact that was the first symptom of a problem that was to plague us for the entire year.

We started out using the engine pan and oil system that Kaplan had developed. But because we had improved the chassis so much, cornering and braking performance had increased to the point where the oil was being forced away from the pump pickup. It was similar to the oil starvation problem we had with the first bigblock Chevy engine in the Lola in 1966, except that in this case it wasn't so obvious. In the Chevrolet, oil would get trapped in the rocker covers and start smoking past the valve guides, but in the American Motors engine there was no warning. Suddenly the oil pressure would just drop to zero, then come right back up again. All it took was an instant, and the bearings were history. We were so certain that it was a mechanical problem that we didn't suspect the oil pan. I suppose it was my fault that we didn't recognize the real problem for such a long time.

We had two cars ready for the first Trans-Am race at Laguna Seca, and Peter and I went there a week early to test. Between us, we lost three motors before the race even started. The best one we had was only good for 391 horsepower, but at that, they were still very expensive. I got a little upset with Peter because he kept on driving when his motor started coming apart. He had relatively little feel for mechanics, and he would drive it all the way into the pits with connecting rods coming out the bottom. Peter and I were contemporaries in racing from 1960, and each of us liked to think he was better than the other. In fact, Peter may have been a better driver, while I was a better developer. But I guess we all knew that there would be some conflict with both of us on the same team. He wanted to drive for Roger Penske because he knew it would be good for his career, even though he didn't like the idea of being the number—two driver. I think whenever he had to make the choice, he preferred to be the number-one driver on a number two team. But both our cars were always the same. There's no reason to ever make one car slower than the other. The awkward situation was that I would set up both cars, and he would just come to the track and get in his and drive it. Roger informed us, though, that if either car broke, I would drive the remaining one, because I was the one who had put all the effort into developing them. Eventually that happened, and Peter got kind of sour about it, but that was the agreement.

In the Laguna race Peter went out with brake problems after hitting some haybales, and I was second to Parnelli Jones. Parnelli won going away, and he was happier than hell. He was taking shots at us for saying we were going to win seven races. Now it was just that much harder. After the race I sat there in my car, totally exasperated. We had designed, built, tested, and brought to the track the best car we could build, and it was second best. We had done more in seven months than most teams could do in years, and in the end we had a mediocre car. It wasn't outstanding in any department. It was just mediocre all around. I was destroyed. Second place may have looked good on paper, but we were so far back that we might as well have been last.

Our low power was bad enough, but the oil starvation was a disease that was hard to diagnose. The engines would run forever on the dyno, and they seemed good in the car . . . and then suddenly one would fail. One would run a 300-mile race, then not last five laps at the next. We started to suspect Traco of carelessness. There was one prevalent thing that bothered me though. The oil temperature was much higher than in the Camaros, and the pressure was sometimes down from sixty to forty psi.

The second race was canceled, which was a blessing in disguise, and the next time out for us was an even worse disaster than Laguna. At Lime Rock Peter blew his engine and spun in his own oil coming into the pits. I fought with Parnelli for a long time, finally taking the lead when he went off the road—and then my engine failed. I finally said, "Look, we can't go on losing motors like this. We've gotta solve this oiling problem."

The first thing we did was to make a removable front cross member so we could change oil pans without pulling the engine. Then we made up about fifty different kinds of pans, with all sorts of trapdoors, baffles, screens, slots, and trays. We took everything to Bryar to prepare for the next race there. I got one of the mechanics to sit in the back of the car and watch the oil pressure gauge while I drove around the track. He was supposed to tap me on the shoulder if the gauge went to zero. It's no wonder we were losing engines—we couldn't go *one lap* without losing oil pressure! The reason I hadn't seen that happen on our skidpad was that it took a combination of extreme braking and cornering and acceleration to starve the oil pump pickup. That may also be why it wasn't happening to many other drivers—who don't combine the three to any great extent. We tried heavier oils and anti-foam oils and all our trick pans without much improvement. Finally, when we had installed external drainbacks and the best-sealed door system we could build, it was marginally better. In the Bryar race Peter and I finished two-three, but at least we finished.

At that point we knew Ford had something tricky in their pans, so we got our spy system working to find out what it was. We ended up with a photograph that showed what seemed to be another oil pump in addition to the stock one. In checking the rules, it seemed that pumps were an open area, so the solution was obvious. We replaced our stock single-rotor pump with one that had a pair of stacked rotors, each having its own separate pickup. The pickup from the second pump scavenged oil from the "uphill" end of the pan, and filled the sump for the primary pump. From then on we never had low oil pressure again. We still had lingering doubts, though, so Roger lobbied with the SCCA until they allowed dry-sump systems for the next season.

In retrospect, the really sad part of the deal was that we could have done something about it earlier had I followed one small bit of advice from Roger. When we realized what was happening, he suggested that we raise the engine a little, so that we could use a deeper pan, and everything might be all right. Our engine *was* lower than the Mustangs or Camaros, which was another reason why they had fewer problems. But I said, "Roger, you've got to be kidding! If we raise the engine it'll bring the center of gravity up—and that will certainly depreciate cornering capability." Unfortunately, the more important problem of the moment was survival. Many times Roger says things that are so profound he doesn't even know it himself, and that was one of the times. But I had put him down. He stopped because I had made his advice look ridiculous. It's always easy to look back and think you see where you made mistakes, but I'm sure there would have been other problems like moving mounts around and cutting the firewall and building new headers. All together we lost twenty-three engines that season. It's hard to imagine what we might have saved in dollars and gained in finishing positions had I listened to Roger with an open mind.

I won the next race at Bridgehampton, even though it had nothing to do with the oiling system. It rained so badly, and the track was so slippery, that

I never could find enough traction to slosh the oil around in the pan. I won solely because I had better rain tires. After the disastrous race in the Camaro at Michigan the previous season, where the Mustangs ran away on their superior Firestone rain tires, I decided we needed to do some development in that area. We had recently put in our own skidpad, and we could wet it down with a firehose whenever we needed. My biggest problem was in convincing Goodyear that their rain tires were no good, and that skidpad testing was the way to develop better ones. Their engineers kept saying that they designed tires for racetracks, not skidpads. Now, of course, they even have their own skidpad. But I convinced them that we couldn't make things worse by trying. They made up some special test tires for comparison, and we spent a few days running the Camaro around on a wet surface. It was soon obvious what designs were best, and by the time we were finished we had a tire that was head and shoulders above the Firestone. Trouble was, we never had an opportunity to use those rain tires the rest of that season. But when the time came—with the Javelin—we *really* needed them. We had lost or not finished five races in a row.

When it started to rain I knew we finally had the Unfair Advantage. Rain makes up for low horsepower and reduces the stress on the car and engine, and we knew exactly how to set up the car for those new tires. A car requires rebalancing whenever you change from one tire to another, especially when you change to rain tires. Since I had done all the development driving, I knew exactly what we needed to do. We adjusted the anti-roll bars and the brake ratio—and won the race. If it had dried out, things might not have gone so nicely.

We had a meeting scheduled at our shops with the American Motors guys after Bridgehampton. We had no idea what they wanted, but it could have had something to do with the fact that we were losing races. I came in from the skidpad all hot and dirty, and we shook hands and smiled a lot. Then one guy said, "I suppose you're wondering why we're here. Well, we had decided to end our contract at this meeting, but since you won Bridgehampton, our management has changed their minds. There's really no reason for us to be here now. Keep up the good work." Roger and I took a really deep breath . . .

I had been at the skidpad because I was continually looking for better tires. Somehow or other, Firestone had again come up with a better tire than we had. It was a carry-over from the design we had borrowed and created such a hassle with in '69. So the Mustangs were ahead not only in power but in their tires, and I just couldn't convince Goodyear that we needed more work in that area. I eventually decided to try a NASCAR Super Modified tire that was smaller than what we had. Actually it was larger in diameter, but because of its narrow tread no one expected much out of it. Sure enough, in the first few laps around the skidpad it was slower. But we had learned to watch tire temperatures and laptimes to make sure each tire was operating at its optimum, and as we let the temperature come up, those tires equaled, then surpassed, our best Trans-Am tires. I was quite excited about our discovery, so I got Goodyear's Ted Loebinger to supply us with enough for the next race, at Donnybrooke.

As soon as our competitors saw those tires they all started laughing and saying, "You're not really gonna run those tires, are you? They're *terrible*!" I just acted like I was resigned to our sorry situation. Ted knew they must be better, though, and he told us that if we ran quicker, we were going to have to share them with other teams. I wasn't about to let that happen, not after all the work we had gone to in attempting to find an advantage. Ted was doing his job in trying to get Goodyear tires on a winning car, but we were behind, and we really needed an Unfair Advantage. I knew that there weren't enough new tires to go around, and the ones that were there happened to be in our truck. So I told Ted we didn't know whether we would use them or not. All through practice and qualifying we ran on the old Trans-Am tires. But we set the cars up—gearing and anti-roll bars—for the new NASCAR tires. Meanwhile, our guys were quietly mounting up the other tires on all the spare wheels we had.

We showed up the morning of the race with the NASCAR tires on our Javelins. No one else had time to try them out, and even if they wanted to, we had forgotten to bring the truck that had the rest of the tires. Ted was furious. I just said, "Sorry, Ted, but we changed our minds last night." Some of the other teams threatened to knife our tires if we were quicker, but I just told them, "You do what you have to do, and we'll do what we have to do." In the end it was all academic, because both our cars failed before we ever got the tires up to operating temperatures.

Peter was really angry with me about that race. First my engine failed in practice. Then I took over his car, and the same thing happened about twenty laps into the race. I don't blame him for being mad, but neither car would have lasted the race, no matter who was driving. That was when we realized that we had another serious engine problem. Over the length of a race the ignition timing would change. It would keep retarding more and more, costing us valuable horsepower. At Donnybrooke it got so bad the engine started backfiring out the exhaust. The headers got so hot they blistered and burned paint, and they damn near set the car on fire. Finally we concluded that the added drag of the extra oil pump was wearing out the drive gears on the camshaft. Since the distributor shaft is driven by the same gears, this put the ignition timing off.

I called Traco the next morning to discuss it with them. I suggested they set up a dummy engine and drive it with an electric motor until they got some gears to survive. Travers said, "We can't do that. That's a major development program, which takes a lot of time." We're pretty good friends, and I didn't want to aggravate him, so I thought, "By damn, I'll do it myself." They sent us all the pieces we needed—block, cam, gears, oil pump, and so on—and I set aside an afternoon to put it all together. It turned out to be a major effort after all.

After a couple of days we had a block and cam and oiling system mounted over a metal tank to catch all the drippings, with an electric motor driving the camshaft through belts and pulleys. It was a big five-horsepower motor, but when we tried to start it up it went "pffft," and burned out immediately. Then we got a ten-horsepower motor, and "pffft," it blew out all our fuses. In desperation we replaced the fuses with metal blocks, and finally we got the cam to turn. It was the messiest and most spectacular thing I've ever seen! It filled the shop with smoke and spraying oil, and with a great shrieking and groaning—the gears lasted about six seconds. We were running the cam about 7500 engine rpm, and we figured we had a severe enough test. If we could get gears to last longer than six seconds they could survive anything.

We had all kinds of special gears built to experiment with. We tried different materials, and we had them chrome plated, cadmium plated, and moly plated. American Motors even gave us some help by providing handmade gear sets. Before long we decided the real problem was that there was no direct oil supply to those gears. By drilling new oil passages in the block and camshaft, we routed a steady stream of oil to them. The combination of better materials and better oiling brought the durability up to about forty minutes, and we figured we were home free.

That was a *big* accomplishment for us. We had a major problem, and we stepped up to it and solved it in a short time. But Cox and I were up until the wee hours of the morning getting it done. The American Motors engineers never even cared. Why should they? It was no problem to them. We were driving a special distributor and two oil pumps at twice the speed that engine normally runs. Anyhow, that was the end of all our engine durability problems. Our next race was at Elkhart Lake, and we knew we had engines that would last and that we had better tires in the bag.

We were still down about fifty horsepower, though. I could be sitting on the pole—and be fifth going into the first turn. Those guys would just pull away from me in the straightaways, and I couldn't pass them in the corners. That was when Roger came up with the staggered pitstop routine that really confused everybody. He knew I could run faster when I was alone and not battling it out in traffic, but the Mustangs could kill us if I ran with them. So he came up with a really clever way to get me separated from the rest of the frontrunners. Everyone usually had to add three eleven-gallon dump cans of fuel during a race. The standard procedure was to add two cans on the first pitstop and one on the second. Roger's new scheme was for me to come in early—as though something was wrong—open the hood and add a quart of oil while one can of fuel was being put in, and put two cans in on the *second* stop.

I was running in second place early in the race, when suddenly I went piling into the pits at 100 mph, the hood was thrown open, oil added, a can of fuel, and I was back out again—way down in the standings. Everyone else forgot about me at that point; they thought I was having trouble and was out of the picture. Meanwhile, I got down to business and started really using those super new tires. I ran as hard as I could for the rest of the race. I never saw anybody or passed anybody—and at the end of the race I was ahead of everybody. People were standing around scratching their heads, saying, "What the hell happened? Where did he come from?" Parnelli was saying, "How could he win the race? I never even saw him."

We did exactly the same thing at St. Jovite, and they didn't figure it out there either. At the next race Ford did it too, without knowing why. They just said, "Donohue comes in early and wins the race, so we've gotta do it too." I suppose they eventually figured out the real reason.

We had no more than solved all our problems when a fresh one came up. Peter dropped out of the Elkhart race with a broken driveshaft. We had been having some difficulty with the driveshaft all along—like whipping and being out of balance—so our natural reaction was that it ought to be strengthened. But the American Motors engineers insisted it was strong enough as it was. When we looked a little closer we discovered that the rear spring perches had broken, and the axle housing had rotated until the driveshaft universal joints had failed. So we thought that the spring perches ought to be strengthened. When we looked at it a little more objectively, and realized that they were already stronger than any we had built before, we decided that rear axle hop in braking was what had *really* caused them to break. Having been through that before with the Camaro, we knew the answer was in modifying the rear shock-absorber valving. We simply increased the "low-velocity leak" characteristics—and no more hop, no more broken driveshafts. You can tell that race cars are *really* getting complex when you can correct driveshaft problems with shock-absorber valving.

We had effectively lost the Championship by then. When Ford got their act together there was no way we could overcome the horsepower deficit. I finished second or third in the last three races, and wasn't even close. The Mustangs were just flat faster, even though we were about equal in durability and tires by the end of the season.

Roy Woods came to us at the last races, though, and said he was interested in buying our cars to campaign the next season. I had already noticed how professional the Woods team looked, considering they weren't a factory effort—especially when one of their Camaros had won at Donnybrooke. I suppose Roy is planning to become another Roger Penske, and he certainly is doing a better job at it than most of the other team owners. He's gotten some good sponsors, he hires good men, and he keeps his cars in good shape. It's just that sometimes he doesn't do the right things. Apparently he isn't quite as dedicated as a team owner needs to be. Sometimes it seems like he's just drifting along. He finally did end up with some sort of American Motors contract in the Trans-Am when we got tired of it. My only regret about Roy was that he wasn't afraid to hire our guys away. He even bought up Gene Owen from Traco, which put one of our development programs behind schedule. But I suppose now we would do the same thing ourselves, just to survive.

We actually built three Javelins in 1970. In addition to the two good racers we had another junkbox car that we used for development. So I told Roy he could have the two race cars right after Riverside. The day after the race we had a little checkout session in my Javelin, with Roy, his co-driver Milt Minter, and Paul Van Valkenburgh. Paul instrumented the car to get driving performance comparisons on all of us, as Bucknum and I had done with the '69 Camaros. It was kind of educational to me, also. Even though none of them was as fast as I was, the recorder charts showed that Milt was noticeably faster in two corners. If we had had time, I might have tried some of his lines.

I didn't feel I had to be as careful with the car anymore. It wasn't just that it had been sold, but that it was going to be totally disassembled and rebuilt before it was raced the next season. After we all had our turns in it, I went back out on the track and really thrashed it. I drove as I had seen Parnelli do with his Mustang. I used more rpms and I shifted with reckless abandon. There's another little trick that Parnelli used in his driving technique. Most racing drivers think that the fastest way around a corner is to just touch the apex of the turn with your inside front tire. Well, when he really got in a hurry, Parnelli would clip the apex with his *outside* front tire. Of course, that sprays a little dirt and gravel onto the track, but I guess he figured the other cars would have it cleaned off by the time he got back around again. I didn't want to destroy the Javelin, but with one thing and another, I was able to knock over half a second off my qualifying time—set when the car was fresh.

Roy seemed really happy with the cars. He talked with Roger and American Motors about it for a long time, and I promised I'd give him all the information and parts and drawings he needed. They stripped the bodies and updated them to 1971 Javelin sheet metal, and as we developed our new car, we made all the latest pieces available. They even used the same Traco engines we had, although they had some externally-caused problems with them. They bitched at Traco a lot—as everybody does. It turned out to be a pretty good deal for both of us, though. They did a good backup job in 1971.

I decided that we had learned enough about durability and performance so that one strong car was all we needed to win the Championship in 1971. Of course, if that car got severely broken we could always buy back one of the nearly identical Woods Javelins. We kept the third junkbox car to use in developing our new 1971 Javelin, and we really did a great deal of work over the winter.

The first thing we tried to do was optimize the front geometry. A-arms had to be basically stock, but in the interests of safety we could use any upright. Not only were we interested in safety, but we wanted to have the stiffest upright possible, and to locate the spindle and all mounting points to give us an Unfair Advantage in geometry. Don Cox designed a beautiful fabricated upright that used a live axle—it rotated in huge bearings *inside* the upright—and adjustable ball-joint mounts top and bottom. Of course, all the steering-linkage geometry was adjustable also. Earl MacMullin, the chief mechanic on that car, spent weeks setting up half a dozen totally different layouts on the surface plate in our shop, so that we could quickly change from one to another at the test track. We had every possible combination of roll center height and equivalent swing-arm length. There was a low roll center, short swing-arm; low roll center, long swing-arm; high roll center, short swing-arm; and so on.

We took the development car and all those alternate geometries to a skidpad we use near Ontario Motor Speedway. After days of switching back and forth, trying to find the optimum static camber, camber change curve, and steering linkage, we came to the conclusion that all of them were about the same, except for two. We rediscovered that a high roll center with long swing—arm caused sudden breakaway due to the "suspension-jacking" effect. And I made a new discovery. A low roll center with short swing-arm may have good skidpad performance, but it is very difficult to drive. The wheels make such rapid camber changes over bumps that the car is hard to steer, and it feels uncontrollable even in a straightaway. After the skidpad work we went to the Ontario road racing course and confirmed our findings. In the end we concluded that there was really no outstandingly good geometry between those two bad extremes. We finally selected what was basically the stock suspension geometry, with the axle raised about three-fourths inch on the upright to get the chassis down where we wanted it. That gave us a roll center at the ground, and an equivalent swing-arm length of about seventy inches. We never did get around to trying anything else on the rear suspension after our "gronked" axle housing failed. There isn't much you can do with a solid axle under SCCA rules. We've always used longitudinal leaf springs with a simple Panhard rod for lateral locating. It's simple, light, cheap, and it gives us a roll center about where we want it.

At the same time we went through another big brake study. I wanted to get away from the booster system, because it was just another area where something could go wrong, and high pressure on the front calipers was causing some overheating. I suggested that we try *two* calipers on each front wheel to give us the proper balance against the single calipers at the rear. Cox said that would never work, because of the high fluid displacements needed and because the extra rotor shielding would block cooling airflow.

But I insisted we try it anyhow, so we set it up for the Ontario tests. In simply breaking in new pads and warming the brakes up, they got so hot that they actually caught the car on fire. What happened was that the heat melted grease out of the suspension, which then ran onto the rotor and ignited. We were testing late in the evening, so Cox was able to see the rotor glowing red hot. I was driving relatively slow, and he came running out to the track, screaming that the brakes were burning up. I had to stop and put the fire out, which caused no great damage since we were using the old 1970 development car with a '71 front end on it. We probably could have solved the cooling problem somehow, but he was right about the excessive pedal travel required. After the brakes warmed up, the pedal was just too low. We left the double calipers on for a while just to confuse the opposition, but they never worked as well as the booster did.

While we were testing at Ontario, Roger drove the car quite a bit, and he really had a good time. He tried and tried, but his laptimes were always way off. I think the problem was that our new "American style" of driving was unheard of when he was racing. And that's a hard track for even current drivers to learn, with a lot of high-speed cornering and changing-radius turns.

The serious work was in trying to find a better Goodyear tire for the '71 season. It's really hard to pick out a good tire for Trans—Am sedans, because those cars are so violent. Hardly anything will hold up to that kind of punishment. We had seen the principle of "fall-off" on our skidpad, where tires would depreciate in performance when they were really "leaned on." Some tire designs literally crumble under abuse. Our first 1970 tires were light and sticky, and they'd smoke and flop around like a rubber band, and even blow out when they got really hot. You could watch the car and see all the compliance. Conversely, the NASCAR tires we had started using were relatively stiff and hard, so all Goodyear drivers were using them by the end of 1970.

The guy who actually identified the proper design was J. M. Smith, a really talented Goodyear tire engineer who kept track of all the tires and data. After a couple of days he just said, "I think these are the right tires for you." We tried them again and again, and no matter how hard I abused them, they never fell off. They were kind of a compromise, but quite a bit better than the NASCAR tire. They did have a lot of compliance like the old tires, but it never got worse as they heated up. It's really not so hard to drive with a tire that's as flabby as a wet dishrag. Once you get used to it, it's just like driving on a tire that's going flat.

That was all the vehicle development we did for the 1971 Javelin. After that, we went back to the shop, started with a new bare chassis tub, and built a new car as perfectly as we knew how. The approach was straightforward. We built one super car that was strong, easy to maintain, and had no major engineering "breakthroughs" that needed to be debugged. It was a fabulous car. From the beginning it was almost bulletproof, and we never had any serious problems with it all season.

Over the winter we also did a lot of power development with the engine on Traco's dyno. We worked especially hard on the exhaust system, finally ending up with four tail pipes that were as short as we could make them, and recessed into the floor for ground clearance. That alone gave us almost fifty horsepower—at lower rpms, anyhow. We ended up with a maximum of only about 440 horsepower at the peak, but we broadened the torque curve a great deal to get the low—end power we thought we needed.

The Trans-Am died about that time, however. There were a lot of reasons, but what hit us the worst was that the rules never stayed the same, and our cost practically doubled every year. The cars became so tremendously complex that they could cost $60,000 just to build and develop. And they were so refined—so sensitive—that we could go from understeer to oversteer with a twenty-thousandths change in the anti-roll bar. Finally, most of the other factories decided not to support the Trans-Am. Ford was an unknown for 1971, though, because there seemed to be a lot of dealer support for a team. But we could tell that there wasn't going to be another dog-eat-dog, drag-out battle.

The season opener at Lime Rock was really a tremendous example of the Unfair Advantage. Parnelli was there in his Bud Moore Mustang, but without factory dollars. In the first few laps he got pushed off the track and the car got bent up, and that was the last I saw of him. He was going to come to the next race, but in fact I guess that was his last professional road race. That really is an unspectacular way to end a career. Follmer was my biggest competitor for the rest of the year. He won the next two races when I had some little difficulties. At Bryar, my carb floats stuck open while I was in the lead, and I couldn't even get back to the pits.

Mid-Ohio was a really terrible drive for me, because of the power brake system. Early in the race it developed a leak between the engine and the vacuum brake booster, making the front brakes almost useless. In the rain it wasn't so bad, but when the track dried out I had to drive like hell just to finish second. The worst incident was in our pits, though. Roger always positions himself exactly where the nose of the car is supposed to stop—to guarantee that I won't overshoot the pit. That's a pretty strong show of confidence in my driving ability; you might say he's putting his life on the line. Well, that particular time it was almost tragic. I really misjudged how much distance I needed to stop with just the rear brakes working. I locked up the rear brakes and went sliding right through the pits. I hit poor Roger, knocked him on the hood, and carried him about fifteen feet. The pit crew always has just one job on their minds—no matter what the circumstances—and they were running along behind, trying to get gas in the car. Paul Van Valkenburgh had the pit next to us, and if he'd been in at the same time, we would have pinched Roger about yea thick.

At Edmonton a spark-plug electrode broke off and fell into the engine. Fortunately I was far ahead, so I just kept going on seven cylinders and still won by a little bit. That spark plug almost caused an embarrassing situation with the mechanics. At the start of the year I had tried hard to convince Roger that Earl MacMullan ought to be crew chief on the Javelin. Roger didn't want to promote him to a number-one car right away, but I said I would work closely with him—sort of taking some of the responsibility myself. At Edmonton, however, I was so exhausted from other programs that I had to leave him more or less on his own. And then that spark-plug problem almost cost us the race. I was out there struggling around the track thinking, "Earl has got to go." I was on the verge of firing him. I managed to cool down after the race, and when we looked more carefully, I realized it wasn't his responsibility after all. Over the years he's continually grown even more capable and responsible, and today he's not only one of the best guys we have, but he's a really close friend. It goes to show that you can't snap-judge people out of their jobs. If you consider your mechanics as people, they'll always do right by you.

After that we won six races in a row and wrapped up the Championship. It was a fairly easy year in the Trans-Am. We had the car ready in the beginning, and we just went and won races with very little drama. It was mostly a matter of Earl and Blaine Ferguson keeping the car maintained and well tuned. There was no development work to be done, and no pressures from the crew. I would just fly in and tell them what to do—and it would be done.

By the end of the season we realized that there was no reason to continue in the Trans-Am. We let Woods have the American Motors contract to continue in 1972. Roger had made a deal to sell our Javelin to a Chevrolet dealer friend of his. It was a gift to his kid who was coming home from the Army. I never met the guy—Bill Collins—because the car was delivered at Riverside while I was driving a USAC race at Trenton. He did fairly well with the car, even though it began to deteriorate after a few races. When we sold the car we said, "Here it is. Keep it like it is and you'll have no trouble." The trouble was that they just didn't know all the little things you had to do to maintain it. Otherwise they had a good operation, but it only lasted one year.

Chapter 17

1970–71

LOLA-FORD (USAC)
Engine Trouble (and Poor Decisions)

In 1970 we were more or less disassociated with Chevrolet products in racing, and at the time the four-cam Ford engine was winning all the USAC races. Roger had been professionally friendly with all the right Ford people during our Trans-Am days, so he went to Detroit and gave them a call. I suppose they were honored, because they seemed happy to have us run a Ford motor for a change. Roger bought some of their motors, and I'm sure they gave him a really good deal. We asked Traco if they wanted to handle our rebuilds on the Fords, but they weren't interested, so we went down the street to Falconer and Dunn. Danny Jones, who had done the development on the turbocharged versions, was with them, and he promised us everything we needed. They were up-and-coming guys, and they seemed to be anxious to have our business.

For the chassis we took our four-wheel-drive T152, which did so well at Indy in 1969, and sent it back to Lola for a rebuild. I told Eric that I wanted another car just like it—only with two-wheel drive and fitted for the Ford motor instead of an Offy. By March we had what we thought was the right combination for USAC. We took the car to Phoenix to test before the season opener there. We were all set up to do our development work to make certain that everything was right for the year.

We couldn't even start the motor! Danny was there—and he could not start it. As it turned out, someone had left a bit of paper between the points of the dual ignition system, and it took a couple of days to figure that out. But even at its best you had to be a magician to start it. You squirt fuel in the intakes, crank it, turn the pumps on, turn them off, close the throttle, open the throttle—it was a nightmare. I sat there patiently for a few days while they messed around, and then I finally became angry. I let them know that I wasn't too impressed with their ability to get it to run. Even when it finally did run, I didn't feel it was that much greater than the Offy. We eventually spent so much time with the motor that we ran out of time to develop the chassis. We forgot about Phoenix and decided to test next at the newly-opened Ontario Motor Speedway.

The motor was performing quite a bit better at Ontario, for short bursts, anyhow. After a few days of chassis sorting, I was able to run a 170-mph lap. We were the first people to do that at Ontario, and it was a big deal at the time. But after that run Danny looked at the motor and said it was running a little rich, so he leaned it down one click, and I went out to break my record. I went one lap and burned a piston. We put in another motor, and proceeded to make approximately the same mistake again. I don't know how many times that happened. We never did get a good figure for exactly what the fuel mixture should be. The fuel injection was a Bendix unit from a Piper Navajo, which senses air flow and meters the fuel accordingly. Apparently it was getting confused somewhere on the track. I could see there was a lot of black magic involved, and that Falconer and Dunn knew as much about it as anyone did—which was virtually nothing.

Somewhere along in there Ford transferred their racing engine business to A. J. Foyt. So then we were dealing with experts at Ford, Foyt's, and Falconer and Dunn, and I'm not sure that anyone really had good control over the operation. The fuel flow problem was so critical that we sent some of our motors to Foyt. Don Cox went there for some of the dyno runs, and he could tell that if anyone really knew what they were doing, they were keeping it a secret. I think Danny Jones was trying to keep everything a big mystery because he didn't know anything about it—and he didn't want anyone else to figure it out. It was a big political hassle between us and Danny, and Foyt, and Falconer and Dunn, and maybe even other competitors. It was hard to get the right story about anything.

Eventually Indianapolis came up, and we were neither too good nor too bad. I had the fastest speed early in the month, but we didn't seem to progress. A lot of other drivers there caught up and passed me by qualifying day. I managed to get fifth on the grid. The race itself was anticlimactic. I just drove around most of the day while other cars fell out, and I ended up second behind Al Unser. Since Al seemed to be fastest, we had copied his body shape, sort of a wedge that George Bignotti had come up with. He was also running a locked differential that year, which we *didn't* copy. We had it on our Trans-Am cars, but we really didn't know enough about Indy

courtesy of Indianapolis Motor Speedway

PENSKE AND DONOHUE, LOLA-FORD

cars to believe it would make any difference on a USAC oval. He was faster going into the turns, and we didn't make the connection. It was a matter of copying the wrong things.

Then we went to the inaugural Ontario 500, and we managed to make things worse. Danny kept telling us that the Ford engine had to have lots of cooling. At Indy it ran hot, and at Ontario it was worse, so I decided that we must have more radiators. We ended up with oil coolers and radiators everywhere—engine, transmission, oil, intake, exhaust—until the car was just one big heat exchanger. Of course, every time we added something the car picked up weight and aerodynamic drag, and it got slower. That was simply misdirection on my part. Instead of taking the time to analyze the problem, and use logic, I just did the simplest thing—I tried to cure the symptoms.

Meanwhile, we read plugs constantly, and we blew engines constantly. My runs were mediocre, and I qualified way down. We were just a mediocre team. I'm convinced that will happen whenever a team doesn't understand what they have in the engine or chassis—and we *didn't*.

The race came, and I lasted about six laps. I came coasting into the pits and the announcer was screaming, "Here comes Donohue in for an early pitstop! He's gonna make a surprise tire change or something." I said, "Roger, the motor is blown." He couldn't believe it. He said, "No it isn't! Put more fuel in and go back out there!" So I ran one more lap. But that was it. There was a big hole in one of the pistons.

For the next year's USAC series, 1971, we went with McLaren's M16. But until we found out how good it was, we kept the Lola-Ford around, and made a deal for David Hobbs to drive it at Indy. The first two USAC races of the year are at Phoenix and Trenton, where everybody runs their old cars while getting their new ones ready for Indy. It was much easier for us to run the Lola-Ford there while we were testing the McLaren.

Phoenix was more trouble than it was worth. I had never driven with those guys on a little one-mile oval before, and that takes a bit of learning. To get around somebody who is only a little slower, you have to set him up for a few laps—running literally inches away—then "slingshot" him out of a turn to get on his *outside*. The idea is to get between him and the wall, and hope he sees you and gives you room. That gives the best line into the next turn. Anyhow, I only qualified ninth, and just motored around in the middle of the field to finish sixth. What made it such a hassle was that the Ontario Questor race was the same weekend, which required a lot of flying back and forth.

Then we went to Trenton, where the transmission failed in the race. At first we thought it was the clutch, because the engine kind of revved up while the car coasted to a stop. I'd never experienced that before, so I didn't think to put it in another gear and drive to the pits. I just parked it in the infield—fortunately. When those transmissions fail under all that strain, a lot of pieces get thrown around in there. One tooth breaks off a gear, and all the rest get peeled off with it. It's much cheaper to shut it off quickly than to destroy a gearbox by driving into the pits.

I think that was kind of an early-warning system that we didn't heed properly. We had already heard that some of the other guys were going to bigger gears. The Hewland gears were breaking, and Ford had made up some stronger ones. We simply didn't pay attention—and a month later the same problem knocked me out of the lead at Indianapolis with the McLaren. In the same race David Hobbs had it happen to him in the Lola-Ford. The gear broke coming out of turn four, and the car slowed so fast that another car had to swerve out around him. The other car hit the wall and rebounded into Hobbs. David wasn't hurt at all, but that was the end of the Lola-Ford.

I was so discouraged over the loss of the race that I couldn't have cared less about the Lola at that point. As far as I was concerned it had always been a failure, in spite of its second-place finish at Indy in 1970. Mechanically and aerodynamically it was a mess, and the cost of rebuilding the five or six Ford motors we broke was just astronomical. But a lot of our problems were my own fault. With all my other racing development programs during those years—with the Javelin, the Ferrari, and the other Lolas—I just wasn't organized enough. We weren't analyzing, we weren't learning, and we weren't gaining. We didn't do a geometry study, we didn't experiment with wings, we never understood the chassis, and the engines were too complicated for anyone to handle. Then I messed it up more by adding too many coolers and continually changing everything around at random. Even if that car never had an Unfair Advantage, and even if it never won a race, hopefully it was a good example of exactly how we *shouldn't* run a racing operation.

Chapter 18

1969–71

LOLA T190/T192 (FORMULA A)
Searching for Wins (and Racing Formula One)

The final race of the 1969 Formula A series was to be held a few days after Christmas at Sebring. It was supposed to be an International race, so all the big-name blokes were going to be there. Andretti had a Lotus-Ford, Savage was in a Plymouth-Eagle, and then there was Hobbs, Cannon, Posey, and all the rest. At that time of year Lola usually comes out with a new car for the next season, and the competition was looking very close between the F-A cars of Lola, Lotus, Eagle, Surtees, McLaren, and Brabham. So Lola's American distributor, Carl Haas, approached Roger with an offer. He said, "Eric Broadley has this fantastic new car, and I'd like to have Mark drive it at Sebring for me." Carl and Roger have been friendly competitors for years, but this one time Roger agreed to work with him. He said he would agree if our mechanics were allowed to prepare the car—just to make sure that we knew what we had. They worked out the financial arrangements relatively easily—about who paid for what—but there was another complication. Roger wanted the car to be painted Sunoco blue and carry our number six, and Carl wanted it to be white with number ten, because that was his driver's identification. So we compromised. We painted it blue and ran number ten, and everybody was happy.

We were saddled with the preparation and transportation, however. Roy Gane had been head mechanic on my Camaro all that year, which had been a very difficult job. It had required tremendous effort on his part, and he had seen enough racing for the year. Toward the end of a season all racing mechanics seem to become tired of racing, and the pressure, and the people, and even the world in general, and Roy was suffering from that disease. But he was still one of the best men we had to handle that race. To give him a hand, we decided to borrow Bill Mayberry from George Wintersteen's team. "Murph" had worked for us before, so we knew he was a qualified guy, and he wasn't doing much over the winter. Roger wouldn't have to pay him for the whole year, and he was taking a load off Wintersteen's racing budget. The trouble with that was that Roy was having trouble coping with a team effort, and Murph figured he was capable enough not to have to listen to Roy.

I expected to get the car fairly well set up from Eric anyhow. He and I talk a lot about design, and I had told him that the short-wheelbase McLaren Can-Am car I drove in 1968 had exceptionally good handling. I said that it seemed to be the hot setup, especially when you have basic understeer problems. If Eric believes something you say, he usually tries it on his cars. In this case he even went a little overboard, in building the new chassis with an eighty-eight-inch wheelbase. It was so short that the driver sat pretty much between the front wheels. Other than that it was relatively conventional for the time, with nose-mounted front wings, and the suspension-mounted rear wing that was still legal. Of course, as has always been the case with Lola, the car didn't arrive at our shops on time.

In the meantime, Traco was preparing a super 302 Chevy to put in it. Al Bartz had left them to start up his own engine shop, and he was becoming famous for powerful motors of his own. He was working with McLaren, and taking away some of Traco's business in Formula A. He's a nice enough guy, but he was claiming some thirty horsepower more than Traco was, which is fairly hard to produce. Traco was feeling the bite, and they saw the Sebring race as a chance to show that their own motors were still pretty good.

The car arrived late, and the engine arrived late, and we started getting everything put together late. Right away Roy and Murph and I got into a debate over whether the wings should have end plates. I had checked them out and decided they were the hot setup, but those guys both had different ideas. They were saying, "Why end plates? Nobody else uses end plates." So the whole project was a fight from the beginning. Murph wasn't working directly for me, and he had some Formula A experience, so he reckoned he knew what was right. Roy was tired of working, period. None of us were getting along well. It was really an ill-fated venture.

After they had installed everything and got it all plumbed up, we couldn't start the engine. We fooled around and fooled around, until finally I called Traco. They knew it was perfect when it left their shops, so we looked for something that had changed since then. Finally I discovered that a control rod between the throttles and the fuel metering valve had gotten

photo by F. David Stone

LOLA T192

in the way during installation, so the guys had rerouted it. I should have realized then that they didn't know anything about the engine, but we were late and we had to carry on.

Because we were late, Murph had tried to come up with a faster way to plumb a fuel filter between the tank and the fuel injection. Mechanics are always looking for the simple way, because it's usually lighter and it makes less work for them. The filter we ordinarily used was big and heavy and required a special container, so Murph came up with a smaller one. He said everyone else was using it, and I didn't know any better. I said okay, just so long as everything got done. Of course, it was just before Christmas and nobody wanted to do anything, and I wasn't going to get into a fight about it. I decided the filter was a mechanic's judgment. As it turned out, it was our downfall.

We left for Sebring, and the weather was terrible, as usual. The airport was closed, the truck was late getting to the track, and no one seemed overly anxious to get everything done. We were a day late through inspection, and everyone else had a day's practice already. I was becoming quietly frantic. It was a terrible situation for me, because I couldn't seem to get control. I was trying to be nice, but we had to get the car ready. And the car was starting to look bad. I had gotten used to having a Penske car that was really clean. So I started to clean the suspension myself. But they told me to go away—they said they would clean it eventually. Except for our new paint job, it looked so terrible that I didn't even want to be involved. It was a grim, frustrating time for me.

Finally I got in some practice, and fortunately the car was good. We never had time to take it to the skidpad and check it out, but Eric said that he had tested it in England. He said to use certain springs and bars and it would be fine. That was my first Formula A race, so I didn't know much about open-wheeled cars with wings, but I tried as hard as I could to learn in a hurry. After some very short lessons, I was fast enough to qualify third behind Andretti and Savage.

The race was made up of two 100-mile heats—and I didn't finish either one. I was much faster in the straightaways, which was making Traco look good, but the fuel filter clogged up and starved the motor. In the first heat I dropped out from second place, and in the second heat it happened while I was leading. We expected it the second time, but there was nothing else we could do about it but put in a clean element. Everything else was looking really good—and we were stopped by an undersize fuel filter.

When it was all over I was really angry. We had showed everyone that we had the fastest car, but we just hadn't put enough time or care into the preparation. At that point I decided Roy and Murph weren't doing the job we expected of them. They just didn't seem to care as much about details, and about winning races, as I did. I didn't need to say anything to Murph—I just decided that we wouldn't use him again, and he went on to be a good mechanic for other teams. Roy was working for us full-time, but he had managed to alienate the guys around him so he had to go. I told him that he was one of the best mechanics we had, but that it would probably be best for both of us if he went where he could work more independently. It was really hard for me to do. Both of them were great guys—Roy even came over to my place a lot—but that was the only way I could see to avoid a lot of hassles and remain friends.

That car—the short-wheelbase Lola T192—went back to Carl Haas, and he sold it to someone else. Lola sold a lot of cars based on our performance, which has helped us maintain a good relationship.

Late in the next season things started looking grim in all our other programs. That was 1970, when I was second at Indy, and we couldn't seem to win any races with our new Javelins. Roger started saying, "We've got to start winning races somehow." Wins are all that count in the business. Seconds are nowhere—especially to our sponsors. We thought that our chances might be better in the Formula A series again. So Roger called Broadley and said, "Hello, how are you? Do you have anything new?" And Eric said, "Yes, we have a new T192 for the '71 series, and it looks good in tests. We would like to try it in some races." They worked out a deal where we would get the test car in time to run the last few races. It was such a quick, low-budget deal, we didn't even take time to paint it blue. That car was white, but at least it carried our number six.

The short T190 was obviously all right, but Eric decided that a longer wheelbase was better, so the T192 was basically the same car, only somewhat longer. But the car was late as usual, and we barely had time to get to Mosport. We quickly ran it on the skidpad, and learned that it wasn't quite as good as the T190. Not having any idea why, or time to fix it anyhow, we took it to Mosport relatively untested. When we got there I realized I could hardly keep the car in a straight line. I was having terrible problems just trying to hang on. I didn't know if it was the overhead wing or the longer chassis or the new low-profile tires. By sheer concentration I was able to qualify it second to David Hobbs' Surtees. I was discouraged. We were supposed to be the super team, but Hobbs was faster and there was nothing I could do about it. It looked as if we were going to take a dump in that series also.

Fortunately for us—it was a godsend—it rained the morning of the race. Everything changes in the rain. The rain tires are much bigger in diameter, and they have a lot more compliance, which smooths out any problems in the suspension. I figured that if I was going to win that race, I was going to have to be first into the first turn. If you're behind someone in the rain at Mosport you're really at a disadvantage, because you can't see to get around. I was on the outside of Hobbs, but I decided I was going to go deeper into the first turn.

At the start I watched David and waited until he braked, and then I braked. Immediately I realized that was too late! They had just put up a guardrail around the outside, and as I slid toward it I was thinking, "Oh Christ! Fifty feet off the start and I'm going to crash!" At least I could keep the car parallel to the rail, so the impact load would be spread out evenly between the front and rear wheels. Somehow I managed to hit perfectly, and the car glanced back toward the track. It was such a jolt that it damn near knocked me out. I knew the car was finished.

But when a race car gets damaged, no matter what bends, the first thing you notice is that the steering wheel is at some odd angle. When I slid back onto the track I realized that the wheel was still straight in my hands. I thought, "Hey! Maybe it's all right after all!" Surprisingly, no one but Hobbs had passed me. They all held back to see where my car was going to go. I was still in second place. I struggled after Hobbs, and caught up to him at the hairpin before the straightaway—where *he* made a mistake, and I slipped by into the lead.

Racing in the rain has usually been a lot of fun for me, because it's relatively slow, the forces are much less—and I frequently win. In that race, tires could also have been a deciding factor, with my Goodyears versus Hobbs' Firestones. But it does take some skill, good vision, and tremendous concentration. At the finish I was almost a lap ahead of Hobbs. That really pumped up the whole team. We were all tremendously happy to win for a change.

After the race I said, "Because of the rain, we were saved. Now we have to find out why the car handles so badly." It was so "darty" I could hardly steer it in a straight line. Because it wasn't so bad in the rain, I was sure that tires were the answer. So I had the Goodyear guys make me some dry tires with characteristics more like rain tires—with more compliance. I figured that in Formula A everybody had bad cars and tires but they just got used to them eventually.

Goodyear had the new tires ready two weeks later for practice at the Mid-Ohio race. I tried them on the car, and on the first lap I could tell they were worse. And the car was just as "darty" as before. But because Goodyear had gone to so much trouble, and because I really wanted those tires to be better, I tried harder. I thought I would drive a few more laps to try and figure it all out. If that wasn't it, I didn't know what the next step was.

I crashed the car again. It got away from me in a tight turn, and I spun across some concrete apex markers. It literally tore the bottom off the car—right where I was sitting. I was *some* sore for a while. The chassis was bent up, the tub was ripped open, and one of the fuel cells was broken. I said, "Well, now what are we going to do?" It was Thursday afternoon, and we had a broken car. We could either run away from the problem and be quitters, or we could try to fix it and come back for the race. So we loaded it into the truck and hauled it back to Philadelphia, where we could repair it faster.

We got Bill Scott, who is good at fixing mass damage, to come in and make a big patch for the tub. Then we put it on our big surface plate and tweaked it back into shape. Harold Cummings, who can talk the ears off a fireplug, was able to get our new fuel cells through air freight on Saturday, without waiting for customs to open. All of us worked night and day to get the car back together late Saturday. The truck pulled back into Mid-Ohio Sunday morning. I warmed up the car for a few laps to prove to the officials—and myself—that it was truly repaired, and I started the race at the back of the grid. I knew we still had the handling problem, but at least it was no worse, and I was able to fight my way up to a third place.

Again I said, "We've *gotta* find out what's wrong before we go any further." We went back to the shops and prepared some other fixes. When we tried them out on our skidpad they looked a little better, so we decided to test again. We went to Summit Point, which was a new and bumpy track, thinking that a solution there would be good anywhere. But the car was getting fragile after my two accidents, and it just barely lasted through the first day. A lower front A-arm pulled right out of the chassis. It happened slowly enough so it didn't cause me any excitement, but we could see that the tub was completely worn out. That particular area had looked scary anyhow. Now the chassis was pretty well destroyed, and we still hadn't found any answers to our handling problems. By then we had decided where the problem *wasn't*—in tires, or wings, or springs, or geometry—but I was truly mystified as to where it *was*.

The last race, at Sebring again, was only a few weeks away. We *had* to win that race. We had put too much effort into that program to let it dribble down the drain. I called Eric Broadley from Summit Point and said, "Look, we've ruined this chassis, and even when it was running, I couldn't keep it in a straight line. Now what?" He asked some questions, and I spent some time going over all those things we had tried already, to prove that it wasn't anything obvious. Finally Eric said, "I think it's in the front track and the chassis. We'll build you a new tub, and you can put all your parts on it for Sebring." I agreed, under the condition that we could have the new tub in one week, so that there would be time to test again. But he had a condition too, that we run with a low, chassis-mounted rear wing. I didn't reckon that a low wing could beat a high wing—but then I didn't think they could get us a new tub in one week either. I later heard a lot about the pressure Eric's shop was under for that week, but they got the job done for once!

When we got the new tub it appeared basically the same—it had to be, to mount our old parts—except for one area. The front A-arms were shorter, and the pickup points were wider, to give it the same overall front track. It was also much stronger at the pickup points. Apparently the problem was simply too much flex in the front suspension. Not only had that caused the handling to be erratic, but it was an explanation for the mounts tearing out. There's no way you can eliminate flex completely, but by shortening the A-arms Eric had reduced the leverage on the chassis. Eric is really clever sometimes, and I admired him for that job. I was lost in the woods, while he was able to interpret what I said and see the forest. With that stiffer chassis, the car was cured. At that point it was transformed into a fantastic vehicle.

Once we knew the basic design was fixed, we resolved to do the rest of the setup right, too. That involved our standard procedure of a geometry check in the shop, going to the skidpad, and finally a track test of the final product. When we got to the skidpad I thought the car was damn good. Don Cox, our new engineer, was in the act on that car, and he wanted to see what a good car felt like, so I let him take it around. Well, it sometimes happens that little stones get kicked up into the throttle bores, which can jam the throttle open. After a few laps that happened to Don, and he went sailing over a mound and bouncing through a field. After that we began taping shop rags over the inlets—there isn't enough airflow to be a problem on the skidpad—but Don was never interested in driving again.

We had just enough time to spend one more day at Summit Point, if we went directly to Sebring from there. I reckoned that the high wing was going to be better, but I wanted to live up to our end of the bargain with Eric, and I thought the car was enough faster that we could make up the difference.

So we set up the car with the low wing. It was a relatively good shape, and it was mounted well back where it ought to be. We worked out the wing angles, camber angles, and ride heights until I thought everything was just right. That was an exciting time for us. Everything was falling into place for a change. We left for Sebring, optimistically hoping that the lower wing might be an advantage in lower drag on the straightaways.

When we got there we made a strategic decision not to let anyone know what we were going to do. There was lots of speculation whether a high wing or low wing was going to be better, but we were already committed. To confuse the issue, we used the high wing for warm-up. Of course, the car wasn't balanced for that wing, and it didn't handle well at all. Then, just before qualifying, we put the low wing on, and qualified on the pole. We really had everybody wondering about that. They all had high wings, and we had the fastest car on the track. A couple of cars got ahead at the start of the race, but I managed to win without too much difficulty. Eric couldn't have asked for better advertising.

That was obviously a great thrill for me, and our team also. Not only did we need the win for Penske Racing, but after the tremendous effort and aggravation, and the heartache of the race the year before, it was a great victory. To come back with a car that was properly tested and sorted—to have the Unfair Advantage—to pull it off . . . it almost made our whole terrible year worthwhile. At that point I thought we had the best-handling, most fun car in the world. Traco was now looking good also. A lot of their customers were coming back because we had done so well. Actually, their greatest advantage all along has been reliability, because no one can really get much more horsepower out of the same basic motor. Everybody usually has all the same parts to work with, whether it's in motors or chassis or tires.

About that time we started hearing about the Questor race at Ontario Motor Speedway. It was to be the challenge race of the year—Formula A cars versus Formula One cars, the Americans versus the Europeans. And it was at a road course none of us had raced on before, although I had tested there. After the Sebring race I figured that the Lola handled well enough, and went fast enough, so we ought to put on a fairly good show against those Formula One blokes. My second thought was that if we *weren't* able to beat them, at least we ought to have the best-looking Formula A car they had ever seen. That was Woody Woodard's car, and I told him to spend all the time and money he needed, to prepare it as beautifully as possible.

Right away, I told him to chrome all the suspension parts. Everyone else said, "No, you don't wanna do that. You'll get hydrogen embrittlement and acid damage." Those were all the logical arguments, but I said, "What do we care? We're just going to run the car in this one race." I insisted, so Woody pulled everything off, Magnafluxed it, polished it, and chromed it.

Then he took the tub apart and painted that, and we had the body refinished and painted Sunoco blue.

In the middle of all that the SCCA changed their roll-bar rules. We had to have a new bar with different braces. Eric knew all about it, and he was making new ones for other 1971 cars, so he said he'd send us one that would fit—but, of course, it would be a little late. We were just finishing up and getting ready to leave, when in came this horrible bent-up piece of junk that looked as if it was hammered out by plumbers in a blacksmith shop. I said I wasn't going to have a thing like that on a car that was so nicely prepared and polished otherwise. So we fit it to the car and then ran it over to the platers. There was scale falling off it, and it was the worst-looking part I had ever seen Eric build. Trouble was, we didn't have time to clean it and polish it like all the other stuff, and when we got it back from the platers, it still didn't look so good. But we put it on the car anyhow—and that was ultimately the reason we lost the race.

I didn't know many of the European drivers—except Hulme and Stewart from the Can-Am—and I hadn't taken a good look at their cars before. They seemed to have about the same power, but they were smaller and kind of funny-looking. For all the sophistication and expense, they didn't seem all that much faster on the track. Traco had made certain we had every bit of power that a Chevrolet engine could put out, so we seemed fairly equal in that department. The Formula One cars had thirteen-inch wheels on the front, compared to our standard fifteen inches all around. It was the first we had seen that, but there wasn't time to experiment. As it turned out, those tires may have been quicker, but they had a chattering problem in the corners, and they were overheating in the high-banked turn one. At that point I decided that the greatest difference between Formula A and Formula One was that their motors had three liters and cost $20,000, while ours had five liters and cost $5000.

Our team was looking good. Unfortunately the other Formula A cars and drivers weren't in such good shape. Our best road racing drivers—Revson, Follmer, Savage, and Posey—were in pickup rides that were neither well developed nor well prepared, and the big-name USAC drivers like Foyt and the Unsers couldn't learn the track fast enough. I had tested there with our Javelin, so I had one Unfair Advantage in at least knowing the track a little better. For all the work we had put into our car, I don't think any of the Europeans even noticed it. I guess they reckon that any car with a production American motor must be junk.

We had a USAC race in Phoenix that same weekend, so I was shuttling back and forth between practice sessions at both tracks. On Saturday afternoon, immediately after the Phoenix race, Mario Andretti and I had to fly to Ontario to qualify. We took a helicopter from the track to the airport, the

STP plane from there to Ontario—thanks to Mario—and a car from the airport to the track. Not surprisingly, neither one of us qualified very well.

In the first-heat race the next day, it seemed as if my car was just a little bit quicker than the Formula cars. It was a game of inches, and I slowly picked up places until I was running third. The rather partisan crowd was excited about an American engine and driver doing so well, but to me it was just another race to try and win. I don't recall any particular awe at being able to pass those great Formula One drivers. After all, Mario's Formula One Ferrari had come up from behind and passed *me*. Then—on the last lap—I ran out of gas! The engine started sputtering, and I barely made it around to the pits. Instead of a strong third, we got knocked down to ninth.

We had the situation in hand for the second heat, though. We put more fuel in and made a little correction in the suspension. The car had been too perfectly balanced at the start, and during the race it began to oversteer just enough so I couldn't gain on Mario or Stewart. In the second heat my car was *really* running right. I moved from ninth up to third behind Mario and Stewart within a few laps. And then my damned engine sputtered and died again, just like it did before!

As it turned out, it hadn't run out of fuel at all. What happened was that the fuel-tank vent had clogged, which kept fuel from flowing out of the tank. And that occurred because it vented into the chromed roll bar, where scale had broken off and clogged the vent. The roll bar cost me a certain third, and the way the car was going, we might even have won the second heat. The interactions on a race car are so complex that you never know where your mistakes are going to come back and haunt you.

I'm glad Mario won the race, but it would have been better if he'd done it with an American engine. It was a good idea and a good race, but it died. If I had won with a Chevrolet, we might have saved the concept. As it was, Ron Grable was the highest-placed Formula A driver—seventh. We cleaned out the roll bar and vent and sold the car to Brett Lunger, who ran it all the next season with no trouble.

Chapter 19

1971

FERRARI 512
What Breaks
(That the Factory Can't Fix)

Our dealings with Ferrari started out with a guy named Kirk White, a used-Ferrari dealer in Philadelphia. He had a lot of contacts with wealthy Ferrari owners, and he wanted to make a big name for himself in racing. I think he was also a bit of a dreamer about what you can get out of racing—compared to what you have to put into it. He thought it might pay off, somehow—or at least not cost anything. Not being a mechanic or an engineer, he didn't know how much preparation we have to put into a car to make it competitive. He went to Roger Penske and told him that he would provide a Ferrari 512 and all the parts if Roger and I would prepare and race it. Roger didn't take him too seriously at first, but then we put some thought into it. Long-distance racing has always been attractive to Roger, and it's not often someone offers us a *free* race car. That was the original thinking, anyhow.

But a characteristic of Roger is to keep changing the ground rules whenever he can see a more profitable way to do something. Through the whole program it never stopped. It was like a running gunbattle between him and Kirk. And then there were the promotion aspects. Kirk had a newsletter to keep his Ferrari owners abreast of racing developments—promoting Kirk White's "world's fastest Ferrari." It annoyed him that Roger kept making *his* name smaller and the *Sunoco* logo bigger on the car. He would say, "Hey, how did Sun Oil Company get in on this deal?" It was a constant battle between them.

When the Ferrari arrived at our shops nobody was very impressed. It was a year-old 512 that Jim Adams had raced on the West Coast for Hollywood Sports Cars. It had a few races on it and was really beat up—by our standards. I wasn't too sure where to begin with it at first, but Roger said, "Do something! *Work* on it." That's easy enough to say. We decided that first we would try it out on the skidpad. It was understeering a little too much, so we rounded up some springs and bars and got it balanced pretty well. Then we decided to use our instrumentation to find out what the aerodynamic lift and drag were like, and to improve them if possible. But where was the nearest place to do it in the middle of winter? Roger was becoming known in Reading because of his Waterbor Truck Leasing company there, so his manager, Lamar Heydt, arranged for us to use the Municipal Airport. We did the best we could, in spite of all the people who were there to watch that strange, loud car. But the runways were too rough to get good lift data and too short to get up to reasonable coastdown speeds, and there were grades and winds. We spent a couple of days getting nothing. Then we went to Summit Point Raceway, which we could rent for five dollars a day, and sat around in the rain. Finally I ran the car once in the cold mist, and we went back to the shops. We didn't discover anything that was too encouraging. We realized that the engine was okay at full throttle and okay at idle, but there were difficulties in between. The fuel-injection cam was going to need development. The plugs were fouling, the oiling system seemed weak, and the dry-sump system looked kind of backwards. Also, it seemed to have a tremendous amount of front-end lift under acceleration, probably due to poor aerodynamics and suspension geometry. If we could have started from scratch, there were a lot of things we would have done differently. At least it could be driven, though. There were no really serious deficiencies.

Winter was upon us by then. The plan was to totally rebuild the car before Daytona, but Woody Woodard was the only guy we had working on it. When we realized we were going to need somebody else, Roger got Lujie Lesovsky to come in. Lujie is a great old guy, a "master craftsman." We can't afford him full-time, and he doesn't like Pennsylvania very much, so whenever we really need him we "rent" him from John Holman, of Holman-Moody. We end up paying roughly double his normal salary, but the guy is *so* good that we can't do it any other way. Sometimes we just can't find anyone else who is that capable, because he seems to be able to do anything better than anyone else. But one of the most outstanding things about him is that nothing ever gets him too angry. Guys who are that talented are usually belligerent—the prima donna. They want to sit at the head of the table. But Lujie is soft-spoken and meek, and he works well with anyone. He's gotten a lot of respect that way. Everybody in the shop likes Lujie. The trouble is . . . he'll come up here to work for a month, and there will be so

photo by Hal Crocker

Ferrari 512

many things for him to do that he'll end up staying for three. It's very expensive, but worth every penny.

We had heard rumors that Ferrari had a new body for the 512, which made it lots faster. So Roger sent some guy to South Africa where it ran for the first time, and he got a bunch of pictures of the new body. Then we had Lujie rebuild our 512 to mount that kind of body. He and Woody stripped the chassis down to nothing and reinforced it where it looked weak. Then Lujie built the entire center section from scratch. It took a new cab, doors, windshield, and fuel tank structure. Even the plumbing and wiring was done our way. We try to prepare our cars from a common-sense standpoint—unlike Ferrari, apparently.

We did make one small misjudgment, though. We tried to make our own bodies again, as we had with the McLaren in 1968. The factory bodies were very heavy and very expensive and didn't fit well, so we went back to Berry Plasti-Glass. They made a mold for us and produced a lighter body—at a tremendous cost. It would have been justified if we could market them, but Roger didn't want to sell to our competitors. The expense made no sense at all for one or two bodies. At the time Roger was thinking that maybe we could run the car in the Can-Am, and that Berry could then produce a lightweight open version of the coupe. That simply turned out to be a poor decision on Roger's part.

At some point Roger decided it would be keen for us to go to Italy to select the extra pieces we needed. He told Kirk we were going to need some bucks, because that was Kirk's end of the deal, and he was still trying to do what was right. So we went to the factory, and we were well received. They were all quite cooperative. They wanted us to make sure we ordered everything we needed. We looked at all their new wheels and bodies and brakes and things. Roger even decided to buy a new Ferrari Daytona for his own personal transportation. I remember them asking me if I wanted one too. But $20,000 for a *car*? I couldn't *conceive* of it! Ultimately Roger even got another one, which really made me envious.

After a day or so we decided we knew what we had to have to get by. We'd selected an extra motor and gearbox, plus suspensions and all sorts of other spare parts. Then they came to us with the bill all totaled up—and we had to start subtracting things. They weren't doing us any favors at all. What we had asked for turned out to be so incredibly expensive that it was completely out of the question. We pared the list down to a bare minimum, and then went to their financial guy and tried to make a deal. Roger finally got some special arrangements, like a spare gearbox as sort of a loaner. With everything ordered, we went home to wait for the parts and to prepare the car. But ordering parts and getting parts are two different things. With a lot of phone calls and telexes, we at least got a new motor fairly soon.

Back in the shop we took the old motor out of the car and sent both of them to Traco. Roger thought we should have the factory rebuild the old one, but I convinced him that the communications and shipping problems were just too great. Traco went through the new motor to see what the clearances were, and they put it back together and pronounced it healthy. But it wouldn't fit on their dyno, so we took it to Champion's dyno and ran it for about a day. We changed the oil pressure and the fuel mixture and fiddled with the timing, and we eventually got a peak of 630 horsepower. That was impressively more than the five-liter American V-8's we were familiar with. Traco rebuilt the old motor to those new specs. Number two only produced about 600 horsepower, with a different fuel-injection setup, but we knew we had two real good motors.

Two weeks before the first race we were to enter at Daytona, we took the car there for a final test. We were late, as usual, so my first laps were run at night. We were all really excited about our new car, especially Roger. I put in a lot of very slow laps, just to make sure everything was right. We were adjusting a wing on the back, and fooling around with the suspension. Roger started worrying about my laptimes, which were about ten seconds slow. But when I was certain that everything was right, I stood on it—and it was *really* fast. Everybody smiled a lot, and Roger was really thrilled. The only thing that bothered me was that the car was a little hard to handle. It had a short swing-arm front suspension, and it felt "twitchy" in braking or on the banking.

We also ran some the next day. It seems that our Ferrari must have been a very newsworthy thing, because there were a lot of people around taking pictures. Perhaps that's a good reason why we usually have late-evening tests the first time out with a car—to make sure we don't look bad to the press while we're getting the car right. Anyhow, everybody was all pumped up about our chances—Kirk White, Sun Oil Company, Goodyear, Sears—and they all got a lot of pre-race publicity out. We still hadn't had time to paint the new cab, though, so to hide it, most of the pictures were taken at an odd angle.

We did a little more testing to determine the right gear ratios, wing angles, and chassis height. In spite of all our experience there on the banks, we were still having spring problems. We had selected about the right rates, but our new springs were collapsing—yielding—under the stress. We also tried some alternate rear-suspension pickup points, and were surprised to learn that the car wanted a relatively high roll center. Don Cox got on the problem and designed some new springs and geometry. With all that in mind we went back to the shop to finish up the car for the race—springs, gears, suspension, paint, pin striping, and polish.

My co-driver that year was going to be David Hobbs. Roger saw him as an up-and-coming young driver who would also be right for our number-two car at Indianapolis. When we told Ferrari, though, they seemed disappointed. When we asked what was wrong, they said it was because he had driven for Porsche and they got rid of him, and he had driven for Ferrari and they got rid of him, and he didn't get the most out of a car, and he got tired, and other wishy-washy comments like that. It didn't matter to us what they thought, as long as we were paying the bills. In fact, I was kind of apprehensive about David making me look bad. I've always been nervous about other drivers on the team being better, because I have to work with the guys in the shop all the time. I have to call the shots, and I feel I've got to be the best driver or they might not respect my decisions. When David went to Daytona with us, I wasn't sure how I was going to handle the situation.

On the first day of practice David went out to run a few familiarization laps. Almost immediately he came coasting back into the pits. He said, "I think . . . even though the shift lever is in fourth gear . . . I think it is in fact in second gear." Sure enough, he was right. There was a compliance problem between the lever and the transmission, and David had sensed something wrong before he let the clutch out in the wrong gear. He could have blown that expensive engine to junk.

Since we were only practicing, we were able to fix it before the race. I was impressed. I thought, "Here is a guy who isn't trying to make me look bad. He is truly trying to take good care of the car and do the best he can." His laptimes were about the same as mine, too—if maybe a little slower and a little less consistent. He always did a great job for us, though. I liked him, the mechanics liked him, and he became good friends with Kirk White.

I think it was because his attitude was so positive. He was always smiling and he always had something good to say about the car—a real pleasant optimist. I think David has found it very easy to sell himself as a driver because he has such a strong, personable image.

The most enjoyable part of the Daytona race for me was in practice and qualifying. Our only real competition was the Wyer Porsches, and we knew we were far faster. They struggled along in practice, changing tires and brakes and suspension, and eventually they reached our time. So I went back out and turned 9000 rpm instead of 8500, and dropped my laptime by about two seconds. Everyone else was trying not to show it, but they were really struggling. When they got close again, I went out and ran 9500 rpm, which was *really* faster. No one had told us what these engines should be limited to, but we generally ran them about 8500 rpm in a race. After qualifying, we acted disappointed about our performance. We went back to the garage area, pulled out that 600-horsepower practice motor, and installed our newer 630-horsepower motor. We really had Porsche worried. We had one car that was faster than all of theirs. The other Ferraris weren't even in the hunt. They had problems with oil pressure and their fuel system, which we had anticipated and solved already.

From our experience at Indianapolis we were familiar with the "dry-break" nozzles they require to avoid fuel spillage. Don Cox had even built a test setup over at Sun Oil where we could try out different systems. So I decided we ought to adapt something like that to the Ferrari, since there were no rules against it in long-distance races. My first idea was to have a dry-break catch tank on the vent also, which would have a vacuum on it to help pull fuel into the cell faster. Roger wasn't for the idea, because it had never been done before and there were too many things that could go wrong. We built a test rig anyhow, just to see how it worked. On the first trial the suction collapsed the fuel bladders inside the frame, sucking fuel into the catch tank before the bladders were full. That obviously wasn't what we wanted. But we decided to leave the dry-break connections on both the filler and the vent, with a clear plastic vent hose to show us when the cell was full. It was the first time anyone had ever done that on a road-racing car, and it was both fast and clean. When the Porsche team saw our rig they complained that we were using two people for fueling, which was against the rules, but they weren't too worried about it. During the race, however, people came around to watch our pitstops. We would plug those beauties in . . . then unplug them . . . and no fuel was ever seen. They were quicker, quieter, and less messy than anything ever done before. That started something—now, that kind of fueling is required everywhere.

It was a close race for a while. I diced with Pedro Rodriguez' Porsche for the lead, feeling it was a "Penske versus the factory" battle. Then both of us came in for our first fuel stop at the same time. My fuelers were so fast I was back out on the track before their crew got Pedro's windshield wiped. Then the race started getting confusing. Little odds and ends started failing on our car—a fuel pump belt, an alternator, the fuel pickup—and gradually we fell back. In spite of the pitstops to fix this and that, we were still running strong, and we could make up a lot of time on the track. Then, at the stroke of midnight, everything went to pieces.

Vic Elford blew a tire and spun his 917 on the banking, and other cars spun into him, throwing up a lot of smoke and dust. The blinking yellow light came on, just as a Porsche 911 and I came around the fourth turn onto the scene. I was coming up very, very fast on the 911—which was in the fast lane—and I instantly had to make a choice between two evils. I could jam on my brakes to avoid passing him, and run the risk of losing control on the banking. Or I could slow down and gradually slide by him in the outside lane. I guess my final decision was that if we *had* to go into an accident, I wanted to be under control, and I wanted to be first so I could pick my own way through. I pulled around him on the outside and began to brake. Suddenly—crunch!—the 911 rammed me from behind. It's hard enough to see another car on the banking in the daylight, because you have to look *up* to see it, and late at night it's far worse. He probably didn't see me until we hit. It wasn't a serious impact, but we were both immediately spinning out of control. All I could think was, "Christ! That was the wrong thing to do." I spun toward the infield, while the 911 tripped and went rolling into the other cars.

Then I made another mistake. In the daylight you can tell which way a car is headed and try to correct it, but at night the headlights are useless while a car is spinning, and it's hard to pick out a reference point. I knew I was into the grass already—and I knew the car was going to hit a barrier somewhere—so I gave up trying to correct it and locked up the brakes. I waited . . . and waited . . . and waited . . . and then—crunch!—the left side of the car slid into the guardrail. The impact wasn't great enough to hurt me, but it tore all the suspension off that side of the car. I was devastated. I had made a deliberate choice, and it turned out to be a serious mistake in judgment. We had put months into that car, and now I had turned it all into thousands of dollars worth of junk.

Somehow I scraped it into the pits on the two remaining good wheels. Woody looked at the car and said it was history. But Roger said, "Let's *try*!" They stripped the necessary suspension parts off another Ferrari that had dropped out earlier and quickly bolted them on our car. Fortunately, the 512 frame was built like a truck. It was made out of 4130 steel, and it wasn't even bent. We patched up the body with ten miles of "racer's tape," fourteen broomstick handles, and anything else we could find lying around.

After a few hours spent rebuilding the car, we went back out and limped around to finish a distant third.

After that I had to try and forget everything that happened at Daytona and start working for Sebring. We sent both motors back out to Traco for a rebuild, while Woody stripped the car and made it new again. All the time we were trying to get parts from Italy. It was a constant struggle—calling, writing, telexing—and they would say, "Oh yes, Mr. Donohue, your parts are on the way." What could I say to that? At that point I must have thought we had the only Ferrari in the world. But now I can understand that they had lots of people calling them for parts, and they just aren't geared for that. We got a lot of used parts from them, too. We would ask for a new halfshaft, and pay for a new halfshaft, and then get a used one. We couldn't put a used halfshaft on a car that had to run a twenty-four-hour race!

We got the older engine back and had the car running in time to go to an early test at Sebring. Besides making sure the car was set up right again, there were three new things I wanted to try. We tested a locked differential—against advice from the factory—and it was faster, as we expected. Ferrari eventually knew we were using it, but they didn't seem to catch on to its value. They reckoned that whatever we did was junk. It's not that they couldn't accept what we did, they just didn't care. They had their own way of doing things, and they didn't want to know our way.

Then we tried a bigger wing, which also made the car faster. We had to replace the small wing that was damaged at Daytona, so Cox said that if we were going to make a new one, we might as well make it bigger and better. He selected a NACA shape and drew it up for Lujie to make. Since it was bigger we didn't have to tilt it up so far, hopefully cutting down on air drag. At that time we weren't aware of sophisticated things like flaps. We didn't even have the wing mounted in a very good location. It probably acted more like a flat plate, or a spoiler, than a wing.

Another difficulty was that we had no way to balance the rear wing forces at the front. We would just crank that thing up until the car had a minimum of understeer on fast bends. It was very easy to go over the limit—to the point where it would lift the nose and give a *lot* of understeer. We were getting so much downforce out of that new wing that the brackets were breaking. We learned valuable lessons about wings then, even though we couldn't say exactly what they were in numbers.

The final thing I wanted to do at the Sebring tests was to change the front geometry. The car still felt "bouncy and darty," which I reckoned was due to the short swing-arm, as we had discovered on our '71 Javelin. We might not make the car any faster, but we could make it easier to drive. Woody didn't want to mess with it though. He figured it was too much work for too little gain. So he went to Roger and said, "Mark wants to do this, but I don't think we should because there isn't enough time." We had to decide who had the authority and who had the responsibility—as far as what we ought to do to our race cars.

That was the beginning of long series of decisions other people made to keep me from jacking around with the cars too much. I would frequently get it thrown back at me when we spent a lot of time on something that didn't work, as opposed to the times when we jacked it around and *did* get the job done. I suppose that's human nature. But you can only expect maybe 30 percent of the new things you try to work right. If you criticize people too much, they're going to stop trying and you'll end up being a copier—a few steps behind. I wasn't mad at Woody for going to Roger, but I was rather discouraged it had to come to that. And after all, Woody had worked very hard to fix the car after I broke it at Daytona. I had to understand that he always works really hard, and he ought to know how much he can get done and still be ready for a race. I let it ride—regretfully.

It looked as if we had a more serious problem for Sebring. By that time we had a lot of hours on our older practice motor, and Traco was having trouble with the newer one. It was hard enough to get the seals and bearings and piston rings to rebuild it, but the heads were leaking. They didn't use a gasket! Ferrari had an unusual design on that motor, where the heads were supposed to seal directly to the block. Traco noticed some leakage there when they tore the motor down, but when we called the factory they said, "Just torque them down properly and it'll be all right." After Traco put it back together, though, we ran it on the dyno—and it only pulled 540 horsepower instead of the 630 we had seen before. We could actually see all the combustion gases whistling out through the gaps. It was one of those last-minute deals, so all we could do was take it to Sebring as a spare. We were stuck with racing our old practice engine, which by then was down to about 580 horsepower.

Then, at the last minute, I sprained my clutch foot. We were loading the car on the truck at two o'clock in the morning, and I stepped in a drain hole. On top of that, we were one man short, so I offered to help drive the truck to Sebring. I felt I had to show them I was willing to put out a great deal of effort myself, after wrecking the car. We left at five in the morning and drove twenty-four hours straight through. We got within 100 miles of the track—and then the truck engine gave up. We had to be towed to the track behind a wrecker.

By the time we got unloaded I was totally destroyed from the lack of sleep and the pain in my foot. So Hobbs practiced with the car and helped the mechanics make last-minute adjustments. Somehow we managed to get the car right, because it was really fast, even with the old junk motor. We sat on the pole and started out well in the lead. Our nearest competitor again was Pedro Rodriguez' Porsche. There was also a new Ferrari 312 there from the factory, for Andretti and Ickx. It wasn't nearly as fast, because of its three-liter engine, but after a few hours it got ahead of Pedro and me because it was making fewer fuel stops. Also, the Porsche people had taken a good look at our quick-fill fuel rig and had come up with a faster system themselves. At the same time, we discovered that we weren't getting all the fuel out of our tanks, which made more stops necessary. The situation looked grim. We had no clear advantage over the long distance. But we were using the quick-brake-change vacuum device that worked so well on the Camaro, so we figured we would get ahead again on the first brake stop.

Being in the precarious position of "behind but gaining," we had to decide what the best policy was. Should we charge for the lead, or relax and wait? I tried to convince Roger that we should hold back for a while, since the other teams could afford to sacrifice a car or two at that pace. He didn't argue, but he was quietly encouraging us to run faster. When I was driving, he continually gave me "interval" signals, such as "minus 20 seconds," then "minus 22 seconds." When he worked on me that way long enough, I got pumped up to reduce the gap. I was trying for every inch of ground I could make up when I pulled up on Pedro in second place.

Our car was so much quicker that I could have passed him any place on the track. But instead of waiting for a straightaway, I decided to pass in a very high-speed right-hand kink. I guess Pedro was surprised when he saw me go by on his inside at that point. That's not unusual at all in oval racing; USAC drivers do it all the time and no one even flinches. But apparently when Pedro saw me next to him in that high-speed turn, he panicked. On top of that, I had to slow down then, because we were coming up on a slower car. Instead of going on back around me, Pedro ran into my outside rear tire. That could have been an accident—but then he banged into me again . . . and again. Finally the tire blew, sending me skidding off the road.

I managed to limp into the pits on the shredded tire, but the loose rubber flailed to death our aluminum fuel vent in the process. I was really very angry with Pedro at that point, and he was mad at me. He came over to our pit and told Roger that I was crazy—*loco gringo*! I had been ahead of him, and I was on the line, but sometimes drivers feel that the best defense is a good offense. So he came around and attacked. I kept to myself, because I didn't reckon there was any sense in discussing it then—what was done, was done. We both lost our chance to win the race as a result. Our car was in the pits for an hour, while we tried unsuccessfully to patch the fuel tank vent. Then, because we couldn't fix it, refueling took much longer on each stop. We just ran as fast and as strong as we could to finish sixth. Pedro had fewer repairs to make, and he took fourth. Later, I began to think that possibly the accident was due to poor judgment on my part. Indirectly it could have been a result of driving all the night before, and having a painful ankle that was all bound up. Sometimes you make the wrong decisions when you don't have a clear mind.

With that, we figured the Ferrari deal was over. Kirk White had run out of money and goodwill, and Roger didn't particularly want to go to the next race, at Le Mans. Everything we had was junk. We had a lot of hours on our old motor, and the new one wouldn't seal. We had used up two gearboxes and all our spare parts, and we had two broken bodies. Kirk and Roger had paid for everything, without the least bit of help from Ferrari. Why should we go to Le Mans? Then we discovered that Kirk still thought Le Mans was part of the deal. He and Roger argued about it for a while, and finally Roger agreed to go if Kirk would pay all the bills—from start to finish. We knew it had to be a real low-budget deal.

We also had to count on Ferrari giving us a new motor to replace the "leaker." Traco rebuilt the old one again to use as a spare, with all new pistons and valves and so on. They even started making their own valves, because of their cost and the vast quantity required. When the new motor arrived, they just opened it up and looked it over, and ran it on the dyno. It was only about 590 horsepower, but still better than our spare.

Because of our other racing commitments, the only extra development we had time for was a little brake work. At Sebring we realized the Porsches were getting a lot more mileage out of their brake pads. Because of our locked differential, I was able to use the brakes more than they could, but they made up the difference in fewer brake changes. The Ferrari brakes weren't fading—the front pads just burned up in a hurry. Once they get over a certain optimum operating temperature, they wear very fast. If you can lower the temperature by 100 or 200 degrees, sometimes you can double their life. Porsche had some real nice brake ducts leading to "cans" surrounding the front rotors. We figured that if they were going to copy our fueling system, we would try their brake cooling system. So Lujie made some stainless-steel shields to go around the rotors, and we ducted more air to them. We still didn't improve durability any, and we never did learn why the Porsches got such long life out of the same pads we had. They must have had good, careful drivers who were very easy on the brakes—or who ran into other cars to slow down. Another possibility, which I considered after we had a Porsche of our own, was that the 917 long-distance car was so unstable in braking that the drivers were reluctant to use their brakes very hard.

Kirk White eventually produced the money we needed, which probably came to about $30,000, and we crated up the car and parts and flew them to France. Peter Reinhart picked them up there and trucked everything to the track, and Woody, Blaine Ferguson, David Hobbs, and I flew over later. I had been there before with the Ford GT program, so I knew my way around well enough to be the team manager. This time I wasn't the donkey. This was my show—and it was one big hassle. There were language barriers, customs barriers, rules barriers—until I thought I wouldn't even be able to find time to drive.

In the first practice session it was obvious that the Porsches were going to be faster. They were doing 240 mph down the straight, while the best we could do was 212. We changed gear ratios and we tried bigger and smaller wings. Nothing made any difference in top speed. It turned out that our total horsepower equaled aerodynamic drag at 212, so that was our terminal speed. Porsche knew all along that they had a good straightaway car, with that long-tailed body. We were now in a "one-down" position.

The Ferrari van was there with all the spare parts we needed—except for more horsepower or a more slippery body. It wasn't supposed to be a factory effort on their part, anyhow. They were just there to help the independents. On the first day of practice I heard a knock in our new engine, and I went to the Ferrari engineers about it. They said, "It's okay. That's just the throttle plates rattling around." But it wasn't my imagination. To make sure other people had the same diagnosis, I hadn't said anything at first. But everyone else noticed it when I started it up in the garage, so I knew I was right. I said, "This factory answer to a maiden's prayers has gotta come *out*! We're not gonna start a twenty-four-hour race with a motor sounding like that." We ran practice with it that day, then pulled it out and put our old one back in. Ferrari was kind of insulted about that. But before long they came around and asked if they could borrow our new "noisy" motor for Michael Parks' Ferrari. I said, "No thanks. That's our motor, and we may have to use it yet. Besides that, I *know* it's gonna fail, and then you'll blame us for it." We were also thinking ahead to one more race, and I wanted Traco to tear it down and fix it before it self-destructed completely. But they kept insisting, "No, no, we know that's a good engine." After a lot of discussion, we agreed to let them use our motor if they replaced it with a *brand-new* one later on. So they took it, put it in Parks' Ferrari, and it broke in the race.

Not that we did much better with the old motor. After four hours I was running strongly in second place when a piece of dirt clogged an oil passage to the cam bearings, and we were out also. In spite of Porsche's speed we were running conservatively and yet staying in the battle until then. Porsche's pace-setters dropped out, and a 917 running behind us finally won. It was just one more frustrating race for us.

Then, instead of giving us a new motor as they agreed to, Ferrari rebuilt the one they borrowed and sent it back to us. We were really getting discouraged with Ferrari. Sometimes we felt we were actually competing against the factory. When Porsche executives asked Roger to meet with them after Le Mans, he was more than willing to listen.

The last Manufacturers Championship race was at Watkins Glen, the same weekend as the second Can-Am race of the season. We had a pretty good idea by then that we had a Porsche deal for the next year. In fact, our chassis development was going to start very soon, even though no one else knew anything about it yet. So we had a couple of reasons for racing the Ferrari at the Glen. It's not far from our shops, making it a relatively inexpensive race. And there was a chance to win some money—especially if we could do well in the Can-Am race there also. Fourth place in the Can-Am would pay better than winning the Manufacturers race. But most important, it gave us an opportunity to see how competitive the Ferrari was in the Can-Am series, and a chance to see the Porsche 917 Spyder we were going to be working with in the near future.

We didn't go to any great effort, beyond general maintenance, to make the Ferrari any better for that race. We knew it was the fastest five-liter car on any track besides Le Mans. Traco overhauled our old engine one more time, and inspected our "new" one from the factory. Maremont spent time with us working on some new shocks, and Goodyear helped us adapt a new tire.

The 917 Spyder was at Watkins Glen for Jo Siffert, who had already done some development driving for Porsche. Roger and Don Cox and I quietly and carefully studied their design. It had a tube frame, nicely designed rear hub carriers, a great many magnesium parts . . . but it wasn't really very impressive on the track. It didn't stand a chance against the McLarens in the Can-Am, with its unblown five-liter motor.

We were looking really good for the six-hour race. I sat on the pole and led the race for as long as the car lasted. Our fuel stops were so good that any fears of the Ferrari 312 beating us on mileage were ill-founded. We were so far ahead that we could afford the extra stops. But about halfway through the race the steering arm broke on the left front wheel, and that was the end of it. There was a steel pin that screwed into the magnesium casting, and we had looked at it and wondered if it was not quite right. But in spite of the fact that we had inspected the casting, no one had ever Magnafluxed the pin. That could have been a very costly mistake. We often worry about pieces that don't seem right, and usually they never break. But it happened once on the Lola spring tower at Daytona, and now on the Ferrari.

We still had a chance to win some bucks in the Can-Am. I managed to qualify sixth behind the 500-inch Chevys and a new seven-liter Ferrari for Andretti. The 917 Spyder surprised me in the race, however. It lapped me once, in the time it took the McLarens to lap me twice. Even without a wing or a turbo-motor, it was that much faster than the Ferrari. We didn't stand a chance to win the Can-Am race in that Ferrari, and I knew it—and I hated it. I'd get stuck behind a backmarker with a big V-8, and I'd have to stay there until he crashed. They would blow me off on the straights, and I couldn't pass in the corners. Then that bloody engine failed again. Andretti was doing fairly well with his seven-liter Ferrari, which made us briefly consider boring our three-liter engines out to that size and running the Can-Am series. But not after that last failure. We decided it wasn't worth the aggravation to deal with Ferrari when all they sent us was junk. The "world's fastest Ferrari" never won a race.

I'm not going to ignore my own contribution to our problems with the Ferrari, as I was mainly responsible for the accidents at Daytona and Sebring. But in spite of that, and in spite of all the careful detail preparation we put into that car, pieces broke and fell off continuously. It couldn't have been all our fault either, because no Ferrari won a race in that series all season, and they finished a distant third to the Porsche 917 and Alfa 33/3 in final points. For not finishing too well, at least we had an Unfair Advantage in laptimes on most tracks, which I think we could attribute to developing a well-balanced car. No one else at that time was aware of such chassis tuning tricks as the skidpad. It was the same old story to us, though.

We had to go through a big hassle over what to do with the car when we were through with it. It was sold, then it wasn't sold, then someone else wanted it. Finally Roger just wanted it *out*, so we trucked it over to Kirk's and dropped it off there. Ultimately it was bought back by one of the guys who had originally owned it. His son had gone to Le Mans and helped us race with it there, and then later had been killed in an automobile accident on the highway. So his dad had the Ferrari restored in his memory. It's now sitting in his garage, as sort of a museum piece.

Chapter 20

1971–72

MCLAREN M16 (USAC)
Winning Indianapolis (After a Lot of Setbacks)

Late in 1970 Roger Penske and I went to Europe to have a look at various cars we might run in the 1971 Can-Am. On the way over we had a discussion about what to do if our prospects didn't look good in the Can-Am—if we couldn't get a competitive car. I told Roger that it might be wise for me to learn to drive the ovals, and go on the USAC circuit. We had done a little of that already, but it was obvious that we needed a better car. Don Cox, our chief engineer, had put some thought into what was necessary. He figured that wings would be the answer, and had worked out a way to adapt them to the Lola chassis.

While in England, talking to Eric Broadley about schedules and costs and designs, we decided to go past the McLaren works. There wasn't much chance that they were going to let us have a new Can-Am chassis, but we had heard that they were working on a new Indy car also. Teddy Mayer, the team manager, was glad to show it to us, because unlike the Can-Am, they were underdogs at Indy, and they might be willing to sell "customer cars" there. The minute I saw it, I knew they already had a better package than what we were discussing with Eric. Gordon Coppuck had designed it with the best features from their experience at Indy in 1970, and some ideas from the Lotus 72. It had a long, flat wedge shape, with side-mounted radiators and integral front and rear wings. They had obviously learned a lot about wings in Formula One, and were applying that knowledge to Indy—as we were planning to do. But they had gone farther, by making it a clean complete package, where our Lola conversion would have been cobbled together. I quietly marveled at their guts, to come up with such a new concept, and it inspired me even more to go USAC racing.

It didn't take us long to decide not to buy a Can-Am car. The 512 Ferrari program began then, and we thought that it *might* be a possibility in the Can-Am later in the year. So Roger started dealing with Teddy. At first we had expressed limited interest. When Roger went back, Teddy wasn't sure whether he ought to let us have one. He had to talk with the rest of the team. He fudged around awhile before saying yes, and then Roger said he wasn't sure. I told Roger again how much potential it had, and finally they came to an agreement.

The first M16 was brought over by McLaren for Denny Hulme and Peter Revson to test at Ontario in January 1971. When they got through we were loaned the car for further tests at Phoenix. Cox and I looked at it and poked at it for a while before deciding on our procedure. We skipped over the usual skidpad tests because that wasn't hard enough work to heat up the tires on a car like that. Phoenix is a relatively slow USAC track, though, so we used it like a skidpad. First we took all the wings off, and we tried to sort out the chassis by itself. We tried all the standard variables—springs, anti-roll bars, cambers, suspension geometry, and so on. We took a careful look at McLaren's asymmetrical camber-compensator link in the rear, and found that it was definitely better—although not so much in laptimes as it was for driver comfort. We tried cross-jacking, or using unequal weight balance on each wheel, and found that the car needed much heavier outside front loading. We also learned that the front springs should be much stiffer than usual. We did a lot of work with a locked differential, too, and found that it was definitely the way to go.

After we had the chassis well set up to my preference, we put the wings back on, and everything was different. However, we had enough chassis experience by then to get it rebalanced fairly quickly. Then we spent a few days optimizing the aerodynamics. We saw right away that the rear wing was much more effective than the front one. We turned both wings up farther and farther until we found the point of stall—where the car just wouldn't go any quicker—then we backed them down a notch to the best position. All together, we spent about a week getting everything the way we wanted it. When our time was up the car was far better, but we still had no idea how it would compare at Indy.

We went there for tire tests in March and got up to 172 mph, which was one mile per hour faster than anyone else. That suddenly got us a lot of attention. The car was really quite good. George Bignotti and a lot of other well-known mechanics came over and looked at our car. They started complaining that the engine was too exposed and that we weren't allowed to have wings. Wings weren't allowed per se, but we had incorporated one into the rear body work, which was required to cover the motor. We had the chief technical inspector over to look at it, and he said it was within the rules, just as front wings were when they were part of the nose. At that point the McLarens obsoleted every other car at the track. Nobody else had allowed for aerodynamic downforce, and they couldn't get their chassis set up in time to use it—even if they could adapt the body. Bobby Unser tried the hardest, with wings and spoilers everywhere, and it got him closest to the three fastest McLarens.

Our old Lola-Ford was there too, for David Hobbs to drive. He was a rookie that year, and he's so entertaining that he got a lot of press. Roger became a little annoyed about it eventually, because he didn't feel David was concentrating enough on the race. We also had to pick up a new crew for that car. Lew Spencer was associated with Hobbs on the Terry Godsall team, so he came over as manager. I knew Lew from the Mustang and GT-40 teams, and even though he was "green" at Indy, I thought he did a great job. We made Bill Blankenship the chief mechanic, since he had done so well under Karl Kainhofer on my car. He became frustrated about not being with the fastest car, however, and started arguing with Roger. He and Roger eventually had a real blowout. They got into a shouting contest over something, and Roger told me that Bill was going to have to go. I stuck up for him for some time, but it kept on—they couldn't cope with each other—and Bill did eventually leave. Even if the boss isn't always right, he's always the boss.

We ran another short test before official practice opened, to get the camber and springs right, and when we came back in May, we set off a bombshell. We unloaded and ran 178 mph almost the first time out. We had raised a few eyebrows at 172, but a jump of six miles per hour was inconceivable. Actually, the car's ultimate capability as built was over 180, but everyone else thought there was some sort of barrier below that. All of a sudden the 1969 "Rookie of the Year" was the focal point. I was like Superman, because no one else had done anything like that before. It was really an enviable position to be in. But I knew I wasn't Superman. I knew others were going to go as fast as I did—but it wasn't a good idea to say it too loud or too often. We went to our garage and sat around wondering what to do next. We were in a state of shock.

About that time Al Unser came over. He knocked and asked permission to come in, because it's an unwritten rule there that no one ever goes into anyone else's garage without asking. Al said, "Look, we've been competitors for a long time, and you have your way of doing things and I have mine, but when you can come here and run six miles per hour faster than anyone else—I gotta shake your hand." I was really impressed. I don't know if I would have been that big a guy to have the courage or sportsmanship to do that. From that time on I've had tremendous respect for Al.

But the nicest compliment came the next day at Lime Rock. I had to fly there for a Trans-Am race, and word of my new record hadn't gotten there yet. Parnelli Jones was there with his partner, Vel Miletich, who was also Al's sponsor. At that point there was some tension between Parnelli and me, because of the Trans-Am accident we had at Riverside, but Vel and I were friendly. So Vel came over and asked how fast I had gone at Indy. I tried not to shout and scream. I just said, " 177.8. " Vel is a great big guy, but he looked like I'd hit him with a bulldozer. He reeled around a little bit, then came back and said, "Of course, you're kidding." I said, "No, I'm not." He reeled around some more, then turned and headed for Parnelli as fast as a guy that size can move. I could see them talking, and Parnelli just sat there gritting his teeth and shaking his head. Vel didn't like being in that position—it was a tremendous blow to his Indy team—but he seemed happy for me anyhow. But the shocked look on his face, and Parnelli's frustration, were the biggest things that happened to me that weekend, even considering that I won the race. Of course, Vel knew I wasn't Superman. He knew that if I could go 178 his team could somehow go that fast too. And, as it turned out, Al Unser did win Indy that year.

By the time I got back to Indy some other drivers had time to realize that it wasn't going to be easy to go 178. Peter Revson and Denny Hulme were driving the two factory McLaren M16's, and they were anxious to find out why my car was faster. Cox and I weren't about to volunteer any information, though, because we had worked long and hard to get an Unfair

McLAREN M16

courtesy of Indianapolis Motor Speedway

Advantage. The McLaren team hadn't done much at Ontario, while we spent a week at Phoenix resolving all the details. I didn't feel at all bad about watching Peter and Denny struggle along.

Then Roger came around and said, "You've gotta tell Teddy as much about their cars as he wants to know. This is a long-term deal, and if you make him mad now, it's gonna mean trouble later. We're ahead now, but they have twice as many people and cars, and what if they find out things *we* need to know?" I could see Roger's reasoning. What good would it be to have the fastest car if we couldn't get parts for it? I reckoned we ought to cooperate—but only when asked. We still weren't going to make it easy for them.

They were smart enough to find out everything they wanted to know anyhow. They agreed on springs, then after a while they agreed on anti-roll bars, and then after another while they agreed on wing angles. We even agreed that the rear wing needed more angle than it had, so Tyler Alexander, their engineer, got their body builders to change the mold for us. That was a genuine cooperative effort between the two teams. There was one thing we didn't agree on, though, and that was the locked differential. Teddy would come over and try to turn one rear wheel, then go off shaking his head. Both Peter and Denny tried it eventually, but they knew it wouldn't work before they drove it, so of course it didn't work.

We practiced some more, and I finally got up to 181. No one else was even close. We were really looking good—until qualification day, anyhow, when we made three big mistakes, or maybe four. In the first place, we were so confident that Roger didn't want us to run any more than necessary. He didn't want to take the risk of an accident. So we didn't go out at all the day before qualifications. Second, we didn't raise the turbocharger boost pressure above what we planned to use in the race. At the time we didn't know how long the motor would run if we boosted it over twenty-five pounds per square inch. Third, when I ran the car in warm-up I thought I felt a little oversteer, but there was so much tension that I just didn't want to touch it.

So I went out to qualify—on a hot morning, with low boost, in an oversteering car—and I ran a very disappointing 177. That was fast enough for the pole, however, so everybody was cheering for me. Then I made the fourth mistake. Teddy came up and asked why I was slow, and I told him that the track was so hot that the car was oversteering too much. I suggested that he use less wing angle in the front of Peter's car. Peter wasn't that close to my times anyhow. He had a lot of engine troubles, and he was in and out of the pits all week.

In the middle of my "polesitter's interview," a tremendous roar went up from the stands, and people started flashing me the number-two signal. In midsentence I realized what had happened, although I didn't know it was

Peter who had done it. It was very hard for me to maintain my composure. Of course, they didn't want to finish interviewing me then. I was destroyed. Later, Teddy said that he had done exactly the opposite of what I recommended on Peter's car, but who knows?

They interviewed Peter then, and he made some comments about that being a fitting comeback for the guy who didn't get "Rookie of the Year" in 1969. We had gone fantastically all month, and we had the pole and the $15,000 award that goes with it, only to have it all snatched away by a guy who badmouthed us a lot. We had helped them set up their cars, and now they were looking better than we were. Later Teddy told me that Peter and Denny were actually better drivers than I was, it was just that I had a better way of developing the car. We were devastated. Our garage was like a morgue.

On carburetion test day we spent a lot of time debating the proper boost pressure. Our engine builder was Davy Crockett, and he was desperate to win that race. That's the kind of attitude I like. But he wanted to turn the boost up, and I was worried about breaking the motor. So we ran a few quick laps to see what there was to be gained in power. The night before the race everybody was leaving the garage except Davy. He said he wanted to hang around a little while. When I asked why, he said he was going to "pat the motor a lot." When I asked him to be more specific, he said, "Well, I think I'm gonna pat the boost screw a little bit too." I said, "Davy, I think that's a real good idea. In fact, why don't you pat it up one more turn for me."

For the race, Peter and I and Bobby Unser were on the front row. I had run with the USAC guys quite a bit, and I knew some of their tricks. I also knew that they were a little annoyed with Peter's attitude. He seemed to be flaunting his position when he went to accept the pole-position award at the drivers' meeting. He was kind of stuck-up about it, which didn't sit too well with the other drivers. At the drivers' meeting everyone is supposed to sit in three rows of eleven seats each, in qualifying order. When Peter went back to his seat, everyone had moved over one place, and Peter ended up sitting on the steps. I think Bobby and I kind of understood each other about how the start would go.

At the start of a race it's very easy to get into a "slingshot contest" with turbochargers. And if two out of three of the front-row cars are together, the third guy is "wrong," whether he's ahead or behind. Going around on the pace lap, Bobby and I went real slow, then sped up together and passed Peter. That seemed to make him angry, so he sped up, and we slowed down. Then he was too far ahead, so he slowed, and we sped up. We were staying out of "sync," which was getting him all screwed up. Finally we got around to the front straight, and Bobby and I gave it a big blast with our motors—and backed off immediately. Peter charged ahead about ten or fifteen car lengths, then looked back and saw that he was too far ahead. He backed off just as our blower pressure was coming up, and as we crossed the start line—all three abreast—we were going about sixty miles per hour faster than he was. It was timed perfectly. He never knew what hit him.

Bobby tried to get around the outside of me in the first turn, but I kind of held on and he didn't make it. I concentrated just as hard as I could for the first lap, and when I looked back at the start-finish line, I could see them back there a ways. So I concentrated real hard for a few more laps, and when I looked back again, I couldn't see anyone. For a minute I wondered if there had been an accident. Then I realized that we were *really* looking good. Almost immediately, a yellow light came out, and we closed up, but I was able to get away again. I was trying to be just as careful as I possibly could. I wasn't taking any chances. I led up to my first pitstop, which went perfectly, and then I repassed Bobby for first place.

On lap sixty-six—how's that for irony . . . the same as my car number—my gearbox broke. I just wasn't prepared for that! I just wasn't ready at all. It happened in the third turn, so I immediately went down into the grass, in case I was trailing oil on the track. I could see that it was all over for me. When the car coasted to a stop, some corner workers came running up and suggested that we push it up next to the infield wall, behind Steve Krisiloff's car, which had been parked there earlier. I didn't care what anyone did at that point. I trudged on back to our pit.

I had hardly gotten back and told Roger about it, when Hobbs' gearbox broke and he got hit on the front straight. We were both out of the race. So I suggested that our mechanics, Woody Woodard and Karl Kainhofer, ought to go back to the fence and watch my car, in case spectators got to it after the race. They got there just in time to see it destroyed. Mike Mosely hit the outside wall and careened into our McLaren and Krisiloff's car in a ball of flame. Our guys were able to stand there first-hand and see our fantastic car destroyed. Karl came back to the garage area with the remains, and he said, "Whatever it takes, we've got to get this car in shape for Pocono—and go there and win the race."

I seldom see Roger out of control of a situation, but I could tell he was really stunned. Not only did we lose the race, but our two $50,000 race cars were destroyed. When he walked past the officials he got really angry, and said, "You *let* that happen! We brought this thing here in a limousine, and we're taking it home in a dump truck." That's the first time I saw him a little desperate.

Suddenly it became obvious that we had done the right thing in cooperating with McLaren—now we needed their help. We sent Karl to England with our broken racer. They set it up on their assembly jigs, grafted on new pieces where necessary, and we had a new tub back within a few weeks. We put it together with exactly the same setup as we had at Indy, and we went to Pocono.

I still had the upper hand there. Peter Revson wasn't around very much, and our car was as much better as it had been at Indy. Bobby Unser had put wings like ours on his car, which brought his speed up somewhat. He went out and qualified faster than I had run in practice. I went out and ran one lap and came in again. I knew I could beat Bobby—but not with all that heat and all that tension. So we pushed the car back to the garage, closed the doors, and just sat around trying to be cool while Bobby was sweating it out. Finally, at five o'clock, I went out and qualified on the pole. That was really enjoyable—to do it in such a careful, calculated way.

The race was a constant strain. Seven times I pulled away from the field, and seven times the yellow light came on and everybody closed up on me. It was like seven separate races. When the last green light came on, Joe Leonard got by me on an oil-slick turn. I repassed him just a few laps from the end, and won my first USAC race. The battle was a little disconcerting for us, but a great thrill for the spectators. Winning the inaugural Pocono 500 wasn't much compared to losing Indy, but it was a good shot in the arm for our team. Woody and Karl were rewarded for all their work, it was the home-state track for Penske Racing and Sun Oil, and I won a new Camaro in the deal.

We went to the next race, at Michigan, and I won again. Bobby Unser took the pole, just because we weren't expecting it and didn't try hard enough. But I got around him in the race and ran away. There were a lot of engine failures there, since it's a high-banked track and everyone can run wide-open throttle more. I almost lost my motor near the end, due to heat and fuel starvation causing it to lean out. I could hear the muffled popping of detonation, so I backed off as much as I could, and eased to the finish.

The race at Ontario was almost a story in itself. We were late, and when I started running the Goodyear tire engineer told me that everyone else had decided on a low-profile twenty-six-inch rear tire. I thought those tires were too stiff and "darty," so I wanted to try the twenty-seven-inch tires. The Goodyear guys won't ever tell what anyone else has discovered because they reckon that's violating a confidence, but sometimes they hint very strongly. He tried to convince me that I didn't want to waste my time with the twenty-sevens. I insisted that it wouldn't take long to run a comparison test, since I had two close ratios in the gearbox that would immediately correct for the diameter effects. We did it, and even though the times were about the same with either tire, I felt better on the twenty-sevens. But more important, I went quicker than anyone else had—which really upset the Goodyear guy. He knew that everyone else would be wanting to switch to the bigger tire. So he asked me to try the twenty-six-inch tires again, just to be sure. About that time Roger phoned us to see how things were going. When I told him we were fastest, he said to put the car away and get a rest.

But I decided to run one more time for the Goodyear people, because they've helped us a lot and they were really anxious. I tried the twenty-sixes, and *no doubt* they were worse. They were very sensitive and unstable entering the turns.

There was time for one last run of the day. I was going to put the twenty-sevens back on and really stand on it, to show myself I was right. The wind was coming up and the sun was going down, so we had to hurry. I burned out of the pits, ran a warm-up lap, and hustled into turn one. I was thinking, "These are really much more comfortable." But I didn't realize that my front tires were still warm from the previous test but the rears hadn't heated up yet. I went into turn three a little faster—too fast—and the rear end started around. There was nothing I could do at that point but try and hit the wall tail-first. I backed into the wall at about 150 mph! The car bounced, hit again, and rolled into the infield. That was it. The impacts tore off the transmission, the wheels, the wings, the nose . . . it was a mess!

They hauled me into the medical office and got a guy to come in and look me over. I was really worried. It was only three days until qualifying, and I didn't want them to think I wasn't fit. The guy started asking me a lot of stupid questions. Then he would get tricky and reask the same question. I got angry and said, "What are you doing?" He said he was testing me for amnesia. So I got angrier and said, "You haven't even put me under X ray. You just ask me a bunch of dumb questions, and my neck is hurting like hell." They gave me some pills and let me go.

I walked back to the garage, and when I saw the car, I *really* hurt. I got into my rental car to go back to the motel—and discovered that I couldn't even hold my head up. The least acceleration caused my head to flop back on the headrest. It was like my neck muscles were disconnected. I had to drive with one hand and hold my head up with the other. I just lay down and rested for a few days.

Meanwhile, Roger sized up the situation. Karl and Woody had been working night and day, so he told them to go and get some rest while he flew in two fresh mechanics from our shop. The four of them worked twelve-hour shifts to get the car back together for qualifying.

Saturday I went out on the track to make sure both the car and I were working right. I was having a hell of a time running 175, while Bobby qualified at 182. Finally I felt comfortable, and I lined up to qualify. I was still on the twenty-seven-inch tires, which no one else was interested in since I had crashed with them. And we turned the blower boost up more than usual. Roger said, "Look, all you have to do is run about 180 and you'll make the first couple of rows." So I came around on my first timed lap at 186 mph! It was so sensational that I consciously slowed down on each following lap, and still had the pole at 185! That was the big payoff for Karl and Woody and all the guys who had worked so long and hard on that car. Everyone on the team was ecstatic.

But that was the race where I ran out of fuel in the lead. We knew that the car would go exactly fifty laps between fuel stops—and no more. So it was at least a three-stop race. I was ahead, driving just as hard as I could as we approached the first stop. I was in traffic, too, which made it hard for me to take time to see the pit board. Roger usually starts giving me warning signs three laps before a fuel stop. In turn four I felt the engine stumble, and when I went past the pits I saw the "in" sign—just as the engine died. I coasted around to the back straight and waited to be towed into the pits.

I don't know how we could have made such a dumb mistake. They had counted each lap up to number fifty, and they knew it wouldn't go any farther. Later I saw Teddy Mayer's lap chart on us, and when he put down "51," he wrote, *"no way!"* When I first realized what had happened I was so angry that I started shouting into my two-way radio. I screamed, "This sonovabitch is out of gas," and then went on from there. I worked in every rotten obscenity I'd ever heard. I was so frustrated that I had to get it out of my system. Some time later I was told that our secretary, Mary Ann O'Donnell, was monitoring the receiver.

We put fuel in it, and I went back out about ten laps down. But running out had leaned the motor enough to damage it, and we didn't finish. By the time it was all over I had calmed down somewhat. I knew it wouldn't be good if the press asked me what went wrong and I said something like, "That stupid Penske let me run out of fuel." It would make Roger mad at me, the team mad at Roger, the sponsors would question our ability—and for what? It wouldn't fix anything. So I took the blame, I said it was my fault. The crew wasn't happy with Roger, but we all make mistakes. I made a mistake and backed the car into the wall, and they all supported me.

We finished out the year by going to a couple of disappointing short-track races at Trenton and Phoenix. I still hadn't perfected the art of the outside pass, which other USAC drivers were experts at. That isn't something you can learn all of a sudden. On top of that, we had more car troubles. The injectors gave us trouble at Trenton, and at Phoenix stones bent the fins closed on our side-mounted radiators until the motor overheated and stopped. I was angry at myself for that, because I knew it was running hot and I didn't try to stop and fix it.

For the 1972 season we sold the M16 and made a deal for two new M16-B's. The second car was for our new driver, Gary Bettenhausen. The new cars weren't much different from the old, except for a wider track, bigger radiator boxes, and a shorter nose that allowed us to move the rear wing back and still maintain the legal length. We tested the prototype at Ontario in January, without learning very much. Don Cox and I were trying to work with McLaren's Tyler Alexander and Gordon Coppuck, but without any real system. Nothing we did seemed to make any difference. The car was about the same in its new state as it was in its old. The problem was compounded by the fact that we never optimized anything. We were bolting on new things and looking for the same six-miles-per-hour step we found the year before—and it just wasn't going to happen. We saw a marginal increase at best. After that, the McLaren guys caucused on their own and decided how they were going to build it. We could take it or leave it, so we took it.

Since the car wasn't changed a whole lot, we decided to skip over the extensive developmen tests we ran the year before. We went to Phoenix and Trenton again. Things still weren't going well for me on the short tracks. I qualified way down and dropped out of both races. At Phoenix, Karl didn't get the right front wheel completely on during a pitstop, and I crashed. He very rarely makes a mistake, but he didn't have the wheel registered on the studs, and when I put the brakes on, the nut just twisted off. Fortunately it was on the yellow light, so I wasn't going fast enough to hurt the car very much.

At Trenton, the fuel injection was so bad that the engine would die in the turns. It got worse and worse until I just couldn't take the frustration any more. What made it even harder for me was that Gary Bettenhausen seemed to be doing a better job than I was. He finished fourth at Phoenix and won at Trenton—in an identical car. I felt so bad about it that I drove home just as soon as I could get out of the track. At the time I was staying in an apartment above the shop offices, and when the rest of the team got back, they came and got me. They said they knew how bad I felt, but that I ought to come down and join them. We never allow drinking in our shops, except for a kind of a party after local races. So I went down and had a few drinks with them. After we got loosened up a little, they started telling me how much they appreciated what I had done to help Gary and the team win at Trenton. We all got very drunk, but I still remember that night as one of the few times when the guys went out of their way to tell me they appreciated my efforts. Of course, everybody always congratulates me when I win, but they were expressing it then when I really needed a vote of confidence.

Right away we had to rebuild the cars and go to Indianapolis for a month of preparation and qualification. That period was *really* depressing for me. I was having to fly back and forth to Germany because the 917 Porsche program was going badly, and we couldn't keep an engine together in the McLaren long enough for me to practice. We had *seven* engine failures before qualifying, and none was ever for the same reason. I lost a rod bearing, a blower, a spark plug, a piston, a valve—and each time we lost a day changing motors. Gary was using the same motors and they were staying together for him. In fact, he was running faster than me, at 191 mph, and he used the same motor up through qualifying,

In the meantime we had heard that the Eagles could go 196, even though they weren't practicing with the rest of us. I'm sure Gurney was promoting false confidence, so that everyone would reckon 192 would be about the quickest. The Eagles never showed up until the last minute, knowing all along that they would take the pole at 196. And I had no chance to practice, to get the feel, to get into the swing of things—or even to think much about Indy. Even when I wasn't off to Germany, Don Cox had the program so well in hand that the only thing I had to do was stand around. I hated not knowing what was going on.

Then, the day before qualifying, I broke our last motor. The only one we had running was one that Gary had tried and rejected in his car. He had found that it was down about 100 horsepower. My only chance was to put the weak motor in my car, but I was resigned to it, since I was so down about my poor showing all that month. The year before I had dominated the place, and now it was a complete turnaround. I was the donkey. I told Roger that it didn't make much difference—that I could at least get in the race. But he wouldn't let me give up that easily. He hunted around awhile and finally found a brand-new Offy sitting in someone else's garage. Thirty-five thousand dollars worth—C.O.D. I told him not to worry about it. I hadn't demonstrated that I could go well enough to deserve it. Roger paced around . . . and paced around . . . and finally he decided to do it. He plunked down the $35,000, we put the motor in my car, and I qualified third on the grid—just ahead of Gary.

The big speed secret at Indy that year was in the blowers. We had the Unfair Advantage in 1971 with better aerodynamics, but turbochargers aren't quite so obvious. We knew there were two available—the 670 everyone ran the year before, and a new 690. What we didn't know was that the Eagles had an even bigger one. My decision was between the 670 and the 690. Because I had lost so many motors I decided to stick with the smaller one, while Revson outran me for second on the grid with the 690 in his otherwise identical car. It didn't really matter very much, though, because Bobby Unser's Eagle had the same four-miles-per-hour advantage over us that we had the year before.

We didn't put much thought to running the bigger blower in the race. I still didn't know why my motors were failing, but I reckoned that the smaller blower was a good way to restrict it. As we got into the race, however, I had second thoughts. Everyone else was just pulling out and passing me at the end of the straights. I told Roger over the radio, "It looks like we made a big mistake."

Bobby Unser, Peter, and Gary just ran away from me. Then Peter broke his gearbox, and he was out. Then Bobby broke his motor, and he was out. Gary was leading the race, with Jerry Grant right behind him in an Eagle.

I started hearing less and less from Roger as he worked with Gary. I was the "other guy" on the team. We came in for pitstops on a yellow light, and because Gary was already there, I had to wait for him to fuel up before I could. I had pretty much given up hope. I had no power, I had a bad pitstop, and I couldn't even see the leaders. Then Gary dropped out—and all of a sudden I was in second place! Roger phoned and said, "You've gotta catch Jerry!"

At that point, for the first time in the entire month at Indy, I really got enthused. I started driving as hard and as fast as I possibly could. Not that I wasn't driving hard before—but then I *really* started taking chances. I was driving way down on the shoulders and taking unusual lines to get around slower cars. In the process, not only did I catch Jerry but I set a new race record. But I couldn't get by him, so it was going to be a battle of pitstops. Then Jerry had to make a stop on the green light, and shortly after that I was able to make a stop on the yellow. I couldn't tell where I was then, so I hollered over the radio, "Tell me where Jerry is!" And just then he slipped by me. But Roger was giving me the " +1 lap" sign that indicated I was a full lap ahead of Jerry because of his bad pitstop.

Roger gave me the signal to conserve fuel then, because he suspected that in fact Jerry had run out. I was so excited I was shouting into the microphone, "Tell me where I am! What's happening? Should I slow down a lot? Should I slow down a little? What should I do?" I had totally lost my cool. After running at the back all month—and through the entire race—all of a sudden I was going to win! I couldn't believe it was really going to happen. I *won* at Indianapolis!

When I drove into Victory Circle I think it was about the happiest moment of my life. They really make quite an occasion of it. They present you with the huge Borg-Warner trophy—and a glass of milk—while everyone crowds around and takes pictures. They even got my mother in there with me, and that was the picture that made the Associated Press. She became famous from it, and was asked to give speeches here and there. Then they took me to the press box and I told everyone about using the small blower. I think I was trying to make it look like we had done it that way intentionally, and I was trying to give an excuse for not running faster in the race. That was one of the few times in my life that I didn't mind winning by default.

But by far the most memorable part of winning was taking the victory lap in the Oldsmobile convertible pace car. A long time had passed since the finish of the race, and the stands were still packed with screaming, cheering spectators. They all looked so happy, like they really meant it. It's impossible to describe the feelings I was having. Roger and Karl were there in the car with me. We had started out together back in 1966, never anticipating that six years later the three of us would still be together as winners at Indianapolis.

People always ask what it's like to race at a track like Indianapolis. I have to distinguish between just driving around in the pack and being in the lead. When I'm behind and not gaining, it's—in one simple word—depressing. But when I'm ahead, and everything is working properly, it's like living in another world. Late in the race the windshield collects a lot of oil from other cars, and it becomes almost completely black. When that happens I don't see a lot. I don't really see the car as such. I can see over the windshield and between the front tires, but everything else is a blur. I'm going very fast, there's a lot of noise from the engine, and I can feel the cornering and accelerating forces rising and falling—as if *I* were the car. By that time I've established a pattern for each lap. I'm working at it without having to think about it. I know exactly how to get the maximum out of the car, and there's no need to try anything new. It's almost relaxing, to know that I'm not on the verge of doing something wrong.

Driving at Indianapolis is like being guided down a corridor by some other force. I get to the end of the straightaway and then its my turn to do my own thing. I do certain things—lift the throttle, brake, turn the wheel. Nothing very fast. Nothing very violent. But everything very precise. Then the car does the rest of the work on its own. I don't ever feel much braking or accelerating, because lateral forces are so much greater. As the car settles into the turn, the lateral forces rise gently to an extreme, then taper off gradually as the car comes out. When tires start working in a corner, the rubber heats up and becomes shiny. As they cool off in a straightaway, they become dull again. As I sit there and watch, the accelerator comes up, the suspension deflects, the steering wheel turns to the left, the suspension rolls, the tires become shiny, the outside wall comes up to meet me then goes away again as the car straightens out. Somehow it seems like I have plenty of time to watch all that. I know all the movements, so while the rest of me is driving the car, my eyes are like a movie camera. It's like running the same reel over and over again, and watching myself do all these things from somewhere else. I don't even see it as a car. I just seem to be part of a well-oiled machine. That's the sensation that's so thrilling to me—knowing that everything in the system is working exactly as it's supposed to. And the longer I'm away from that, the harder it is to understand or describe it. Most people who have never been in that position will *never* understand it.

That's when I lose sight of the fact that racing drivers do something. There is no conscious skill involved at that point, and I feel what I'm doing is the obvious, natural thing to do. The driver is simply doing what the car wants to be done. But you'll never get to that point if the car is screwed up somehow in the engine, or tires, or handling. It's only when the car and I have run a long distance and everything is still working perfectly that I get that funny feeling of standing aside and watching the movements.

The post-race celebrations at Indianapolis were something else. There were tons of people coming around to our garage with congratulations and cocktails. I was trying hard to be polite and thank everybody and still keep my composure. One spectator wasn't able to reach me, but she did give an interesting message to one of the crew. She said, "Tell Mark that if he wants to, he can have my body tonight," and she wrote down her address and phone number. I never did have the nerve to call and thank her for the offer—but *there* was a gal who was truly down-to-earth! Then there was the opposite extreme. I was the last person to leave the garage, and the area was deserted except for one guy waiting at the gate. He told me he was an old racer from Florida who had come up to see me win, but his friends had left without him and he had lost his wallet. He wanted me to give him enough money for the bus ticket home. I don't know how good his story was, but what else could I do? I had just won a few hundred thousand dollars, which I wasn't sure I deserved. So I reached in and gave him thirty dollars. I felt pretty good about that. But there have been times when I wished I could find that girl or that old man again.

It was a long evening. I changed and went to a bar to meet the rest of the team for a television interview. But they were late, and while I was sitting there having a drink, the bartender came up and asked if I wasn't Mark Donohue, the guy who had just won the race. When I said yes, he became so amazed about me being all alone on my big night that he bought me another drink. Pretty soon, everyone else at the bar heard about it and bought me one also, so I had a whole row of drinks running down the bar and around the corner. By the time we got to the television studio I was weaving. We did the show, but I heard later that not only was I pretty funny but that I was a little too gross for television, and they had to edit the tape somewhat. Then we had dinner, which most of us slept through, and I went to bed—alone. When other racers asked how the night ended and I told them, each one of them said, "Boy! When I win Indianapolis I'm gonna spend the night hookin' it up everywhere!"

But the next day everything always goes back to normal again. When the clock strikes midnight it throws you back down on the ground. We had to get both cars ready for Milwaukee. That was another short track and I had never raced there before, so I just watched Gary and did what he did. I still wasn't very good on short tracks, but late in the race I got around Gary to take second to Bobby Unser. After that I wasn't the latest big USAC winner any more. A serious accident in my 917 Porsche caused me to disappear for a few months.

After I won at Indianapolis one of the most frequently asked questions was, "How did it change your life?" Not much, really. Maybe it would have done a lot for me if it hadn't been for the accident. For a while it looked as if I was going to get some good speaking engagements, and some endorsements, and some other long-term deals. But all that stopped while I was in the hospital. When I reappeared, the enthusiasm had died down. Roger took advantage of the win and made some real smart moves, and all our sponsors were happy, and it helped the morale of the team. But not much happened to me personally. I got a lot of congratulations, but it seemed as if most of them were directed to Roger. I'm not bitter about the way things turned out. It's just that everybody seems so disappointed when I tell them that "success" didn't change my life very much. The nicest, and one of the most frequent, compliments directed to me was that I was a "gracious" winner.

My next USAC race was at Trenton. Gary had broken his arm in a sprint car accident, and I felt I had to get back in action after three months in the hospital. Roger did me a favor by arranging a test there, so I could get in some practice and find out if my leg was strong enough. I was particularly anxious to avenge my terrible performance at Trenton in the spring. I didn't qualify well, and I had a hard time getting back into the swing—getting close, being aggressive, and passing on the outside. I was also having trouble with my left leg. It was still so weak I couldn't hold it against cornering forces, and it kept falling over on the brake and accelerator pedals. That hurt my performance quite a bit until I found a way to wedge it behind the clutch. Toward the end I started getting the feel again, and I made a late-race comeback, working my way up to second.

At Phoenix I was looking even better. Through sheer effort I was able to qualify on the pole for the first time at a mile track. But then I jumped the start too much, and when they sent us around for another lap, Andretti and both Unsers jumped me. Bobby Unser, who is the master of the outside pass, was long gone. Finally I settled down and concentrated on the correct technique of passing. First I practiced on slower cars, then faster cars, and eventually I began to get comfortable at it. Then the blower failed while I was running third, and I was out. Don Cox saw what I was up to though, and said, "You may not have finished, but that's the best race you've ever driven on a short track." Roger didn't see it that way. He decided after that race that I should stop driving on the short ovals. As far as he was concerned, I was relatively noncompetitive in that area. I knew what it was that I had to do, and I was learning how to do it, but Phoenix was the last short-track oval I ever drove. It was also the last time I drove the McLaren—an anticlimactic end to our great Indianapolis-winning combination.

Chapter 21

1971

MCLAREN M19 FORD (FORMULA ONE)

European Drivers Aren't Supermen (Any More than Americans Are)

Some time after the Formula A-Formula One Questor race in 1971, Roger started thinking about running a Formula One car at Watkins Glen. I suppose he's always had Formula One in the back of his mind, and since we ran so well with the A-car we thought we might stand a chance. Because the Mosport race is sort of a preliminary to Watkins, we could run two Grands Prix if we could get a car. Roger started looking around at different manufacturers. The Tyrrell seemed to be fastest. March and Ferrari were very close—except that we'd had enough of Ferrari with our 512, and March was unproven. Because of our good established relationship with McLaren at Indianapolis, that seemed the obvious tie-in. We had always gotten good cars and parts from them relatively inexpensively. And, after all our development work, we had shared enough information at Indy for them to run as fast as we did. We were already cooperating successfully.

Eventually Roger made a deal with McLaren for us to run one of their cars at Mosport and Watkins Glen. Roger must have been paying something for our sponsors, but I don't know how those deals work. At the time, Denny Hulme and Peter Gethin were driving for McLaren. But when Peter heard he was getting bumped for two races, he quit the team and went to BRM. Things weren't going so well with McLaren at that point anyhow. It looked as though their M19 needed more development.

Teddy and Tyler Alexander, their chief engineer, came to me and suggested that if I was going to race the car, maybe I ought to go to England and help them sort it out. That was their first season without Bruce McLaren, and they seemed to have a need for a good driver-engineer. Roger was a little worried about that. He was concerned that when we exchanged information they might gain more than I did. That didn't bother me, because I didn't think I knew enough about those cars to tip McLaren off to any great secrets. They had been building cars for a long time, and I felt that we could learn something valuable from each other. And we would both probably interpret what we learned in different ways—and go off in different directions from there. It was going to be sort of a technical workshop—a fair exchange where neither of us got a better deal. During that time I got to know their designer, Gordon Coppuck, who is quite knowledgeable about cars and a very clever guy. I think we agreed that it's impossible for a new guy to come in one day with all the answers. My biggest contribution would probably be to drive the car and simply interpret what it was doing in engineering language. Not everything I thought was correct, and not everything they thought was correct, but we agreed on many different things.

That was also McLaren's first season with something called a rising-rate suspension. The springs and linkages were arranged so that as the suspension deflected, the spring rate increased very rapidly, until it was extremely stiff. The idea was to allow a soft rate for small bumps, and yet prevent the car from ever bottoming on the suspension or the ground. In addition, the suspension seemed very wide compared to what I had driven before. And the car had a sort of Coke-bottle shape, and an unusual rear wing. Instead of being a wing with flap, it was two little wings, one ahead of the other. The four-cam three-liter Ford motor was supposed to be the ultimate in racing engines, but in spite of all the thrashing around and the noise it made, it didn't seem to do anything more than our pushrod Chevrolet motors could do.

When I agreed to do the tests I told them the first thing I wanted was to go to a skidpad. They didn't understand anything about a skidpad, and they didn't want to know about a skidpad. But I insisted, and they found one on a military base somewhere. It was bumpy, and a different radius than ours—which prevented laptime comparisons—and of course it was wet most of the time. We spent a day there without learning anything.

The car seemed to be understeering, but when we changed springs and anti-roll bars, nothing happened. It was just totally unresponsive. It didn't make any difference what we did—it always felt about the same. Sitting still, it was soft enough to push up and down, but on the skidpad it acted as though the suspension was locked. It was the strangest thing.

I gave up and decided that maybe we ought to go to a track after all. We weren't ready, but what else could we do? The skidpad only shows a few things, and we had to keep hunting and exploring for possible answers. We went to Silverstone, and the car was just as bad. It didn't seem to understeer all the time, nor did it seem to oversteer all the time. It was a

photo by F. David Stone

McLaren M19 Ford

"nothing" car. Denny had raced it all season without much success, and nobody else had any answers either. Now, there I was—the great test driver who was supposed to sit in the car and tell them what was wrong with it—and I just couldn't feel a thing. After a day at the pad and a day at Silverstone the car wasn't one way or another. It had so many variables that it was impossible to work with. Not only did it have the normal complications, but the rising-rate suspension made it beyond comprehension. I suggested that we go back to their shop to have a closer look at it.

In time I eventually began to see that as the spring rate rose it rapidly approached an infinitely great rate. No matter how soft the springs we put in, they would still go to this very high rate at the end of their travel. That was probably why none of the softer springs we tried seemed to have any effect. I said that the first thing we had to do was try to adjust the rising-rate curve, to get away from the extreme changes in it. There were some links that could be shortened or lengthened to change the point at which we were operating on the rate curve. Of course, the interactions meant there were other effects—like raising the car and changing the camber—that also had to be dealt with.

At the same time I reckoned a rising-rate suspension *might* be all right in front, but it was probably wrong for the rear. In the front suspension a big problem is bottoming when cornering or braking, and certainly rising-rate springs should help that. The problem is in the rear, where the spring rate gets stiff while accelerating out of a corner—which can cause oversteer. With rising rate at both front and rear, it's almost impossible to predict. The car can go from understeer to oversteer depending on the acceleration or braking pitch angle. The only way you could cope with all those things happening at once is with a computer program.

I suggested we try just one thing at a time. The front suspension was an integral part of the car, but the rear suspension was mounted on a removable cross member. They scrounged up parts from another car and mounted up a rather conventional layout for the rear. That gave us a chance to work on the front rising rate without complications from the rear. We finally got way off the rising-rate curve, and softened up the spring rate a great deal. I was having a hard time, coming in there as a new driver and asking them to change everything around. I tried to be very careful not to offend anybody. We took the car to Goodwood with all those revisions—and it really felt much better. Then we put the old setup back on and it was worse again. Finally we could see some progress.

It isn't easy to test a new car on a new track. In the first place, it takes some time to learn where the track goes. At Goodwood the biggest problems are that you can't see where you're going, and there are a lot of high-speed bends that are hard to memorize. Otherwise it's kind of fun to try to figure out the right line. I think everybody was standing around saying, "Here comes Mark Donohue, and he's gonna smoke everybody off." I wasn't about to smoke anybody until I felt comfortable, and I couldn't get comfortable in that car.

Denny Hulme was there too, and he drove some, but he just sort of stood back and watched quietly. He didn't even seem particularly interested in what we were doing. While we were working he would go lie down in the pits, with an I-couldn't-care-less attitude. He was very nice to me, but I interpreted his actions as laziness. I guess he was doing a lot of things between Formula One and the Can-Am, and that was his time to relax. That seems to be a way of life for some race drivers. They reckon they're gonna be driving forever, and that if they just stumble along everything will be all right. Why become overly sensitive, or concerned, or turned on by any particular program? It was hard for me to understand that kind of attitude, because I could never be that way myself. Maybe that's how some drivers burn themselves out, and some go on racing—somewhere down in the pack—forever.

There was one thing that Teddy did to Denny's car that really shook me. He put a stiffer anti-roll bar on the front, and it *reduced* understeer. When I saw that—and it worked!—I threw up my hands and said, "Boy! We are *really* screwed up. I just can't understand how everything we do could be working backwards. Certainly the law of gravity hasn't been reversed." We were really in the woods when that happened. Eventually we managed to come up with a reasonable explanation. Apparently the roll resistance of the stiffer bar prevented the chassis from rolling over onto a sudden infinite spring rate on the outside wheel—which would give automatic terminal understeer. Maybe that wasn't what was happening, but it was the best explanation we could think of.

After two weeks of testing in England we really didn't come up with much of anything. We did manage to determine that we ought to go with conventional suspension on the rear and rising rate on the front. I also quietly figured that maybe we shouldn't have rising rate in the front either, but it was beyond changing at that point. Since we had simply stuck an arbitrary suspension on the rear, we probably could have made it better. We could have moved points around a little to tailor it to the car if we'd had time. But English weather and racing dates stopped us, and we resolved to continue development later at Mosport.

We started our Mosport tests two weeks before the race, assuming that would be plenty of time to get everything fixed. We were prepared to stay with the rising-rate front and the conventional rear, and just try to get the best out of them. The first day I tried to get the car softer in front to reduce the understeer—and it worked, for a change. But then, apparently, I went too far, and it seemed to oversteer at high speeds. I was hoping to correct that by optimizing the rear suspension—forgetting, for the moment, the possible effect of the rear wing.

Unfortunately, that test session was cut short also. Going down the hill into turn five, a 180-degree hairpin, the brakes failed. They were there for an instant—then nothing at all. There was no time to do anything but drive straight into the embankment outside the turn. Luckily the car just plowed up the face of the embankment like a bulldozer and nosed over the top. It was a bit scary, though, coming down that steep hill toward the corner and not being able to stop. The problem was simply poor preparation. Fluid was leaking out of a loose fitting in the front brakes. After that ride the suspension was all disconnected and the tub was folded up a little. We stopped testing and took it to our shop to rebuild. At that point the executive decision was made to paint my car Sunoco blue. There had been a conflict between Sun Oil and McLaren's Gulf Oil sponsors, but eventually Teddy conceded instead of Roger, because he was having some problems with Gulf.

As we rebuilt it, I was thinking that as bad as it was, we ought to stay with the springs, bars, and wing angles we had found already. But now we had the opportunity to go to our own skidpad. When we did, I still saw the terrible low-speed understeer. The car was only doing about 1. 1 "g" lateral, when it should have been up to about 1.4 with Formula One tires. So we worked, and fought, and tricked bars and springs and cambers all around, until we got it up to about 1.3 "g." Then we went to Mosport—and I couldn't even drive it. It just felt *terrible*. That meant, of course, that I could expect to qualify in the middle of the pack—which I did.

Just before the race the rain came. Again it was a blessing that saved me from terrible embarrassment, as it had with the Formula A car. I told the team, "I don't know what you normally do in the rain, but there are certain things I like to do." We put all the wings up to their maximum angle, we put large-diameter rain tires on and lowered the car as much as we could, we adjusted the camber so that the tires ran on their inside corners, we took the front anti-roll bar off to reduce understeer, and we taped up the front brake ducts. I was under the impression that all those Europeans were expert rain drivers. I figured I was going to get smoked no matter what I did, so I had nothing to lose. I tried everything I could think of.

After a few laps of slithering and spinning in the race, everybody else slowed down and I found myself in third behind Jackie Stewart and Ronnie Petersen. I was looking good. I was even closing on them, before my goggles fogged up and I had to pit for dry ones; apparently the turbulence in the cockpit was causing water to get in behind the lenses. I didn't lose a position with that, but it put me too far back to challenge the leaders—and then a spin made it worse. I settled down and accepted third. The biggest problem was not being able to see going up the straightaway. Everyone was throwing up a sheet of water, which made it quite hard to get by. Denny doesn't seem to do well in the rain, but toward the end he decided that going around the *outside* of the groove was faster, and he worked up to fourth.

My impression of the race was mostly surprise. I thought guys like Jackie Ickx, and Clay Regazzoni, and François Cevert, and Emerson Fittipaldi were supposed to be outstanding in the rain. They didn't seem so fast to me. No one ever passed me. But the most outstanding thing I noticed was that they made a lot of mistakes. Maybe they didn't know how to set up their cars, or maybe it was a matter of having the right tires. Maybe they were trying too hard, or perhaps they didn't care. Everyone told me how great it was that I finished third in my first Formula One race—but it wasn't so great to me. It was only because of the rain. I was still disappointed in the car, and in my lack of ability in getting it developed.

For the Watkins Glen race I knew that we must come to a solution. We went to a test session there and I tried a nonrising-rate front suspension—which didn't seem to work. And really stiff rear springs—which didn't seem to work. Then we tried different wing angles, and we jacked the car all around. Nothing seemed to do the job. Eventually we just put it back about like it had been at Mosport. Then, at the last minute, I wasn't able to drive it because a rained-out race at Trenton was scheduled for the same day. We brought in David Hobbs, and I sort of worked with him in practice and qualifying. But somewhere in there I began to wonder if the team hadn't uncovered the real problem and not told me. Denny qualified third and led the race until he had tire troubles and hit a guardrail. David came in tenth in my car.

I felt that I had truly failed as a development driver in that car. I never did understand what was wrong with it. Some months later, when it was all over and I had some time to think about it, I came to the conclusion that the final problem was aerodynamic. Only one time that I drove the car did I ever see the rear wing working. It was possible to look in the mirrors and see it at high speed, and only once did I see it depressed. If we had cured that we probably could have gone from our skidpad to Mosport and had the car set up right. But because I was so deeply involved in one area—the suspension—I lost sight of the whole package. Consequently I got off on a tangent, and when we *did* get the wing right at Watkins Glen, other things were wrong. In all my running back and forth between different cars and different races, somewhere I had gotten confused.

I later told Tyler Alexander what my analysis was. I said that I thought the M19 was really a good car as we had it at Mosport, but that for some reason the rear wing wasn't working right. It could have been in the wrong location, or a poor design, or simply at the wrong angle of attack. I just offered that impression for what it was worth—it didn't matter to me at that point. Eventually they made a winner out of that basic configuration. They never explained how they did it, but from what I learned later about wings, I decided that they had a poor shape then. It was more like a flat plate working at a high angle.

I was through with Formula One. I had enough other racing cars to try and cope with so I didn't need to worry about my failure with that group. There was something I noticed at the Watkins Glen race, though, while I was helping David Hobbs and participating in a drivers' seminar. It became obvious that a lot of Americans wanted me to race in Formula One. That was the first time I realized how much enthusiasm there was for American drivers to compete against the Europeans. Of course, Andretti was driving for Ferrari, and Revson was in a third Tyrrell car for the Watkins Glen race, but the comments seemed aimed toward me. I still don't know whether the encouragement was meant for me as Mark Donohue or me as another American. But naturally I was honored, and impressed, and flattered. My ego was really pumped up.

In fact, when I was in England testing the McLaren the thought of racing for them in Europe *had* entered my mind. I was honored that they considered me valuable enough to work with their cars, even though I knew very little about Formula One. I was certainly not an expert in that field. They were either very desperate or they thought enough of my ability to ask me to be involved.

I started hinting around with Teddy. I knew he would never ask me outright to drive for him, because he just wouldn't do that to Roger. But he knew there were some bad times between Roger and me, and that I was often frustrated in certain operations. So Teddy made it clear that some kind of a deal could be a possibility. And I subtly asked him about the financial considerations. I said, "How much money could a Formula One driver expect to make in a season? Is the profit picture better in Europe?" It would make little sense to go to Formula One for half the money. Teddy was deliberately vague, but he did make an interesting comment: "A Formula One driver certainly shouldn't make over one hundred thousand a year. There's no way a guy can be worth more than that." So I reckoned that's the way it was. I would never be one to try and negotiate finances at that point. But I felt that if that was the maximum potential in Europe, it wasn't a smart thing for me to do. Why should I drop all my present programs for the prestige—and unknown circumstances—of European driving?

So Mosport was the only Formula One race I ever ran—to a third-place finish, which I considered a gift.

Chapter 22

1972–73

MATADOR
Trying NASCAR (and Getting Humbled Again)

The idea of racing an American Motors Matador in NASCAR superspeedway races came about in a meeting we had following the 1971 Trans-Am series. We had easily won the series for American Motors, so they were happy with us and we were happy with them. But Roger wasn't interested in running the Trans-Am again the next year. He seems to have a good sense of the right time to stop a program. Roy Woods wanted to continue at it with his race team, though, so he and Roger and AMC all made a deal among themselves for Woods to keep racing the Javelins. That was one of the few policy meetings at which I was present, and we were all sort of thinking out loud about where we would go from there. I said, "Why don't we try NASCAR racing?" We didn't know enough about NASCAR to have any idea what was involved, but we reckoned we could hire a guy to build us a chassis and show us the tricks. Then we could race the car for American Motors. They might have gone to someone who was already established in stock car racing, except that they didn't want to gamble on another racing team, and we didn't want to lose our relationship with a large American automobile company.

Roger didn't say much about it at first, but he thought about it for a few months and finally decided it was a good idea—in some modified form. In SCCA racing we knew the game, and we knew what we could get away with. But NASCAR rules are so vague it's hard to know what to do. It would be foolish to read the rule book, build a car, and go to the track with a $60,000 mistake. Also, we were all tied up with our extensive Porsche and USAC programs for the next season. Finally, we decided it would be best to more or less subcontract the deal out to a stock car builder, while we took on the responsibility for American Motors.

Roger and I and Chuck Cantwell, who was going to be team manager on the project, all went to Holman-Moody to talk to them about building the first car. After a lot of discussion about what it would cost, what pieces they would use, and when we could have it, they agreed to build it. They would just do the first step for us. It was up to us to go on from there. John Holman and Ralph Moody were breaking up, though, so we also talked with some of their people. Dick Hutcherson, J. C. Elder, and Port Thompson were thinking about forming their own company, called Hutcherson and Pagan—like a new Holman-Moody. Roger agreed that they could subcontract the racing team operations from us. He and Hucherson never quite saw eye-to-eye about the financial end of the deal, though. Hutcherson was a little shaded in his views from the days with the Ford racing programs, when everyone was working on a "cost-plus" basis. He saw the American Motors factory, and he saw Roger Penske Racing Enterprises, and he thought, "Oh boy, here it is!" So there was always a bit of a cost problem between us, although it probably would have cost us more in the end to try and do it all ourselves.

We had a lot of time on American Motors' V-8 engine, so we hoped that part would be easy. I had Traco build us a standard 305-inch Trans-Am motor for our first tests, and I also asked them to build a 366-inch version of it. They said, "No, that would require a lot of development with different bores and strokes and things." But I knew that the 305 had a relatively short stroke, so I told them to just stroke it to 366 and we would gamble. "Who knows whether it'll have any power or whether it'll pitch apart at 6000 rpm. Let's just do it." I didn't even know exactly what the stroke was, but I didn't think that was out of the question. As it turned out, that was basically our most successful engine.

When the car was first put together, we all went down to Charlotte to look it over and run it on the superspeedway there. I spent about three days driving it around the track, while Hutch, Port, and J.C. tried to teach me all the tricks of the trade. First we ran the springs they recommended. Then they showed me how cross-jacking with different springs affects the handling, and I tried out every other spring they had—before finally coming back to their setup as the best. They showed me a little about ride heights, and how rake affects the aerodynamics, and what sort of a line was best on those tracks. And all the time I was thinking, "Boy, if only we had prepared the car ourselves. . . ." I reckoned the roll cage was wrong, and it had all rubber bushings in the suspension, and it had drum brakes that were just totally inadequate by my standards. The plan had been to start with their ideas first and go on from there. It seemed to be such a basket case that I knew we could improve it at our own shops before the first race.

Nevertheless, the car was fast, and everyone was very happy and enthusiastic. It ran "reel good," as they say in the South. In fact, we never again ran quite as fast as we did at that test, even with the same engine. It only amounted to about one tenth of a second out of a thirty-five-second lap, though, and tires and tracks have changed a lot since then.

The first race at Riverside was only weeks away, so J.C. and Port brought the car to our shops and did their maintenance there, while we did our thing. We changed the suspension a little, and reinforced the frame here and there, and fitted disc brakes. I was saying that there was no way we could go to Riverside without disc brakes. That was going to be our Unfair Advantage. Don Cox, our engineer, stepped up to the challenge and produced new hubs, flanges, discs, and brackets to mount the calipers on. It required tremendous effort on everyone's part, but we reckoned that was the only way to go. It was the only way, of course, and it still is. But as long as a car isn't winning, no one else is likely to learn anything from it. We ran the car on our skidpad also, trying to get it to respond better than it did at Charlotte. But we couldn't see any improvements. It understeered a lot with rear tires on the front, as we had seen before, but there was nothing much we could do about it besides just recognize the situation for what it was.

In practice at Riverside the car looked good. In qualifying, however, it was not so good. We had hoped to be quickest on a road course, but we soon learned that you can't walk in and immediately be the best in such a highly specialized area as stock car racing. As Junior Johnson told Roger, we aren't

MATADOR

photo by F. David Stone

Supermen. Everybody has to serve an apprenticeship in a new racing game. After all that work, and all that hoopla, I was only able to qualify with the fourth fastest time. Richard Petty and David Pearson and I fought it out for the first few laps, and at one point on the track I even had the lead. But it didn't last very long. The car started getting sick in the first laps, and it got progressively worse until I had to stop. The locating linkage for the rear axle pulled right out of the frame. Roger was very upset, of course, and right there he decided we were going to have to build a new car, with more things done our way.

While that was being done we went to Daytona to see how we compared in horsepower on the high-speed ovals. In a short qualifying race I started seventh and finished fifth, and in the Daytona 500 I started tenth and lost the motor. It was obvious that the car was junk. When everyone else was running laps at 185 mph, I was at 171. Our 366 motor was at a great disadvantage to their 427's, even with restrictor plates, and our aerodynamic drag was terrible with that big, boxy shape. I just held my foot to the floor all the way around the track for as long as it lasted. The driver meant nothing. You could put a robot in there to do the steering.

While the second car was being finished we went to the Ontario NASCAR race, just to keep our hand in, in case we could run for the Championship. I qualified seventh again, and we weren't even in the hunt. In the race I was running back in the second pack when Bobby Isaacs came up behind me. I was driving as hard as I could to stay ahead, but he was closing on me because of his power advantage. I went into turn one as deep as I could before braking—and he ran into my inside rear fender. It put us both out of control, and I spun around and backed into the wall rather hard. Isaacs hit pretty hard also, and we were both stunned for a while. I don't know if it was my fault for braking too hard or his fault for being so close if he didn't have any brakes, but it wasn't any sort of planned "NASCAR initiation." It was just one of those things that happens—not anything either one of us wanted. My car was shortened up a lot, and his car was destroyed also. My body was really sore for a while, but that's all, thanks to the special high-impact safety seat I had in my car.

There never did seem to be any difference in body contact between NASCAR and any other racing I've done. There may be a little nudging, and some brushes with the wall, but those stock cars won't take the outright ramming you hear of. They do get very close to each other, but the drivers aren't reckless, and it never seemed to bother me. I never really had any problems with NASCAR drivers in that respect. They never said they made a mistake, and I never said I did. They all accepted me very easily because I wasn't running in their league. If I had been as fast as they were it might have been a different story, but I had a car that was about five miles per hour slow. There I was, a big-shot champion from SCCA, and I couldn't even keep up. They were happy to see me, because it made them look better. The promoters told me that they loved to see me come to NASCAR races and take a big dump, because it made their drivers look good. Believe me, I was trying like hell not to let that happen.

After the accident I went off to Indy and the SCCA, while our guys finished building the new Matador. The only major difference in the second car was that it had Chevrolet truck trailing arms on the rear axle. That was supposed to be the hot setup, because that's what Bobby Allison's Monte Carlo had. Roger said, "Allison has it, and he's going faster, so we've gotta have it too." Later there was some question whether that was the answer, so Roger had Hutcherson patch up the old wrecked car from Ontario, and we made an A-B comparison at Charlotte. Another stock car driver named Dave Marcis drove them, but he wasn't able to tell whether the new suspension was any better. At least it wasn't any worse.

Unfortunately I wasn't involved in the Matador program as much as I should have been. I was so tied up with the Porsche and Indy cars that we were leaving the Matador mostly up to Hutcherson-Pagan. I figured that since I couldn't be there constantly, knowing what went into the car from start to finish, I ought to let them alone. If a driver is going to be involved, he has to know the entire car by heart. I couldn't just drop by and put in my two cents here and there. I can't keep the thousands of little details from a number of different race cars separate in my head. Maybe Roger can do that with his business, but I'd have to write everything down, and that would take forever. If those guys asked me what I thought about some detail, I'd tell them, but stock car guys tend to be very set in their ways. They reckon something should be done a certain way, and they go right on and do it.

We got the car ready for Atlanta and went early for a little testing. I still thought I knew what I wanted the car to feel like, but as it turned out I really didn't have enough experience yet. Each time we practiced the car would be understeering. Then we would adjust it too much, and in the race it would oversteer. I refused to pay attention to all the old rules of thumb they had, like: "You never put a sawed-off forty-five-inch trammel bar on the car at Darlington." They knew everything from years of experience on all those tracks. I felt the car should handle a certain way, and I would work for that. But because of the weight and the oversize front tires, it just wouldn't handle like a road-racing car. The behavior was quite sluggish, and it wouldn't respond to treatment. Besides that, those cars run all the time at wide-open throttle, and usually at peak cornering forces with a lot of suspension deflection. You end up with entirely different circumstances from road racing. I had been on the banks at Daytona in sports cars, but that wasn't the same experience at all. The stock car has to be set up so that you can relax at some point. They're so big that they can almost get away from you before you realize it. I was really out of my element, and because of my stubbornness—my refusal to play their rules—it took us a long time to learn how to do it.

For the start of the Atlanta race I had the car oversteering so badly that I couldn't control it for very long. At one point it got away from me, and I spun it down the front straight. Then the engine lost water and started to overheat. I had to come in for water about a dozen times. It was really a bad scene. I started eleventh, and finished fifteenth. It would have saved us a lot of embarrassment had it just blown up.

After the race we did a little more basic research into the situation. We spent another four days at Charlotte, trying to put our finger on the problems. It appeared that a lot was lost to the high-air-drag shape, but we were hoping to find something to be gained in suspension geometry. Cox did go through a geometry study, and concluded that even though everything looked about right, there were a few things wrong. The Matador has "dive" in the front, instead of anti-dive, and there was the same roll-center height and swing-arm length situation as on the Javelin. So we tried lots of camber change, less camber change, high and low roll centers—and nothing seemed to show any effect—as on the Javelin. We decided that there wasn't any way to build it any better, as long as we did it as good as everyone else.

At that point Roger said he wanted me to concentrate on other programs until we could work out a winning combination with the Matador. We had Dave Marcis around at the tests, and Roger hired him to drive the car for the rest of the season. He gave Chuck Cantwell sole responsibility for the NASCAR team. They sort of fizzled out the year.

For the last race of the season I went to Rockingham just to watch them race, and I learned more that way than in all the races I had driven. I could take time to talk to people about how it was done, and I could see what everyone was doing on the track. I could watch their strategy, and their drafting, and see how they passed by choosing a different line. Before that, all I could do was watch how they all went around me. I learned how a driver would determine what was wrong with his car's balance, and have the mechanics correct it during a pitstop. I might have been able to figure out how to drive better if only I had been humble enough to watch them at the outset. I look back on my first NASCAR experiences as some of my unhappiest times.

Over the summer Traco looked to the motor. As time went on we had decided that it was our only hope, with the body limitations we had. Finally we tried opening it up from 366 to 427 inches, even though a 427 with a NASCAR restrictor plate showed no horsepower advantage over the smaller motor. It didn't seem right, but it was decided to try it anyhow.

Much later, after a year of engine failures, we finally had to face up to the fact that 427 inches was too big for that block. Since then we've been limited to 366, and that's *it*. Restrictor or not, that little motor won't live at anything over 366 inches.

As we all know, however, power and aerodynamics are far less important at a road course like Riverside. You have to separate NASCAR races into oval tracks versus Riverside, which was the only road race they ran at that time. Because I had won some sedan races there in the Trans-Am, I understood what was needed. The Matador was somewhat like our Javelin, only much heavier, slower, and with the wrong tires on the front. I figured we could be lookin' good for Riverside, anyhow.

Riverside was the only NASCAR race where we had even one Unfair Advantage, and we made the most of it. If our Matador didn't have low drag or high horsepower, at least we had the brakes. Our Girling calipers were from the long-distance Lola, and they were the biggest, stiffest, best design made for automobiles of any kind. We also had the biggest, stiffest rotor we could find, which happened to be off a Lincoln. Another advantage to that disc is that it has the least offset, which, as we had learned, reduces heat cracking. But even with the right pieces, you have to understand brakes from an engineering standpoint.

It wasn't that I could outbrake other cars in any one particular corner, but that we could make our brakes last longer. On any one lap, everyone else's brakes would stop their cars at the same rate, but no one's—not even ours—could lock up the wheels of a 4000-pound car forever. Once you understand how the brakes absorb and dissipate the heat, you can drive in a way that gets the optimum performance out of them. The stopping capability of our system for long periods was about one-half "g," which, believe it or not, was far greater than their drums could do. On the other hand, there are certain low-speed turns where I could use them up to about 0.7 to 0.8 "g," because there was less heat input, or a long straightaway afterward to cool them off before the next application. If you drive like that, you'll have brakes to the end. But once they get overheated, lining wear can double. I wasn't stopping much quicker than the drum-braked cars early on, but because they were running hotter, their brake lining soon wore out. They tried to adjust them, but you can only go so far before the material is gone. Most NASCAR cars finish that race with literally no brakes at all. None! But they get used to it, and it doesn't seem to bother them very much. They use engine braking to slow down early, and they slide around a lot to scrub off speed. You'll see one of them headed toward a boiler-plate wall, just pumping his brake pedal like crazy to build up pressure. When you don't have brakes at a place like Riverside, you just go slower and slower, and try to survive.

In spite of our advantage we didn't have anyone particularly worried.

Again I qualified with the fourth fastest time. The problem was that I hadn't been working with the NASCAR team very much, and their maintenance had deteriorated toward the last part of 1972. I got in the car at Riverside expecting it to be "Penske ready," and it wasn't. The brakes were out of balance and the clutch was slipping—which I thought was inexcusable preparation. I got really angry with the guys, and I let it be known that just because the car hadn't been winning races didn't allow them to be careless. They got behind me, and by race time the car was as perfect as they could make it.

The race wasn't even a contest. We all ran together to about the halfway point, where I still had the same brakes I began with but everyone else was out of it. I was able to win easily, even though I lost almost an entire lap when Allison's Chevrolet was allowed to close up on me with a yellow flag deal near the end. I was hardly using my brakes at all—and still staying way ahead. Of course, another Unfair Advantage was that we could change pads during the race. We had our vacuum-retractor system from endurance-race experience, and we could change pads just a little more slowly than changing tires. We projected that we would only have to change the front pads. We could change the left front when we added left-side tires, and the right front with right-side tires. After they got the left front pads off, though, the crew carefully measured how much material was left, and they concluded that I could go the distance on the less-used right-side pads. It would be touch-and-go, but Roger didn't want to take the chance of something going wrong in the pits. That made me worry a little, which is why I was taking it so easy near the end. In fact, the right front pad material was worn down to the backing plate in one place at the end of the race.

Some of the NASCAR people were impressed by my being able to run twenty or thirty laps in a row, all faster than my qualifying speed. But there were a lot of reasons besides the poor condition of the car when I qualified. At Riverside, 500 miles takes about five hours in those cars, and I was naturally going to improve after two or three hours of experience. And they only allow two laps to qualify in. You can't afford to make a mistake by taking any chances. Then too, I had learned years ago that the mark of a good driver was being able to run hard consistently, without overusing the brakes. All those years I drove with poor brakes—and Cox's engineering experience with brakes—taught us how to handle that particular situation.

But those brakes cost us a lot of money, especially in body damage. Our Matador was in four accidents because it could stop when others couldn't. It happened to me at Ontario, and Marcis was hit in the rear three times. So it's been a disadvantage—-except in avoiding front-end damage—but I can't justify taking off our brakes just because other cars can't stop.

It was really unfortunate that we couldn't apply our aerodynamics experience to the '72-'73 Matador. In the first place, the springing was so stiff, and the tracks so bumpy, that we weren't able to measure lift or drag accurately enough to see improvements. And secondly, you can't make many improvements under the rules. Years ago everyone else cheated, until some very explicit rules were put in the books. Now about all you can do is add a two-inch spoiler on the rear or a four-inch spoiler under the nose. Since they had standard body-shape templates that we had to fit, we spent a lot of time trying to get the fenders and hood exactly where they had to be. It seems to be a big game they play. You droop the nose, chop and narrow the body, and then try to puff it up to fit the templates. We didn't even know for sure that it made any difference in performance. We tried a little and couldn't tell, but everyone else thought so, and they knew more than we did. Our cars were always finished so nicely that I hated to keep changing body panels around. The kind of body and paint work we must have makes it very expensive. All we could do was try to keep the car as low as possible and yet raked forward at a good angle.

After two seasons in NASCAR we have a good idea how to play their game, and the 1974 Matador is a better car to work with. We even know the best place to get the knowledge we need. Experience is good, of course, but NASCAR people must be the friendliest racers in the business. They love to talk, and they always seem to want to help—they did while we were so far behind, anyhow. Our job is to try and filter the truth out of the bullshit. We served our apprenticeship in a highly embarrassing position, and now it's time to show what we learned. I may not have been successful as a driver in NASCAR, but I still have a chance to go back and try again as a team manager.

Chapter 23

1973

LOLA T330-AMC (FORMULA A)

Disaster into Mediocrity (with a Lot of Wasted Effort)

There were a number of reasons why we went into the Formula A series in 1973. American Motors was interested in getting into a series where they were more competitive than the Matador was in NASCAR. At the same time, Sunoco liked Formula A because it involved real open-wheel race cars that burned gasoline—unlike USAC cars, which burned alcohol. And it looked to us like an easy way to pick up some wins. All we had to do was buy a competitive chassis, stuff our proven AMC 302-inch Trans-Am motor in it, and go out and collect the money—or Roger would, at least. I didn't know much about the series, but Don Cox was going to Europe for us, and he could look at the various chassis that were available. McLaren didn't have one. Trojan was going to, but they weren't ready yet. March offered one that Cox didn't like. So we ended up back at Lola, where Broadley was building a Formula A chassis that looked like a winner.

Fitting our AMC motor in the standard Chevrolet engine space turned out to be a hassle. Cox handled the engineering and packaging, and Karl Kainhofer went to England to help get everything together right. The big problems were that the AMC motor had its distributor and oil pump in the way at the front, the water pump stuck out more, and it needed a different dry-sump pump mount. But Eric has always done very well for us, so by the time I saw it everything looked about right. It was even painted Sunoco blue at the factory.

Of course, the first thing to do was to take the car to the skidpad. I figured it would be easy to get it into shape. We would select the right springs

courtesy of Penske Communications (photo by Floyd D. Harvey)

Lola T330-AMC

and anti-roll bars, tweak the motor and the wings, go to the races, unload the car from the trailer, and win all the money—and then walk off into the sunset. But we couldn't run on our own skidpad in the middle of winter, so we took the car to California to test right after the Riverside NASCAR race. We ran on Digitek's skidpad, and sure enough, it understeered too much. We did the usual. We softened the front and stiffened the rear. Nothing happened. Eventually we got to the point where we had the stiffest springs and anti-roll bars available in the rear, and the softest springs and bars up front—and the lap times still hadn't changed very much. It was still slow and it was still understeering.

Because time was running out and we had no more ideas to try, I decided to take it to Riverside and see how the engine and aerodynamics were. Not knowing anything better to do, we left the rear stiff and the front soft. The first thing I realized at the track was that the fuel-injection metering cam was wrong. It was an old case of "on or off—nothing in between," which Traco should have taken care of already. But even as it was, I could tell immediately that the suspension wasn't right. When it's bad on the skidpad, and unstable in the straightaway, it's really a pail of worms. It was understeering all right, and yet it felt as if it was "hunting" on the straights—as if it wanted to pivot about the front wheels and oversteer. I was baffled. I thought that maybe the chassis was twisting, because it did look kind of flimsy, or there was something else basically wrong that we couldn't see. It was so depressing to get nowhere with the chassis or engine, and I was so tired from running 500 miles at Riverside the day before that I went back to my motel room.

A couple of hours later Karl and Haig Alltounian came to my room and woke me up. They had been working on the oil-pump bracket in the Goodyear garage at the track. I said, "Gee, are you finished already?" They looked kind of strange, and Karl said, "No. We have some bad news.

The whole thing is gone. The garage is still burning and the Lola is history." They told me how a spark had ignited some gasoline, they couldn't get a fire extinguisher to work, and the flames set fire to the race tires that were stored there. They weren't hurt themselves, but they were really shook. I drove out as fast as I could. Les Richter, the track owner, was there, but there was nothing to say, except that it had been an accident and it was fortunate no one was injured.

In some ways I felt it was a good thing. We already had the Porsche in Can-Am, the Eagle and the McLaren in USAC, and the Matador in NASCAR, and we didn't have enough time or people to spare. Besides that, there were the handling and motor problems, which I didn't know how to cope with. As far as I was concerned, that was it.

So what happened? Our troubles were merely put off until later in the season, then resurrected again. In May Roger came around and told us that we were going to race in Formula A after all. By then American Motors had seen that they weren't going to win any superspeedway races with the Matador. There was nothing I could say, except that we would do our best. We ordered another car from Broadley, exactly like the first one. It was so late by then that I was a little sad about it. That was the sort of thing we would have done six years before, when we were new and inexperienced not as professionals.

I was hoping that the basic problem was too much flex in the chassis. When the next car arrived we set it up on our surface plate, replaced the springs with solid bars, and tested its torsional rigidity. Woody spent a week at it, anchoring one end, twisting the other end with hydraulic jacks, and measuring the deflection with dial gauges. It turned out to have a stiffness of about 4000 foot-pounds per degree, which ought to be perfectly adequate for a race car. We could see a little bending in the middle, though, so we added a couple of extra braces between the roll bar and cylinder heads.

Since that wasn't it, we looked to geometry. We made the standard bump-steer measurements, and determined that it was bad at the rear. We didn't have time to run a computer analysis to find out why, but the trailing arms didn't look right. Instead of converging to the front, or at least being parallel, they converged to the rear. We moved the front points, and the bump steer came out better. Then we made a longer upper camber link, because I felt that the short ones Eric preferred made the car twitchy from a too-rapid camber change curve. We also made a new split-flap rear wing, like the one that was working so well on the Porsche. It was a real "shade-tree" operation. We had to do as much as we could, as fast as we could.

This time we went to Atlanta for a test. The car didn't feel quite as unstable as it had at Riverside, but it was still understeering far too much. We added more anti-dive angle in the front suspension so we could use even softer springs—and *still* it understeered. At least we were encouraged by the fact that the Lola was faster than the past year's record Formula A time. By then I was convinced that the understeer problem was due to the front track being so narrow. We trucked back to the shops and spent a week widening the front suspension. It was no small step, either, as the increase was about eight inches. We tried it out on the skidpad and it seemed a little better, so we went back to Atlanta. Not only did it understeer about the same as before, but the arms were so long that everything was flexing to the point of instability. I wanted so badly for it to be better that I tried too hard, and spun into a fence. The damage was slight, but I felt the guys were angry with me for making such a big change that turned out to be wrong. We got a little response by going to a *really* stiff anti-roll bar from the 917 Porsche, but in the end we went back to a relatively stock Lola setup. After all that work we still weren't much better off than when we started.

At that point we had to go to the next Formula A race, at Mid-Ohio. I didn't feel we were ready, but Roger had a contract with American Motors, and everyone had agreed to that as our first race. Roger was wondering why I still hadn't gotten the car sorted out. Sometimes he doesn't realize all the work that's involved when we're working on so many different programs. He figures that with all my experience I ought to be able to look at a car—or at least drive it once—and have all the answers, right *now*. He gets angry when we seem to be wasting time.

When we got to Mid-Ohio we could see immediately that the car wasn't right, but we were stuck with what we had. Because Indianapolis had been rained out the week before, we didn't get to the track until Saturday. My best time—right out of the truck—was four seconds off the pole. I felt my engine had as much power, and yet I couldn't stay with other drivers out of the turns, and the understeer limit was driving me berserk. I drove my heart out, and finished third. Brett Lunger was there, and at the time he was running fastest he came to me and said, "This is really great racing, isn't it? We have great cars, and we're having a great time." I just nodded my head and thought, "Brett, these cars are shitboxes, and when you get in a nice one, you're really gonna go a lot faster." We had no more time to test, so we just kept going from race to race, getting nowhere.

At Watkins Glen the best I could do was a fourth, so I had the crew put *all* the stock Lola stuff back in for Elkhart Lake. It understeered so badly that way that it almost went straight off at the corners during warm-up. I didn't know what to do but stiffen the rear bar and boost the rear brakes so that I could jam them on to get the tail around. It was so embarrassing to me it was pathetic. I couldn't wait for the day to be over so I could get out of there. I was supposed to be the expert, and all I could do was limp around to a poor sixth-place finish.

On the Skidpad

courtesy of Penske Communications (photo by J. Sheridan Evans)

It wasn't all in the handling, either, because Traco still didn't have the fuel-metering unit right. At any part-throttle condition, or even on a shift, the engine would sputter and wheeze and gasp. I eventually had to work it out on the dyno with them. We ran the engine at various part-throttle conditions, and hand-ground the metering cam to suit. We knew the AMC motor wasn't the major problem, though, because Traco had gotten some of our competitors' Chevrolet motors to rebuild, and we compared them on the dyno. They were outpowering us at the low end—the 5000-rpm range—but we could blow them off at the top. At 8000 rpm our best was 497 horsepower, while 480 was all we could get out of the Chevrolet. We had already done all the necessary development on the fuel injection, headers, intake lengths, diameters, and camshafts, which has to be done to a new engine. So I asked Traco to add some power at the bottom of the rpm range, even though it meant taking off some twenty horses at the top. We thought that the only difference we couldn't overcome was the fact that our AMC motor was about 100 pounds heavier than the Chevrolet. What we didn't know at the time was that certain of our competitors had experimental new Chevrolet heads with better port shapes, which were worth some unknown additional horsepower.

Something else that was worrying me was a comment someone made at Elkhart Lake: "The only difference between you and the other Lolas is that you have a locked differential. It's gotta be that." But I thought, "Dammit, all our experiments have shown there is no difference on the skidpad. I know a locked differential has gotta be better." When we ordered the car, Broadley asked if we wanted it locked, and I said, "Oh yeah, sure. We always run that way." He didn't argue, and I forgot about it. Why should that be a *disadvantage* all of a sudden?

If springs, and bars, and track width, and torsional rigidity, and the engine didn't make any difference, then what could? My next step was tires. We had all been on thirteen-inch-diameter wheels front and rear, and then everyone went to fifteen-inch wheels in the rear. I thought that if larger diameter was better on the rear, it ought to reduce understeer at the front. I talked to the Goodyear guys about it, but they said that the Formula One cars ran on those tires, so they had to be perfect. I went to Roger's Goodyear tire store with a tape measure and looked around for myself. Pretty soon I found a tire that was the same except for a three-inch larger diameter. It was a rear tire for a Formula B car. We mounted a pair and took the car to the skidpad. As it came from Elkhart Lake, the best it would do was about 1. 1 "g's," but when we put the Formula B rear tires on the front—with no other changes—it went almost 1.4 "g's." It was really fast on the skidpad. Then I decided to try unlocking the differential on it. We put the old tires back on and installed a Z-F differential—and it went about 1.3 "g's." So I had a choice. I could unlock the differential and run small front tires, just like everyone else. Or I could keep my locker and run the larger front tires—and possibly be able to corner faster.

Then I could tell what had been happening. The greatest difference was in our driving styles. Formula A cars were basically set up for the "European style" of separate braking, cornering, and acceleration. To drive with the "American style" of combining all three, as we had learned at Chevrolet, I had to have a locked differential. But when I put it in, the Lola didn't have big enough tires on the front to prevent understeer. It was incredible how simple it seemed at last!

We could have gone to their total setup, and I could have adapted to their style of driving, but I had good reasons not to. With an unlocked differential the brakes can't be used as hard. An inside rear wheel will lock up and make the car unstable—if not stall the engine. The next day I had the locked differential put back in, and I went back to the Goodyear guys. I told them I needed a tire that was bigger yet, and asked them if they could build me one in a front tire design. There's a slight difference in shape between a front and rear tire design, so the ones I had were slightly too convex across the tread. They said they probably couldn't do it but would check with the factory. A while later they came back, looking kind of sheepish, and said I could have them within a week. When I asked how they were able to do it so fast, they admitted that they were already being designed for Formula One racing. As it turned out, there was sort of a competition between the American and European race-tire engineers within Goodyear, and the American group was building those tires to beat the other design at the Watkins Glen Grand Prix. They knew from their Indianapolis experience that bigger was usually better on the front, and they were going to try it on

Formula One cars. They had exactly what I wanted—but it's interesting that we had both come to the same conclusion from unrelated experiences.

We went to Atlanta with that setup. Those huge tires looked ridiculous on the front, but finally the car was starting to feel right. Of course, none of the other drivers caught on. They thought that going back to large diameter tires was a step in reverse, and since I didn't have the fastest car, they weren't about to copy it. Actually, the tire contact patch on the new tires was a little narrower. I didn't quite understand why the tires were better, but I suspect that they were showing us something we should have understood. The car still wasn't quite as fast as we expected, though. I was about half a second off the pace, and I finished second because I still didn't have enough acceleration to pass in traffic. I reckoned that the final problem was the power-to-weight ratio of the motor. A 100-pound disadvantage is quite a bit in those little cars.

The next race at Pocono was a disaster because there was no time to do anything to the car. The mechanics were doubling up on my USAC Eagle, and we had a Can-Am and the Ontario 500 in there also. In fact, Pocono was the day after Ontario, and they're about 3000 miles apart. We were lucky to keep me and the car together for a sixth-place finish.

The car was closer, but still not where it should be. At least it was responding to treatment the way it should, and we could go back and develop it properly. Once we were rid of the horrendous understeer we could drop the rear spring rate from 700 pounds per inch—which is ridiculous on that kind of car—to a more reasonable 400-pound rate. It began to feel like it ought to, and I could drive it with my normal "American style." It was a comfortable car. We went to the last race at Kent and finished second to one of the trick motors from Chevrolet.

Everything began to fall into place all right, but too late to win anything. Our next step in the normal progression of development would have been to do a complete suspension optimization. We needed a front geometry that was designed for the high-profile tires, and we needed to modify it to allow even wider front tires. Then we could go through the aerodynamics and get the wing angles right. And finally, we might have been able to get some weight out of the motor. It would have been a thrill to win even with that Unfair *Disadvantage*.

As we worked through the Lola and it changed from being undriveable to being a potentially great car, I began to feel that it wasn't much different from a Formula One project. Combined with my performance at the Formula A-Formula One Questor race, and the development of the McLaren Formula One car, I realized that the Europeans aren't Supermen. I had always thought that they were the experts who knew everything about everything—the world's best cars and drivers. It made me want to take an

American car to Watkins Glen, or even Europe, and try our education and experience against them. I learned a great deal about cars from that Lola—even though it almost killed me. When we were running way behind, I was totally distraught, although it didn't seem to bother Roger so much. He said to just keep working and we'd get there eventually. But I wasn't satisfied with running third—I wanted to win. Maybe I was spoiled, but going to a track knowing that you're going to be twelve miles per hour slow on the straightaway is not my idea of professional racing. It began to make me feel that it might be time to start thinking about retiring.

Chapter 24

1973

EAGLE-OFFY (USAC)
The Last Development Job (Left Unfinished)

In March 1973 we took a new McLaren to Indianapolis for tire tests. It hadn't been changed a great deal, but where it had been—a longer wheelbase, a shorter nose, and a different cowl—it was going to require some development. We spent a week working on everything, and when we got through, we still had a 185-mph car, while the Eagles were easily going 192. But we were committed to McLaren, and we already had two new cars on the way for Gary Bettenhausen and me. By then, however, it was possible to buy a new Eagle from Dan Gurney. They were "customer cars" in 1973, and a lot of USAC drivers were buying them. While we were waiting for our McLarens, I talked to Roger about the possibility of getting an Eagle ourselves. We were the only racing group around who could hedge our bets by running two different chassis. It wouldn't be hard to find something to do with our second McLaren. Roger had already talked with Bobby Allison about being a third driver for us at Indianapolis. It was very late to be changing our program, but Roger talked to Gurney and got him to make us a car in kit form, on a real-quick-hurry-up basis.

Karl Kainhofer went out to California and gathered up all the necessary pieces and brought them back to our shops. We only had about a month, so Karl had just enough time to put everything together and get the car to Indy. We knew absolutely nothing about how it handled or what it would respond to in chassis tuning. I talked to Dan on the phone, and he gave me a rough idea of what they had already done. There were things about it that were nice, and some things that weren't so nice. It was heavier, but everything seemed a little more precise than our McLarens. We took it to Indy without ever having run it.

That was the first time we had ever tried to run a three-car, three-driver team, so we tried to split up the responsibility. Don Cox would work with Bobby Allison, Roger would work with Gary Bettenhausen, and I would be alone on the new Eagle. That was fine with me—as long as I was *truly* separate. I said that I didn't want it to be like the past, where I would end up getting a lot of interference and criticism, and I'd also have to do a lot of work on the other cars. Roger and Don agreed. They figured everyone had a fair share of the responsibility and authority.

I set up my Eagle just like Dan said to, and it didn't feel good at all! It was constantly changing attitude. The nose wouldn't go down, then it would stick down. The tail would go up, then it wouldn't come down. The solution wasn't obvious, and I didn't know where to start looking. Time runs out so fast at Indy that my first decision was to push out to the line with fifty gallons of fuel. That way I could make a series of five or six tests without stopping to refuel. I ran—and ran—and ran—constantly trying everything I could think of to make the car respond. Because of all the fuel I was going relatively slowly, and Roger made a few comments about that, but it was *my* program. I only had two weeks to learn everything—including what happens between a heavy and a light load of fuel.

Roger and Gary were working well together in their own way. Roger was determined to make him fastest, as he usually does it, by asking around with his friends to find out what setup was quickest. Allison passed his rookie test with no problem, and qualified with no problem, but he didn't seem too awfully interested in Indianapolis. Cox was doing a great job, even though he was annoyed at being a "clerk-manager-executive" instead of a race-car engineer/designer, where his real talents are. And Roger was always around, always criticizing his attitude, so they were constantly sideways with each other. Indianapolis is very difficult for us, because Roger is so intense about it. He's always there, trying to keep control and frequently changing the program—sometimes reasonably, sometimes unreasonably. It's perfectly understandable, because that's our single most expensive race. The cost of running three cars there is so high, it's almost beyond comprehension. Somehow, it's worse than three times the cost of a one-car effort. And the complexity is mind-boggling. Trying to organize people, when their jobs can't be well defined and everything keeps changing, is like carrying water in a sieve. You tell a guy to do "this, this, and this," based on the best available information. So he does the first "this," then discovers he can't do the last two until he does "that." He goes his own way doing "that," not knowing someone else is already doing it. When both guys find out they're doing the same thing, the second guy says he'll do "another thing"—which

photo by F. David Stone

EAGLE-OFFY

was never on the program in the first place. Then someone from the other car sees him and starts doing it too. And a whole new program starts.

Meanwhile, I was groping around with my new car. There seemed to be something wrong with the ride rate, but when I tried to describe it to Dan, he reckoned it wasn't a problem. Either I wasn't conveying it properly, or they just ignored it, or I wasn't coping with it correctly. It was some kind of an aerodynamic "ground effect," where the nose would "lock down" at some height and stay there. But if it was up, it could stay there, too, and begin to "fly the nose," as they say. That was something I could see happening to most of the new Eagle drivers, but not with Gurney's factory Eagles. Some of the cars looked like motorboats. I had seen something similar to that on the Porsche 917 at very high speeds, but since it didn't happen so often on that car, I hadn't tried to understand it or correct it.

It was during that period, I think, that the first serious thoughts of retirement came to me. I was sitting in my car in the pits after running some practice laps, and I was completely lost. There were so many things I had to think about—driving the car, solving its problems, managing my crew, traveling to other tests and races—that I was having serious trouble coping with all of it. And yet I couldn't feel sorry for myself, because it was a situation I had consciously created. I had asked to be let alone on the development of that car—and when I got it, I didn't want it. It was always the same. Car after car after car had to be sorted out and developed. Some turned out successfully and some didn't. But as I thought about it, I realized that if I had my choice to be any other person at Indianapolis, I couldn't improve my position any. I didn't know what the procedure would be—how I would stop and what I'd do next—but I decided that the Eagle was going to be my final project, the last straw. However, while I was there I had to do the best job I knew how.

Dan's theories about making a car fast were: the lower the better, and soft springs gave better road holding. Since speeds don't vary much at Indy, he put in very soft springs, jacked the car way up, and let it sink down on the springs at speed. To prevent bottoming in the turns, he used very stiff anti-roll bars. That's a good enough idea, but his particular spring rate wasn't quite right for me. When I changed it, everything else in the suspension was out of order. Finally we took the car to the garage, removed all the springs, blocked the chassis half an inch off the ground, and aligned the suspension with zero camber at that height. We didn't worry about where it was while sitting still with the springs in. At the minimum turn speeds it was going to be pressed back down to that half-inch clearance.

Still, while I was running 190, the rest of the Eagles were up to 195. I was looking bad—but knowing all along that I couldn't expect to be too fast with fifty gallons of fuel. Once I got the camber right, I selected my own spring rates. I raised the front rate enough to make it stable, then raised the rear rate to keep it from bottoming, and finally selected anti-roll bars to balance the understeer. There was just enough time left to trim the wings, and that was it. It was time to qualify. Karl Kainhofer had measured everything very carefully all month, and his assistant, Haig Alltounian, had kept very precise records of everything we did. So I was confident that I could go out there with the car exactly right. I did, and I went 197 mph, the fastest I'd gone all month. It didn't put me on the pole, but I had won the year before from a front-row starting position.

I felt the Eagle was good enough. Johnny Rutherford's McLaren was on the pole, and Bobby Unser's Eagle was between us, with a total spread of about one mile per hour. Maybe I could have gone faster, but I was pleased with what I had. Early in the race I ran right behind Bobby, and we walked away from everybody else until I lost the motor. We were just beginning to run into a new engine development problem. If the throttle was lifted in the middle of a turn because of traffic, the fuel injection would go lean and burn a valve or a piston. Allison had already gone out in the first lap, but Gary went on to finish fifth in our other McLaren.

The same engine failure put me out of the next race at Pocono, but that wasn't my greatest problem there. Somehow—for the first time in my life—I felt I was being spooked by a race car. I thought I had the Eagle well understood and well developed from Indy, and yet I couldn't even drive it down the straightaway. It felt as if the rear end was swaying back and forth. We went through the car time and time again, and never found anything wrong with it. I began to wonder if there was something wrong with my mind. How could a car begin to handle so badly if nothing had been changed? It's hard to describe what I was going through. I thought I knew all about race cars, and yet there was something that had never happened before, and I didn't know what to do.

I never did qualify well. I started way back in the twenty-third spot, partly because I didn't qualify the first day. In the race, everything was fine. I even led the race at one point, before the motor broke. Since we hadn't found any particular problem, I was even more convinced that it had to be me. I wasn't afraid of the car—it was more like I was mad at it. Then I became mad at myself because whatever was happening was beyond my control. I began to feel more and more as if it was meant to be—for me to stop driving. It could have been some minor thing, like the chassis or suspension being at some odd angle. But trying to sort it out was the most terrible experience of the year for me.

Whatever it was, it carried over into the Ontario race. Again I didn't qualify well, and in the early stages I fell even farther behind. In trying to work my way back up, the motor failed again.

There could have been a number of reasons for my poor performance. I still wasn't too happy about the Eagle's aerodynamic characteristic of "sticking" up or down. It was very sensitive at the last few critical miles per hour, and I just didn't have the time to put into it. I was also racing the 917 Porsche and the Lola-AMC—which, in fact, I had to race the day after Ontario on the East Coast. Everyone else in USAC has a lot of time to devote to one car in one series—a luxury I never knew in my entire professional racing career. Any problem can be solved in time.

But worst of all, I was down on myself. Because I was so far back in the pack I felt I had lost my ability and I was on my way down. Whatever it was I had before that allowed me to run up front was lost somehow. At that point I was in the "also-ran" category. The minute a driver starts to have an attitude like that, it's devastating to his ability. Racing is a game of inches. If a driver is a little dull, he'll be way back in the pack.

The Eagle was a good car. Other drivers proved that. But I never could get it to do what I thought it should. The "ground effects" were too weird, which taught me that I still didn't know everything I needed to know. We never had an Unfair Advantage with that car, other than hoping we could be better prepared. As it turned out, we just bought it and ran it, very unspectacularly.

Chapter 25

1972–73

PORSCHE 917-10, 917-30
A Monument to Effort (Wisdom and Tragedy)

Our program with Porsche began at Le Mans in 1971, while we were there with the Ferrari. The people who control Porsche, Mrs. Piech and her sons, Ferdinand and Michael, asked to see Roger Penske for lunch one day. We were quite impressed by the invitation, assuming that it was based on our reputation in making our Ferrari so much faster than anyone else. At that meeting the Piechs expressed a desire to go racing in the Can-Am. When Roger told me, my first impression was that it was too good to be true—that it was something we should have to fight to get. We didn't know exactly what they wanted, or even what kind of car they wanted to race, but there were certain things that both of us had to have.

Roger followed up on it by flying to Germany about four or five times, and eventually they began to hammer out a contract. The deal almost died over the contract, but because of all the dollars at stake, we couldn't work from a handshake. By fall, it became obvious that all the changes and rewriting were narrowing down to the details. They always asked for absolute secrecy while we were negotiating, possibly because they didn't want to be deluged with unsolicited offers from other teams. We didn't want to say too much either, while we were working with McLaren in USAC. Word did leak out among European journalists, though, which prompted McLaren's Teddy Mayer to ask questions. We told him that since they wouldn't sell us a new Can-Am chassis, it was entirely possible that we might make a deal elsewhere.

I saw the first version of what we were going to race at the 1971 Watkins Glen Can-Am. Jo Siffert was there with a roadster version of the 917 coupe series. My immediate reaction was, "If we're gonna race it, why does Siffert have it?" I didn't know him very well, but I had the impression that he didn't know much about setting up a car. Since Don Cox was involved in the engineering, he was there to have a look also, and we quietly 'scoped the car over. If nothing else, it had to be the ugliest car in the entire world. Not only was it a patch-up job of putting a stub-nosed roadster body on a coupe, but it was very, very dirty. It had a big air-cooled engine, an aluminum space frame, and heavy-looking suspension and hubs.

Then we looked at the McLaren, with its modern monocoque and aluminum Chevrolet engine, and I said to Roger, "I wonder if this is such a smart thing to do after all?" We knew that McLaren's motors were good for 750 horsepower, and the best we could hope for was about 650 out of a normally aspirated, five-liter, air-cooled engine. Besides that, we were sick of our Ferrari deal. We were tired of working with foreigners a million miles away. Cox said, "What a fine mess you've got us into, now that we finally have the Javelin squared away in the Trans-Am." Roger became angry. He said, "If you don't want the deal, tell me now. I'll stop everything." He wouldn't have, of course, but we said we would do whatever it took—as usual.

Once the contract was signed and everything was arranged, the next step was for Roger, Cox, and me to go to Germany and meet all the people on that end. We didn't know what to expect, but we had to see what equipment they had and decide what we were going to do. The first people we met were Ferdinand and Michael Piech. They introduced us to Helmut Flegl, the engineer who was to be our only contact at the factory. He, and no one else, was to make all the decisions at their end. That was fine with us. So we sat down with Flegl and tried to resolve the schedule. Roger was the deadline guy, and he was saying when we needed this and that—while I was thinking that we didn't even know what it *was*.

After a while we went to lunch with some other engineers we would be working with. We were eating in the company dining room, and I was astounded when we were offered cocktails with the meal. If that was done in the GM dining room everyone would go crazy, but that sort of thing is accepted in Germany. We met a Mr. Bott, a Mr. Falk, and Dr. Ernest Fuhrmann, who was seated next to me. I didn't know what Dr. Fuhrmann's role was. I just learned that he was returning to Porsche after a number of years, he was very well liked and respected, and that he had designed one of their six-cylinder engines. Later we learned that the Piechs had hired him to take over the operation of Porsche, and he eventually became such a powerful individual that the entire company now revolves around him.

That afternoon we got a tour of their facilities. They were just completing a new plant, which incorporated a road-racing type of test track right next to their engineering shops. Roger didn't appreciate what we saw, except that he related to the fact that it was like the GM or Chaparral Racing Team setups—with a track right next door. But Cox and I recognized immediately that it was a miniature Chevrolet Research and Development. In our short tour we saw that they had everything we could possibly need—dynos, component test machines, tire testers, chassis shakers, hot rooms, cold rooms, door latch testers, and so on. It was just smaller than GM. They had five racing engineers, instead of five thousand. There was a separate area where they kept old Le Mans cars, customer cars, experimental cars, and cars under restoration. We were truly impressed. We reckoned that all we had to do was put the operation in the proper gear, push it forward, and we would have unlimited success.

Cox and I spent a lot of time discussing the situation that night. We saw that as the opportunity of a lifetime, if it was handled right. Cox knew from his experience between Chevrolet, the Chaparral Racing Team, and us, that we had to establish the right relationship from the beginning. If we let them ship us a car two weeks before the first race, it would be a disaster. We had to convince Flegl that we could work closely together in a joint effort, and develop the car with our old, stock approach. They would apply their technical expertise and facilities, while we used the techniques of skidpad, track testing, and aerodynamic development. If we could communicate, the sky was the limit.

Right away Cox started laying the groundwork with Flegl. As we looked at their facilities and talked about testing, he related things to his race-car engineering experience at Chevrolet. It became obvious to Flegl that we weren't just a bunch of bullshitters. We knew a lot about the engineering they were doing, and we had already come to some of the same conclusions. He had been engineering race cars for some years, and as he began to realize that we could relate, I could almost see a spark come into his eyes. There are certain things that are of interest only to racing engineers—like lateral acceleration in "g's," aerodynamic downforce, centers of mass—and we spoke the common language. We began to convince him that we were not like any other race team he had ever worked with.

Then the time came to take a car to the test track and have a lot of publicity photos taken. The car was a little different from the 917 Spyder we had seen before. It had a Le Mans nose on it, and a small wing was mounted between the fins at the rear. So I put my driver's suit on, and we stood around and posed for pictures. When that was all over it was time to eat. There were about forty people there—the press, the Piechs, Dr. Porsche, everyone's wife and children and dogs, plus some factory workers who had walked over. It was a regular cast of thousands. There was a professional cook, with a grill set up, and we all stood around and ate hot dogs and drank a lot of beer and wine.

Porsche 917-10 *courtesy of Penske Communications*

After lunch they asked if I would drive the car, to give the photographers some action shots. I didn't expect to have to *drive* it right then! It had been a hectic few days. We were out drinking late the night before, and we had to get up early for our meetings. I had no desire to drive at all. But it seemed to be such an important thing to them that I got in the car, fired it up, and took it out on the track. I thought they just wanted some motion, to make the car or scenery blurred, or whatever, so I went around at a reasonable speed for a few laps.

Just driving around, my initial reaction wasn't too favorable. In the first place, I was hung over, and I didn't want to go too fast. But even at that speed the car was *terrible*. It was "hunting" back and forth on the straightaway as if it had an inch of toe-out. I had to jam my legs against the steering wheel to keep it in a straight line at 150 mph. And I couldn't shift it well because the gears were in odd locations and there weren't any definite gates. I came in thinking, "Christ! I'm glad that's over with. They have their pictures and we can all go home." I was ready to take the car to the skidpad and start over from scratch. Flegl walked over to the car and said, "You went around in 53 seconds. The record for this car is 51.5 seconds. What do you think is wrong?" I looked over and there were five mechanics standing there. Suddenly it hit me that they were expecting a command performance—some new lap records, right there! Then I remembered the huge "record board" they had on a wall at the factory. It had a map of the course, and lists of the lap records set by various cars and drivers. I had never driven the track before, I had never sat in the car before, and they expected me to break the lap record. Germans are very tough people. They expect the maximum from everybody at all times.

I got out of the car thinking, "I've gotta play for time. I've gotta prepare myself mentally for this." I didn't know what to say. The car was terrible, but I couldn't tell them that. So I told them to adjust the accelerator pedal up or down—whatever, it didn't make any difference, really. Since I didn't know anything about the car, I didn't know what to change. While they were doing that, I tried to pull myself together. I got back in and tried really hard—and got down very close to the record.

I came in again and Flegl said, "What do you think now?" I said, "Well, I wouldn't have done it quite this way." He looked kind of surprised and said, "What do you mean?" I couldn't say what I meant, because I didn't know how they got where they were. Since I always set up my own car, I know where every adjustment is—toe-in, camber, steering geometry, spring rates, wing angles—everything. I had to ask Flegl what all those settings were. When he told me, I made a quick analysis of the situation, and stabbed at an answer. It was basically an understeering car, but it was oversteering in the high-speed bends. And it had instability in the straights. I said, "I think it will be better if we stiffen the rear anti-roll bar, increase the wing angle, and reduce the toe-in at the front." Flegl became really angry. He said, "You tell the mechanics what to do, but you don't tell me what the car does! What is *my* job? Obviously, you don't need me." I had made a political mistake already. His bosses were standing around watching while I appeared to be doing his job. They were all used to the concept of separating the driver, the engineer, and the mechanics. They weren't prepared for a driver to have some engineering knowledge.

But they did all the things I asked, I went back out, and I was immediately under the track record. That was all they wanted to see. All the bosses and executives started leaving. They saw us demonstrate that we could do the job and that they had made a wise decision. Everybody was happy—except Flegl. He and test driver Willi Kauhsen had put *1500 miles* on that car the week before, developing it as far as they could, and in a few hours I had made it faster. Flegl figured I had gotten him fired. But because Cox had already done a good job convincing him of our combined-forces approach, we were able to keep the relationship from falling apart.

We decided right then that we would start development the next day. I went over there for three days—and ended up staying three weeks. Everyone else left, while Flegl and I tried everything we could think of to make the car better. In addition to the track, they had two skidpads, a small one with a 100-foot radius and a large one with a 400-foot radius. First we spent a week on the small skidpad, getting the suspension optimized. Then we went to the large skidpad and balanced out the aerodynamics.

All that time people were going to Flegl and saying, "Why do you go to the skidpad? Why do you not go to the track? You know that a car set up on the pad will oversteer on the track." First the little guys came—and got nowhere. Then their bosses came—and got nowhere. And finally the Piechs came around. But Flegl stuck up for us. He had confidence that the engineering approach would succeed. I began to realize that he was a very valuable guy to work with. The two of us could discuss the situation in engineering terms and reach a stronger conclusion than either of us working alone. It was much easier on me, because it freed my mind somewhat, to concentrate more on driving. Flegl constantly kept elaborate records of precisely everything we did, and how it affected the car.

Over a period of a few weeks we learned everything there was to know about the setup of that particular vehicle. We went through the standard development procedure, but we were able to do it much faster and more completely because of all their mechanics and facilities. We tested springs, anti-roll bars, shocks, ride heights, wings, and all possible variations in suspension alignment. It became obvious that all their suspension geometry was wrong. I could tell by looking that the front was wrong, because it had such a short swing-arm radius. That's why it was hunting so badly on the straightaway.

At the rear, the problem was apparent in tire wear. The inside two inches of the tread would wear out almost immediately. I pointed that out, and they agreed that it was obviously wrong. But none of us had any idea what the answer was. As we got to the end of our tests, we started looking at the engineering drawings, and computer curves of the geometry. It became apparent then that the rear roll center was too low. In fact, it was underground. When the original chassis was built, they hadn't anticipated all the aerodynamic downforce that could be generated. Now, in a turn, cornering forces were causing the rear suspension to fall, causing too much camber and wearing the tires out wrong. I couldn't convince them of the seriousness of the problem, but I knew that once we had the car at our own shops, we could modify the geometry ourselves. We could run an A-B test, and let them know how it turned out. I also tried to convince them that we needed a locked differential, and they fought that too. I figured that the sooner we got a car to America, the better.

We never went back to their test track until the last day I was there. After all that work, the car was half a second faster. I was tremendously disappointed. I expected it to be about two seconds better. It was a great victory for Flegl, though. He stuck to our way of doing things, and he showed everyone that it was better. Without making any design changes in the vehicle, we had produced a new lap record for their wall. Then everyone said, "Flegl, maybe you *do* know what you're doing."

While we were at the track a truck showed up with another 917. It looked like the Spyder we had seen before at Can-Am races—an ugly, dirty, beat-up old thing—except that it was longer. It turned out to have a sixteen-cylinder motor that they wanted me to try. I was told that it was built by special order from the Piechs, and it was quite expensive. The chassis was easily stretched the extra two cylinders' length, but the motor required a new case, a new crank, new manifolds and fan housings, and lots of other pieces. They didn't tell me much about it, but I clearly got the impression that it was a possible alternative to the turbocharged twelve, or that it could even be turbocharged itself—for something like 2000 horsepower. So I drove the thing for them, and it was a real monster. The motor was so long that you could hear one end start up before the other. There were exhaust pipes sticking out everywhere. Although it wasn't set up properly to try for any lap records, it was truly impressive in a straight line. They just wanted me to feel the motor, anyhow, and when we were through they stuck it back in a barn somewhere. I was honored that they went to all the time and trouble to get it out and running just to show to me. It gave me something to think about.

While Flegl and I were doing the chassis development, I had one of our best mechanics, Woody Woodard, come to Germany to learn all about maintenance of the car. He worked in the shops with the Porsche mechanics, rebuilding transmissions and engines and hubs, and going over all the little details that are so important. We figured it should take about a month, but after two weeks he said he had learned everything he needed to know. The factory guys were amazed that he was so motivated and able to catch on so rapidly. He was anxious to leave, and I figured that since he was ultimately responsible, it was his decision. Our eventual finishing record shows how successful he was. He's really good at doing all those mechanical things the proper way.

The first thing we did when we got our 917 test car in our own shops was to prepare some bigger and better rear wings. The small Porsche wing was tilted up as high as it would go without stalling, and we thought we could use even more downforce at the rear. We built two new wings, one the same shape as Porsche's, only twice as big, and one with the modern split-flap design. I figured that if the drag was too much greater with them, we could always level them out for the same downforce.

The car we got was identical to what we had ended up with in Germany—still without the turbocharged motor we had been promised. We took it to Atlanta in December for its first American tests. Not much happened on that trip, except that we proved our wings to be much quicker, and we broke the motor. It was such a surprise that we sent it back to the factory and asked them to tell us what had gone wrong. They telexed back that it wasn't the motor's fault—it had just run out of oil. Woody went back to the car and looked over his records, and finally said that it was quite possible. The tank was hard to read, and it needed a lot of oil to avoid starvation. We telexed back that quite likely they were right, that it was our mistake. I got the impression they were amazed that we would admit we were wrong. Most mechanics become incensed when they feel they're being accused. But that's the only way to get anywhere—to admit an error rather than try to cover it up. I felt that was a stepping stone in our relationship.

While we were waiting for a new motor Woody prepared an alternate front suspension, which incorporated the long swing-arm. It was designed and set up in the shop so that it could easily be switched with the original suspension at the test track. It wasn't exactly what I wanted, but it was the best we could do within the structural limits we had. The rear roll center was still too low, but we had an unstable, understeering car. The best policy is to get one thing right at a time. We could look to the rear after we got the front suspension working right. We went back to Atlanta in January, bolted on the new suspension, and I was immediately one second faster. The first thing I did was to telex Flegl. I told him what the new geometry was in inches and degrees, and then I told him how much faster and more stable it was. They then had three choices. They could disbelieve it. They could accept it and do nothing. Or they could suspect that there was more to be gained, and suspect that the first try was certainly not the best. They took the third choice. They went even farther with the same idea, and eventually produced exactly what I wanted.

The second time we ran at Atlanta my laptimes were reasonably good. With the new split-flap wing, new front suspension, and some changes in the springs and anti-roll bars, I went half a second under the track record. We were really happy. I thought maybe we wouldn't need the turbo-motor after all. Maybe we could just lighten the chassis, optimize everything, and be competitive as it was. Roger was a little more realistic, though. He said, "Don't kid yourself. Atlanta is a twisty, winding track where horsepower doesn't count for much. Take the car to a high-speed track like Riverside and see what happens."

While we were in Germany looking at our car for the first time, the last Can-Am race of 1970 was being held at Riverside. I had Paul Van Valkenburgh go there and record the fastest times set by the McLaren cars on every section of the track—breaking down the corners and straightaways separately. We could go back there in a private test session and determine where our car was faster or slower. Our 917 went directly from Atlanta to Riverside. Unfortunately, it was so far off the pace there that it wasn't necessary to distinguish between corner times and acceleration times—except that we were only 4 percent off in the corners, compared to 8 percent in the long straightaway. We tried really hard, and we were still five seconds slower than the McLarens. Because we had already tested the car so extensively, we knew there wasn't much left in it. We could get a few percent here and there, but we couldn't make up for the 150 horsepower advantage the McLarens had on us.

One thing we did discover at Riverside was that we finally had enough downforce at the rear—with the new wing—but that we were going to have trouble getting enough at the front to balance the car. We started by mounting the front stub wings from our Indy McLaren on the nose of the Porsche, and got nothing at all. Then we realized that the flow split laterally at the nose and went over the wings at an angle. So we turned the wings inboard, which only made the car "darty" at high speed. We went fastest with no wing at all on the front, and with the rear wing trimmed out considerably below its best downforce position.

We realized then that we had to have the turbo-motor, and as soon as possible. I told Flegl that we must have one to test in America, because of the weather problems in Germany in the winter. Since we had never even *seen* the turbocharged version before, they sent their engine guy, Fritz Springler, with it. There wasn't any space problem, with the turbocharger mounted out in the rear, but it was pathetic how little we knew about its operation. It looked like they had put a lot of thought into it—sizing the blowers, lowering the compression ratio, selecting cams, pressure gauges for the inlet and exhaust, and so on.

We went back to Atlanta with the first turbo-motor in February. But it was cold there, and the motor wouldn't start. Eventually we towed it around the track a few times before we got it to run at all. Then, once it started, we damn near couldn't keep it running. By really working on the throttle—blipping, opening and closing—I could almost keep it going. I tried to drive it a few laps, and discovered that the throttle worked like an ignition switch—it was either wide-open power, or off. It wouldn't run at any part-throttle condition. I had to open the throttle all the way when coming out of a turn, and wait for the boost to come up. To start with, it was a few seconds slower than the unblown motor, but after a banzai effort, I got down to about the same laptime—with 300 more horsepower. Then we tried a 200-mile durability run, and I discovered that after about ten laps I couldn't keep up with the anticipation that was necessary. In addition to that, the brakes were fading from trying to cope with the odd blower problem. Toward the end of the durability test the blower failed, scattering parts into a cylinder and ruining the engine. We sent it back to Germany with a long dissertation on the problem, and possible solutions they could try.

Another engine arrived shortly, with Flegl and their head engine guy, Val Schaffer. We installed it and went back to Atlanta for the fourth time. In the meantime, we had sent the car out and gotten it painted up for an L&M press showing. It cost us $3000 for all the body preparation and paint, but it was the most beautiful job ever. All kinds of promoters and the press were at Atlanta taking photographs that time—and everything went exactly the same. We had to tow the car to get it started, and it wouldn't run at part throttle. I was getting exasperated. I showed Flegl and the engine expert what was happening, and they said they understood, but neither one knew what to do about it. We finally made up a variable-ratio linkage between the throttles and the fuel metering device, which for all our experimenting got us nowhere. The engine failed again in the same way. Still we had learned nothing.

I decided that it was foolish to waste any more time in the States. I told Flegl that I'd have to go to Germany and work with their engine men personally. I would have to fly back and forth for races and appearances, but it would be faster to use their facilities and their test car.

Our first runs in Germany were exactly the same. We tried bleed valves, and the Bosch injector guy came and told us how he could make it do anything we wanted—and nothing made any difference. Unfortunately, the turbo was faster on their track, because the turns were so simple that I could have the car in a straight line when the boost came on. They said, "Why worry? The car has more horsepower and it is faster. You want too much." But I was the one who had to drive the car, and I would decide when it was right. I knew it could be made to run at any part-throttle condition because it had been done to our Offys. In the first place, it still wouldn't start or idle correctly, and I told their engine men that I didn't know how they could be proud of a racing engine that wouldn't idle.

I told Roger that we were going to get smoked by McLaren if we couldn't get the turbo-motor to run right. So he went to Germany and watched me struggle with it on the track. He recognized that it was truly a handful to drive. We went to dinner with all the top Porsche guys, and Roger made an announcement. He said, "I think we should decide now not to go to the first race." They all looked shocked. "Mark has shown me that the engine is not ready, and it is better that we not go to the first race and look bad. We had better make the announcement now, so that our sponsors will be prepared." We all agreed to consider that alternative.

I came back a week later, after they had a chance to 'scope it over. They said it was exactly the way it should be—but it was exactly the way it had been. From a technical or a language standpoint, we just weren't understanding each other at all. I was totally exasperated. I said, "We are wasting our time on the track. Now we must take the engine out of the car, put it back on the dynamometer, and I will try to *show* you what is wrong." While they were doing that, I looked at their dyno output curves. They had all the necessary data—torque, rpm, boost pressure, and so on—except that the curves started at 5000 rpm. I said, "Why are there no curves up to that point?" They said, "The motor does not run there." I thought, "Christ! That's what I've been trying to tell you for a month!" I couldn't believe it was that simple. I couldn't believe that they had simply calibrated the fuel injection for wide-open throttle with full boost, and had totally ignored any part-throttle operation. Flegl and I sat down and designed a dyno program to get the information we needed for proper calibration.

We had to find out what the proper fuel flow needed to be at different rpms, pressure boosts, and throttle openings. The first thing I recognized was that we would have to run the motor with no blower. They said, "But it is a turbo-motor. It will have no power." Finally I convinced them that there were times when the boost was very low and yet the engine must keep running. When we took the blower off—it wouldn't run at all! When we tried to accelerate above idle, it just died. So we fitted the motor with two control levers—one for the throttle butterflies and one for the fuel-flow meter. The engine guys were a little angry. They were mumbling in German, "He runs in America with the blower and is not happy. Then he runs here with the blower and is not happy. Then he runs on the dyno with the blower and is not happy. Now we run on the dyno *without* the blower and he is *still* not happy. We are going backwards." By the time we got a fuel-flow control lever the engine was so fuel-soaked inside that it wouldn't even idle right. They decided to clean the plugs out by revving it up, but when they gave it wide-open throttle, it just went "burble-burble-bump-burble . . ." I was furious. I told Flegl, "Look, you may be able to afford to ruin a $30,000 motor, but I can't afford the time. If those guys are too lazy to change the plugs, give them a coffee break and I'll change them myself."

We got it to run, and we made a complete map of what fuel the motor wanted, in steps from 2000 to 8000 rpm, with throttle angles from ten to ninety degrees open. From that data we could make a fuel-control cam to regulate the fuel at all nonblown conditions. Then we reinstalled the turbocharger and ran similar fuel-flow maps with different boost pressures. From that, we could design a diaphragm-operated fuel valve to allow extra fuel as it was required for various boosts. All the time we were doing that, I had to be very careful not to let them know I had never done anything like it before. If they knew I was simply working from intuition, rather than experience, they never would have listened to me. But I knew one thing. If we didn't get the job done, there would be no hope in the Can-Am. I had nothing to lose by trying.

When we had a complete map of all the fuel-flow points required under all conditions, we called the Bosch guy back again. He looked at the curves and said he could give us what we wanted—now that we could *tell* him exactly what we wanted. He went away to redesign the fuel-injection metering system, while we went back to the test chassis with an unblown motor.

They had produced the third-generation front suspension by then, with an even longer front swing-arm radius than I had suggested, and it worked very well on the track. Then we began looking to the rear suspension. We came up with many good ideas over a bottle of cognac in Flegl's office. If we had done that in America, we would have been pitched out on our ears.

But there, as long as you do your job, it's fine. I suggested that we could easily raise the rear roll center by spacing the lower outboard A-arm ball joint down. When we did that, the rear swing-arm radius was shortened and the car was not so fast, but at least we improved the edge-wear problem on the tires. So we lengthened the rear swing-arm radius back to where it was by raising the upper-inner ball joint location. When we were through, it ran about the same speed, but we had cured the wear, and it was easier to drive.

All that time I was looking at the spring travel in the rear suspension. I asked if it was bottoming, and they said it was all right. I had already shoved them far enough, so I figured it was something we could look into at our own shops.

Then the Bosch guy came back with the injection system. We put the turbo-motor back in and went to the track. I tried to get them to run it on the dyno first, but they insisted that it was right and there was no reason to check it. I started the engine and right away it idled perfectly. Then I tried to drive off—and it died! It wouldn't run at any other throttle position. I could see some bad looks in their eyes, and I was getting quietly desperate myself. But we had spent enough days on the fuel system so I could make an educated guess that it was too lean. I had them open the fuel-flow meter by fifteen clicks—that increases it all across the band—and it ran well enough to get me around one lap. But it was snapping and banging, so we opened it another ten clicks. Suddenly, it was right! It started, idled, accelerated, and had immense torque over a wide throttle range! The fastest we had ever gone on their track with a badly calibrated turbo-motor was 49.7 seconds. Almost immediately I was down to 48.9 seconds. I came in and said, "I am quite happy with this fuel pump." They were elated. They were so pleased they never let go of that pump, which became known as the "happy pump." They kept it at Bosch, and it was used for the calibration of all other fuel-injection systems we used. Whenever there was a problem, they would always go back to the "happy pump." I immediately sent a telex that read:

JUST RAN WITH RECALIBRATED FUEL INJECTION. VERY MUCH IMPROVED ENGINE NOW RUNNINGAT ALL THROTTLE POSITIONS. NEW LAP RECORD 48.9. MUST STILL MAKE INTERMEDIATE RANGE CHECKS ON DYNO TOMORROW. THE WRITER IS VERY ENCOURAGED. PLEASE INFORM CAPTAIN OF MAJOR BREAK THRU. MARK.

I had a copy of that telex posted over my desk for the next two years, because that was truly the turning point in our Can-Am program. The front suspension was right, the rear suspension was right, and the motor was right.

The first time I drove the car with the motor working the way it should, I came in and said, "Boy, this is one strong mother!" None of the Germans were familiar with the term, so I had to explain that it meant "very, very, powerful." From then on they used the expression quite a bit without knowing its real derivation. They asked me if it had enough power then, and I said, "No. It will never have enough power until I can spin the wheels at the end of the straightaway in high gear." They were aghast at that. They had never seen motors put out even as much power as we had. As they reached 800 horsepower, they literally burned out one of their dynamometers. By the end of the year the five-liter engine was up to 880 horsepower, and the best 5.4-liter engine in 1973 was eventually good for 1190 horsepower. All the time they kept asking, "Now does it have enough?" And I kept saying, "I still can't spin the wheels all the way down the straightaway."

After the engine was developed we went back to aerodynamics. They thought the 917 was really tremendous as it was, and Cox couldn't convince them how important it was to work on aerodynamic downforce. After we tested at Riverside, I said there was only one way to show them what we were going to be up against. I sent them a year-old McLaren to run against our test car. Roy Woods had one for sale, so I called him and said, "We would like to rent your McLaren, and we will return it in perfect shape—as long as you don't ask any questions." I air-freighted it to Germany, went over and showed the Porsche engineers how to run it, and let them look it over for a while. I had to be somewhere else for a race or two. They drove it on the skidpads, measured it completely, weighed everything, and even looked inside the monocoque because they thought there must be a space frame inside it. Eventually they broke the motor by trying to run it on a chassis dyno, which made me a little angry about the extra expense. But the trip wasn't in vain. It woke them up to the fact that the McLarens had some merits after all.

We could get all the downforce we needed at the rear with monster wings mounted way back on extended fins. But we were having trouble balancing it at the front. The first idea was to mount a series of wings ahead of each front wheel hump. There were vertical end plates going forward from the wheel openings, with four split-flap wings mounted between them and the radiator duct. It was the meanest, wildest, ugliest race car nose in the entire world. It worked well in the wind tunnel, but since the weather wasn't good enough for a track test in Germany, we had to test it at Atlanta. We couldn't make it do a damn thing. I was so convinced it ought to work that we wasted a lot of time on it. We sent it back to Germany, ran it on the high-speed skidpad, and proved conclusively that it was no good. All that time I was telling them that if we could glue the nose down like the tail was, we ought to get *two* "g's" lateral acceleration out of it. Finally, in desperation, we took a huge *rear* wing and stuck it out in front on special brackets. I couldn't even see past it, but we had to get something better. We turned it up all the way—and *still* nothing. We had to conclude that a wing is not a wing when it's mounted in front. Piece by piece, we cut away everything we had on the nose, and when we were down to the radiator duct and the convex surfaces ahead of the wheels, it was best of all. The only other thing we did was to add a lip around the base, which increased downforce a little bit more. And that was the way we went to the first Can-Am race at Mosport.

Indianapolis was two weeks before Mosport, though, and we were working closely with McLaren there. They had a reputation for always designing the perfect car—and then testing it simply to prove it was perfect. But we heard that they had designed their new Can-Am car around a huge wing in the nose, and radiators which were moved back to the sides. Air works the same in England as it does in Germany, and because of all the development we had done on our car, I knew they had made a big mistake. When I saw the McLaren guys I said, "You may think our Porsche is a big joke, but if what we learned is true, and if what we hear you're doing is true, then you've been screwed and you don't even know it." I wasn't so smart myself—I couldn't have done it without a lot of help—but that was one time I had to get my licks in.

I was about as far on top of the world as I could get. I won at Indianapolis, I had developed a car that I knew would win the Can-Am, and I had just rewarded myself by buying a new Cigarette—a twenty-eight-foot, dual 350 Chevy-engined offshore power boat. It was terribly expensive, but it was my first extravagance, my first diversion, since I began racing professionally. Flegl, my boat expert, Jay Signore, and I went running berserk in it—and ran it high and dry on a sandbar off Sandy Hook, New Jersey.

We went to Mosport a week before the race, just to check everything out. I didn't hold anything back, and ended up going about three seconds faster than the record. Then a gear broke in the engine, and we had to go back to the shops. By the time we returned for practice the word had leaked out, and we were mobbed by everyone—spectators, the press, and our competitors.

Our biggest problems from then on came from other Porsche owners. Racing customers and "friends of the factory" are very important to Porsche. People like Vasek Polak and Peter Gregg have strong Porsche dealerships, and the factory doesn't like to make them angry. Both of them were very upset when they heard how fast our car was, and that they wouldn't be able to buy one like it. But Roger had been explicit about that in our deal with the factory. We were putting a lot of time and money into the development, and we wanted a head start on other Porsche racers. We weren't worried about running against someone else with the same equipment as much as we wanted the impact and publicity of having the first, one, and only. Gregg really tried to dynamite us by spreading rumors that he was about to get a car like ours, but Roger made a stand. We had lived with the car, we were most qualified to race it, and we were going to win with it—exclusively.

What really bothered them was that we had *two* 917–10 Porsches at the race. At Mosport our old test car stood by with an uncharged engine, in case it rained and the turbo-motor was undriveable. We had decided early in the year that we would always take two cars, with one solely as a spare. We weren't going to the expense of hiring another driver and another crew to keep it in shape, but it could be pressed into service if the race car got broken. It didn't have the same tender loving care—the inspection, maintenance, and cleanliness. It was just a lot of spare parts that happened to be assembled in the shape of a car. After Mosport, we decided that the turbo-motor would work in the rain, so we also put one in the backup car.

When the McLarens showed up at Mosport we weren't surprised to learn that we were easily two seconds faster. We were so much quicker that we decided not to practice on Friday. But the promoters came around and told us that a big crowd had come to see the car run, and wouldn't we please take it around. So we fired it up, and I took a few slow laps at the end of the day. I even talked with the McLaren guys a little, but I didn't rub it in too much. Before the race, I couldn't be sure what was going to happen, and after the race it would be academic. But as far as I was concerned, the entire Can-Am series was already over. We were so much faster that there was no way they could ever catch up. They acted confident, but I think they were a little shocked.

Everyone was complaining about the front tires. They were a low-profile design that we had developed with Goodyear, to help optimize our long swing-arm, low roll-center front suspension. There were a lot of comments about excessive understeer with those tires, but I rather suspect that McLaren's understeer problem was due more to their unworkable front wing.

In the race itself I was looking good—for a while. After about twenty easy laps in the lead, a turbocharger valve stuck, and we spent three laps getting it free. I was so discouraged that I started to walk away, but Flegl got mad, and Roger told me to go back out there and win some money. As it turned out, I finished second to Hulme's McLaren. Flegl later said he was disappointed in me—that I wanted to quit just because it looked like I couldn't win. That was good criticism. I had made that mistake before, and Flegl put me back in my place.

Because of the failure at Mosport we all wanted to make sure everything was right for Atlanta. We went there a week early to do some testing with both cars. We were trying to do too much, I guess. While the guys were changing gear ratios in the backup car, I decided to take the race car out and warm up a new motor we had in it. It was just going to be a few casual laps.

On lap one I just puttered around. On lap two I warmed it up against the brakes. On lap three I was still keeping the rpms down, but coming out of the turns harder. I accelerated out of turn seven, up the long back straightaway, over the crest of a hill at about 150, and . . . *crack*! . . . there was a tremendous noise from the rear. I felt the rear of the car rise up and start rotating around to the left. Because it happened going over a hill, I was sure I had broken a rear half-shaft, as I did in the Lola at Bridgehampton. So when the car had rotated 180 degrees, I lined it up to back into the embankment. It hit *very* hard, and spun back onto the track. I didn't know whether the wheels and suspension were still connected, but I was thinking I could straighten it out on the track, release the brakes, and roll to a stop. What I didn't know was that I had lost the entire rear bodywork, and the car was dangerously unstable. When I released the brakes it was like someone drop-kicked me into the air. The whole car jumped right off the ground and started cartwheeling end for end.

To me, everything had been relatively serene up to that point. Even sliding backward at over 100 mph, there are a few seconds to analyze the situation. The impact wasn't enough to knock me out, and then I was sliding again. But all that time the car was on its way up. When I released the brakes, all hell broke loose. I remember going into the air, and then looking down at the guardrail. The car came down nose first on it with a tremendous shrieking and crying of metal. Then it flipped over and I was looking *up* at the rail and posts flying past. Each time the car hit the ground I'd black out, but I recall thinking, "This is going to be bad." And then I was thinking, "This really *is* bad, because I'm hurting a lot." And I was trying to pull myself into a ball so that my arms and legs wouldn't fly around so much.

I don't remember seeing much of the front end go away. Suddenly the bodywork was gone and I could see twisted tubes and bars. Then the right front wheel just kind of went away from me. I don't know if it was up, down, or sideways at the time, but it went away like a slow-motion dream. I didn't see the frame, or dash, or steering wheel go, I was trying so hard to pull myself into my seat. And then there was silence.

I looked around—and I was sitting on the grass, still strapped into my safety seat, with the motor right behind me, and *nothing* ahead of me. No front end, no frame, no wheels, no body, no fuel tanks—just me, my seat, some tubes, and the roll bar. I looked back and saw a small fire in the turbocharger, and thought I'd better try to get away. Then I noticed that my left leg was bent at a funny angle. It bent 45 degrees at the knee, and was lying on top of my right leg. I thought, "This isn't so bad. The only thing wrong is that my leg is broken. But I've gotta get away from the car without getting a compound fracture." I wedged my left leg against my right foot, unfastened the harness, and pushed myself out of the seat. In an accident like that, there has to be some mental confusion—if not shock—and I thought it was possible that what was left of the car might blow up. I dragged myself clear across the track by my hands. By that time I was hurting so bad I just couldn't believe it.

The guys heard the accident clear back in the pits. Woody said that first he heard the engine rev way up and blow the rev-limiter with a "bam!" Then there was the wailing of the tires and the rumble of the car being destroyed. They ran to the standby ambulance and came after me. Dual, the ambulance driver, had been around us for some time, and he was really shook up. He didn't know how badly hurt I was, but he put a pressure splint on my leg and got me back to the pits. He and Woody were debating whether to take me to Atlanta or Gainesville, and trying to get the air-conditioner to work. I started shouting, "Goddammit! Just get going to *any* hospital! I can't stand the pain much longer."

So we went hauling into a hospital in Gainesville, all sweaty and dirty. They took the splint off, X-rayed the leg and told me it wasn't broken, and gave me some pain pills. I was also bruised up quite a bit, but they never looked at anything else. Then I called my wife—even though we were separated, I thought she ought to know I was all right—and I called Roger. But I had so much Demerol in me by then that I didn't know if I was on foot or horseback. The doctor said I could put an Ace bandage on my knee and leave, but Woody thought I ought to stay in the hospital for a while. I agreed, because I thought I was going to die just from the pain.

The next day I tried to take a wheelchair to the whirlpool bath, but I passed out and fell in the hall. The day after I made it to the whirlpool, but it didn't seem to have any effect. We had no idea how bad the knee was at that point, so we were hoping that maybe I could drive that weekend. By Thursday I realized it was getting worse. I called my friend Burge Hulett, who can find out anything about anything, and asked him to get me the best muscle doctor available. He found one in New York who said he would be glad to help me if I could get to New York in the next week. That wasn't quite fast enough, so Woody asked around and came up with a Dr. Funk, who was team physician for the Atlanta Falcons. When I called him he said he had heard about the accident, and if I could come to his emergency ward that night, he would have a look. I checked out of the hospital and got someone to drive me to Atlanta. Dr. Funk put the knee under X ray, pulled and twisted it a lot, and told me I had to have an operation right away—and that I was going to be in a cast for two months. I said, "I can't do that! This is my big season. I can't take time off." He reckoned I could do what I wanted, but I was like anyone else—if he didn't operate, it might not ever heal. I agreed to go ahead with it. But first I had to go back to the track and give the team a hand.

In the meantime Woody had gotten the test car out and prepared it for the race, and Roger had George Follmer come to Atlanta just in case I wasn't able to drive. I got a motel room that night, somehow pulled myself together enough to shower and shave, and went to the track Saturday morning. I showed George everything I knew about the car—how to start it and warm it up, and how to drive it. We drove around the track, and I showed him where and how to adapt to the blower lag.

By then I knew my leg was in really bad shape. Whenever I rode in a car, I had to hold my lower leg to keep it from falling away at the knee. But what made me even sicker was seeing George drive that beautiful car, which I had spent so many months building exactly the way I wanted. It must be like seeing another man in bed with your wife.

Before I left to go back to the hospital I had to see the remains of the other car. The guys didn't want me to see it, since it was all balled up and packed away. But that was a big thing in my life. I couldn't go away not knowing what had happened. They did tell me that the tail had come off, but I wanted to know why; we might learn something that would prevent George from getting hurt. So we climbed into the truck, closed the doors, and pulled out all the pieces. The frame was kind of brittle, and it had just broken apart. The frame rails were sheared off right next to the seat, and the roll bar was crunched and cracked. There had been about twenty-five gallons of fuel in one tank, but it broke away cleanly and never caught fire. The fire extinguisher, which had been in the nose, was gone also. My safety seat, which was designed by Paul Van Valkenburgh, was fastened to the firewall and the floor, and it was all that was left forward of the engine. The accident was similar enough to the one that killed Bruce McLaren that I reckoned it was a miracle I was still alive. Milt Minter later had a serious accident in Al Holbert's Porsche with one of my seats, and Al told me that it kept him from being badly hurt.

As I looked at the remains of my car, I kept asking myself, "How did this happen? What was different from all the other times?" After a while Woody said, "Mark, I really screwed up! When you went out on the track, all the pins weren't in the tail section." The rear half of the body, including the wing, was held on with eight lock pins, but because we had installed some new brake ducts, two of the pins wouldn't fit. Woody wasn't working on the car then, but he still felt responsible. Since I was in the car with the motor running at the time, I had no way of knowing some pins didn't fit. But no one realized the consequences then. Woody was beside himself. The car—and my safety—were up to him, and he took full responsibility for the error. How could I be angry with Woody when he readily admitted it was his fault? He went way up in my book, for being man enough to do that. Whatever he may have lost, he's earned back many times. He pulled himself together and got the other car going, when other guys would have fallen apart. It's a burden he has had to live with for a long time.

That tail problem was something I was already nervous about. The tail wasn't put on quite right in our pitstop at Mosport, and I had seen pictures of the body lifting just behind the doors. The fiberglass had deformed so that there was a noticeable gap there. We were already working on it in small stages, by making an aluminum lip and taping the gap. Finally it opened enough to rip the whole tail off when just two pins were missing. We couldn't make an announcement that our crew was to blame, so we said there was something wrong with the ducts.

I heard about the race at the hospital after my operation. George Follmer qualified right behind Denny Hulme, and won easily when both McLarens went out in the first few laps. Hulme's car went upside down at about the same place mine did, but instead of cartwheeling, it just slid on its top and stayed together.

After my accident I never again had the same kind of control over Penske's racing operations. That was something I had built up slowly since 1966, when I first went to work for him. I had become the person who called most of the shots. Suddenly I wasn't there any more, and my influence stopped entirely. I was so doped up with Demerol I couldn't even manage myself. I'm sure Roger had anticipated something like that happening, because he was well covered with employees like Don Cox, Chuck Cantwell, the mechanics, and even himself. It certainly showed me that no one is indispensable. Even when I went back and drove again, I never had quite as much authority. Everyone else stepped up to their new responsibilities, and when I came back there was no reason to give them up.

Porsche 917-10 wreck at Atlanta

courtesy of Penske Communications

Things didn't go so well for the team in the next race at Watkins Glen, however. Porsche chartered a plane and flew a bunch of their head guys over—including Dr. Ferry Porsche—plus a lot of European journalists. It was the third race, but sort of an official debut. I was still in the hospital, and Roger called me a couple of times to tell me what was going wrong. First it seemed the new motor wasn't as strong, so they put the Atlanta motor back in. Then the handling wasn't right. I was so doped up that I wasn't capable of any constructive suggestions. George qualified third, pitted to have a blower valve unstuck, and drove a very poor race to finish fifth. Roger was blaming Flegl, and Flegl was saying George was no good. Someone at Porsche called Roger and suggested he get another driver. They said to contact Andretti, or they would get Ickx. Roger called to ask what I thought.

I thought Roger had made the right decision with George. The car wasn't so tricky or unusual that no one but me could drive it. With proper guidance anyone could do a good job with it. But I didn't want another driver coming in. I knew I could work with George, and I didn't want to run the chance of anyone else trying to take my position on the team. I told Roger that George could do the job if anyone could. Roger agreed to stay with George if *I* would go to the next race and help him sort the car. I was just out of the hospital and barely able to hobble around in my cast, but Roger has never been afraid to ask me to do a difficult task. I agreed to go to Mid-Ohio and help. It was George's last chance.

We had all day Wednesday to test, then a day off, and official practice began on Friday. The first thing we tried was a change in the turbocharger, since there had been a response problem at Watkins Glen. I told Flegl and Schaffer, their head engine guy, that the problem would be worse on a shorter track if they couldn't find some smaller "exhaust snails." The exhaust turbine housing is shaped like a snail shell, and its size determines blower response. They brought two smaller snails, we tried them out—and we could tell just by listening to the motor that George's laptimes were better. That was a real breakthrough.

Then we tried wider rear wheels and tires. We had always used seventeen-inch rims, even though Porsche had provided us with spare nineteen-inchers. The problem was that Goodyear didn't have any tires wide enough to fit the wider rims. We tested some at Riverside but they weren't right, and I asked Goodyear to make them in another compound. We put them on at Mid-Ohio, and they were definitely quicker. But George was still complaining that the car was both oversteering and understeering at different places on the track.

I had suspected that there wasn't enough bump travel in the rear. I asked Woody to check it, and he told me there was two inches of ground clearance with the shocks bottomed. I didn't know if that was right, and I didn't know how to find out in a hurry. When we put the wider tires on, they were rubbing on the wheel openings—but they didn't wear very far into it. I knew then that the rear was bottoming, causing temporary oversteer. I also began to understand what had gone wrong. The car was designed for twenty-five-inch-diameter rear tires. But they had grown by stages to twenty-eight inches with the latest wide tire. As the chassis was progressively lowered for the same ride height, the suspension travel became less and less.

We had run George to exhaustion by then, and the day was up, so I told Woody that he was going to have to raise the shock mounts. It was a lot of work, but Woody knew it was coming. They took the car to Micky Rupp's shops to use their heli-arc, and did a real clean job. When we knew what to look for, the answer was obvious. In official practice the car no longer had sudden oversteer, but then it understeered too much—as I expected. So we boosted the rear spring rate, and George said that was better. Finally, between practice and qualifying, I made the decision to go even stiffer. The McLaren team was amazed that we were faster and still changing things around.

George qualified on the pole and led every lap to a win. Part of that was due to Roger's good judgment. It rained off and on during the race, and while Hulme came in four times to change tires back and forth, Roger kept George on dry tires. When it was all over, everyone was happy. I realized then that I could relate to George—I could understand his comments and get the car sorted that way. All the Porsche guys were satisfied that we could get the job done. Roger was satisfied that our team was still working together right. And George kept his job. I shed a tear when I wasn't asked to go to the victory celebration, but it helped me understand the rest of the team. That was the first time I wasn't up there taking all the credit. It was good for me to realize what the other guys live with all the time.

Elkhart Lake went about the same. George started way down because he was commuting back and forth for the Ontario 500, and it rained during his qualification period. But he went right to the lead and won, as both the McLarens dropped out again. I decided then that I was going to drive in the next race. I was out of my cast and off the pain pills by that time. I was drinking a lot too, but it wasn't so much for the pain as to reduce the anxiety and frustration of being out of action in the middle of one of my best years. I drank a lot of vodka, which isn't as bad as some alcohol—but it still kept me rather drunk. It wasn't hard to stop when I decided I was going to drive again. All along I had been exercising my leg as much as its movement and the pain would allow. It had shrunk up like a beanstalk when the cast came off, and I needed a lot of therapy.

In the meantime Roger had arranged to get another chassis. Hardly anything was salvageable from the wrecked car—except for two extra lock pins—so we built the second car out of all our spare parts. At first I told Roger it wasn't necessary for George to continue. It was my job to win the Can-Am. But he convinced me that since George had the lead, we couldn't take a chance on me, especially since we didn't know how well I had recovered. I didn't want Roger to go broke running two cars, but it was important for me to get back in the car that bit me, as soon as I possibly could. Roger said he wanted me to do it, although it cost him a great deal of money.

We went to Donnybrooke prepared to race both cars. Karl Kainhofer was working on my car, but without much enthusiasm. It was a slapdash affair, without enough time or money to do it the way Karl thought we should. Since it was virtually untested, I had some difficulty sorting it out. It seemed to be oversteering too much. We changed around springs and bars until I was comfortable in it, and I sat on the pole, just barely ahead of George. As it turned out, though, my car had a fictitious setup. After being out of action for three months, I had lost my touch. It's critically important to have the feel of a car, especially something as sensitive and powerful as the turbo-Porsche. Midway through the race I began to get the feel back, and I realized that, in fact, I had the car understeering too much. George and I traded the lead back and forth, but I was driving my tail off—an unfortunate pun at that point—while George seemed to have the situation in hand. Then my left rear tire developed a slow leak and started going down. I didn't recognize what was happening, except that the car was understeering less—and going slower.

There was one place where I was definitely faster than George—the high-speed right-hand bend at the end of the straightaway. He wasn't taking any chances there, while I was going through it flat out. But low tire pressure was causing the left rear tire to overheat, and in the middle of that turn the tread peeled off and it blew out. I spun right in front of George. There I was, going sideways through a turn at 190 mph with the rear end flopping around. I thought, "Oh, *shit*! Here we go again!" The back of the body was being torn up by the tire, and I was afraid the car was going to go over. I just couldn't take another scene in the hospital at that point. Definitely not in Brainerd, Minnesota. On one loop I saw that George was going to hit me if I didn't get off the road, so I got off the brakes, pushed the clutch in, and let it careen backwards off the turn. I figured it wouldn't be too bad an impact with the engine behind me. Fortunately, or due to good planning, there was an open field there, with nothing to run into. But it was a very scary ride. It was my first time back, and I had another accident, which I could have prevented by recognizing the problem. It was a dumb mistake, and I had only myself to blame. Then George ran out of gas on the last lap and finished fourth.

We had one truck and one good car, so the guys had to go back to our shops to fix my car before going on to Edmonton. A bad situation developed at that race, which made me angry about having a two-car team. Near the end I was leading the race and could see George closing up behind me. I was trying to keep ahead, and mad that we were having to run both cars so hard when we were far ahead of the McLarens. Then George passed me. On the next lap I saw Roger give him the signal to back off and let me go by. I had mixed emotions about that. I was upset about having to race against him in a car that I had developed, but I figured George ought to win fair and square. So on the last lap I slowed down and motioned for George to repass me before the finish. What I didn't know was that George was a lap down on me! He had had to pit to change a leaking tire, and when he passed me, he was merely unlapping himself. I won the race!

For Laguna Seca I tried really hard to be in better shape, so that I could keep up with George. Our qualifying times were identical, but I had a stronger motor for the race, and I was able to pull ahead. Roger had told us before the race that he didn't want us fighting it out. If it came down to it, he would signal us as to which car should take the lead. So I tried to build up a large margin on George, to make it hard for Roger to justify letting him go by me. I don't like to boil down to those tactics on a team, but when it comes to winning races, I'm a selfish race driver. About three laps from the end Roger gave me the signal to let George win. I didn't understand that at all, because George could have won the Championship with a second place. But I slowed down out in the back and let him by. I think that was an unpopular decision to the crowd and to our crew. I was certainly devastated.

At Riverside it was the other way around. George was faster because we put my motor in his car, and my new motor turned out to be weaker. When George made a sarcastic comment in the pre-race ceremonies about the pace car *I* was going to win, I knew that Roger had told him to hold back. I said, "Wait a minute, George. The race isn't over yet." But halfway through the race, while I was running second, George slowed down and let me by, right at the start-finish line where everyone could see him do it. John DeLorean came up after the race and said that George's move ". . . showed absolutely *no* class." George stayed right behind me up until the end. With a few laps to go, he pulled up very close and started weaving back and forth. I thought something was wrong with my car. It felt like a tire was going flat again. I was afraid I was going to make another mistake like I did at Donnybrooke. The cars were already sold, and I couldn't afford the risk of smashing up one or both of them. I pulled in to have the tires looked at—they were all right—and George went on to win. That move dropped me from second down to fourth in the final Can-Am standings.

I was sick. I went back to our motorhome and secluded myself. Pretty soon, Porsche's Dr. Fuhrmann came around and said, "We are very happy that Porsche won the Championship, but you should have won this race. Let us have a drink together." He went out and found a new bottle of Bourbon. We had no ice, or glasses. We just drank right out of the bottle until it was dry. That cheered me up some, but mostly it showed me how much someone appreciated what I had done. It showed me what a fabulous, down-to-earth guy Fuhrmann was, to help me when I was really hurting. There was the head guy from Porsche, sitting there drinking out of the bottle with a lowly "fourth-place" driver.

That weekend we made our deal for the next season with Porsche. They liked the idea of us running two cars and two drivers, but again Roger convinced them it didn't make sense financially. We knew we could beat McLaren with a one-car team, even though the rumor was that Chevrolet was going to help them with a turbo-motor. We didn't know then that they weren't going to run against us the next year. Part of our deal was an explicit agreement that we would have exclusive use of the new car we developed. Anyone else could have a 917-10, but we would work on a 917-30, which would be basically the same except for slight improvements. That was what we understood the deal to be in 1972. The factory didn't want to build a lot of experimental pieces to sell during the year, while we were still proving them on the track. Whenever we came up with something new, everyone would want it at once, and the factory wasn't geared for that. So Porsche told other teams like Polak, Gregg, and Rinsler that they could buy what existed, but we would have some new developments that were entirely up to us.

Our two 917-10's were sold to Bobby Rinsler at Laguna Seca. I think we would have preferred to sell them to Roy Woods, but Rinsler came up with an offer first. Woody Woodard went with one car to help Charlie Kemp with it at the American Road Race of Champions (ARRC) runoffs at Atlanta. Rinsler had some Southern stock car mechanics working on his cars, and Woody tried to show them how to maintain the various precise bits and pieces. But he was worried that as he went through the gearbox and suspension, nobody was writing anything down. Those guys left the team very soon, and Rinsler tried to hire Woody. He was even calling at our shops, which kind of annoyed me, but we try to give our people the best overall deal they can get anywhere. Eventually Rinsler hired some mechanics from the factory, which couldn't have made Porsche too happy. We had asked if we could do that, and they discouraged us because of the money they had invested in training them.

We saw immediately that Rinsler was going to be a problem. He went over to the factory and wined and dined all the right people, trying to get a better deal than we had. Roger was concerned that he might be able to push us out. I told Roger not to worry. The ultimate performance of those cars depended on all the minor details in the engine and chassis. Everything had to be perfect, and Rinsler's team wasn't capable of doing it the way we could. All we had to do was take care of ourselves and let the record speak for itself. Still, we knew Rinsler was going to be a thorn in the ointment when he hired George Follmer to drive for him.

Since Rinsler hadn't paid for both cars right away, we decided to take one back to the factory to baseline it against our 917-30 development. Rinsler wanted it over there anyhow, so that he could run some European Interseries races. The car was a little faster than the factory-development 917 had been—on the skidpad and on the track. Then we took our 5-liter motor out and put in the new 5.4-liter version, and the car was exactly half a second faster, with no other changes. That gave me some idea of what kind of opposition we had to face in 1973 with the car in Rinsler's hands.

We set to work developing our 917-30. Porsche had hired a French aeronautical company to produce a new aerodynamic shape called the "Paris body." They had been working on it ever since we first went with Porsche, and the first molds were produced in late 1972. Finally it was available for testing, so that we could find out whether it was actually better in downforce and reduced drag.

I had also been talking about having a longer wheelbase, but neither Flegl nor I had any idea exactly what it should be. The factory couldn't justify an arbitrary increase in length without trying some out, so they adapted a 917 chassis that could be quickly stretched at the firewall. When the press saw that they naturally assumed we were going to vary the length for different tracks. Another change I asked for was a wider front track. When we had gone to nineteen-inch rear rims, we automatically increased the rear track width by four inches, making it much wider than the front. I suspected that was why the car was very hard to balance correctly if it was slightly off in oversteer/understeer.

In December our 917-30 test car became a reality, with the Paris body, a stretchable chassis, wider front suspension, and the 5.4-liter engine. I had just enough time to run it on the small skidpad one time before the weather became really bad. I waited around for a week, came back to the United States, went back and waited some more—and finally we decided to take the car to a warmer climate. Flegl said that the Paul Ricard track in France usually had nice weather. Their new Carrera was about ready for testing also, and we still had our old 917-10, so we moved practically their entire operation to France. We had trucks, cars, people, tools, spare motors, gearboxes, and bodies. The trucks were slow and we had to pass through various customs stations with all that paperwork and the inspections—it was almost a week-long trip. That was about the time of Porsche's annual

Porsche 917-30 *photo by F. David Stone*

racing awards dinner in Stuttgart, which Flegl and I were invited to attend. We tried to get the company pilot to fly down and pick us up, but he said that was impossible for one reason or another. So Roger and George went to accept the awards.

We baselined the old 917-10, ran the Carrera some, and proved out everything on the 917-30 test car—everything but the new body. With the car the same except for the new body, it wasn't any faster. On top of that, it seemed to have a high-speed oversteer, no matter how high we turned the rear wing up. It was a funny-looking wing shape. It was almost flat on top and very round on the bottom. It looked a lot like the Porsche setup we tried unsuccessfully in our first development car, but since they had paid a great deal for the design, we felt obligated to give it another chance. We had no way of knowing the relative value of the new front versus the new rear, so we put the old tail back on, and discovered that combination was best of all. At least the new nose configuration was better. Still, the top speed was limited at 212 mph.

It started to snow about that time, so we all sat around the restaurant/rooming house/hangar/bar drinking a lot of Calvados and wondering where we could get more speed. I knew that their long-tailed Le Mans body had allowed the same basic car to run 240 mph, but Flegl didn't even want to think about it. He had been primarily responsible for that car, and it had been a big mark in his career. But it had been such a bad experience in development that he wanted to forget it. It was an unstable design, and it took a lot of work to make it driveable. But finally, after a lot of drinks, Flegl began to relate that experience to the Can-Am, and he began to get enthused about utilizing all that accumulated knowledge in another area.

While we were waiting for the snow to stop, Flegl got a great old racing mechanic named Mimler to cut up some tubing and sheet aluminum and graft it onto our old tail. It was the worst piece of cobbled-up junk I'd ever seen, but it was about the right shape. When we got it on the track we smeared black droplets of oil on it to see what the air flow looked like, and changed the shape where we could see it was wrong. We had to keep going higher and higher in gear ratios to reach peak rpms on the straightaway, but ultimately the car went 240 mph with no other changes. The mid-speed cornering was a little slower, though, which indicated that it had less downforce. The weather shut us off then, but that tail had so much potential that we decided we would make it work somehow. While I went back to the United States, they cut a tail off a Le Mans body, stuck it on our car, raised and lowered it until the position was about right, and finalized it at that. It was a tremendous gamble to make final bodies from an untested shape, but I had confidence in Flegl.

We tried the new car for the first time at Atlanta. It had looked good on our skidpad, but at Atlanta it wasn't balanced properly. It seemed to need still more downforce at the rear. For all our trick stuff—suspension, body, motor, and tires—it still wasn't any faster than the old car. We couldn't seem to get the aerodynamics balanced. The nose had a big lip around its base, which worked great up to certain speeds, where it would "grab the ground" and create high-speed oversteer. So we had to find more rear downforce to balance that out.

We no more than got the problem resolved when our test was suddenly cut short. I was driving down the back straight—about where I had my accident before—and I thought, "That's funny. Something doesn't feel right." I didn't know if it was just my nerves or if something was really wrong. So I decided to stop in the pits and have a look. I applied the brakes to pull into the pit road—and the right front A-arm broke! The entire wheel, suspension, and brake hose were torn off and got wedged under the chassis. There I was, still going about 100 mph, sliding along on top of a tire, with no control and no brakes. Finally the wheel worked its way back to the right rear tire, which caught on it and catapulted the car through the air. As I flew into the air and started to roll over, I thought, "Oh, Jesus, here it goes again." But it didn't quite make it over, and I bounced back down—rightside up. When we had redesigned the front suspension, someone had decided to make all the components out of aluminum. It wasn't the material, though, but simply a bad weld that had failed. I called Flegl and told him to make me some steel A-arms. We had three weeks to get the car repaired for the first race at Mosport, and we couldn't take any more chances.

While we were down, Flegl took another body back to the wind tunnel and tried a bunch of different flaps—actually they were right-angle lips—on the wing and the trailing edge of the body. He sent me the information that certain sizes produced large amounts of downforce for a minimal increase in drag. I selected what I thought would be about right, and we took the car to Mosport.

Jody Scheckter was there with Vasek Polak's 917-10, and it looked as if he was going to be the star of the show. He was faster in practice, while we finished balancing our aerodynamics with the lip that Flegl recommended. Finally I sat on the pole with about 1½ seconds over Jody. At least the McLarens weren't there to worry about.

At the start of the race Jody got away in the lead. I was a little nervous about everything being just right in my car—especially after having had three accidents in 917's—and I didn't know anything about Jody's style. I had heard he was a wild driver and that he hung the tail out a lot. I had raced against him the week before in Formula A cars at Mid-Ohio, but that had been our first race with the Lola-AMC and I never got close enough to even see Jody. He beat me there in his "European style" cars, and I was anxious not to let it happen again in my kind of cars.

Eventually I passed Jody on the long straightaway. But popping over a hill in the middle of it, we came up on a much slower car. He saw me coming and tried to get out of my way. I went right—he went right. I went left—he went left. We were just 180 degrees out of phase. I barely clipped him, and went off the left side of the track. It's hard to control those cars on the grass at 220 mph. It seemed like I went about forty-five miles before getting slowed down. That wouldn't have been so bad except that there was an access road at a right angle to the track, with a three-foot-high embankment. When I hit that at some reduced speed, it launched me into the air—*again*! Coming down, the nose rotated over until I thought I was going to augur in vertically. But I hit, bounced, and rebounded a few times, and just about everything stayed attached to the car. I was able to drive into the pits with the nose sticking up into the air, and a front ride height of about fourteen inches.

Roger and Flegl insisted that I go back out and finish the race, even though we couldn't do anything about the nose. But there was so much front-end lift that way that when I got up to a certain speed, the front end would just lift right off the ground. I could see the tires through the bodywork, and they'd drop down lower and lower until they hit the rebound stops and I'd lose all steering control. I could turn the wheel from side to side and nothing would happen. I motored around forever, and finished seventh, seven laps down. I was very disappointed, but at least all of my strongest competitors broke, and none finished ahead of me.

Before our next race back at Atlanta I had a disastrous nonfinish in a USAC race, and a miserable fourth-place finish in a Formula A race. It was beginning to look as if it might be a poor season after all.

We went to Atlanta—and neither broke nor crashed. I qualified about two seconds faster than Follmer, and won the Saturday heat by a big margin. On Sunday, however, for the big-money race, we reenacted an old scene. On the warm-up laps I discovered that the fuel cap was leaking when the tanks were full. I was hoping that it would stop when the fuel level dropped.

But I was already soaked with fuel, which becomes very painful, and the leak showed no signs of stopping. So I pulled into the pits in the first few laps. They retightened the cap, poured water on me, and I went back out again. It was still leaking, so I came in again and they replaced the cap. By then I was two laps down. Eventually I unlapped myself and finished second to George, but it was an incredibly painful race after the water evaporated. It's one thing to be ahead and in unbearable pain, but when you're a lap down it's somehow much worse.

When we went to Watkins Glen I was really nervous about winning, since we'd taken a big dump at the first two races. Right away, a crankshaft broke in practice, and the guys had to change motors real quick. When I went back out again, a rear A-arm broke going over the hill at high speed. The car was all over the road—finally backing into a guardrail and bending the suspension up a bit. We towed the car back and got our spare car out of the truck. The guys really stood on the gas, and they got it ready in time for me to qualify on the pole with ten minutes to spare. Cox diagnosed the suspension failure as a poorly-designed spring mount with a high-stress offset. He designed some new A-arms with the load path positioned better, and we never had the problem again. In fact, we hardly had another problem with those cars all year.

I won both heats at Watkins Glen by about a lap. But I was trying so hard, and it was so hot, that I thought I was going to pass out. I talked to the track physician about it, and he said that I would be all right. But as we talked, he watched me more closely, and he finally admitted that he'd never seen a person sweat so hard. I told him that it didn't seem that unusual to me, or to any other race driver I knew. There he was, a race doctor, and he didn't recognize the true physical effort required to drive those cars for a couple of hours.

Mid-Ohio was a little more exciting—for the spectators. I won the first heat again. But George bumped me going into the first turn of the second heat and got ahead. He was taking up so much road that I stayed behind for most of the race. With just a few laps to go, the crew—Roger had excused himself to get married that weekend—held up a sign that said "Boost!" which meant for me to turn up the turbocharger regulator screw. I turned it up a little—and nothing happened. I turned it up some more, and nothing happened. Finally, I turned it *way* up. That, combined with the fact that George missed a shift, got me by, and I was home free. Everyone gave me credit for playing with George the whole time, as though I had planned it that way. But I was actually worried that I couldn't get by, or that the boost-screw trick wouldn't work.

That was an innovation that Bobby Rinsler actually had on his cars first. We had talked about adjustable boost pressure on our turbo-Offy Indy cars, where the durability versus passing ability problem is even greater.

But the Rinsler cars started the season with a complicated device that turned the screw with an electric motor. We eventually put together a simpler device in which manifold pressure was valved to operate the regulator diaphragm. The first and last time I used it was at Mid-Ohio. I never needed it again.

The rest of the season was rather uneventful. I was always quicker by some large margin. But because of that, other teams became discouraged and didn't try very hard to beat us any more. Jody and George actually became slower. At some tracks George was slower than he had been in the same car the year before, even though his motor was bigger and more powerful. That had to show that the Rinsler team was stepping backward in the preparation of their cars. At the same time, I don't think George knew enough about the cars to be able to tell the mechanics what to do. They were probably changing things that they shouldn't have. It wasn't so much that we were a lot faster as that they were getting slower.

Edmonton was a bad race for me, even though I easily won both heats. I knew I was going to retire soon, so I was starting to be more friendly with other drivers. Hurley Haywood—or Haywood Hurley—had made the jump from a 911 to a 917 turbo-Porsche, and I could see he was having trouble adapting. I had suggested that he bring his car to our skidpad so that I could help him sort it out. But first he didn't have time, and later I didn't have time. The morning of the race, "Hayley" and I were sitting around talking about our futures—about his desire to become a successful racer and mine to perhaps have a dealership someday, perhaps in partnership with him.

In the first few laps of the race his car hit an embankment and went upside down. It laid there with its wheels in the air for the entire race, while I worried about what happened to him. I was in the lead, but every time I came around and saw his car I thought, "There's a guy who was really trying hard. I could have helped him, but now his car is destroyed, and he's probably hurt real bad." I felt awful. Then I got mad at myself for letting it worry me while I was driving a race. That was the first time it ever bothered me to see a crashed car. I don't know whether it was because I had been in that position myself and could empathize, or whether it was because I had finally become friendly with another driver. I was really relieved at the end of the race to learn that he was going to be able to finish the series. In fact, he ended up third in the point standings.

We had a little trouble at Laguna Seca. In the first heat a stud broke and let all the oil out. The motor wasn't broken, but we couldn't fix the stud in the car. And we couldn't race the backup car in the second heat because of the rules. So everybody pitched in, and we changed motors in record time. I started in the back of the pack, and eventually worked my way up to first. I was slowed a little when Charlie Kemp got in my way as I passed him.

I don't know whether I couldn't get around because my rear anti-roll bar was broken and the car was understeering too much, or whether he was blocking me. But it did seem like he only moved over for me when he was going faster. On the other hand, I was helped when an accident brought out the pace car and let me close up on the leaders. George Follmer made it easy when he blew his motor while I was trying to pass him for the lead.

We were making a big mistake by flaunting our Unfair Advantage at those last few races. As long as we left the backup car out of sight in the truck, everyone accepted us as merely having a faster car. But by the end of the year the guys had gotten the backup car in as good shape as the race car, and to insure the Championship, I was practicing in both. They were so much alike that I could go out and lap two seconds faster than anyone else in either car. Then the other Porsche teams started getting angry. They went to the factory and complained that they ought to get one of our cars to race if we weren't going to run both. There were a lot of hard feelings over that, but we worked hard for our Unfair Advantage and we weren't going to give it away.

By Riverside we had won the Championship. But there were still dollars and our reputations at stake. I knew I was going to announce my retirement there, and no one else seemed to be even trying to beat us. So we tried one last trick on the car. We replaced the broken rear anti-roll bar with one that could be adjusted from the cockpit. After I got way out in front, I began playing with the bar, turning it up to oversteer, and broadsliding the car around the tighter turns. I really had a good time sliding all over the place—knowing that I could rebalance the car at any time—and more importantly, knowing that it was my last Can-Am race.

Chapter 26

1973

PORCHE 911 CARRERA

Equality in Race Cars (Could Prove the Driver)

When all the Porsche executives were at the 1972 Riverside Can-Am race, they asked George Follmer and me if we would like to race a new 911, to be called the Carrera. They would send two cars to the United States for endurance races at Daytona and Sebring. George and I would have one, and Peter Gregg and Hurley Haywood would have the other. I said I'd love to do it, as long as Flegl and I could do the development work as we had on the 917-10. I didn't want the car to be a complete stranger when I saw it for the first time at a racetrack. There wasn't even a contract on that deal. It was just a loose arrangement where I would help develop the car over there in my spare time, and they would send it to us ready to race, painted Sunoco blue.

At the time we made the agreement I had only driven one high-performance 911 before, when the factory was demonstrating a fabulous new anti-skid braking system. I first saw the system when it was mounted on a 917 they'd been testing. Their other race drivers hadn't liked it very much—partly because of some failures and crashes—but I became so enthusiastic that they put more work into it. The problems on the 917 had been electronic interference from the engine electrical system, and a slight delay during emergency applications. There was such a great hydraulic length between the pedal and the brake that it took just an instant too long—which can be a real problem in a high-powered car.

So they installed it in a 911, which we drove to the Paul Ricard track in France on a test trip. Whenever rain or snow held up the 917 tests, we drove the anti-skid 911 on the track. It was just unbelievable! I could drive into a turn until there was no possible way to make it, then put on the brakes and turn the wheel—and the car would just steer right around. But it took a lot of practice to be able to put enough trust and faith in it to come anywhere near its ultimate capabilities. At first, I would go to a reasonable braking point, jam on the pedal—and almost come to a complete stop before I ever got to the turn. I spent at least two hours at it, going deeper and deeper into the turns without reaching the limit. It was eerie. I knew exactly what was happening, and what I should do, but it takes a lot of time and confidence to jam your brakes on in a slippery corner when all your instincts are telling you not to. We turned the system off, and the car became normally uncontrollable. I realized the potential in racing when I saw I couldn't take full advantage of it myself.

They kept the system on that car for other drivers to try in normal use, and eventually they found one really bad mode of operation. When the wheels were out of balance or going over a high-frequency "cobblestone" surface, the sensors would think they were locking up, and reduce the braking. They had to make the system absolutely bulletproof, but there was no apparent solution to that problem so the project was temporarily shelved. They're the best people to decide when it's safe enough to use in production, or on a race

PORSCHE 911 CARRERA

photo by F. David Stone

car. Since it doesn't do much for ultimate braking capability in a straight line on a dry surface, it's hard to say whether it can reduce laptimes very much, considering how little time is spent in braking. The greatest advantage will be in braking deeper and more stably into the turn, especially on a wet track. But it's definitely a thing of the future. It will be absolutely unbelievable to watch. Properly driven, the car will charge into the corner until everyone—spectators and other drivers—will say, "There's no way he's gonna make it!" And the car will just brake and turn, and go. It will be the true Unfair Advantage. Unfortunately, it's a "threshold of science" thing like the turbomotor was, and it's going to require a *lot* of development.

While Flegl and I were getting ready to test the new 917-30 at Paul Ricard, we discussed what we ought to try on the 911 Carrera also. Since I had never driven one really seriously before, I had no idea what to expect. We looked the car over as it was set up. It had the same brakes as our Can-Am car—which made a lot of sense. The Carrera actually weighed more, and there were a lot of pieces available which we already understood. The car had a good roll bar in it, but I wanted a full roll *cage*. They had never seen a roll cage in a car before, and they didn't know about the advantages in chassis stiffness. So we looked at the original torsional test on that body, and it turned out to be over 2000 foot-pounds per degree, which I decided was adequate for a coupe of that weight. I wasn't anxious to push them into something that would be a lot of work and yet not show much in performance. They had already done some anti-roll-bar work, but because of the difficulty in changing torsion bars in the suspension, they had never done much about spring rates. I suspected we were going to have to do some work in that area. Flegl decided it would be easier to add coil springs around the shock absorbers—which they already had a wide selection of from other race cars. The only other things they had done to the basic 911 were to put solid bushings in the suspension and fit bigger tires. The car was obviously going to need some help.

When we got to Paul Ricard I met two other drivers who would also be testing with us. Herbert Muller and Giis Van Lennep had both driven 917's in the Manufacturers Championship, but now they were to concentrate on the 911. They were to do the basic testing, while I would spend most of my time on the 917-30 and act as a consultant to them. I was a little uneasy about that, because I'd never shared my testing duties before.

The tests lasted two weeks, and I had to leave over the weekend to race in the United States. Also, I was saddled with the information that some other Porsche driver had already been there with a lowered Carrera, and he set a lap record that was hard to match. Every time I suggested we try something, they would say, "But the other driver didn't do that, and he was faster."

I had my own ideas about what's usually wrong with a car that's being set up for racing. A production car usually lacks bump travel when it's lowered. If it's sitting on the bumpstops, it doesn't matter what springs and bars and shocks are used. The results will be confusing and frustrating. I've learned it the hard way time and time again. Sure enough, the Carrera didn't have enough travel. It wasn't even close. They spent four days simply moving things out of the way and raising the front spindle on the MacPherson strut. We recognized that we were also changing the roll center and the geometry, but those effects were minor compared to the problem of a rigid suspension.

When I finally drove the car it felt fairly well balanced, but the outside rear suspension was falling down in the corners. It felt as if it wanted a stronger rear anti-roll bar or stronger springs, which would naturally cause too much oversteer. Whenever you see a 911 Porsche in a corner, it's usually lifting the inside front wheel. That's because they've tried to get rid of high-speed oversteer with a heavy anti-roll bar in front and soft springs in the rear. We fiddled back and forth for a while, until we were obviously fiddling without any direction.

Eventually Flegl suggested we start working on the geometry. There wasn't a lot we could do with the Porsche trailing-arm rear suspension, though. It had a lot of bump steer and a very low roll center—which was causing the "falling" coming out of a corner. So we decided to do whatever was needed to raise the roll center. The mechanics pulled the motor out, and hacked and welded until they got the inner pivot points raised. It was a terrible job, and the bump steer was no better, but the end result was that the car was a lot flatter in the turns. There were no major breakthroughs in development. We just made small improvements in durability, suspension geometry, springs, and bars until we had exhausted all our ideas.

Then we looked to the aerodynamics. It was kind of a fictitious test, because we could only race the body as it was homologated. The factory had already measured aerodynamic downforce and drag, both in the wind tunnel and on the road, which is where the "tongue" on the rear deck and the front spoiler came from. But we played around with it anyhow.

We found that drag could be reduced by extending the front spoiler all the way down to the ground. As illogical as it appeared, we had already proved it on our Camaros, and we simply verified it by getting another five miles per hour out of the 911 on the straightaway. Of course, that added to the high-speed oversteer, so we then worked with bigger tongues and wings on the rear deck—as eventually appeared on the 1974 Carreras. The 911 tests weren't as spectacular as those for the 917-30, but we tried a lot of different things, and we learned enough so that the Carrera was eventually very successful as a race car. Unfortunately, it wasn't that successful for me, in the early stages.

The two cars that Porsche shipped to Daytona were very, very well prepared. They were obviously race-prepared just for us, with great workmanship and care, and all the spare parts we needed. Peter Gregg may have seen his car for the first time at Daytona. He was upset that I had done all the factory development work on the car, since he sees himself as the all-time 911 expert. At least I get that impression from listening to him tell me how to set them up. But there's no doubt that he *does* know a great deal from all his years of experience.

I learned that right away, when our flywheel fell off and ruined the practice motor. I talked to Gregg's mechanic for a while, and he told me that it would happen unless the flywheel was put on in a certain way. At that point I became worried that Gregg's guys knew lots of little things that we didn't. We might have to learn the hard way—by pitching motors apart. Those were the first 2.7-liter motors, and because of durability problems, they had rev limiters set at 8000 rpm for practice and 7500 rpm for the race. By putting the race motor in early, we were at a disadvantage in qualifying.

On the other hand, our chassis was a little more tricked up. There was some debate whether we would be able to run it as a production car or not, so we had an alternate suspension available. Ultimately the car was not homologated in time, so we ran as prototypes and used the better suspension. All that was involved was the relocation of one ball joint in the rear and installation of longer lower front A-arms to get a better camber angle. Otherwise both cars were identical.

After looking at Gregg's car to see what tires he had been using, I decided that we had to have a bigger rear tire. I asked the Goodyear guys to dig up some old Trans-Am front tires, which I was familiar with and knew would work. But somewhere between the tire shop and our car, they went back and got dismounted. I was standing around waiting and asked where they were. One of the guys told me they wouldn't fit. I said, "What do you mean they won't fit? I didn't try them on the car. How can you say they won't fit?" By backing up a little ways, I discovered that Peter Gregg had come along and asked what they were doing. When they told him, he said that the tires wouldn't work. Because he was the Porsche "expert," they took his word for it. I became angry and said, "Let Peter do his thing to his own car, and I will make the decisions on our car." We put the tires on our car, and they did fit—of course. And the car was faster—of course. And immediately Peter wanted to put them on his car also. Naturally, I told him they wouldn't fit!

The Goodyear guys came back and asked if I would like to try some racing radials. B.F. Goodrich was running them on race cars and getting a lot of good advertising out of it, and Goodyear was interested also. I didn't like the looks of them—they were narrower, taller, and heavier—but I had tried some before that performed very well on the skidpad, so I gave them a try on the Carrera. Even though they looked like street tires, they were only about 1.5 seconds slower. I started thinking what a perfect opportunity that could be to make Goodyear happy at no cost to us. We didn't stand a chance going for an overall win in the prototype class anyhow, and what was a second or two per lap in a twenty-four-hour race? I got together with Roger, and after some persuasion, he agreed that it could be a keen deal. There was one small advantage in that those tires gave us a slightly higher gear ratio. We had the tallest differential available and we were getting close to the rev limiter in high gear already. I knew from experience that the natural draft during a race would raise the potential speed another few hundred rpms.

While I was making the executive decision to run on the radials, I never even considered Gregg. At that point I thought of him as a Porsche teammate. George Follmer, my co-driver, wasn't entering into the decisions either. He said that he would go along with it, however I wanted the car set up. In qualifications, Gregg's higher rev limiter and better tires made him about 0.6 seconds faster.

At the start of the race I wasn't too excited. There were about ten legitimate prototypes—Matras, Mirages, and Lolas—ahead of us, and they were much faster. But as I watched Gregg pull away, it started bothering me. I didn't want to let that happen. We had an Unfair Advantage of quicker pitstops, with quick-fill oil and fuel nozzles, and the vacuum brake retractors, so I caught up somewhat on each stop. Then Hurley Haywood and George got in the cars, and they were about equal also.

While George was driving, Roger and I sat down and worked on our strategy. I had worked out a chart of mileages and points at which various things needed to be done. We knew just when to add oil, change tires, change brake pads, and so on. If anything got out of order, we could predict how the entire schedule would shift. I had also worked out the most efficient combination of changes to make on each stop. For example, if the brakes would go eight hours, we would change left tires and left brakes at six hours, and right tires and right brakes at eight hours. It was arranged so that only one side of the car had to be jacked up at a time. In addition, we started fitting Gregg's pitstops to our chart, so that we could anticipate what his next move was going to be.

By the time I went back out again we were running very close together. I could see that Gregg's car was about two seconds a lap quicker. We were simply keeping up by having faster pitstops, and by driving harder. There was a problem in that, too, because the radials would overheat when really pushed to the limit, and they were less consistent in the turns. Then I got ahead on one pitstop and Gregg came up behind me and spent some time trying to pass. He would draft me down the straights, but he couldn't pull out and pass because of his lower gear ratio and the rev limiter. I could hear his motor cutting out.

Eventually he got ahead again, and I concentrated on driving as carefully as possible and not making any mistakes. Occasionally Gregg would make a mistake in traffic and fall back in my sights again. I could see that he was staying ahead partly by taking unnecessary risks and bashing into other cars. I thought he had the wrong attitude about how to treat someone else's car. He was abusing his Carrera a lot more than I would in a twenty-four-hour race. Especially when we were close together, I thought he was being a bit rude to me, as another driver. I became angry and decided that we *must* get ahead.

In the meantime all the faster prototypes had dropped out, and Gregg and I were running one-two. It became obvious that we were really having a race between us. Gregg was anxious to show us up in front of all the Porsche factory guys who were there. But we had another Unfair Advantage—a two-way radio between the car and the pits, so that Roger and I could work out our strategy on the run. I called up Roger and told him that we had to beat Gregg. The guys in the pits recognized that the only way we were going to win was in our pitstops. They stepped up to the challenge and really did a tremendous job. On the next stop I went into the lead again.

It was nearly midnight, and we were leading Gregg by about half a lap. Steve Beizer was giving my intervals on the pit board so that I could tell how much Gregg was gaining on me, while Roger and I talked about other things over the radio. We could see exactly what was happening. I was driving as hard as I could, and I knew that Gregg was trying tremendously hard also. We were scheduled to make a brake change on the next stop, and that would put Gregg ahead again. But I knew that if we could stay ahead through the next pitstop we might be able to stop his charge. It would break his back.

I thought about it for a while. Because I had made up the charts myself, I knew them by heart. I didn't need to look at the sheets to know how the schedule went. Finally, I called Roger and told him that we needed a whole new plan. The charts were a little conservative, so we could shift the brake change back by one pitstop. The next time we came in for fuel, we would make no other changes. I would even stay in the car instead of taking time to trade with George. We would probably be even further ahead if the stop went well. I reckoned it ought to destroy Gregg, when he saw it was going to take him a couple of hours to catch up again. It was like tank warfare.

Roger said, "Wait. Will you go through that again?" I was driving around the banks at 170 mph, and explaining very slowly and carefully just what it was that we had to do. I went through it about three times, just to make sure he understood. Finally Roger agreed that we could do it. He got off the radio and told Woody that I had decided not to change anything at that time. Woody looked at Roger and said, "What's Mark doing, deciding what to do in the pits while he's out there driving around?" He just couldn't believe that I could be leading a race at one o'clock in the morning, and figuring out pit strategy at the same time.

We did it that way. Gregg made a mistake in his pits, and we got two laps on him. It was all over at that point. We figured that we'd won the race. No matter what speed we ran, Gregg drove about the same speed, and he stopped chiseling away at the margin. I was feeling good about being able to communicate with Roger like that, and we were all really excited about leading a long-distance race in such an outclassed car.

However, after we led for about six hours I came in and traded off with George. He went out, and on the first lap I told Roger that I thought I saw smoke coming out of the car. Then George got on the radio and said that it wasn't running right. It was down on rpms. We could hear it running on five cylinders. He pulled into the pits in a huge cloud of smoke. Compression was gone in one cylinder, and there was oil everywhere. It wasn't George's fault. Porsche told us later that a valve relief in one piston had been machined improperly, and after eighteen hours it burned through. We were out, and Gregg and Haywood won the race overall. We had been so far ahead that they backed off and just coasted to the finish.

We didn't go to Sebring, because it wasn't an International race that year and Porsche wasn't interested. Our Carrera was sold to Al Holbert, the son of Bob Holbert, who was a friend of Roger's and a famous former Porsche racer himself. I ended up driving the car one more time for Al at Watkins Glen on a weekend that was free, somehow. I didn't really want to do it, but they were good friends, and I had kept in touch enough so I knew the car was still safe and in good shape. Besides that, Peter Gregg was going to be there in his Carrera.

It was raining on the morning of the race, so Al decided to let me start and drive when conditions were worst. Of course, that meant I had to start way down in his qualifying position. We no more than got going, and the rain stopped. So I came in for dry tires and a load of fuel, and stayed in the car to try to make up the lost time. I drove really hard for a long time, and after fifty-six laps I somehow worked my way up to the lead. At that point I pitted for fuel and to let Al take over. Six laps later, the sky fell in. Rain started pouring down, and the fog got so thick that the drivers couldn't see the course. Al drove into the pits with the whole front torn off the car just a couple of laps before they stopped the race. We were given credit for an eighth place, while Gregg took second.

I ran one other race in a factory Carrera. There was a six-hour manufacturers race on Saturday before the Can-Am at Watkins Glen. Jackie Stewart was going to be driving a prototype Capri, and Porsche wanted us to defend their honor. That time, they built a pair of true prototypes for Gregg and Haywood and Follmer and me. They had *really* wide wheels and tires, three-liter motors, and wings mounted on the rear. We were so involved with the Can-Am, though, that all we did to ours was paint it blue. Fortunately, they were very well set up the way they arrived. The wing at the back did a good job of balancing out the high-speed aerodynamics.

As it turned out, Stewart didn't make the race because the Capri wasn't prepared well, so we had our own race between the two Carreras. Gregg drove a very good race, with the two of us running nose to tail for a few hours. I couldn't get away from him, because he had so much more speed on the straightaway that he could just pull out and pass. Finally he dropped back with a broken axle or something, and the two Carreras finished in sixth and seventh positions. Right after the race our Carrera was sold to some people from Mexico for $20,000—in cash. They had a twelve-year-old kid carrying hundred-dollar bills in a suitcase. I was a little amazed, but they said it was safe because they figured no one would mug a kid.

All along, a deal of Roger's called the International Race of Champions was materializing. He had said before that he wanted to try a racing series for the world's best drivers—all in identical cars. But he didn't know what kind of cars to use. He talked about Formula Fords, or Mustangs, or Javelins, or Camaros. But there were questions of who would build them, the cost, and their reliability. Shortly after I did the Carrera development work at Paul Ricard, it began to look as if his race was going to become a reality. So I told him, "Roger, there's no question about it. The only way to go is with factory-built Carreras." In the first place, he wouldn't have to build them. Second, they wouldn't be anywhere near as expensive as any other completely race-prepared car. Third, they had to be as identically equal as any race cars ever built. And fourth—and foremost—the Carrera had to be the most reliable car available.

Dr. Fuhrmann had told me once that the car couldn't be broken—as long as it wasn't over-revved and as long as it was shifted correctly. And that was really quite true. They come with Can-Am brakes, dry-sump lubrication, fuel injection, good ignition, oil coolers, stainless-steel exhaust pipes, and a lot of other nice things that only racing people can appreciate. They also have all the stock upholstery and instrumentation. Of course, they sell for $20,000 or $30,000, but there's no way we could ever build such a good race car for that amount of money. I always liked those cars because they could be driven hard without worrying about breaking anything. They're so strong, and so well engineered, that there isn't much a driver can destroy but the gearbox. The Carrera is—without a doubt—the very best off-the-shelf production race car available at any price. At least as long as there's a competitive class to race it in. And Roger was going to make that happen.

After listening to me for a while, he decided maybe I was right. He went to the factory and tried to tell them what he had in mind. He even had them build him a car, so that he could see for himself what it was like. It was actually a Targa, with all the right Carrera bits in it. It had wide tires and fenders, a special motor, and hillclimb gears. He drove it for a while, as his personal transportation, and then he gave it to his wife. I thought it was such a great car that I was even kind of jealous.

That was the prototype for his IROC Carreras. He went back to Germany and had Porsche make a production run of fifteen perfectly identical cars for his races. He hired Peter Reinhart, a former employee who raced one of our Camaros in Europe, to keep tabs on the operation over there. Peter took the cars and Porsche mechanics to Riverside and spent a couple of weeks getting everything set up right. The trouble was, he wanted to personally test drive all the cars. That was all right, except that he didn't drive them hard enough to really heat the tires up. At the last minute Goodyear brought in Milt Minter to check out the tires. He immediately overheated them and blew one out, tearing the side off one of the cars. Goodyear needed a crash program to produce another couple hundred tires for the three races. In the meantime, Roger had signed up Allison, Fittipaldi, Follmer, Foyt, Hulme, Johncock, McClusky, Pearson, Petty, Revson, Bobby Unser, and me. He also tried to get Al Unser and Mario Andretti, but their contracts with Firestone prevented that. Roger even made a big pitch to Firestone, saying those guys could run without any Goodyear identification on their cars, but he was turned down.

Other than that, I wasn't close enough to the program to know what was happening. At the outset Roger told me, "Don't get involved with those cars, and don't talk to anyone who is working on them. Don't even *look* at them! If you so much as touch one, you could ruin the whole deal." When he was trying to sign up drivers, they all said, "No thanks. Somehow, Mark will end up with the best car." There was a lot of unrest among the other drivers, and feelings that I would have a deal worked out with Roger. He told me personally that he hoped I would win, but he said, "You stay away from those cars!" Eventually I think everyone was satisfied that there was no possible way in which it could have been rigged by anyone.

At the first practice session three of the fifteen cars were provided for all of us to practice in. I did just as Roger said. I sat around with my helmet in hand, waiting for someone to tell me what to do. I was really *completely* out of it. After all, we had the 917 there, and I had other things to do. I didn't talk to Roger, or Peter Reinhart, or even the other drivers. Finally someone told me to take one of the cars out.

We were each supposed to practice in all three cars, but one was apparently slower. Roger told me to take it out, since no one else wanted to. I went quickest in it, and everyone wanted to drive *that* car.

After I drove I started to walk away, but Roger came up and asked me what I thought of it. I said, "If it was my car, I'd change it, but you told me not to talk about it." But he persisted. "Well, if it *was* your car, what would you do?" I told him that it was obviously oversteering, and it needed a bigger anti-roll bar in front. He said, "Hmm. Everyone else is complaining about that too." Apparently the change in tires had upset the balance. Roger made the executive decision to take all the cars in and make the bars stiffer.

Fittipaldi qualified on the pole, with me right next to him, and the first six drivers all within a second of each other. But before we drew numbers for our cars, Fittipaldi and Follmer were penalized to the back of the pack for being late to the drivers' meeting. I started next to Revson.

Everybody knew it was going to be a race of mistakes. Just before we pulled out, I told Revson I was going to pace the start at 5000 rpm in *second* gear. Normally we only used third, fourth, and fifth gears, so starting in second meant we all had a chance to miss the two-three shift—and lose from the start. Peter gave me a hopeful "3" signal on the pace lap, but he had no choice at that point.

It was a slow start all right, but I managed to pull away, literally by inches. I tried really hard never to turn the steering wheel any more than necessary—to keep from scrubbing off speed—and I always shifted very carefully. Since I was far enough ahead that I never had to race against anybody else, the few million people who watched the race on television know more about it than I did. There was a lot of close racing and changes of position, but I was well ahead at the finish.

By winning the first race, I had to start at the back in the second race. But the throttle stuck in the car I got for that one, and I was the first person out. There was something wrong with the throttle bores—sand in them, or heat warpage—which took a couple of cars out.

That, of course, put me on the pole for the third race, in the car that Follmer drove to a win in the second race. In the beginning Roger had told everyone that he "hoped" we all stayed close together throughout each race. Before the last one, he came up to me and said, "The second race was a real good show, because there were some lead changes, and they were close together at the end. If you get ahead again, don't get so *far* ahead. It doesn't look good." I didn't really care about the show at that point. I knew

I was going to retire, and I wanted to win that race by as large a margin as any other race I'd ever run. At the start I pulled away again, and I stayed as far out in front as I could without taking any chances. And that was it for the time being. I won two of the three races. Because I didn't finish the second race, Follmer and Unser beat me on total points, but I was guaranteed an invitation to the final race at Daytona.

When I pulled in after the third race it was really anticlimactic. There's usually a big deal with a lot of people in the winner's circle. But that race was planned for television, so there was no ceremony at all. It was as if no one cared. So many people had predicted that I was going to win anyway that no one was even surprised. I felt a little confused. I didn't have much time to think about it, though, because I had to immediately get ready for my last Can-Am race that afternoon in the 917.

It was really great to win those two races, not necessarily for the prestige, but because I needed the prize money. At the same time, I felt kind of bad that maybe I did have the Unfair Advantage before the race started. I had done enough of the original development so I understood the car and its capabilities and what technique to use in driving it. On the other hand, George won most of the points, and he had spent a lot of time in Carreras himself. While he was driving Formula One and Interseries races in Europe, the factory provided him with a Carrera for other races over there. So he had more competition experience in them than any of the rest of us. Still, I didn't want the other drivers to be mad at me. Inside, I was happier than hell, but I wasn't going to show it.

The cars had arrived at Riverside directly from the factory, but before the Daytona race they all had to be rebuilt somewhere. The motors were all shipped back to the factory, while the chassis went to our new Penske Racing shops. By then the other drivers' fear of me getting the Unfair Advantage in selection was gone. They realized that no matter who prepared the cars, they were all identical on the track. And the car selection method was such that the mechanics couldn't do any special last-minute work to any of them. Car numbers were drawn out of a hat with just enough time before the race to put the names and numbers on. At that, the fastest qualifier had to draw last.

The cars had to be changed for Daytona. For one thing, the banking there requires stiffer springs, to keep the cars from grinding away on the pavement. The factory sent over some recommendations for spring rates, and what they thought the proper front/rear ratio should be. I was asked to take a look at their figures, and they seemed too stiff to me. So I dug out all our old records on cars we had run there before, how much they weighed in comparison, and what wheel rates we had used. From that I made an educated guess as to what the spring rates ought to be. The guys working on the cars ordered the springs and fitted them to the cars. They also went through the standard "Penske preparation" of balancing wheel loads on the scales, and checking ride heights and geometry on the surface plate. For Daytona, Al Holbert and Peter Gregg did all the test driving, and the spring setup I recommended turned out to satisfy them.

There was also some question about the aerodynamic balance of the cars. Al and Peter tried a little lip on the back of the rear spoiler, and found that it made the cars a little slower but reduced a tendency for them to wander on the straightaway. It would have been more of an advantage to me without it, but it did make the cars more stable and easier for the other drivers, so it stayed on. They also found the brake problem that some drivers had complained about at Riverside. In some cars the brake balance bars were out of adjustment. When the pedal was pushed really hard, the bar would bottom and increase pressure to the rear brakes only. That was probably why Fittipaldi lost control a couple of times. The guys got that adjusted right, and added more balance to the rear to compensate for more downforce there. The preparation was tremendous. The cars were more identical at Daytona than ever before. Al drove all the cars as hard as he could, before anyone else saw them, so they were all very well tuned. Nobody complained about the handling or power on any of them.

The race really gave me an odd feeling—to know that it was finally going to be my last one. I had a feeling that all six of us—Follmer, Foyt, Pearson, Revson, Unser, and I—would be able to turn almost identical laptimes. I knew the cars were perfectly identical, and all of us had a similar amount of experience at that track. The course wasn't as tricky as Riverside, where Follmer, Revson, and I might have had an advantage. I also felt funny about having a mixed role, because one minute I was the team manager of our Matador in the Daytona 500, and the next minute I was putting my driver's uniform on for the Carrera race. But I was looking forward to the fun of driving again.

I was quickest in qualifying by about a second, which was a little surprising. But that race was very, very important to me. Again, I didn't care about the show—I wanted to go out with the best performance I could put on. And I needed the $41,000 the winner would get. I don't think I've ever before tried *so* hard to qualify on the pole. I was taking a lot of chances that I would have considered unnecessary previously, hoping that my reflexes would cover for any slipups. I was diving just a little too deep into turns, for example, and relying on my reflexes to correct in time if a wheel locked up. It wasn't important to be on the pole to win that race, but I had decided ahead of time that I was going to do it. It was a real "white-knuckle" deal.

The strategy of the race was that the leader was always at a disadvantage, because any closely-following car could easily pass him by drafting down the straightaway. At the start of the race I immediately fell back to third or fourth, as a number of cars drafted right on by. But then I had the advantage, and drafted back up to the front again. Foyt was out almost immediately, when he shifted from third to second, instead of fourth, and broke his motor. Pearson dropped back also when he missed a shift and destroyed third gear. It was just a matter of drafting strategically, and not making mistakes. I knew there was going to be a lot of close racing for a while, with all of us in a pack. But after four or five laps Follmer and I somehow managed to break away from Revson and Unser.

I reckoned that rather than stay behind Follmer I would get ahead as soon as I could. But once I got into the lead, I could see that no matter how hard I tried to get away on the infield, he could draft back up on me. But he wasn't trying to pass. He just sat there on my tail until it was obvious that he was setting me up to shoot by on the *last* lap. I decided I had to cause him to make a mistake, so that I could break away.

I knew I had an advantage on at least one part of the course. I was braking later than George going into turn one, a decreasing-radius turn going off the banks into the infield. There was no difference in the cars. It was just the old brake-and-turn technique that allowed me to go deeper into the turn. But I was going so deep that I was having a hard time keeping everything under control. As the laps went by, and George kept following me, I could see that he was getting the knack of it. He was learning from me.

So I thought, "Now I'll have to do something unusual." He and I had done exactly the same things for five or six laps. I had to break his train of thought—to confuse him somehow. I decided to let him think I had lost my brakes going into turn one. I braked early, and not very hard, which caused me to overshoot the turn by a few feet. It wasn't enough that he could tell exactly what I'd done, but he probably got the message that my brakes were weak. That put him right on my tail for the next turn. He reckoned that I would brake early again, and he was positioned to shoot by on the inside. That time I went about twenty-five feet deeper than I'd ever gone before. Naturally I couldn't make it on a good line, so I went wide, got a little sideways, and left a big hole for him. He wasn't prepared for that. On the third turn I decided to pull a trick he's played on me a lot. I braked normally, went into the turn pretty much on the proper line—then deliberately put my inside front wheel off the edge and ticked up a little dirt and dust cloud. When I looked around, there he was, backwards.

When that happened I was long gone. Apparently George had settled down to comfortably follow me for the rest of the race, and he didn't realize that he was following what I did *too* closely. He was used to seeing me be so precise—just as I'm used to seeing him be so precise—that when I started doing unusual things, it was all over. I realized I could back off then and let the others close up on me a little, but it would have been very easy to lose that way. I wasn't worried about my car lasting, because I *knew* it wouldn't break if I didn't miss a shift. George ran some distance behind me for a while, before he broke his gearbox, and Revson and Unser had a close battle for second.

Again, that was a television race and there weren't many people around. But those who were there knew it was my last race. On my last lap the corner workers held up a huge banner that said, "Goodbye Mark, we'll miss you." I started getting kind of emotional about it then. In the victory circle Chris Economaki—a reporter who always seemed to be picking on our team—said how much he appreciated what I'd done for the sport all those years. I was having a hard time keeping control. Then Jackie Stewart, who had gone through almost the same experience of retirement that year and well knows what it feels like, said, "Mark, this is a fabulous moment. You are really going out in style. The way you retired is truly a mark of class."

Chapter 27

EPILOGUE

After it was all over, I began to wonder if I'd made a mistake in judgment. I thought maybe I had underestimated myself. I'd always been told that a lot of my successes came from having the best car. Still, I knew that in the International Race of Champions all the cars were equal, and yet I'd won three races out of four. It's possible that sometimes our team *didn't* have the best car, and we won on my ability as a driver. Everyone in the IROC races had about the same driving capabilities, but I won because I made fewer mistakes. I've made plenty of mistakes in racing, especially in the beginning when I crashed a lot, and I've made engineering misjudgments and strategic errors. Every one of them was incredibly expensive. But Roger seldom criticized me for them, and I learned a lot that way.

An *Autoweek* story implied that the IROC races may have proved me to be "driving champion of the world." But nothing is ever cut-and-dried like that. On any given day any driver can be slightly off his edge or a little out of his element. All any other driver had to do was make one little mistake and he was history. Still, those races surprised me more than anyone else. One major reason I was retiring was that it seemed I was past my peak. What made me so sure were intended compliments from the team like, "You aren't falling off. You've just *leveled* off." That was the clue that I wasn't improving any longer, and I had to get out before I began to drop. The downfall of many racing drivers is continuing when they're past that peak. After I stopped and looked a little closer, I could see that I had something left—I still had some valuable capabilities as a driver. I could see how important the driver is to a team, and that I could still be an asset as a driver. But it was too late to second-guess.

It might have been easier to retire after my Porsche crash in 1972, except that I didn't want to be known as a guy who would quit with his first serious accident. I made a great effort to come back after that—and I did it. I feel that no accident had any effect on my retirement. From mid-1971 until my crash in mid-1972 was my peak year; I won twice as much prize money as in any other year of my career. But that was also about the time I began to realize how overextended I was. I knew I was burning myself out. As you get older something happens. I don't know whether you become less durable, or you become wiser and less willing to put up with the pressure. But I'm sure I can't push myself as hard as I did five years ago. If it was just a matter of getting in the car and driving, it would have been easier, but all the outside hassles wore me down. When I ran out of energy, I had to keep going anyhow, because race dates can't be put off or rescheduled by a few weeks. Then, about the time I would think I had everything in hand, along would come a new car or a new guy who showed a lot of talent, and I'd have to work harder to be competitive. It was very discouraging to know that sooner or later they were going to get me.

If all I had had to do was run a one-car team—in addition to driving—I could have coped. Or I could have kept up with a car in two or three series. But somehow, the more Roger and I won, the more we had to expand. Over the winter of 1972 I worked with seven cars: two Porsche 917's, a Carrera, two McLaren M16's, the Lola T330, and the Matador; plus four other drivers: Follmer, Bettenhausen, Allison, and Marcis. There was less preparation time and no development time. And I was not only the number-one driver but had overall responsibility for the whole team. Then someone wrote an article about our team and made the comment that our weakness was in having no *depth*—that I was the kingpin, and if anything happened to me, the team would collapse. It's funny that no one ever mentioned that before, and we were a great success. Then someone came along and said, "Hey look! Your barn's on fire!" and we had to start rearranging things.

About then, I began to realize that I'd had just about enough of race-car development driving. All the enthusiasm and drive and interest that's needed to go through the same problems in car after car after car was gone. You can only do that for so long. I found that I was almost hating it. Of course, there was the possibility that I was just tired—that it was a freak feeling that would go away in better times. So I didn't say anything about it then. But sorting cars is a lonely, dangerous business. Sometimes I enjoyed the feeling of accomplishment when everything went together right, but those times were becoming rarer. It's unfortunate that I couldn't have separated the fun of racing from the pain of development.

There were so many mixed emotions going through my head that I had to talk with someone who really knew what I was facing. I've always had a lot of respect for Dan Gurney, and he had gone through the retirement thing just a few years before. So I "sponsored" Dan to dinner with the express purpose of just talking about ourselves—no business or race cars. That was one of the few times I ever got close to another driver, and it was a good experience. We had our own little "has-beens" club . . . but as Jim Travers says, "Better a has-been than a never-was." Jackie Stewart had also retired by then, although in his case it seems to have been due to the personal tragedy of losing close driver friends. I think you're almost asking for it when you become friends with people in such a dangerous business. When Peter Revson was killed right after I retired, I was terribly upset, but it wasn't such a personal thing.

I asked Dan how he retired, and what his feelings had been. From what he said, I got the impression that it was going to be harder than I anticipated. He liked to race as much as I did, and many times he wanted to get back in his Eagles to see what was happening. But we were also alike in the knowledge that we couldn't keep driving just because we enjoyed it. We had to keep winning or stop entirely. His circumstances were a little different, but the feelings were the same. A person might say we were spoiled kids—if we couldn't win, we'd go home—and maybe that holds some water. But there are also the professional career aspects to consider. I had to make the right financial decisions, regardless of how I may have felt. I had to face the fact that no matter how much money I'd made, I wasn't a wealthy man. Somehow, I'd always figured that if all my interests were left alone, or left up to a management group, everything would take care of itself. It didn't work, of course.

It wasn't as though I was totally trapped, though. Roger knew what I was going through, and it was in his best interests to help me in any way he could. So I had a number of choices. I could keep going until I was totally burned out as a driver. Or we could reduce our programs and I would just run in fewer series or fewer races. I could stop driving entirely, and stay on as the race-team manager. Or, finally, I could leave completely, and go off into my own business. I knew that once I stopped driving, even if I were a race-team manager, I would slowly disappear. There's no perfect solution in that respect. Few people can put up with the pressures of being famous, and yet no one wants to be anonymous either.

I shouldn't have been surprised at the salary Roger offered me to stay on as President and General Manager of Penske Racing. Roger ought to know what I'm worth. I'd been running his racing shops for eight years, and I could probably get more out of our guys with less effort, and win more races, than any other person he could hire. Few people realize that our biggest enemy is wasted man-hours. A racing team has irrevocable deadlines to meet, and if mechanics stand around not wanting to work, or not knowing what to do or how to do it, the race is lost before it starts.

Toward the end of the season Roger was seriously shopping around for drivers, which was very hard on me. Even under the circumstances—it was my decision—I didn't like the feeling of being replaced. But Roger had to get started, because the next season's plans have to be drawn up early for our sponsors. If I was going to be team manager, it was also very important that I have a say in who the number-one driver was. It would have to be someone I could relate to in engineering terms. All a driver would have to do one time is jump out of a car and say, "It's a shitbox. Fix it!" and it would be all over. At the same time Roger knows that the right driver might be too expensive for us. We still have to watch costs in this business, and there's no sense in paying extra for a reputation. We already have that. At one point in our discussions, I told him it might be easier if I just kept on driving. There was a long silence at that point. I wasn't sure whether my mind was made up or not. Was it such an irrevocable decision?

I thought a lot about other drivers who passed their peaks. Most of them never came back—but there were some good examples who did. Jerry Grant peaked and then practically disappeared. Then he came back and almost won Indianapolis. In 1968 Bobby Unser won Indianapolis, and he was king. He didn't do a damn thing through 1969 and 1970, then he went with Gurney and became the star again. He stuck his neck out, kept plugging, and he made it back. I kept telling myself that if *they* could do it, *I* could do it.

What was the right thing to do? It was the biggest conflict I'd ever faced. Was I quitting because I was becoming a donkey, because I'd had enough, or because it was time to go on to a position with more potential for growth?

All that time, while all that conflict was going through my mind, I knew I was racing out my last season. Knowing that it was my last race on each of those tracks gave me a different outlook. It gave me insights that I'd never realized before. I began to honestly accept congratulations from the spectators, even though I still knew they had no real comprehension of what I was doing. I was almost cherishing their comments, knowing I would never hear them again. I had worked for many years to fulfill my own ambitions, only accidentally becoming a "hero" for other people to relate to. It didn't come easy, and a lifetime of competition was hard to give up.

Perhaps I first realized what the public and I meant to each other when we took our Lola-AMC to Elkhart Lake. We were looking terrible, and yet when we unloaded the car, there was a bigger crowd around us than anyone else at the track. I went out and qualified twelfth, and the crowd became even bigger. If I had been fastest, it would have been natural, but we seemed to have a following that didn't care if we were twelfth. I ran sixth in the race, until I lost the water and melted a piston. The car stopped at turn four, and the spectators there were so enthusiastic they offered me beers, asked me for my autograph, and wanted to know when we were going into Formula

One. Why did they care so much about a guy who didn't even finish the race? Maybe there *is* something more important than just winning races.

Of course, there weren't more than half a dozen people who knew it was my last season—right up to the last Can-Am race at Riverside, where I made the announcement. A few people *had* to know in advance because of our business arrangements, and they were good at keeping it secret. It was very important that nothing interfere with the concentration necessary for an ordinarily hectic racing operation. If I had said I was retiring on a certain date, people would have been counting the weeks and races, and bugging me with questions and interviews. There was plenty of time for that after the season was over. Plus, it was my last opportunity for sensationalism—to surprise the press and the public. You only get to do something like that once in a lifetime, and I wanted it to be a memorable event.

In the last few days it became harder to hold the secret. Our secretary got a hint, and she asked the mechanics if it was true. Woody Woodard and Heinz Hofer figured it out pretty quickly, and told me they would be sure to prepare the car the best they ever had, for our one last race at Riverside. Then Flegl figured it out and told Dr. Fuhrmann. They came to me and asked why I was doing it. They wanted to be assured that it had nothing to do with Porsche. I appreciated their concern, although I didn't quite know how to express my feelings at the time.

On the morning of the last race, I told Dan Luginbuhl, Roger's public relations guy, about my retirement so that he could prepare a press release. I had planned to make the announcement at the awards banquet that night, but Dan said it would ruin everyone's evening. The press guys would run out to get the story on the wire. So we decided that I would have a special press conference right after the race.

At first I thought I would write out my farewell speech, to make sure I said everything exactly the way I meant it. And I did try to write it, but I just couldn't. I had gotten in the habit of always speaking right from the heart, and that was all I could do.

When everyone was assembled in the press tower after the race, I noticed that a hush settled over the place. Usually everyone is talking and there's a lot of typewriter and telephone noise. I realized then that they knew I was going to say something of importance—to me, anyhow. They had all gotten the word. I can't remember exactly what I said, but I was annoyed, at first, that I had lost my chance to really surprise them, just because some of my friends couldn't keep quiet about it. But the guys I know in the press didn't get where they are by being oblivious to what's going on around them. It's their job to dig out secrets, and they're good at it.

I was thankful for one thing, though, and that was being able to really quit on top. Dan Gurney retired right after the 1970 Riverside Trans-Am in which he finished fifth—an anticlimactic end to a great career. But I won three very important races on my last weekend.

And that was it. It was all over. Gone were the apprehensions, the sudden failures, the hard-earned successes, the victory celebrations, the fans, the admiring kids, the enthusiasm, the congratulations. I had a lot of great memories to look back on. Many wonderful people and many exciting Sunday afternoons. It was a history of unbelievable happenings—great and sad—in a guy's life between the ages of twenty and thirty-six.

By coincidence, I seemed to be going out at the end of a great era in automobile racing. I could look back and say that I raced under the last "knife-fight" rules. We will probably never again see unlimited 1200-horsepower motors, exotic aerodynamics, engineering freedom, giant leaps in racing technology, and continually higher speeds and lower laptimes. The individual driver's performance and safety are rightfully becoming more important, but I'm glad I didn't miss all the rest.

When I became President of Penske Racing, I got total responsibility for all racing projects, which meant that in addition to running the shop and the engineering programs, I had to associate more with outside contacts. Everyone began seeing me more as a boss than a friend, and I made a lot of mistakes as I learned how to run a business.

I also had to face up to a new emotion that many retired drivers have to cope with. It was the mental anguish at not being able to get back in the car when necessary, to find out what was *really* happening out there. I had to listen to drivers complain about what the car wasn't doing right—when I was sure that I could take it out, as it was, and go a few seconds faster. Or were they right? I tried to get closer to the drivers, to teach them the language and in turn to relate to them.

As a team manager, I began to realize just how important the driver really is. Sometimes, I'd had the idea that I was just another donkey on the team. I would try my damnest to qualify on the pole, and everyone would take it for granted. That was what I was *supposed* to do. I got so used to it, I developed the idea that I was simply a mediocre driver with valuable engineering skills.

I realize that retirement is inevitable. That eventually young spectators will have to ask, "Who was Mark Donohue? What kind of car did he drive?" All race drivers return to the obscurity they came from—but it was still possible that I could put that day off a while longer.

I feel like I succeeded at retiring. I really did retire—from a way of life—if not from racing. Sure, I'm driving race cars again, but it's not so much that I changed my mind, as it is that I'm starting over. I'm in the Formula One Championship now, which is only casually related to all the racing I've done before. It's a different series, on different tracks in different countries, with different drivers in different cars, and it takes a different approach. I've even got a different attitude.

I was kind of embarrassed about it at first. I was wishing I could change my name so that I wouldn't have to explain why I was "unretiring" after the tremendous send-off I got. And I wouldn't have to make apologies for not winning races again for a while. But again, it was my own decision. I had to decide what's right for me, and I had a lot of reasons to consider.

Most of the reasons turned out to be positive. The year I spent out of the driver's seat gave me time to stand back and look at myself. I could look back over the story of my career as it's written here, and see it in better perspective. One of the things I realized is that one person can only do so much. And I learned that everyone doesn't blame the driver when he loses. He doesn't carry *all* the responsibility.

I used this new perspective to learn to separate my feelings from my business deals. I can now be more objective about the value of my efforts, my enthusiasm for my "work," and what I ought to be getting out of it. In other words, I was able to negotiate a better contract once I knew what it was like to be "out." I changed things so that I can now operate under a lot less pressure, and I've made better salary arrangements so that my future is a little more secure. The net result of all this is that I feel like I've gotten more control over my life.

Of course, there were some negative concerns. For one thing, I'm putting my life on the line again, and many people have shown some disappointment that I'm driving again, for just that reason. And to be quite honest, I needed the income. When I was racing, I never looked to the money. I hardly *considered* it. But when I retired I tried to get an automobile dealership, and learned that it would take some fraction of a billion dollars to get started. Maybe I'll still do that some day, and there's no faster way for me to come up with the cash than by driving.

I do still have a lot of problems though. I have to face up to the fact that I'm not going to be winning any races for a while. At one time, winning wasn't the most important thing—it was the *only* thing. Now I'm in new territory, I'm out of practice, and I'm out of shape. But some good drivers have to lose. I've seen them do it, and it doesn't take them apart. So I'll have to put winning to the back of my mind for a while. I've got a fresh attitude, Roger sees to it that the pressures on me are reduced, and I think I can cope with it mentally. We will be using our old familiar systems of development and maintenance, and trying to adapt to Formula One as rapidly as possible. Just like in USAC and NASCAR, we'll have to serve an apprenticeship. And hopefully, in a few years, I'll have another story to tell.

MARK DONOHUE CHRONOLOGY:
A life mastering the science of speed

A list of victories and short sentences only begins to do justice to a racing life as rich as Mark's. The variety of cars and significance of his accomplishments is the story of a man who availed himself of every advantage—fair and unfair.

1937 Mark Neary Donohue, Jr. is born to Hazel and Mark Neary Donohue, Sr. in Summit, NJ on March 18.

1952–1959

First Car to First Win (and getting an education).

Highlights

- First car at age fifteen.
- BS, Mechanical Engineering—Brown University
- First win at Belknap, New Hampshire hillclimb. *1957 Corvette*

In **1952**, at age fifteen, Mark finds his first car, "a cheap 1937 Ford from which someone had cut off the top and the fenders."

Graduates from The Pingry School in **1955** and enters Brown University to study mechanical engineering. His summers are spent on Martha's Vineyard working at a gas station.

At 20, with financial help from his father and technical assistance from his lifelong friend, Dave Lawton, Mark buys a new **1957** Corvette equipped with two four barrel carburetors and 245 horsepower. In the spring of that year, as Dave's guest, Mark enters and wins his first competitive event—a hillclimb at Belknap, NH.

Graduation from Brown in **1959** is followed by a job, a few graduate courses and some ice races with the Corvette. He begins to contemplate racing with the Sports Car Club of America.

Introduced by a mutual friend, Mark gets advice from someone already finding racing success. He is told that if he is going to go racing, he should only go first class. The advice comes from Roger Penske.

Donohue's first car, a 1937 Ford.

Donohue Collection

Donohue's 1957 Corvette.

photo by Dave Lawton

1960–1966

Amateur to Professional (to Penske).

Highlights

- E-Production Championship *Elva Courier*
- Lime Rock Formula Libre Win *Cooper-Offenhauser Midget*
- Formula C Championship *Lotus 20*
- B-Production Championship *Mustang Shelby GT350*
- 3rd at 24 hours of Daytona, 2nd at 12 Hours of Sebring *Ford GT40 MKII*

Races an Elva Courier in SCCA F-Production in **1960** and begins the climb upward. The car is reclassified in **1961** to a tougher E-Production. Mark wins the national championship against drivers such as Peter Revson.

Throughout **1962** Mark competes in the SCCA with his Elva Formula Jr. In **1963** he tries a Daimler in C-Production. He "loses" his amateur status after winning the Formula Libre race at Lime Rock, in a Cooper-Offy Midget that same year.

A ride in Jack Griffith's Cobra results in Mark's first national victory at Virginia International Raceway in early **1964**. Mark does some modifications to a Walt Hansgen hand-me-down MGB and wins the 500 mile race at Bridgehampton. Walt Hansgen mentors Mark and helps him to his debut endurance race in a Ferrari 275 at the 12 Hours of Sebring.

By **1965** Mark is driving the proper line in his development as a professional with class championships in both a Formula C Lotus 20 and a B-Production Shelby GT350—the Mustang being the first car he refers to as a "program."

Hansgen's friendship and recommendation results in a Ford deal and a drive in a GT40 in **1966** that continues into the next year. Invited by Penske to try out his new Lola T70, Mark spends the year juggling the Mustang, the GT40, the T70, and a "real" job. Races in the USRRC and FIA net only two wins, but he manages to finish second in the Can-Am championship with Penske Lola.

Donohue poses with his parents in 1966

Donohue Collection

Donohue working on his Elva Courier (with a claw hammer!) at an SCCA race at Thompson

Donohue Collection

1967–1969

Racing Everything and Everywhere (and winning it all).

Highlights

- Joins Penske Racing
- Two USRRC Championships *Lola T70, McLaren M6B*
- Two Trans Am Championships *Camaro Z28*
- Wins 24 Hours of Daytona *Lola T70 coupe*
- Indy Rookie of the Year *Lola T152*

Racing full-time for Penske in **1967**, Mark begins a Trans-Am Camaro program. Three wins in the Camaro, six wins and the USRRC championship in the Lola T70, and seven Can-Am races make his first year with Penske a busy one. Still doing development and race driving for Ford, Mark races at his 2nd 24 Hours at Le Mans. He co-drives a Ford GT40MK IV with Bruce McLaren, and the duo finishes 4th.

1968 brings the Trans-Am championship and some beautifully crafted advantages. Vacuum assisted brake pad changes—among others—remain masterpieces in rules interpretation. The USRRC championship is Mark's again and a USAC program is begun. Mark continues the Can-Am effort in the McLaren M6B, finishing 3rd in the championship.

1969 begins with a win in the 24 Hours of Daytona, soon followed by the Rookie of the Year trophy at Indy after Mark qualifies fourth and finishes seventh in his first 500. Led by clues from early data acquisition instrumentation and advantages from a quickly banned 20+ foot tall fueling rig, the Camaro takes another Trans-Am championship with six wins. The year ends with Mark finishing 7th in the Lola T190 at his first Formula A event—the Sebring Continental.

Trans-Am

Year	Starts	Wins	In top 5
'67	10	3	7
'68	13	10	12
'69	11	6	8
'70	13	3	9
'71	10	7	9
totals:	**57**	**29**	**45**

The '68 Camaro is polished and ready at Penske's Newtown Square shop.

Donohue Collection

The '66 Lola T70 at mid-Ohio. Note his pit crew (from left to right): Roger Penske, Al Holbert and Bill Scott.

Photo by Dave Arnold

1970–1972

Trans-Am to Can-Am (with a stop at Indy).

Highlights
• Wins Trans Am Championship *AMC Javelin*
• Wins Pocono 500 and Michigan 200 *McLaren M16*
• Wins Indy 500 *McLaren M16B*

1970 saw a 2nd at Indy in the Lola-Ford and a new association with American Motors. The AMC Javelin nets three wins from some of Mark's most determined development. "Donohue" edition Javelins are built for the street. At the wheel of the Lola T192, Mark wins two out of three Formula A starts.

Mark dominates Trans-Am in **1971** with seven wins and the championship. In addition, Mark teams up with David Hobbs for four endurances races in the Ferrari 512M; places third in his first Formula One race, at Mosport in the McLaren M19; competes against the European F1 drivers in the Questor Grand Prix; and racks up 2 USAC wins at the Pocono 500 and the Michigan 200 after a heart-breaking DNF at Indy.

1972 is remembered for victory at Indy, but of perhaps greater significance, Mark becomes a formidable contender in the Can-Am series with the Porsche 917-10. He finishes 4th in the championship despite sitting out four races with a broken leg; it would only be a matter of time before Mark would dominate the series. Also notable this year is Penske Racing's first NASCAR effort, with Mark at the wheel for four of the ten Penske starts in the AMC Matador.

Indy		
Year	Starting Position	Finish Position
'69	4	7
'70	5	2
'71	2	dnf
'72	3	1
'73	3	dnf

The Ferrari 512M during the early morning hours at Daytona in 1971.

Photo by Pete Lyons

The winner's circle at the 1972 Indy 500

Photo by Barry Tenin

1973–1975

"Just ran with recalibrated fuel injection . . . please inform Captain of major break thru."—*Mark* (Getting it perfect).

–from telex sent to Penske team during Porsche development work in Germany.

Highlights

- Can Am Championship *Porsche 917-30*
- Wins NASCAR Western 500 *AMC Matador*
- Inaugural IROC Champion *IROC Porsche 911*
- Sets world closed-course speed record *Porsche 917-30*

The words Can-Am Champion almost seem to be an understatement when remembering **1973**. No other driver/car combination have so dominated a series and captured the imagination of the racing world as did Mark and the Porsche 917-30. Mark simply owned Can-Am. Still racing other programs, Mark began the year with a win in a Matador at the NASCAR Western 500. He also started in three USAC races in an Eagle-Offy, three endurance races in a Porsche 911 Carrera, and six Formula 5000 races in a Lola T330.

A new series began that year pitting the world's great drivers against one another in equally prepared cars. Mark won three of the four races and the inaugural IROC championship, leaving no doubt about his driving mastery.

After a short retirement in **1974** as manager of Penske Racing, Mark returns to the driver's seat for two Formula One starts.

In **1975**, Mark's autobiography, *The Unfair Advantage*, is published. This year also begins Penske Racing's participation in a complete F1 schedule. Mark is reunited with the 917-30 on August 9th and sets a new world closed-course speed record of 221.12 mph at Talladega Speedway.

One week following, in morning warm-up for the Austrian Grand Prix, an accident results in a cerebral hemorrhage. Mark Donohue dies two days later, on August 19th.

In the cockpit of the Porsche 917-30 before the start of the first 1973 Can-Am race at Mosport.

Photo by Barry Tenin

Three of the best drivers in the world in 1973: (from left to right) Donohue, Hurley Haywood, and Jody Scheckter.

Photo by Dave Arnold

INDEX

CONTRIBUTORS TO NEW EDITION

Arnold, Dave

After some years as an Ohio newspaper writer, during which time his interest in road racing gestated and grew, Dave Arnold handled the media relations at the Mid-Ohio Sports Car Course from 1969-84, where he got to know Mark Donohue. He encountered David Donohue at his first professional race, an IMSA Firestone Firehawk series event at Mid-Ohio, while handling media relations for the Firehawk series. Dave now lives in Big Flats, N.Y., just a 20-minute drive from the famed Watkins Glen International circuit, where he owns Arnold Communications, a media relations and PR firm specializing in road racing clients.

Biro, Pete

Pete Biro, born in Oakland, Calif., began motorsports photography in the 1950s, chasing sports cars up and down the West Coast. His work appeared in most of the automotive magazines as well as *Time, Sports Illustrated* and more recently on Web sites. He photographed Mark Donohue's win at the Pocono 500 for *Sports Illustrated* and covered Donohue's career for editorial and advertising clients, including Goodyear, Sunoco and Roger Penske. Biro's first coverage of Penske's efforts was when Roger himself was driving the famed Zerex Special. Biro covered all of Team Penske's ten wins at the Indianapolis 500 as well.

photo by Tony Mezzacca

Brandle, Bob

During the seasons of 1973 through 1975 Bob Brandle was a competitor of sorts to Mark Donohue, in that he was on the Warren Agor Racing Team (73-77), which raced in the Trans-Am, IMSA Camel GT, and Can-Am Series. He was a designer, fabricator, pit crew and photographer on the team. Additionally, he attended the Formula One U.S. and Canadian Grands Prix during the years that Mark raced for Penske. Bob remembers of Mark, "I was always thrilled at and appreciative of Mark's abilities and success as a driver and an engineer, having been up close, at times, while on the Warren Agor Racing Team, as well as an enthusiastic spectator and photographer of road racing."

photo by David Donohue

Cobb, Bill

Bill Cobb grew up following Mark Donohue's career and enjoyed the challenge of writing the chronology for this book. In 1994, he was a crew member of David Donohue's first professional championship winning team. A consultant and writer, Bill currently spends most of his time around, in and under the cars of BMW—as a member of PTG's M3 racing team and caretaker of BMW's historical cars as Mobile Tradition specialist for North America.

Crocker, Hal

courtesy Team Unicorn, Inc.

After determining that the hustle and bustle of real estate did not offer a requisite amount of excitement, Hal Crocker gravitated to motorsport photography as the 1960s drew to a close. During Mark Donohue's reign, Crocker was the primary photographer for Porsche's racing efforts in North America. Thus, he covered many of Donohue's major wins. Now, over thirty years later, Crocker is still involved in motorsport photography. As the leader of Team Unicorn, he still maintains his strong relationship with Porsche Motorsports North America. He still resides in Roswell, GA where he maintains the largest private archive of motorsports images in North America.

Daytona Racing Archives

Daytona Racing Archives is located in Daytona Beach, Florida and is a department of ISC Publications, a division of International Speedway Corp. The department was founded in 1988 at the suggestion of Anne B. France (Mrs. Bill France, Sr.). It contains over 2 1/2 million photos going back to 1903 and it houses a video library of over 170,000 hours and numerous artifacts. The public is welcome to inquire concerning the obtaining of photos. Head Archivist, Buz McKim, is a life-long Mark Donohue fanatic.

photo by Barry Tenin

Hobbs, David

On page 224 of the book, Donohue writes of David Hobbs, "...He always did a great job for us . . . I liked him, the mechanics liked him . . . I think it was because his attitude was so positive. He was always smiling and he always had something good to say about the car—a real pleasant optimist. I think David has found it very easy to sell himself as a driver because he has such a strong, personable image." A former Formula One driver, Hobbs is currently an announcer on Speedvision where he covers all the Grand Prix races, as well as many other motorsports events.

Jeanotte, Ray

Ray Jeanotte has been shooting automobile and motorcycle racing since 1966. His early photography was in *Autoracing* magazine. He lived in Europe from 1970-1989 and his work from this time can be found in *Motocourse*, *Time*, the book *Two Seats* by Janos Wimpffen, Pete Lyons' *Can-Am Photo History*, and many other books from Germany and France. Of his days photographing Mark Donohue, Ray reminisces, "I have fond memories of Mark Donohue. He was a hero that you could relate to! He was fast and Chevy-powered and that was America in the sixties, for me. He was in a class with guys like Dan Gurney and Dave MacDonald. Mark could beat anyone, British, New Zealander or otherwise. He was fast and smooth to watch. I feel very proud to be part this book." Ray currently lives in Seattle, Washington.

Kemper, Su

In the late 60s and early 70s, Su Kemper, a member of the Chicago Region SCCA, was a freelance photographer specializing in the big series of the era—the Can-Am and Trans-Am—and covered a few of the Formula One Grand Prix races at Watkins Glen, New York. During that period her work appeared in *Automobile Year* (Switzerland), *Rennreport* (Germany) and a variety of U.S. motoring magazines.

courtesy camera arts studio

Kennison, Harry

As an amateur motor sports photographer in the '60s and '70s, Harry Kennison grew to appreciate the extraordinary talents of Mark Donohue as a driver. At Michigan International Speedway in 1969 he watched Mark put his Camaro inches from the concrete wall at the top of the banking lap after lap in a driving rainstorm. In recalling Donohue's career, Kennison comments, "Mark may have had an 'unfair advantage' in being able to set up a car better than anyone else, but first and foremost, he was a racer as demonstrated by his courage and finesse in trying conditions."

Lawton, Dave

When Dave Lawton took some of the earliest existing photos of Mark Donohue's racing career, he was simply taking snapshots of a good friend. "Mark and I enjoyed a close friendship from age fourteen on Martha's Vineyard during the summers because of our common interests. We learned to drive fast boats and fast cars at the same time. Mark pit crewed for me first at a hillclimb event, after that I usually pit crewed for him during the amateur years. We spent countless hours experimenting and coaching each other in driving and exploring the mechanical mysteries of the automobile. Later, it was a tremendous thrill for me to watch a close friend reach the pinnacle of success in racing."

Photo by Charles Best

Ludvigsen Library

As a New York resident in the 1960s, Karl Ludvigsen was often at the Bridgehampton Racetrack, as was his Canadian friend and photographer Stanley Rosenthall. Rosenthall was a frequent companion of Ludvigsen's on and off the track. When Rosenthall returned to his native Canada, Ludvigsen acquired his archive, including these photographs of Mark Donohue. These photographs are part of the Ludvigsen Library collection.

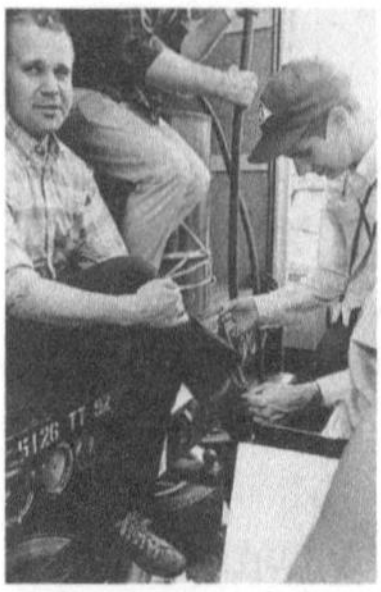

photo by Barry Tenin

Luongo, Peter

Photographer Pete Luongo (right) ties up loose ends for Mark Donohue (left) at Lime Rock in 1968. Luongo was the first professional photographer hired by Penske Racing's public relations agent to capture the team in action. He learned about organization, preparation, and the importance of appearance as he recorded the scene from 1968 to 1972. Pete Luongo can be reached by e-mail at *autofoto@aol.com* or Box 605, Skokie, IL 60076.

photo by Lorna Lyons

Lyons, Pete

Motorsports journalist Pete Lyons covered much of Mark Donohue's career, from the early USRRC days through the Trans-Am, Can-Am and Indy golden years, to the tragic F1 experience. He remembers Mark as a profoundly intelligent and serious man with a contrasting sense of pixyish humor. Lyons has detailed Donohue's racing exploits with the powerful Porsche Panzer in his two books, *Can-Am* and *Can-Am Photo History*. A freelance writer for such publications as *AutoWeek, Racer, Road & Track, Vintage Racecar Journal,* Pete and his wife, Lorna, make their home in Big Bear, California.

Markle, Don

Don started photographing sports car racing in the late '50s at Harewood Acres, a disused airport track in Ontario. Mosport Park, opening in the early '60s, became his "home" track. He considers the '60s and '70s to be the Golden Age of racing. Don currently resides in Mississauga, Ontario, Canada.

photo by Arthur Godfrey

Mezzacca Motorsports Photography

Tony Mezzacca, owner of Mezzacca Motorsports Photography, fondly remembers the '60s and '70s as a different era of motorsports, when the primary exposure for racing was generated by the printed media. "At the peak of his career, Mark was a media favorite with a wonderful smile. His success was thrilling for a young photographer to capture," recalls Tony. Photographing Mark Donohue was especially meaningful to Mezzacca, as they both hailed from the same area of New Jersey.

Donohue Collection

McKeon, Tom

Tom McKeon worked for Sun Oil Company Refinery as Fire Chief and Safety Supervisor for 30 years before retiring from the company. One of his more interesting assignments for Sun Oil was the duty of safety inspector at the Penske team's skid pad. This was a very small circular track built just for Mark Donohue to use for development testing of shocks, springs and suspension on the Penske race cars. It was built at Sun Oil's refinery facility at Marcus Hook, Pennsylvania, and McKeon was part of the Sun Oil crew sent to the skid pad to keep curious spectators from interfering with Donohue on the track. McKeon remembers being amazed as he watched Donohue drive the track at maximum speed, then pull out his slide rule and calculate the necessary adjustments to the car.

Oursler, Bill

Bill Oursler has been involved with motorsports professionally since 1968. As a photographer he covered Mark Donohue's career in the Trans-Am, Can-Am and sports car series for such magazines as *Car & Driver* and *Road & Track*. Today Oursler lives in Charlotte, North Carolina where he is a partner in RBJ Communications, Inc.

courtesy Penske archives

Penske, Roger

Once honored as the Sports Car Driver of the Year by *Sports Illustrated,* the *New York Times,* and the *Los Angeles Times,* Roger Penske is better known as a successful racing team owner, manager and constructor. His cars have won ten Indy 500s, a record 100 Indy car victories, numerous Winston Cup races, Can-Am and Trans-Am championships, and even a Formula One Grand Prix. During the late '60s and early '70s he and Mark Donohue dominated Trans-Am and Can-Am racing and went on to score victories at Daytona and Indianapolis. Roger Penske was also inducted into the Motorsports Hall of Fame.

Picard, Ed

As a worker with the SCCA and USAC, Ed Picard considered himself very fortunate to witness Mark Donohue's progress and achievements. Picard noticed Donohue's natural driving ability at his very first competition, a hillclimb in New Hampshire. "Donohue's infectious smile, pleasant personality and a highly developed sense of humor won him many friends," recalls Picard.

photo by Peter Luongo

Posey, Sam

In describing the early Penske Camaro team, Donohue says of Posey, ". . . We also had Sam Posey driving our backup car, and he regularly picked up thirds and fourths. He was a good person to have around because he was an up-and-coming guy at the time, he wanted very much to drive for Roger, and we didn't have to pay him very much" (p.102). Posey went on to have a very successful racing career before becoming an announcer on Speedvision, for whom he currently covers all the Grand Prix races.

Smith, Carroll

Carroll Smith was chief engineer for the Ford factory team and met Donohue while he was driving for Ford (1966-67). Donohue describes Smith's technical skill on page 68: "Carroll Smith knew more about chassis setup, though, so he and I spent a lot of time talking about calculating spring rates, anti-roll bars, roll couple, how drivers could tell what was right or wrong, and that sort of thing . . . . Carroll always tried to work from some prior knowledge. He tried to keep some degree of sanity in the operation. We had long, interesting technical discussions about what went into those cars, and I learned a lot by listening to Carroll. He was always quite straightforward with me, and I liked him for it."

Stropus, Judy

Judy Stropus was the official timer and scorer for the Penske Racing team from the late Sixties through the mid-Seventies. She was a part of the team during its history-making years, including Trans-Am, Can-Am, 24 Hours of Le Mans, and winning the Indy 500.

Photo by Hal Crocker

Tenin, Barry

In 1968 Barry Tenin was attending a college where one of his classmates was Walt Hansgen's son, Rusty. Barry was already photographing professionally when he decided to attend the Daytona 24 hour race during semester break. At Daytona he walked up to Mark, introduced himself and handed him a handwritten note from Rusty that said, "This guy's a friend of mine and a good photographer—take care of him." With that Mark let Barry into the Penske garage, which even in those days of looser security, was still off limits to most of the press. It was also the beginning of an extended (auto racing) family that on race weekends worked, ate and partied together. These days, Barry works as a corporate and magazine photographer with specialties in annual reports, motorsports, and yachting (including several America's Cup Races). Barry's pictures have appeared on covers as well as inside books and magazines. He has worked on assignment for *Time*, *People*, *Sports Illustrated*, and *National Geographic*. He is a contributor to two other recently released books by Bentley Publishers: the new version of *The Speed Merchants* and *A French Kiss With Death*, both by Michael Keyser.

Tronolone, Bob

Von Trebra, Dale

Warren, Cam

As a notable motorsports writer and photographer of the era, Cam Warren covered many Can-Am races for *Road & Track* magazine, in addition to other major events from Grand Prix to off-road races in Baja. His work has appeared in many publications, both in the U.S. and abroad, including *Newsweek International.*

ABOUT THE AUTHOR

photo by Bob Tronolone

American auto racing champion Mark Donohue used to joke—was he joking?—about installing an "unfair advantage" in his cars. In fact, he was born with the sharpest edge a racer can enjoy: his mind.

Motorsport is rich in personalities with a natural talent for driving fast. Rarer are those who fully understand how they do it. Donohue was among the first of the modern driver-engineers who seek speed through science. His racing record argues that he may have been the greatest.

Mark was 21 in 1958 and still a student of mechanical engineering at Brown University when he took his everyday street ride, a '57 Corvette, to victory in his first official speed event, a New Hampshire hill climb. It was characteristic of the thoughtful young man that he regarded the win as a fluke; it was equally characteristic that he resolved to eliminate any fluke from then on. Tearing into his race cars with his own hands, restlessly and relentlessly trying one experiment after another and coolly analyzing the results, Mark learned exactly what made them faster, and what didn't. He took an equally serious approach to his driving.

While many of his contemporaries relied on their innate ability at the wheel, Donohue the engineer strove to understand the dynamics behind high performance, and then to perfect his skill in extracting it. Where others prepared their cars well, he was obsessive about preparation. All good drivers are dedicated; Donohue was driven. And he never stopped thinking, thinking, thinking.

The results: three Sports Car Club of America amateur national championships, and two years as a pro on Ford's mighty Le Mans team. Joining Roger Penske in 1966, Donohue helped establish one of the most dominant organizations in racing history. Twice Mark took the United States Road Racing Championship, added the Canadian-American Challenge Cup (Can-Am), and brought Trans-Am series titles to manufacturers Chevrolet and American Motors a total of three times. He also was a winning co-driver of the 24-hour sports car enduro at Daytona, and he set a world's speed record at Talladega. Oh, and in 1972 the image of this boyish and fun-loving road racer went onto the Indianapolis 500 trophy.

Of course, racing has been called "the cruel sport;" Mark suffered many losses and disappointments too, both public and private. His life ended tragically at the age of 38 after a 1975 Formula One accident in Austria. But his legacy remains timeless.

In fact, every successful driver today owes a debt of knowledge to Mark Donohue's pioneering work in applying science to speed.

Pete Lyons
September, 2000

Selected Books and Repair Information from Bentley Publishers

BMW

Memoirs of a Hack Mechanic
Rob Siegel ISBN 978-0-8376-1720-6

BMW 3 Series (E46) Service Manual: 1999-2005 *Bentley Publishers*
ISBN 978-0-8376-1657-5

BMW 5 Series (E60, E61) Service Manual: 2004-2010 *Bentley Publishers*
ISBN 978-0-8376-1689-6

BMW Z3 (E36/7 E36/8) Service Manual: 1996-2002 *Bentley Publishers*
ISBN 978-0-8376-1617-9

BMW X3 (E83) Service Manual: 2004-2010 *Bentley Publishers*
ISBN 978-0-8376-1731-2

Porsche

Porsche 911 (993) Service Manual: 1995-1998 *Bentley Publishers*
ISBN 978-0-8376-1719-0

Porsche 911 (996) Service Manual: 1999-2005 *Bentley Publishers*
ISBN 978-0-8376-1710-7

Porsche 911 Carrera Service Manual: 1984-1989 *Bentley Publishers*
ISBN 978-0-8376-1696-4

Porsche 911 SC Service Manual: 1978-1983 *Bentley Publishers*
ISBN 978-0-8376-1705-3

Porsche: Excellence Was Expected
Karl Ludvigsen ISBN 978-0-8376-0235-6

Porsche—Origin of the Species
Karl Ludvigsen ISBN 978-0-8376-1331-4

Volkswagen

Battle for the Beetle *Karl Ludvigsen*
ISBN 978-0-8376-1695-7

Volkswagen Rabbit, GTI (A5) Service Manual: 2006-2009 *Bentley Publishers*
ISBN 978-0-8376-1664-3

Corvette

Corvette: America's Star-Spangled Sports Car *Karl Ludvigsen*
ISBN 978-0-8376-1659-9

Corvette by the Numbers: The Essential Corvette Parts Reference 1955-1982
Alan Covin ISBN 978-0-8376-0228-2

Zora Arkus-Duntov: The Legend Behind Corvette *Jerry Burton*
ISBN 978-08376-0858-7

Driving

A French Kiss With Death: Steve McQueen and the Making of Le Mans
Michael Keyser ISBN 978-0-8376-0234-9

Alex Zanardi - My Sweetest Victory
Alex Zanardi with Gianluca Gasparini
ISBN 978-0-8376-1249-2

Sports Car and Competition Driving
Paul Frère with foreword by *Phil Hill*
ISBN 978-0-8376-0202-8

Going Faster! Mastering the Art of Race Driving *Carl Lopez*
ISBN 978-0-8376-0226-4

Engineering

Supercharged! Design, Testing, and Installation of Supercharger Systems
Corky Bell ISBN 978-0-8376-0168-7

Maximum Boost: Designing, Testing, and Installing Turbocharger Systems
Corky Bell ISBN 978-0-8376-0160-1

Race Car Aerodynamics *Joseph Katz*
ISBN 978-0-8376-0142-7

Scientific Design of Exhaust and Intake Systems *Phillip H. Smith & John C. Morrison* ISBN 978-0-8376-0309-4

Physics for Gearheads *Randy Beikmann*
ISBN 978-0-8376-1615-5

Mechanical Ignition Handbook: The Hack Mechanic Guide to Vintage Ignition Systems *Rob Siegel* ISBN 978-0-8376-1767-1

The Hack Mechanic Guide to European Automotive Electrical Systems
Rob Siegel with Bentley Publishers
ISBN 978-0-8376-1751-0

Classic Grand Prix Cars *Karl Ludvigsen*
ISBN 978-0-8376-1735-0

Classic Racing Engines *Karl Ludvigsen*
ISBN 978-0-8376-1734-3